COLLECTED ESSAYS

H. P. LOVECRAFT: COLLECTED ESSAYS

COLLECTED ESSAYS
VOLUME 2: LITERARY CRITICISM

H. P. Lovecraft

Edited by S. T. Joshi

Hippocampus Press

New York

Library of Congress Cataloging-in-Publication Data

Lovecraft, H. P. (Howard Phillips), 1890–1937
  [Essays]
  Collected essays / H.P. Lovecraft ; edited by S.T. Joshi. --
1st ed.
    v. cm.
  Includes bibliographical references and indexes.
  Contents: v. 1. Amateur journalism -- v. 2. Literary criticism.
  ISBN 0-9721644-1-3 (v. 1 : hardcover) -- ISBN 0-9721644-2-1
(v. 1 : pbk.) -- ISBN 0-9721644-4-8 (v. 2 : hardcover) -- ISBN
0-9721644-9-9 (v. 2 : pbk.)
  I. Joshi, S. T., 1958– . II. Title.
  PS3523.O833A6 2004b
  814'.52--dc22

2004000766

Select unpublished texts have been published by permission of the Estate of
H. P. Lovecraft and John Hay Library, Brown University.

Published by Hippocampus Press
P.O. Box 641, New York, NY 10156.
http://www.hippocampuspress.com

Cover art by Virgil Finlay, used by permission of Lail Finlay.
Hippocampus Press logo by Anastasia Damianakos.
Cover design by Barbara Briggs Silbert.

First Edition
1 3 5 7 9 8 6 4 2

Cloth: ISBN 0-9721644-4-8
Paper: ISBN 0-9721644-9-9

CONTENTS

H P. Lovecraft would have been the first to admit that he was not a literary critic by trade. His critical essays were in almost every instance the product of a given occasion—either a request by a colleague, an article by friend or foe that required rebuttal, or the perceived need to bring readers' attention to the work of an associate. The great majority of his critical essays, as with his essays as a whole, were generated in and for the amateur press—exclusively so up to 1924.

These early essays partake of the bookishness, dogmatism, and antiquarianism that dominated Lovecraft's temperament during this time. Nurtured on eighteenth-century prose and verse, Lovecraft actually felt that such issues as "metrical regularity" and the "allowable rhyme" were vital topics in 1915. In accordance with his fantasy (nurtured, in part, by his mother) of being a poet, many of his early essays are devoted to poetic technique and subject-matter. It was, however, not long before his prejudices were compelled to confront an equally dogmatic set of prejudices inspired by the revolution in poetry in the first decades of the twentieth century—a revolution that has given us free verse and the downfall of orthodox rhyme and metre. Lovecraft's response was predictably hostile (see "The Vers Libre Epidemic"); and yet, his simple utterance in "Metrical Regularity"—"The 'language of the heart' must be clarified and made intelligible to other hearts, else its purport will forever be confined to its creator"—is a strikingly astute indictment of the entire tendency of twentieth-century poets toward obscurity and obsessive contemplation of their own psyches. Lovecraft's devotion to Graeco-Roman classicism is evident to a fault in both "The Literature of Rome" and "The Case for Classicism." It was a devotion Lovecraft never renounced, although he would gradually modify it at least to the extent of allowing a place in the realm of aesthetics for weird literature, a mode not exhaustively treated by the ancients.

Lovecraft's essays of the early 1920s become directed toward single individuals, whether they be his amateur colleagues—Winifred Virginia Jackson, Lilian Middleton, Jonathan E. Hoag, Frank Belknap Long—or recognised figures such as Lord Dunsany. The articles on the amateur poets Jackson and Middleton sound like nothing but the effusively flattering reviews on women poets written by Poe; they are not so much critical analyses as testaments to friendship. It was, however, at this time that Lovecraft's aesthetic horizons were undergoing significant, perhaps radical, revision: inspired in part by his young friend Long, Lovecraft was making an attempt to investigate, and in limited measure to adopt, the tendencies of contemporary writers and thinkers. He himself would later chart his development in striking terms:

> I can look back ... at two distinct periods of opinion whose foundations I have successively come to distrust—a period before 1919 or so, when the weight of classic authority unduly influenced me, and another period from 1919 to 1925, when I placed too high a value on the elements of revolt, florid colour, and emotional extravagance or intensity.[1]

---

1. HPL to August Derleth, Saturday [7 December 1929]; quoted in Joshi, *Life* 307.

Crudely, these are Lovecraft's "Classicist" and "Decadent" phases. The essay on Dunsany is a critical document in the chronicling of the transition from Classicism to Decadence. Lovecraft no longer believes that he can bury his head in the sand and pretend that he is still living either in republican Rome or in Augustan England: the modern world must be faced. That modern world, with its advances in all the sciences (something Lovecraft devoted a lifetime in charting), was forcing artists to come to terms with the brute fact that many formerly viable aesthetic modes were now becoming outworn. One of the greatest casualties of this increased scientific knowledge was what Lovecraft called romanticism—the lending of a false or spurious glamour to emotions that Freud and others had shown to emerge from motives and sources that were anything but lofty. As Lovecraft himself was highly hostile to this kind of romanticism, his transition from Classicism to Decadence was made the easier: in effect, he was, aesthetically, skipping the entire nineteenth century in an attempt to recapture a modified classicism approximately of the sort that certain modern thinkers—in particular, Lovecraft's *bête noire* T. S. Eliot—were seeking to fashion. But Eliot, Amy Lowell, and others had gone too far in repudiating the past. This is why Lovecraft, in his "In the Editor's Study" column of 1923, began with a remarkable utterance—"What is art but a matter of impressions, of pictures, emotions, and symmetrical sensations? It must have poignancy and beauty, but nothing else counts. It may or may not have coherence"—but then drew back nervously with the caveat that he was "no convert to Dadaism."

There is no question that Lovecraft's chief virtue as a literary critic resides in his analysis of the foundations of weird fiction and in his meticulous charting of its history in the two centuries prior to his own day. His first foray into the subject is found in the *In Defence of Dagon* essays of 1921 (see CE5), but the most significant document is, of course, "Supernatural Horror in Literature." Begun in late 1925 at the request of Lovecraft's amateur colleague W. Paul Cook, the essay underwent continual revision up to the very time it appeared in the *Recluse* (1927); and even then Lovecraft refused to lay the work down, taking notes for a possible revision that partially materialised in the *Fantasy Fan* serialisation of 1933–35. Without question, Lovecraft is the preeminent theoretician/practitioner of the weird tale: no other writer has simultaneously produced so distinguished a body of creative work and so thought-provoking a body of analytical work. "Supernatural Horror in Literature" does what no treatise up to that time had done: establish a coherent historical outline of weird fiction from antiquity to the present day, an outline that later critics have largely followed, however much they may have amplified it. The various notes written by Lovecraft in the early 1930s—the product of a severe crisis in his writing engendered by painful rejections of some of his best work by pulp editors—may appear fragmentary and undeveloped, but they are prodigiously suggestive in their recording of the central themes and concerns of weird writing. An important appendix to this theoretical work is "Some Notes on Interplanetary Fiction" (1934), in which that burgeoning genre is subject to severe but hardly unfair criticism.

After this vibrant work, it is somewhat sad to come upon "Suggestions for a Reading Guide"—not because that work is inadequate or insignificant, but because of the painful toil it required of a man who was already afflicted with a terminal illness. The thankless job of revising Anne Tillery Renshaw's *Well Bred Speech*, a hopelessly mediocre manual on English usage and elocution, sapped Lovecraft's energies grievously in the fall of 1936 (at one point he worked for sixty hours without a break to meet the final deadline); insult was then added to injury when the majority of his revisions were omitted from the final version. Nevertheless, "Suggestions" remains a sound guide to general reading up to the time it was written, and non-specialists could do far worse than to follow its guidelines for those subjects (chiefly the sciences) that have not undergone radical revision by the advance of knowledge.

With the passing of years, Lovecraft returned to his first love—poetry. Such later essays as "Notes on Verse Technique" (1932) and "What Belongs in Verse" (1935) show how far he had come in a literary career of less than two decades. By this point, both Classicism and Decadence had been repudiated, or at least reined in; Lovecraft's new views on poetry as a mode that must reflect living speech and contemporary subject matter—evident in rudimentary form so early as the preface to Bullen's *White Fire* (1927), and exhaustively chronicled in letters to Elizabeth Toldridge and others in the later 1920s and 1930s—are themselves embodied in his own verse of the period, such as *Fungi from Yuggoth* (1929–30) and "The Ancient Track" (1929). Works of this kind bring Lovecraft's career full circle, demonstrating what can be accomplished by a keen mind that always remains open to new influences, new ideas, new aesthetic and philosophical conceptions. It is this quality of constant mental engagement that, perhaps even more than the actual literary works produced under its aegis, may be H. P. Lovecraft's greatest accomplishment.

—S. T. JOSHI

A NOTE ON THIS EDITION

This edition is based upon rigorous consultation of the first publications of Lovecraft's essays as well as of relevant later appearances; the texts are based upon the first appearance unless otherwise specified. At the end of each essay, an editor's note supplies bibliographical and other information that readers might find useful for placing the item within the context of Lovecraft's life and work; footnotes elucidating specific literary, historical, and other data in the essay follow the editor's note. The texts for "Supernatural Horror in Literature" and "Suggestions for a Reading Guide" have been prepared using a somewhat different principle: in these works, Lovecraft's citations of literary works have been systematised in accordance with modern conventions, e.g., italics for book-length works (novels, short story collections, long poems, treatises, etc.) and quotation marks for shorter works (short stories, short poems, articles, etc.). A bibliographic appendix has been appended to "Suggestions for a Reading Guide," supplying bibliographical information on all works cited in that text, with indications as to Lovecraft's ownership of them in his personal library.

Abbreviations used in the notes are as follows:

AHT	Arkham House transcripts of HPL's letters
AMS	autograph manuscript
AT	*The Ancient Track: Complete Poetical Works* (Night Shade Books, 2001)
CE1–5	*Collected Essays* (Volumes 1–5)
DH	*The Dunwich Horror and Others* (Arkham House, 1984)
DPC	"Department of Public Criticism" (*United Amateur*)
FP	first publication
JHL	John Hay Library, Brown University (Providence, RI)
Joshi, *Life*	S. T. Joshi, *H. P. Lovecraft: A Life* (Necronomicon Press, 1996)

LL	S. T. Joshi, *Lovecraft's Library: A Catalogue,* 2nd rev. ed. (Hippocampus Press, 2002)
LNY	*Letters from New York* (Night Shade Books, 2004)
MM	*At the Mountains of Madness and Other Novels* (Arkham House, 1985)
MW	*Miscellaneous Writings* (Arkham House, 1995)
NAPA	National Amateur Press Association
SHSW	State Historical Society of Wisconsin (Madison, WI)
SL	*Selected Letters* (Arkham House, 1965–76; 5 vols.)
TMS	typed manuscript
UAPA	United Amateur Press Association

    I am grateful to David E. Schultz, Steven J. Mariconda, Perry M. Grayson, Scott Connors, and Marc A. Michaud for assistance in the preparation of the text and notes. My research was chiefly done at the New York Public Library, the Fossil Collection of Amateur Journalism (formerly housed at New York University), the American Antiquarian Society, the John Hay Library of Brown University, and the University of Washington Library.

—S. T. JOSHI

METRICAL REGULARITY

"Deteriores omnes sumus licentia."
—*Terence.*[1]

Of the various forms of decadence manifest in the poetical art of the present age, none strikes more harshly on our sensibilities than the alarming decline in that harmonious regularity of metre which adorned the poetry of our immediate ancestors.

That metre itself forms an essential part of all true poetry is a principle which not even the assertions of an Aristotle or the pronouncements of a Plato can disestablish. As old a critic as Dionysius of Halicarnassus and as modern a philosopher as Hegel have each affirmed that versification in poetry is not alone a necessary attribute, but the very foundation as well; Hegel, indeed, placing metre above metaphorical imagination as the essence of all poetic creation.[2]

Science can likewise trace the metrical instinct from the very infancy of mankind, or even beyond, to the pre-human age of the apes. Nature is in itself an unending succession of regular impulses. The steady recurrence of the seasons and of the moonlight, the coming and going of the day, the ebb and flow of the tides, the beating of the heart and pulses, the tread of the feet in walking, and countless other phenomena of like regularity, have all combined to inculcate in the human brain a rhythmic sense which is as manifest in the most uncultivated, as in the most polished of peoples. Metre, therefore, is no such false artifice as most exponents of radicalism would have us believe, but is instead a natural and inevitable embellishment to poesy, which succeeding ages should develop and refine, rather than maim or destroy.

Like other instincts, the metric sense has taken on different aspects among different races. Savages shew it in its simplest form while dancing to the sound of primitive drums; barbarians display it in their religious and other chantings; civilised peoples utilise it for their formal poetry, either as measured quantity, like that of Greek and Roman verse, or as measured accentual stress, like that of our own English verse. Precision of metre is thus no mere display of meretricious ornament, but a logical evolution from eminently natural sources.

It is the contention of the ultra-modern poet, as enunciated by Mrs. J. W. Renshaw[3] in her recent article on "The Autocracy of Art" (*The Looking Glass* for May), that the truly inspired bard must chant forth his feelings independently of form or language, permitting each changing impulse to alter the rhythm of his lay, and blindly resigning his reason to the "fine frenzy" of his mood. This contention is of course founded upon the assumption that poetry is super-intellectual; the expression of a "soul" which outranks the mind and its precepts. Now while avoiding the impeachment of this dubious theory, we must needs remark, that the laws of Nature cannot so easily be outdistanced. However much true poesy may overtop the produce of the brain, it must still be affected by natural laws, which are universal and inevitable. Wherefore it is possible for the critic to assume the attitude of the scientist, and to perceive the various clearly defined natural forms through which the emotions seek expressions. Indeed, we feel even unconsciously the fitness of certain types of metre for certain types of thought, and in perusing a crude or irregular poem are often abruptly repelled by the unwarranted variations made by the bard, either through his ignorance or his perverted taste. We are naturally shocked at the clothing of a grave subject in anapaestic metre, or the treatment of a long and lofty theme in short, choppy lines. This latter defect is what repels us so much from Conington's really scholarly translation of the Aeneid.[4]

What the radicals so wantonly disregard in their eccentric performances is unity of thought. Amidst their wildly repeated leaps from one rough metre to another, they ignore the underlying uniformity of each of their poems. Scene may change; atmosphere may vary; yet one poem cannot but carry one definite message, and to suit this ultimate and fundamental message must one metre be selected and sustained. To accommodate the minor inequalities of tone in a poem, one regular metre will amply lend itself to diversity. Our chief, but now annoyingly neglected measure, the heroic couplet, is capable of taking on infinite shades of expression by the right selection and sequence of words, and by the proper placing of the caesura or pause in each line. Dr. Blair, in his 38th lecture, explains and illustrates with admirable perspicuity the importance of the caesura's location in varying the flow of heroic verse.[5] It is also possible to lend variety to a poem by using very judiciously occasional feet of a metre different from that of the body of the work. This is generally done without disturbing the syllabification, and it in no way impairs or obscures the dominant measure.

Most amusing of all the claims of the radical is the assertion that true poetic fervour can never be confined to regular metre; that the wild-eyed, long-haired rider of Pegasus must inflict upon a suffering public in unaltered form the vague conceptions which flit in noble chaos through his exalted soul. While it is perfectly obvious that the hour of rare inspiration must be improved without the hindrance of grammars or rhyming dictionaries, it is no less obvious that the succeeding hour of calmer contemplation may very profitably be devoted to amendment and polishing. The "language of the heart" must be clarified and made intelligible to other hearts, else its purport will forever be confined to its creator. If natural laws of metrical construction be wilfully set aside, the reader's attention will be distracted from the soul of the poem to its uncouth and ill-fitting dress. The more nearly perfect the metre, the less conspicuous its presence; hence if the poet desires supreme consideration for his matter, he should make his verses so smooth that the sense may never be interrupted.

The ill effect of metrical laxity on the younger generation of poets is enormous. These latest suitors of the Muse, not yet sufficiently trained to distinguish between their own artless crudities and the cultivated monstrosities of the educated but radical bard, come to regard with distrust the orthodox critics, and to believe that no grammatical, rhetorical, or metrical skill is necessary to their own development. The result cannot but be a race of churlish, cacophonous hybrids, whose amorphous outcries will waver uncertainly betwixt prose and verse, absorbing the vices of both and the virtues of neither.

When proper consideration shall be taken of the perfect naturalness of polished metre, a wholesome reaction against the present chaos must inevitably occur; so that the few remaining disciples of conservatism and good taste may justly entertain one last, lingering hope of hearing from modern lyres the stately heroics of Pope, the majestic blank verse of Thomson, the terse octosyllabics of Swift, the sonorous quatrains of Gray, and the lively anapaests of Sheridan and Moore.

EDITOR'S NOTE FP: *Conservative* 1, No. 2 (July 1915): 2–4. HPL's first attack on modernist literary radicalism, although his chief targets appear to be the careless poets of the UAPA who could not be troubled to write in correct metre but who were probably not consciously striving to write in free verse. See "The Vers Libre Epidemic" (pp. 19–20) as well as such poems as "The State of Poetry" (1915; *AT* 215–17) and "Amissa Minerva" (1919; *AT* 234–37).

Notes

1. "We all are the worse through license." Terence, *Heauton Timorumenos* 483 (*sumu'* for *sumus* in Terence).

2. See Dionysius of Halicarnassus, *On Literary Composition*, and W. G. F. Hegel, *Lectures on Aesthetics*.

3. I.e., Anne Tillery Renshaw, a longtime amateur journalist and colleague of HPL. For HPL's further comment on the essay, see DPC (September 1915; *CE1*).

4. *The Aeneid of Virgil*, translated into English Verse by John Conington (New York: W. J. Widdleton, 1867). Conington (1825–1869) translated the *Aeneid* in iambic trimeter.

5. See Hugh Blair (1718–1800), *Lectures on Rhetoric and Belles Lettres* (1783). HPL owned a Philadelphia (1829) edition (*LL* 102). Blair was a leading literary critic in the 18th century.

THE ALLOWABLE RHYME

"Sed ubi plura nitent in carmine, non ego paucis
Offendar maculis."
—*Horace.*[1]

The poetical tendency of the present and of the preceding century has been divided in a manner singularly curious. One loud and conspicuous faction of bards, giving way to the corrupt influences of a decaying general culture, seems to have abandoned all the proprieties of versification and reason in its mad scramble after sensational novelty; whilst the other and quieter school, constituting a more logical evolution from the poesy of the Georgian period, demands an accuracy of rhyme and metre unknown even to the polished artists of the age of Pope.

The rational contemporary disciple of the Nine, justly ignoring the dissonant shrieks of the radicals, is therefore confronted with a grave choice of technique. May he retain the liberties of imperfect or "allowable" rhyming which were enjoyed by his ancestors, or must he conform to the new ideals of perfection evolved during the past century? The writer of this article is frankly an archaist in verse. He has not scrupled to rhyme "toss'd" with "coast", "come" with "Rome", or "home" with "gloom" in his very latest published efforts, thereby proclaiming his maintenance of the old-fashioned poets as models; but sound modern criticism, proceeding from Mr. Rheinhart Kleiner and from other sources which must needs command respect, has impelled him here to rehearse the question for public benefit, and particularly to present his own side, attempting to justify his adherence to the style of two centuries ago.

The earliest English attempts at rhyming probably included words whose agreement is so slight that it deserves the name of mere "assonance" rather than that of actual rhyme. Thus in the original ballad of "Chevy-Chase", we encounter "King" and "within" supposedly rhymed, whilst in the similar "Battle of Otterbourne" we behold "long" rhymed with "down", "ground" with "Agurstonne", and "name" with "again". In the ballad of "Sir Patrick Spense", "morn" and "storm", and "deep" and "feet" are rhymed. But the infelicities were obviously the result not of artistic negligence, but of plebeian ignorance, since the old ballads were undoubtedly the careless products of a peasant minstrelsy. In Chaucer, a poet of the Court, the allowable rhyme is but infrequently discovered, hence we may assume that the original ideal in English verse was the perfect rhyming sound.

Spenser uses allowable rhymes, giving in one of his characteristic stanzas the three distinct sounds of "Lord", "ador'd", and "word", all supposed to rhyme; but of his pronunciation we know little, and may justly guess that to the ears of his contemporaries the sounds were not conspicuously different. Ben Jonson's employment of imperfect rhyming was much like Spenser's; moderate, and partially to be excused on account of a chaotic pronunciation. The better poets of the Restoration were also sparing of allowable rhymes; Cowley, Waller, Marvell, and many others being quite regular in this respect.

It was therefore upon a world unprepared that Samuel Butler burst forth with his immortal "Hudibras", whose comical familiarity of diction is in grotesqueness surpassed only by its clever licentiousness of rhyming. Butler's well-known double rhymes are of necessity forced and inexact, and in ordinary single rhymes he seems to have had no more regard for precision. "Vow'd" and "would", "talisman" and "slain", "restores" and "devours" are a few specimens selected at random.

Close after Butler came John Oldham,[2] a satirist whose force and brilliancy gained him universal praise, and whose enormous crudity both in rhyme and in metre was forgotten amidst the splendour of his attacks. Oldham was almost absolutely ungoverned by the demands of the ear, and perpetrated such atrocious rhymes as "heads" and "besides", "devise" and "this", "again" and "sin", "tool" and "foul", "end" and "design'd", and even "prays" and "cause".

The glorious Dryden, refiner and purifier of English verse, did less for rhyme than he did for metre. Though nowhere attaining the extravagances of his friend Oldham, he lent the sanction of his great authority to rhymes which Dr. Johnson admits are "open to objection". But one vast difference betwixt Dryden and his loose predecessors must be observed. Dryden had so far improved metrical cadence, that the final syllables of heroic couplets stood out in especial eminence, displaying and emphasising every possible similarity of sound; that is, lending to sounds in the first place approximately similar, the added similarity caused by the new prominence of their perfectly corresponding positions in their respective lines.

It were needless to dwell upon the rhetorical polish of the age immediately succeeding Dryden's. So far as English versification is concerned, Pope was the world, and all the world was Pope. Dryden had founded a new school of verse, but the development and ultimate perfection of this art remained for the sickly lad who before the age of twelve begged to be taken to Will's Coffee-House, that he might obtain one personal view of the aged Dryden, his idol and model. Delicately attuned to the subtlest harmonies of poetical construction, Alexander Pope brought English prosody to its zenith, and still stands alone on the heights. Yet he, exquisite master of verse that he was, frowned not upon imperfect rhymes, provided they were set in faultless metre. Though most of his allowable rhymes are merely variations in the breadth and nature of vowel sounds, he in one instance departs far enough from rigid perfection to rhyme the words "vice" and "destroys".[3] Yet who can take offence? The unvarying ebb and flow of the refined metrical impulse conceals and condones all else.

Every argument by which English blank verse or Spanish assonant verse is sustained, may with greater force be applied to the allowable rhyme. Metre is the real essential of poetical technique, and when two sounds of substantial resemblance are so placed that one follows the other in a certain measured relation, the normal ear cannot without cavilling find fault with a slight want of identity in the respective dominant vowels. The rhyming of a long vowel with a short one is common in all the Georgian poets, and when well recited cannot but be overlooked amidst the general flow of the verse; as, for instance, the following from Pope:

> "But thinks, admitted to that equal SKY,
> His faithful dog shall bear him COMPANY."

Of like nature is the rhyming of actually different vowels whose sounds are, when pronounced in animated oration, by no means dissimilar. Out of verse, such words as "join" and "line" are quite unlike, but Pope well rhymes them when he writes:

> "While expletives their feeble aid do JOIN,
> And ten low words oft creep in one dull LINE."[4]

It is the final consonantal sound in rhyming which can never vary. This, above all else, gives the desired similarity. Syllables which agree in vowels but not in final consonants are not rhymes at all, but simply assonants. Yet such is the inconsistent carelessness of the average modern writer, that he often uses these mere assonants to a greater extent than his fathers ever employed actually allowable rhymes. The writer, in his critical duties,[5] has more than once been forced to point out the attempted rhyming of such words as "fame" and "lane", "task" and "glass", or "feels" and "yields", and in view of these impossible combinations he cannot blame himself very seriously for rhyming "art" and "shot" in the March *Conservative*; for this pair of words have at least identical consonants at the end.[6]

That allowable rhymes have real advantages of a positive sort is an opinion by no means lightly to be denied. The monotony of a long heroic poem may often be pleasantly relieved by judicious interruptions in the perfect succession of rhymes, just as the metre may sometimes be adorned with occasional triplets and Alexandrines. Another advantage is the greater latitude allowed for the expression of thought. How numerous are the writers who, from restriction to perfect rhyming, are frequently compelled to abandon a neat epigram or brilliant antithesis, which allowable rhyme would easily permit, or else to introduce a dull expletive merely to supply a desired rhyme!

But a return to historical considerations shews us only too clearly the logical trend of taste, and the reason Mr. Kleiner's demand for absolute perfection is no idle cry. In Oliver Goldsmith there arose one who, though retaining the familiar classical diction of Pope, yet advanced further still toward what he deemed ideal polish by virtually abandoning the allowable rhyme. In unvaried exactitude run the couplets of "The Traveller" and of "The Deserted Village", and none can deny to them a certain urbanity which pleases the critical ear. With but little less precision are moulded the simple rhymes of Cowper, whilst the pompous Erasmus Darwin likewise shews more attention to identity of sound than do the Queen Anne bards. Gifford's translations of Juvenal and Persius shew to an almost equal degree the tendency of the age, and Campbell, Crabbe, Wordsworth, Byron, Keats, and Thomas Moore are all inclined to refrain from the liberties practiced by those of former times. To deny the importance of such a widespread change of technique is fruitless, for its existence argues for its naturalness. The best critics of the nineteenth and twentieth centuries demand perfect rhyming, and no aspirant for fame can afford to depart from a standard so universal. It is evidently the true goal of the English, as well as of the French bard; the goal from which we were but temporarily deflected during the preceding age.

But exceptions should and must be made in the case of a few who have somehow absorbed the atmosphere of other days, and who long in their hearts for the stately sound of the old classic cadences. Well may their predilection for imperfect rhyming be discouraged to a limited extent, but to chain them wholly to modern rules would be barbarous. Every individual mind demands a certain freedom of expression, and the man who cannot express himself satisfactorily without the stimulation derived from the spirited mode of two centuries ago should certainly be permitted to follow without undue restraint a practice at once so harmless, so free from essential error, and so sanctioned by precedent, as that of employing in his poetical compositions the smooth and inoffensive allowable rhyme.

EDITOR'S NOTE   FP: *Conservative* 1, No. 3 (October 1915): 3–6. A somewhat antiquated piece defending HPL's use of the archaic practice of the "allowable" rhyme (i.e., grove/love) against strictures made by Rheinhart Kleiner (1892–1949), an amateur poet and critic living in New York City and a correspondent of HPL's since 1914. HPL was specifically addressing a criticism found in Kleiner's amateur paper, the *Piper*, May 1915, p. 6: "Our critic's anxiety that the laws of correct verse be upheld will be shared by every true artist. But even he is inclined to be a little too lenient, perhaps, in the case of 'allowable' rhymes, using the standards of another day, in fact, as his authority. The metrical art in the hands of comparatively recent writers has attained to such finish that we have every right to expect unvarying conformity to these requirements in the work of all who aspire to the name of poet. Such rhymes as 'far' and 'war,' for instance, were sometimes used by the bard when reduced to the last extremity, and in the past he did so without scruple. But to-day there is a tendency to frown upon such apologies and evasions on the part of the poet and to expect him to adhere to every law of his art."

Notes

1. "But where many things shine in a poem, I will not be offended by a few blemishes." Horace, *Ars Poetica* 351–52 (*Verum* for *Sed* in Horace).

2. See HPL's poem "John Oldham: A Defence" (*United Co-operative*, June 1919; AT 130), a reply to Kleiner's poem "John Oldham: 1653–1683," published on the same page of the *United Co-operative*.

3. The "vice/destroys" rhyme does not appear in Pope.

4. The first quotation is from *An Essay on Man* (1733–34), 1.111–12; the second from *An Essay on Criticism* (1711), ll. 346–47.

5. HPL alludes to his many contributions to DPC (see *CE1*).

6. The rhyme appears in the poem "The Simple Speller's Tale" (*Conservative*, April [not March] 1915), ll. 9–10 (AT 204). Kleiner had written (*Piper*, May 1915, p. 6): "In Mr. Lovecraft's verses entitled 'The Simple Speller's Tale' the word 'art' is rhymed with 'shot.' This could not be considered 'allowable' even by a very liberal interpretation of the poet's own theory."

THE PROPOSED AUTHORS' UNION

It has been more than once remarked, that there is an intangible bond of kinship betwixt the highest and the humblest elements of the community. Whilst the bourgeois complacently busy themselves with their commonplace, respectable, and unimaginative careers of money-grabbing, the artist and the aristocrat join forces with the ploughman and the peasant in an involuntary mental wave of reaction against the monotony of materialism.

Never has this kinship been more plainly exhibited than in the present movement among a certain class of American professional authors to band themselves together in an honest workingman's union, and to affiliate with that peerless palladium of industrial independence—the well-known and far famed American Federation of Labour.[1] That the professions of the average modern author and the day-labourer are remarkably alike in intellectual requirements, The Conservative has long been convinced. Both types shew a certain rough vigour of technique which contrasts very strikingly with the polish of more formal times, and both seem equally pervaded with that spirit of progress and enlightenment which manifests itself in destructiveness. The modern author destroys the English language, whilst the modern strike-loving labourer destroys public and private property.

Nor can the ambitious author afford to despise the prodigious power to be gained by entrance into the ranks of organised labour. Since our obliging executive Mr. Wilson[2] has established the precedent of national surrender at the least crook of Labour's gnarled finger, it may be justly assumed that the Writers' Brotherhood, as the most voluble and volatile of all the various bodies of workmen, will have complete power over all departments of the government; at least, until March 4, 1917.[3] From this immeasurable height, our professional scribblers may brandish the quill of authority over a submissive Congress, and extort by due process of law every conceivable sort of advantage over the publishing fraternity, as well as over their less enterprising fellows— the non-union writers. It is barely possible that a strike of authors might be slightly less effective as a threat, than a strike of railway men; but so fond is our present idealistic executive of the beauties of rhetoric, that he would without doubt do much for the cause of fine words.

The place of literary radicals and imagist "poets" in this Utopian scheme demands grave consideration. Since the trade union movement requires at least an elementary amount of intelligence in its adherents, and is applied mainly to SKILLED labour, these deserving iconoclasts of the Amy Lowell school would seem to be left, Othello-like, without an occupation.[4] But a moment's reflection serves to dissolve the difficulty. Here, indeed, is ideal material for that vague and awe-inspiring industrial "Mano Nera" known as the "I. W. W."![5] The benefits of such a coalition of "vers-libristes" and anarchists are patent to all. Since, save for its law and window breaking, the I. W. W. is in a condition of perpetual idleness, its leaders being generally out on strike, or out on bail; its imagistical recruits would naturally be constrained to follow the general example, inaugurating amongst themselves a sympathetic "walkout", and thereby delivering the public ear and the editorial waste basket from the annoyance of their effusions.

It is quite probable that the Brotherhood of Simplified Spellers would have to be created separately from both the American Federation of Labour and the I. W. W. Certain members of these learned societies, including expert hod-carriers and pick and shovel engineers, find difficulty enough with our language as now written, and could not possibly tolerate the presence of those reformers who are adding variability to its other faults.

The burning question of contemporary literature apparently concerns the eight-hour day for historians and the minimum wage for sonneteers. These things, and countless others which fret the artistic brain, could easily be solved by unionism. For instance; shall poets be paid by the hour or by the line? The one system discriminates unjustly against such careful workmen as Tom Gray, who consumed seven years on a job only 128 lines long, called "An Elegy Written in a Country Churchyard"; whilst the other system is too partial to speedy labourers like Sam T. Coleridge and Bob Southey, who, working together, built the poetic drama of "The Fall of Robespierre" between seven o'clock of an evening and the next noon. Also, pay by the line is unfair to writers of Alexandrines like Mike Drayton,[6] while it unduly favours tetrameter bards like Sam Butler and Walt Scott, and leaves a bitter dispute to be settled amongst the ballad-mongers; who sometimes reckon their verses by long lines of fourteen syllables each, and at other times double the number of lines, the long heptameters being split up into alternate lines of eight and six syllables, respectively.

Amateur journalism, because of its free avenues of expression, would doubtless be suppressed as a hotbed of "scabs" by the Gomperses and Giovanittis of organised literature.[7] Since it is the prevailing notion of trade unionism that no man has the right to labour without supporting a union and assuming the insignia of industrial blackmail, it may easily be deduced that literary unionism would utterly forbid all thought or expression by outsiders; and that it would, if necessary, resort to violence in cases of stubborn authorship by United members. Whether this violence would consist of stoning or of satire, is as yet uncertain.

A rather perplexing aspect of the case is afforded by the classic authors. These writers, having lived before the dawn of the New Slavery, are all necessarily non-union, wherefore a man who reads their work must logically be boycotted or placed upon the "unfair list" by the modern Knights of Grub-Street. The manner of establishing such a boycott would be interesting to determine; but the action will probably never be necessary, since but few up-to-date persons ever touch or peruse classic literature.

Looking ahead, as is the custom of all good radicals, the student may discern an age in which the whole domain of art—literary, pictorial, sculptural, architectural, and musical—will be placed upon a strictly union basis. Indeed, the modern Huns are already proving their efficient progressiveness by destroying the offensively beautiful non-union architecture of mediaeval religion in Belgium and northern France. "Down with the cathedrals, Comrade von Teufel," cries Bill Hohenzollern, head of the Berlin Butchers' Local No. 1914, "for they bear not the union label!"[8]

Concerning trade unionism among authors as a whole, The Conservative will not venture here to render an opinion. Be it sufficient for him to say, that it would at least interest him to behold a new folly in a field whose potentialities of fatuity he had thought already exhausted.

EDITOR'S NOTE FP: *Conservative* 2, No. 3 (October 1916): 7–9 (unsigned). Part of the column "In the Editor's Study." A clever satire on contemporary efforts by writers to organise themselves into a union, in which HPL manages to combine his loathing of unionism with his scorn of professionalism in literature. The movement had begun in the 1890s with a succession of short-lived writers' groups; in 1912 the Authors League became the first significant writers' group in the US.

Notes

1. The American Federation of Labor (AFL) was an association of trade unions organized in 1886.

2. HPL's hostility to Woodrow Wilson was of long standing; see, e.g., "Lucubrations Love-craftian" (*CE1*).

3. HPL alludes to the date when the winner of the 1916 presidential election would be inaugurated. Wilson in fact won the election, much to HPL's displeasure.

4. For further comments on Amy Lowell, champion of Imagism and free verse, see "The Vers Libre Epidemic" (p. 19–20).

5. "Mano Nera" is Italian for "Black Hand," referring to a Serbian secret society formed in 1911 and implicated in the murder of Archduke Ferdinand of Austria on 28 June 1914, an event that triggered World War I. The I.W.W. (Industrial Workers of the World) was a radical labor organization founded in 1905. HPL attacks them again in "Bolshevism" (1919; *CE5*).

6. See HPL's poem "A Summer Sunset and Evening" (1917?; *AT* 290), subtitled "In the metre (though perchance not the manner) of the Poly-Olbion of MIKE DRAYTON, ESQ.", referring to the Elizabethan poet Michael Drayton (1563–1631).

7. HPL refers to Samuel Gompers (1850–1924), president of the AFL for the majority of the period 1886–1924, and Arturo M. Giovanitti, an Italian-American labor organizer and orator who also wrote poetry and plays.

8. The individuals are mythical or symbolic: *von Teufel* means "of the Devil," while *Hohenzollern* refers to the German princely family that became the royal house of Prussia and Imperial Germany.

THE VERS LIBRE EPIDEMIC

The alarming prevalence in contemporary periodicals of "poetry" without shape, wit, or artistic beauty, has caused no little alarm amongst the true friends of verse, and has given rise to the apprehension that the Aonian art has entered upon a definite phase of decadence. It is the belief of The Conservative, however, that the situation is more complex and less basically menacing than it appears from superficial indications.

It must be remembered that despite the kinship between human fancy and its mode of expression, there is a sharp distinction betwixt radicalism of thought and ideals, and mere radicalism of form; and that while the most notorious specimens of free verse represent complete chaos both of sense and of structure, the majority of that which gains admission to reputable magazines is decadent only in technique. The poetical fraternity have a new plaything, and all must needs have their hour of sport with it; but the better sort of bards possess too much inherent good taste and sanity to wander too far afield. They will soon be writing real verse by accident, in spite of themselves, for they cannot defeat the natural laws of rhythm in poetical expression. Even now, the work of these poets is replete with occasional reactions to normal rhyme and rational metre. Our fellow-amateur Mrs. Renshaw, a superlatively good poet despite radical theories, has recently composed a piece of apparent vers libre which is really a well-defined iambic composition with variation in the length of the lines. The innate poet has unwittingly triumphed over the radical theorist! We may, then, safely trust to time to bring the really gifted experimenters within the fold again.

The second or wholly erratic school of free poets is that represented by Amy Lowell at her worst; a motley horde of hysterical and half-witted rhapsodists whose basic principle is the recording of their momentary moods and psychopathic phenomena in whatever amorphous and meaningless phrases may come to their tongues or pens at the moment of inspirational (or epileptic) seizure. These pitiful creatures are naturally subdivided into various types and schools, each professing certain "artistic" principles based on the analogy of poetic thought to other aesthetic sources such as form, sound, motion, and colour; but they are fundamentally similar in their utter want of a sense of proportion and of proportionate values. Their complete rejection of the intellectual (an element which they cannot possess to any great extent) is their undoing. Each writes down the sounds or symbols of sounds which drift through his head without the slightest care or knowledge that they may be understood by any other head. The type of impression they receive and record is abnormal, and cannot be transmitted to persons of normal psychology; wherefore there is no true art or even the rudiments of artistic impulse in their effusions. These radicals are animated by mental or emotional processes other than poetic. They are not in any sense poets, and their work, being wholly alien to poetry, cannot be cited as an indication of poetical decadence. It is rather a type of intellectual and aesthetic decadence of which vers libre is only one manifestation. It is the decadence which produces "futurist" music and "cubist" painting and sculpture.[1]

If concrete examples of the two sorts of unmetrical verse—the really poetical and the distinctly abnormal—be needed to illustrate their difference, the reader may compare Richard Aldington's "Inarticulate Grief" (The Poetry Review, August, 1916) with the following bit of sober nonsense, written by one of the so-called "Spectrists"[2] without any idea of humour, but found by The Conservative in one of the whimsical paragraphs of a New York "colyum conductor"; where its complete ridiculousness and irrationality recommended it for citation. Mr. Aldington is a poet of genuine depth and feeling despite his awkward medium; the reader may judge of the following without aid of critic or commentator:

> Her soul was freckled
> Like the bald head
> Of a jaundiced Jewish banker.
> Her fair and featurous face
> Writhed like
> An Albino boa-constrictor.
> She thought she resembled the Mona Lisa.
> This demonstrates the futility of thinking.[3]

And the futility of accepting the chronic free "poets" as serious factors in the literary situation today!

EDITOR'S NOTE FP: Conservative 2, No. 4 (January 1917): 2–3 (unsigned). Part of the column "In the Editor's Study." HPL's most exhaustive attempt to refute the principles of Imagism and free verse. In the end he somewhat sophistically argues that such verse is foreign to the very essence of poetry and is therefore no indication of poetic decline.

Notes

1. Futurism was a short-lived aesthetic movement founded by the Italian poet Filippo Marinetti in 1909 and purporting to address directly the phenomena of the modern world by attempting to depict movement rather than static still-life. As a movement in music, Futurism was chiefly associated with the work of Francesco Pratella (1880–1955) and other Italian composers of the 1910s and 1920s. See HPL's poem "Futurist Art" (1917; AT 223).

2. The Spectrist movement was a parody of avant-garde poetry movements staged by Arthur Davison Ficke (1883–1946) and Witter Bynner (1881–1968). They assembled a volume, Spectra (1916), as by "Emanuel Morgan and Anne Knish." In their introduction they wrote "Spectric connotes the overtures, adumbratrions, or spectres which for the poet haunt all objects both of the seen and the unseen world,—whose shadowy projections, sometimes grotesque, which, hovering around the real, give to the real its full ideal significance and its poetic worth." Many poets and critics were taken in by the hoax until Ficke revealed it; HPL apparently never saw through it. See his "Amissa Minerva" (1919): "Here Librist, Cubist, Spectrist forms arise; / With foetid vapours cloud the crystal skies" (ll. 56–57; AT 236).

3. The poem, titled "Opus 195," appears in Spectra as by Anne Knish, but was actually written by Arthur Davison Ficke.

POESY

The writer perused with no little interest Tryout's[1] comment upon Pearl K. Merritt's opinion regarding the place of poetry in literature.

Lack of appreciation of verse can be attributed to nothing save defective aesthetic perception. Poetry, with its delicate blend of imagination and melody, fulfils a natural and definite artistic function, and could not be replaced by any other species of expression. To cavil at the grammatical licence of the bard is to display much ignorance of the art in question; for the latitude allowed to versifiers is by no means considerable, and is governed by rules as rigid as those which govern prose composition.

Miss Merritt's argument, as a whole, exhibits an unimaginative mood but a step removed from the plebeian attitude which decries all literature and even all liberal culture as worthless and lacking in utility. Such prosaic stolidity grates unpleasantly upon the sensitive reader, and does much to justify Tryout's comment of Miss Merritt's present literary work.

Her recent essays, though undeniably well written, and praised by at least one critic as being "Elia-like",[2] reveal a commonplaceness of subject, narrowness of interest, obviousness of thought, and colloquialism of treatment, which make one almost wonder why they were composed at all. True, they shew keen observation, gentle humour, and sound common sense; but their nearly total lack of imaginative grace, artistic atmosphere, and spiritual elevation, plainly proclaims their author's need of that very influence which she now affects to despise so thoroughly. Amateurdom is indebted to Tryout for its timely and adequate reply.

EDITOR'S NOTE FP: *Tryout* 4, No. 7 (July 1918): [13–14]. A defence of the aesthetic status of poetry that descends into an attack on Pearl K. Merritt, a longtime amateur author and editor. She later married HPL's good friend James F. Morton.

Notes

1. HPL refers to Charles W. ("Tryout") Smith (1852–1940), editor of the *Tryout.*
2. Charles Lamb (1775–1834), British essayist and poet, was the author of *Elia* (later titled *The Essays of Elia*).

THE DESPISED PASTORAL

A mong the many and complex tendencies observable in modern poetry, or what answers for poetry in this age, is a decided but unjust scorn of the honest old pastoral, immortalised by Theocritus and Virgil, and revived in our own literature by Spenser.

Nor is this unfavourable attitude confined alone to the formal eclogue whose classical elements are so well described and exemplified by Mr. Pope.[1] Whenever a versifier adorns his song with the pleasing and innocent imagery of this type of composition, or borrows its mild and sweet atmosphere, he is forthwith condemned as an irresponsible pedant and fossil by every little-wit critic in Grub-Street.

Modern bards, in their endeavour to display with seriousness and minute verisimilitude the inward operations of the human mind and emotions, have come to look down upon the simple description of ideal beauty, or the straightforward presentation of pleasing images for no other purpose than to delight the fancy. Such themes they deem trivial and artificial, and altogether unworthy of an art whose design they take to be the analysis and reproduction of Nature in all her moods and aspects.

But in this belief, the writer cannot but hold that our contemporaries are misjudging the true province and functions of poesy. It was no starched classicist, but the exceedingly unconventional Edgar Allan Poe, who roundly denounced the melancholy metaphysicians and maintained that true poetry has for its first object "pleasure, not truth", and "indefinite pleasure instead of definite pleasure".[2] Mr. Poe, in another essay, defined poetry as "the rhythmical creation of beauty",[3] intimating that its concern for the dull or ugly aspects of life is slight indeed. That the American bard and critic was fundamentally just in his deductions, seems well proved by a comparative survey of those poems of all ages which have lived, and those which have fallen into deserved obscurity.

The English pastoral, based upon the best models of antiquity, depicts engaging scenes of Arcadian simplicity, which not only transport the imagination through their intrinsic beauty, but recall to the scholarly mind the choicest remembrances of classical Greece and Rome. Though the combination of rural pursuits with polished sentiments and diction is patently artificial, the beauty is not a whit less; nor do the conventional names, phrases, and images detract in the least from the quaint agreeableness of the whole. The magic of this sort of verse is to any unprejudiced mind irresistible, and is capable of evoking a more deliciously placid and refreshing train of pictures in the imagination, than may be obtained from any more realistic species of composition. Every untainted fancy begets ideal visions of which the pastoral forms a legitimate and artistically necessary reflection.

It is not impossible that the intellectual upheaval attendant upon the present conflict will bring about a general simplification and rectification of taste, and an appreciation of the value of pure imaginary beauty in a world so full of actual misery, which may combine to restore the despised pastoral to its proper station.

EDITOR'S NOTE FP: *Conservative* 4, No. 1 (July 1918): 2. An unconvincing essay, more wish-fulfilment than argument, defending pastoral poetry as still relevant in the modern age. Among HPL's pastorals can be numbered such seasonal poems as "Spring" (1917) and "Ver Rusticum" (1918), chiefly imitations of James Thomson's *The Seasons* (1726–30).

Notes

1. Pope's "Pastorals" (preceded by "A Discourse on Pastoral Poetry") were written in 1704 and published in Jacob Tonson's *Miscellanies* (1709).

2. The statement is from "The Philosophy of Composition" (*Graham's Magazine*, April 1846).

3. From "The Poetic Principle" (*Sartain's Union Magazine*, October 1850).

THE LITERATURE OF ROME

"The centre of our studies, the goal of our thoughts, the point to which all paths lead and the point from which all paths start again, is to be found in Rome and her abiding power."

—*Freeman*.[1]

Few students of mankind, if truly impartial, can fail to select as the greatest of human institutions that mighty and enduring civilisation which, first appearing on the banks of the Tiber, spread throughout the known world and became the direct parent of our own. If to Greece is due the existence of all modern thought, so to Rome is due its survival and our possession of it; for it was the majesty of the Eternal City which, reducing all Western Europe to a single government, made possible the wide and uniform diffusion of the high culture borrowed from Greece, and thereby laid the foundation of European enlightenment. To this day the remnants of the Roman world exhibit a superiority over those parts which never came beneath the sway of the Imperial Mother; a superiority strikingly manifest when we contemplate the savage code and ideals of the Germans, aliens to the priceless heritage of Latin justice, humanity, and philosophy. The study of Roman literature, then, needs no plea to recommend it. It is ours by intellectual descent; our bridge to all antiquity and to those Grecian stores of art and thought which are the fountain head of existing culture.

In considering Rome and her artistic history, we are conscious of a subjectivity impossible in the case of Greece or any other ancient nation. Whilst the Hellenes, with their strange beauty-worship and defective moral ideals,[2] are to be admired and pitied at once, as luminous but remote phantoms; the Romans, with their greater practical sense, ancient virtue, and love of law and order, seem like our own people. It is with personal pride that we read of the valour and conquests of this mighty race, who used the alphabet we use, spoke and wrote with but little difference many of the words we speak and write, and with divine creative power evolved virtually all the forms of law which govern us today. To the Greek, art and literature were inextricably involved in daily life and thought; to the Roman, as to us, they were a separate unit in a many-sided civilisation. Undoubtedly this circumstance proves the inferiority of the Roman culture to the Greek; but it is an inferiority shared by our own culture, and therefore a bond of sympathy.

The race whose genius gave rise to the glories of Rome is, unhappily, not now in existence. Centuries of devastating wars, and foreign immigration into Italy, left but few real Latins after the early Imperial aera. The original Romans were a blend of closely related dolichocephalic Mediterranean tribes, whose racial affinities with the Greeks could not have been very remote, plus a slight Etruscan element of doubtful classification. The latter stock is an object of much mystery to ethnologists, being at present described by most authorities as of the brachycephalic Alpine variety.[3] Many Roman customs and habits of thought are traceable to this problematical people.

It is a singular circumstance, that classic Latin literature is, save in the case of satire, almost wholly unrelated to the crude effusions of the primitive Latins; being borrowed as to form and subject from the Greeks, at a comparatively late date in Rome's political history. That this borrowing assisted greatly in Latin cultural advancement, none may deny; but it is also true that the new Hellenised literature exerted a malign influence on the nation's ancient austerity, introducing lax Grecian notions which contributed to moral and material decadence. The counter-currents, however, were strong; and the virile Roman spirit shone nobly through the Athenian dress in almost every instance, imparting to the literature a distinctively national cast, and displaying the peculiar characteristics of the Italian mind. On the whole, Roman life moulded Roman literature more than the literature moulded the life.

The earliest writings of the Latins are, save for a fragment or two, lost to posterity; though a few of their qualities are known. They were for the most part crude ballads in an odd "Saturnian" metre copied from the Etruscans, primitive religious chants and dirges, rough medleys of comic verse forming the prototype of satire, and awkward "Fescennine" dialogues or dramatic farces enacted by the lively peasantry. All doubtless reflected the simple, happy, and virtuous, if stern, life of the home-loving agricultural race which was destined later to conquer the world. In B.C. 364 the medleys or "Saturae" were enacted upon the Roman stage, the words supplemented by the pantomime and dancing of Etruscan performers who spoke no Latin. Another early form of dramatic art was the "fabula Atellana", which was adapted from the neighbouring tribe of Oscans, and which possessed a simple plot and stock characters. While this early literature embodied Oscan and Etruscan as well as Latin elements, it was truly Roman; for the Roman was himself formed of just such a mixture. All Italy contributed to the Latin stream, but at no time did any non-Roman dialect rise to the distinction of a real literature. We have here no parallel for the Aeolic, Ionic, and Doric phases of Greek literature.

Classical Latin literature dates from the beginning of Rome's free intercourse with Greece, a thing brought about by the conquest of the Hellenic colonies in Southern Italy. When Tarentum fell to the Romans in B.C. 272, there was brought to Rome as a captive and slave a young man of great attainments, by name Andronicus. His master, M. Livius Salinator, was quick to perceive his genius, and soon gave him his liberty, investing him according to custom with his own nomen of Livius, so that the freedman was afterward known as Livius Andronicus. The erstwhile slave, having established a school, commenced his literary career by translating the Odyssey into Latin Saturnian verse for the use of his pupils. This feat was followed by the translation of a Greek drama, which was enacted in B.C. 240, and formed the first genuinely classic piece beheld by the Roman public. The success of Livius Andronicus was very considerable, and he wrote many more plays, in which he himself acted, besides attempting lyric and religious poetry. His work, of which but 41 lines remain in existence, was pronounced inferior by Cicero; yet must ever be accorded respect as the very commencement of a great literature.

[Andronicus was the first of a large group of dramatic writers who flourished in the third and second centuries B.C. Cnaeus Naevius, a native Italian, produced his first play in B.C. 233. His subjects, both tragic and comic, were Greek, but his medium was the old Saturnian verse, and he lamented the Hellenistic tendency of his day. He also wrote the first Latin epic, a Saturnian poem on the First Punic War, highly praised by Cicero, but now regrettably lost. His satirical comedies gained him imprisonment and banishment, and he died an exile, though later hailed as "last of the native minstrels".

Quintus Ennius, born B.C. 239 of mixed Greek and Oscan ancestry, was a friend of Cato, the Censor, and wrote many tragedies and comedies besides the epic for which he is famous. The latter, based on the legends of old Rome, is now lost to us save for 600 lines, though it survived to the Middle Ages as a masterpiece of genius. Ennius was the first to supersede the old Saturnian verse with the classical dactylic hexameter of the Greeks; a measure which at once became the standard heroic metre of Latin literature. This metre may best be illustrated to the modern reader as that in which the poem of "Evangeline", by Longfellow, is written. Classical metre was based on quantity, not stress, and poems were entirely devoid of rhyme.

Whilst Naevius followed Aristophanes in the old Greek comedy of personal ridicule, T. Maccius Plautus, 254–184 B.C., the leading comic poet of his aera, adopted the New Comedy of Menander, which dealt with social customs and general traits of humanity. His principal successor, P. Terentius Afer, commonly known as Terence, was once called by Caesar only a "half-Menander", owing to his liberal borrowings from the celebrated Greek.[4] Terence was by birth a Libyan. Coming to Rome as a slave, he was educated and freed by his generous master, and produced his first play when only twenty-one. His comedies are marked by keen wit and much delicacy; one of them containing that famous sentiment beginning "Homo sum",[5] which was so enthusiastically received by the audience. In general, the early dramatic period declined after Terence. It was the first flowering of a literature destined to mature in other forms.]

Latin verse continued to depend largely on Greek models, but in prose the Romans were more original, and the first celebrated prose writer was that stern old Greek-hater, M. Porcius Cato (234–149 B.C.), who prepared orations and wrote on history, agriculture, and other subjects. His style was clear, though by no means perfect, and it is a source of regret that his historical work, the "Origines", is lost. Other prose writers, all orators, extending from Cato's time down to the polished period, are Laelius, Scipio, the Gracchi, Antonius, Crassus, and the celebrated Q. Hortensius, early opponent of Cicero.

Satire, that one absolutely native product of Italy, first found independent expression in C. Lucilius (180–103 B.C.), though the great Roman inclination toward that form of expression had already found an outlet in satirical passages in other sorts of writing. There is perhaps no better weapon for the scourging of vice and folly than this potent literary embodiment of wit and irony, and certainly no author ever wielded that weapon more nobly than Lucilius. His aera was characterised by great degeneracy, due to Greek influences, and the manner in which he upheld failing Virtue won him the unmeasured regard of his contemporaries and successors. Horace, Persius, and Juvenal all owe much to him, and it is melancholy to reflect that all his work, save a fragment or two, is lost to the world. Lucilius, sometimes called "The Father of Satire", was a man of equestrian rank, and fought with Scipio at Numantia.

With the age of M. Tullius Cicero (106–43 B.C.)—the Golden Age—opens the period of highest perfection in Roman literature. It is hardly necessary to describe Cicero himself—his luminous talents have made him synonymous with the height of Attic elegance in wit, forensic art, and prose composition. Born of equestrian rank, he was educated with care, and embarked on his career at the age of twenty-five. His orations against L. Sergius Catilina during his consulship broke up one of the most dastardly plots in history, and gained for him the title of "Father of His Country". Philosophy claimed much of his time, and his delightful treatises "De Amicitia" and "De Senectute" will be read as long as friendship endures on earth, or men grow old. Near the end of his life Cicero, opposing the usurpations of M. Antonius, delivered his masterpieces of oratory, the "Philippics", modelled after the similar orations of the Greek Demosthenes against Philip of Macedonia. His murder, demanded by the vengeful Antonius in the proscription of the second triumvirate, was the direct result of these Philippics. Contemporary with Cicero was M. Terentius Varro, styled "most learned of the Romans", though ungraceful in style. Of his works, embracing many diverse subjects, only one agricultural treatise survives.

In this survey we need allot but little space to Caius Julius Caesar, probably the greatest human being so far to appear on this globe. His Commentaries on the Gallic and Civil Wars are models of pure and perspicuous prose, and his other work, voluminous but now lost, was doubtless of equal merit. At the present time, passages of Caesar's Gallic War are of especial interest on account of their allusions to battles against those perpetual enemies of civilisation, the Germans. How familiar, for instance, do we find the following passage from Book Six, describing German notions of honour:

"Latrocinia, nullam habent infamiam quae extra fines cujusque civitatis fiunt, atque ea juventutis exercendae ac desidiae minuendae causa fieri praedicant!"[6]

[C. Sallustius Crispus (86–34 B.C.), commonly known as Sallust, is celebrated for his histories of the Jugurthine war and Catilinian conspiracy, written in the style of the Greek Thucydides, with long imaginary speeches in the mouths of the characters. His prose is admirable, and his works are extensively read in schools.

Turning to the poets of the same period, we come upon one of the greatest thinkers of all time. Lucretius, 98–55 B.C., was the author of "De Rerum Natura", a didactic poem in about 7500 lines, expounding the Epicurean philosophy, and in particular seeking to explain the cosmogony and phenomena of the natural world. The majority of his conclusions accord well with the most advanced scientific thought of today, though some of them have sources as old as Democritus. As poetry, "De Rerum Natura" is altogether admirable. Lucretius sought to reconcile man to the natural order, enjoining rational pleasure and philosophical reflection.

Contemporary with Lucretius was the celebrated lyrist and amatory bard, C. Valerius Catullus (84–54 B.C.), who may be said to have introduced lyric poetry amongst the Romans. His Greek models were Sappho and the Alexandrian Callimachus, and after their manner he produced a large array of verses, the most famous of which are addressed to one "Lesbia", supposed to be a sister of the infamous P. Clodius. From his pen there came also a remarkably weird poem called "Atys" or "Attis".[7]]

The next generation of authors fall within what has been termed the "Augustan Age", the period during which Octavianus, having become Emperor, encouraged letters to a degree hitherto unknown; not only personally, but through his famous minister Maecenas (73–8 B.C.). The literature of this period is immortal through the genius of Virgil, Horace, and Ovid, and has made the name "Augustan" an universal synonyme for classic elegance and urbanity. Thus in our own literary history, Queen Anne's reign is known as the "Augustan Age" on account of the brilliant wits and poets then at their zenith. Maecenas, whose name must ever typify the ideal of munificent literary patronage, was himself a scholar and poet, as was indeed Augustus. Both, however, are overshadowed by the titanic geniuses who gathered around them.

[Foremost of the Augustans, and next to Homer perhaps the world's greatest poet, was P. Vergilius Maro (70–19 B.C.), commonly known as Virgil. Born of honest rural stock in the tiny village of Andes, near Mantua, Virgil has often been affectionately termed "The Mantuan Swain". His education took place at Cremona and Rome, and at the age of 22 he commenced the Eclogues or pastoral poems modelled after the Greek Theocritus, which form the earliest of his surviving efforts. Being dispossessed of his farm when the countryside was apportioned to the soldiery who had battled against Brutus, Virgil was reimbursed by the generous Emperor Augustus, whose praises he sang in his later eclogues. At the suggestion of his friend and patron Maecenas, Virgil next exercised his Muse in the composition of an agricultural poem called the "Georgics", whose precepts are sound, and whose poetry is exquisitely finished. But the poet's crowning work is his "Æneid", a sublime epic in twelve books designed to glorify the Roman people and Caesar's line by tracing them back to Æneas, a mythical survivor of conquered Troy who was said to have settled Italy. The Æneid is modelled mainly after Homer, though Virgil also drew upon the best of his Roman predecessors. The story of the epic is too well known to require description. To the present writer nothing in all the range of poetry seems to stirring and impressive as Virgil's account of the prophecy of Anchises, Æneas' father, respecting the future glories of Rome, which ends with those memorable lines today applicable to our own Anglo-Saxon race if we but substitute *Britanne* for *Romane*:

> "Tu regere imperio populos, Romane, memento;
> Hae tibi erunt artes; pacisque imponere morem,
> Parcere subjectis, et debellare superbos."[8]

Most modern in spirit of all the classic authors—so modern, in fact, that nearly every bard of today makes occasional translations or imitations of his witty lines—is the lyrist and satirist Q. Horatius Flaccus (65–8 B.C.), commonly called Horace. Though the son of a former slave of Venusia, he enjoyed the advantages of an excellent education, and never lamented his humble birth. After a brief and ignominious military experience in the cause of Brutus, which resulted in the confiscation of his possessions, Horace resided in Rome as an obscure clerk, till the excellence of his poetry recommended him to the notice of Virgil, who introduced him to Maecenas and Augustus in B.C. 39. Thereafter he was part of the intimate literary circle of the court. As a present from Maecenas he received a Sabine country farm, where he spent much of his time, and which he has immortalised in verse. As a poet Horace is always subjective and autobiographical. He followed various metres, sometimes the dactylic hexameter, sometimes the lyric forms of Sappho and Alcaeus. His works consist of satires, which are without exception mild, tolerant, and written as if by a man of the world who shares the follies he ridicules; epodes, or individual satires; and odes, from which he derives his greatest fame. The odes are of extreme literary excellence, and so vividly reflect the light, trivial, fundamental commonplaces of human nature, that they have survived with unimpaired popularity to the present day, and amply fulfil their author's pardonable boast, 'that he had reared a monument more lasting than brass'.[9] Occasionally Horace casts aside the commonplace, but it is as an amiable and sophisticated bard of the average man that he is mainly to be considered. His friendship with Virgil was very close, though he was never distinguished by that shining virtue and impeccable moral purity which characterised the great author of the "Æneid".

Last of the Augustan bards, and least of the trio which he forms with Virgil and Horace, is P. Ovidius Naso (43 B.C.–17 A.D.), commonly called Ovid. Born at Sulmo, of an equestrian family, he went early to Rome to secure a legal education; but his greater fitness for poetry soon becoming apparent, he was permitted by his father to go abroad for study and travel. Upon his return, Ovid commenced his career as a poet by writing a tragedy, now lost, entitled "Medea". At the same time he indited the "Amores", a collection of verses whose low moral tone excited unfavourable notice even in an age when Rome had sunk far below her ancient standards of virtue. A succeeding effort, the "Heroides", was of higher quality. The next Ovidian product, "Ars Amatoria", with its sequel "Remedia Amoris", marked a serious relapse of the poet's taste, and later proved a pretext for his still inexplicable life banishment by the Emperor in A.D. 8, to the desolate village of Tomi, in Thrace, on the Black Sea near the mouth of the Danube. Before his banishment, however, the poet produced his famous work, the "Metamorphoses", a collection of pleasing myths involving miraculous changes of form, such as that of Cygnus into a swan.[10] Interrupted by his banishment was the "Fasti", a description of celestial phenomena and of Roman festivals, with an account of the latter's legendary origin. After his banishment Ovid wrote the "Tristia", poems of lamentation, and several minor effusions, including an elegy on Augustus, couched in the newly learned language of the barbarians amongst whom he dwelt. Ovid's work exhibits marked decadence as compared with that of the earlier Augustans, but he is always facile and entertaining. The "Metamorphoses" have all the pleasing piquancy and simplicity of fairy tales, though conforming throughout to the strictest requirements of classic verse.

The sole great prose writer of the Augustan aera is the historian, T. Livius (59 B.C.–17 A.D.), commonly called Livy, who was born at Patavium of an ancient patrician family. Going to Rome in B.C. 31, he soon became so famous as a scholar, that a Spaniard is said to have come all the way from Gades just to behold him in person. The life work of Livy is a prodigious history of Rome from legendary times to the author's day, entitled "Annales", on which he laboured for forty years. It contains 142 books, and was published in instalments, each covering a decade of history. Livy's death interrupted the labour before he had time to cover the Augustan aera itself. At present only 35 books survive; a circumstance most tantalising and regrettable historically. The style of Livy is of utmost elegance, though as an historian he is marred by too great credulity in legends and unreliable authorities. His narrative flows along with all the ease and liveliness of fiction, and makes reading of the most pleasing sort.]

Succeeding the Golden Age, and extending down to the time of the Antonines, is the so-called "Silver Age" of Latin literature, in which are included several writers of the highest genius, despite a general decadence and artificiality of style. In the reign of Tiberius we note the annalists C. Velleius Paterculus and Valerius Maximus, the medical writer A. Cornelius Celsus, and the fabulist Phaedrus, the latter a freedman from Thrace who imitated his more celebrated predecessor Æsop.

[In the Silver Age of Latinity are included two eminent epic poets, Lucan (39–65 A.D.) and Statius (61–96 A.D.). Lucan was by birth a Spaniard, nephew of the celebrated philosopher Seneca. He was educated at Rome, and was at one time an intimate friend of the Emperor Nero. Later, having incurred imperial disfavour, he was condemned to death by his own hand. His fame arises from his poem "Pharsalia", which celebrates the civil war betwixt Caesar and Pompeius.[11] Its style is ornate, and according to some critics bombastic; though in past times it has enjoyed comparison even with the Æneid. Statius was a Neapolitan, the son of an eminent grammatical scholar. His masterpiece, the "Thebaid", is founded on the Greek myth of the Seven against Thebes, and was twelve years in the process of composition. Modern critics place Statius above Lucan as an author, and consider the "Thebaid" the greatest of post-Augustan epics.]

The satirist, A. Persius Flaccus (34–62 A.D.), is the first eminent poet to appear after the death of Ovid. Born at Volaterrae of an equestrian family, carefully reared by his gifted mother, and educated at Rome by the Stoic philosopher Cornutus, he became famous not only as a moralist of the greatest power and urbanity, but as one whose life accorded perfectly with his precepts; a character of unblemished virtue and delicacy in an age of unprecedented evil. His work, which attacked only the less repulsive follies of the day, contains passages of the highest nobility. His early death terminated a career of infinite promise.

In the person of D. Junius Juvenalis (57–128 A.D.), commonly called Juvenal, we behold the foremost satirist in literary history. Born at Aquinum of humble but comfortably situated parents, he came to Rome as a rhetorician; though upon discovering his natural bent, turned to poetical satire. With a fierceness and moral seriousness unprecedented in literature, Juvenal attacked the darkest vices of his age; writing as a relentless enemy rather than as a man of the world like Horace, or as a detached spectator like Persius. The oft repeated accusation that his minute descriptions of vice shew a morbid interest therein, may fairly be refuted when one considers the almost unthinkable depths to which the republic had fallen. Only a tolerant or a secluded observer could avoid attacking openly and bitterly the evil conditions which obtruded themselves on every hand; and Juvenal, a genuine Roman of the active and virtuous old school, was neither tolerant nor secluded. Juvenal wrote sixteen satires in all, the most famous of which are the third and tenth, both imitated in modern times with great success by Dr. Johnson.[12] Contemporary with Juvenal was the Spaniard, M. Valerius Martialis (43–117 A.D.), commonly called Martial, master of the classic epigram. Unsurpassed in compact, scintillant wit, his works present a subjective and familiar picture of that society which Juvenal so bitterly attacked from without.

[Of the prose writers of the Silver Age, the first and perhaps the greatest was L. Annaeus Seneca (4–65 A.D.), a moralist, Stoic philosopher, and literary man whose fame has never diminished. Born in Spain, the son of a famous orator, he was educated at Rome, and became tutor to the Emperor Nero. By order of that tyrant he was eventually condemned to death by his own hand. Seneca was eminent in nearly every field of letters. In youth his oratory was justly praised, and in later life he wrote moral epistles, philosophical disquisitions, poetical tragedies, and even a satire. The style of Seneca is not to be compared with that of Cicero, being tainted with a degree of artificiality and meretricious adornment which clearly reveal the incipient decadence of the period. Seneca is described as ushering in a "Spanish Age" of Roman literature; for he, Lucan, Martial, and Quintilian were all natives of Hispania.

C. Plinius Secundus (23–79 A.D.), commonly called Pliny the Elder, was the most eminent naturalist and scientist of antiquity. Born at Comum, he remained there during his boyhood, coming later to Rome for a rhetorical education. He was during his life a soldier, a proconsul, and a naval commander; but above all he was a scholar. He commenced his labours each day at 1 or 2 a.m., and was always followed by a servant ready to record in shorthand any piece of composition he might find an opportunity to evolve. He deemed it a duty to spend every spare moment in study, and thought it almost criminal to be without a book or writing materials. His motto was "No book so bad but that something good may be gleaned from it."[13] Pliny died of suffocation in the terrible Vesuvian eruption which destroyed Pompeii, having approached the stricken region for a scientific observation of the phenomenon. The work of Pliny consists of an immense "Natural History" in 37 books. This compendious treatise covers a prodigious field, and represents practically all the scientific knowledge of antiquity. Its merit, however, is somewhat impaired by errors and by the author's credulity in accepting popular fallacies. The nephew of Pliny, C. Plinius Caecilius Secundus (62–114 A.D.), is usually called Pliny the Younger. He was a pupil of the rhetorician Quintilian, and distinguished himself in military and civil life, twice attaining the consulship, and once serving as governor of Bithynia. He was ever an advocate of the oppressed, and is gratefully remembered as a true friend of virtue. Pliny the Younger is known chiefly as a letter writer, his personal and official correspondence being of such elegance, urbanity, and interest, that it is today a model of epistolary style.

Rome's foremost rhetorician was M. Fabius Quintilianus (35–95 A.D.), usually called Quintilian. Of Spanish birth, he received a Roman training, and became a tutor to the nephews of Domitianus. His great work, the Institutes of Oratory, is still a standard text-book and guide to taste. In style Quintilian emulated Cicero, and decried the decadence of his own times.

A mighty figure is P. Cornelius Tacitus (54–118 A.D.), one of the greatest, if not the greatest, of Roman historians. Born of a good equestrian family, he enjoyed a number of public honours, and became a son-in-law of the celebrated commander, C. Julius Agricola, whose biography he wrote. With the younger Pliny he was cordially intimate. Besides his biography of Agricola, Tacitus wrote an account of the German tribes, whose savage virility and rude virtue he held up in scornful contrast to the effeminate and decadent society of imperial Rome; histories and dialogues; and a work in 16 books entitled the "Annales", which records the lives of the Roman emperors. The style of Tacitus is not unlike that of Sallust, though it has numerous idiosyncrasies characteristic of a writer of the Silver Age. An inferior contemporary of Tacitus was C. Suetonius Tranquillus whose lives of the "Twelve Caesars" display a terse biographical and anecdotal prose style.

Last of the authors of the Silver Age, and in literary style unquestionably the worst, is L. Apuleius (born 124 A.D.), whose romantic fiction foreshadowed the novel of the present aera. Apuleius was of Numidian birth, but probably of Roman blood, and was educated at Carthage and Athens. His most celebrated work is the "Golden Ass", a tale which treats of the fantastical adventures of a dabbler in magic; who, endeavouring to change himself into an owl, becomes a donkey by mistake.]

We come now upon one of the most distressing spectacles of human history. The mighty empire of Rome—its morals corrupted through Eastern influences, its spirit depressed through despotic government, and its people reduced to mongrel degeneracy through unrestrained immigration and foreign admixture—suddenly ceases to be an abode of creative thought, and sinks into a mental lethargy which dries up the very fountains of art and literature. The Emperor Constantinus, desirous of embellishing his new capital with the most magnificent decorations, can find no artist capable of fashioning them; and is obliged to strip ancient Greece of her choicest sculptures to fulfil his needs. Plainly, the days of Roman glory are over; and only a few and mainly mediocre geniuses are to be expected in the years preceding the actual downfall of Latin civilisation.

[Of the poets following the Silver Age, we may mention D. Magnus Ausonius (310–390), a native of Bordeaux, who wrote some fair miscellaneous poems, most famous of which is "Mosella", a description of a voyage from Bingen, on the Rhine, to the Moselle, and up that river as far as Treves. A peculiar interest attaches to the setting of this poem, as we read that "American forces occupied the west bank of the Moselle River today." Mr. Edward H. Cole, in a most acute and interesting article entitled "Ausonius, the Nature-Lover",[14] points out in this poem a curiously modern attitude toward natural beauty, which shines through the usually classical fabric of the sounding hexameters.

Claudius Claudianus, or Claudian, an Alexandrian Greek who came to Rome in 395, is the last of the really classic poets. Claudian is a really great poet, and was quoted voluminously by Mr. Addison and other literary men of our own Augustan Age, but his work is at present under a cloud of deficient appreciation. It is from Claudian that we derive the famous quotation, "Nunquam libertas gratior exstat, quam sub rege pio."[15]]

It is interesting, in a melancholy way, to trace the course of Roman poetry down to its very close, when it is lost amidst the darkness of the Middle Ages. Claudius Rutilius Namantianus, who flourished in the fifth century, was a Gaul, and wrote a very fair piece called the "Itinerarium", describing a voyage from Rome to his native province. Although inferior to his contemporary, Claudian, in genius, Rutilius excels him in purity of diction and refinement of taste. At this period, pure Latin was probably confined to the highest circles, the masses already using that *eloquium vulgare*[16] which later on formed the several modern Romance Languages; hence Rutilius must have been in a sense a classical antiquarian.

[Ammianus Marcellinus (330–410) was the last great Roman historian. A Greek by birth, he served as a soldier under the Emperor Julian, and continued the history of Tacitus in a masterful manner, though displaying much crudity of style.

Of the later philosophers, the greatest was Anicius Manlius Severinus Boethius (475–525), styled by many "The Last of the Romans". He followed a brilliant public career, though it ended in unjust imprisonment and execution by Theodoric, Ostrogothic King of Italy. During his imprisonment Boethius composed his immortal work "On the Consolation of Philosophy", which has raised him above all other writers and thinkers of his age. This volume was translated into Saxon by Alfred the Great, and into English by Chaucer.]

The end draws near. Compilers, grammarians, critics, commentators, and encyclopaedists—summarising the past and quibbling over technical minutiae—are the last survivors of a dying literature from whence inspiration has already fled. Macrobius, a critic and grammarian of celebrity, flourished in the fourth or fifth century, and interests us as being one through knowledge of whose works Samuel Johnson first attracted notice at Oxford. Priscian, conceded to be one of the principal grammatical authorities of the Roman world, flourished about the year 500. Isidorus Hispalensis, Bishop of Seville, grammarian, historian, and theologian, was the most celebrated and influential literary character of the crumbling Roman fabric, save the philosopher Boethius and the historian Cassiodorous, and was highly esteemed during the Middle Ages, of which, indeed, he was as much a part as he was a part of expiring classicism.

Now falls the curtain. *Roma fuit*.[17] At the time of Isidorus' death in A.D. 636, the beginnings of mediaevalism were fully under way. Authorship had disappeared in the broader sense; learning, such as it was, had retired into the monasteries; whilst the populace of the erstwhile Empire, living side by side with the invading barbarians, no longer spoke a language justly to be called classical Latin. With the revival of letters we shall see more Latin writings, but they will not be Roman; for their authors will have new and strange idioms for their mother-tongues, and will view life in a somewhat different manner. The link of continuity will have been irreparably broken, and these revivers will be Romans only in an artificial and antiquarian sense. He who calls himself "Pomponius Laetus" will be found to have been baptised Pomponio Leto. Classical antiquity, with its simple magnificence, can never return.

In glancing back over the literature we have examined, we are impressed by its distinctiveness, despite its Greek form. It is truly characteristic of the Roman people, and expresses Rome's majestic mind in a multitude of ways. Law, order, justice, and supremacy; "these things, O Roman, shall to you be arts!"[18] All through the works of Latin authors runs this love of fame, power, order, and permanence. Art is not a prime phase of life or entirely an intrinsic pleasure, but a means of personal or national glorification; the true Roman poet writes his own epitaph for posterity, and exults in the lasting celebrity his memory will receive. Despite his debt to Hellas, he detests the foreign influence, and can find no term of satirical opprobrium more than biting than "Graeculus". The sense of rigid virtue, so deficient in the Greek, blossoms forth nobly in the Roman; making moral satire the greatest of native growths. Naturally, the Roman mind is most perfectly expressed in those voluminous works of law, extending all the way down to the Byzantine age of Justinianus, which have given the modern world its entire foundation of jurisprudence; but of these, lack of space forbids us to treat. They are not, strictly speaking, a part of literature proper.

The influence of the Latin classics upon modern literature has been tremendous. They are today, and will ever be, vital sources of inspiration and guidance. Our own most correct age, that of Queen Anne and the first three Georges, was saturated with their spirit; and there is scarce a writer of note who does not visibly reflect their immediate influence. Each classic English author has, after a fashion, his Latin counterpart. Mr. Pope was a Horace; Dr. Johnson a Juvenal.[19] The early Elizabethan tragedy was a reincarnation of Seneca, as comedy was of Plautus. English literature teems with Latin quotations and allusions to such a degree that no reader can extract full benefit if he have not at least a superficial knowledge of Roman letters.

Wherefore it is enjoined upon the reader not to neglect cultivation of this rich field; a field which offers as much of pure interest and enjoyment as of necessary cultural training and wholesome intellectual discipline.

EDITOR'S NOTE FP: *United Amateur* 18, No. 2 (November 1918): 17–21, 35–38. A survey of Latin literature, written as part of the *United Amateur's* "Reading Table," initiated by Verna McGeoch (who had written an article on Greek literature for the September 1918 issue). In DPC (January 1919; *CE1*), HPL states: "Through the process of editorial abridgment, much of the original essay was relegated to the back of the volume [i.e., pp. 35–38] in the form of supplementary notes." In this edition, the editor has conjecturally inserted the paragraphs of this "supplementary" section into their presumed positions within the body of the essay; these paragraphs are enclosed in brackets.

Notes

1. Edward Augustus Freeman (1823–1892), prolific British historian. The quotation has not been located.

2. HPL no doubt alludes to the widespread Greek practice of homosexuality. Cf. *SL* 4.234: "I always knew that paederasty was a disgusting custom of many ancient nations."

3. In using the terms "dolichocephalic" (long-headed) and "brachycephalic" (short-headed), HPL is employing theories of cranial measurement as a means of distinguishing racial groups that had already been discredited by the end of the 19th century.

4. The comment (*O dimidiate Menander*) is found in a poem by Caesar included in a life of Terence attributed to Suetonius.

5. *Homo sum: humani nil a me alienum puto* (I am a man: nothing human is alien to me). Terence, *Heauton Timoroumenos* 77.

6. "Robbery that occurs beyond the borders of each city is not considered shameful, and they [the Germans] claim that it exists so that youths can gain exercise and reduce idleness." Caesar, *Bellum Gallicum* 6.23.6.

7. Cf. The citation of "Atys" in "The Rats in the Walls" (1923).

8. "Remember, Roman, to rule the people with your power; these will be your arts; to make a habit of peace, to spare the defeated, and to beat down the proud." *Aeneid* 6.651–53.

9. *Exegi monumentum aere perennius.* Horace, *Odes* 3.30.1.

10. HPL translated the first 88 lines of the *Metamorphoses* as a boy; see "Ovid's Metamorphoses" (1900?; *AT* 5–8). He imitated the poem in numerous later verses, e.g., "Hylas and Myrrha" (1919).

11. *Pharsalia* is now regarded as an inaccurate title for the work of Lucan's now titled *Bellum Civile* (*Civil War*).

12. HPL refers to Johnson's *London* (1738) and *The Vanity of Human Wishes* (1749). The latter was, after a fashion, imitated by HPL in his juvenile poem "On the Vanity of Human Ambition" (1902; *AT* 13).

13. The comment is found in Pliny the Younger's *Letters* 3.5.10.

14. Edward H. Cole (1892–1966) was a longtime amateur (chiefly affiliated with the NAPA) and associate of HPL's since 1914. Cole's article was published in the *Emissary* (July 1914); see HPL's comment on it in DPC (March 1915; *CE1*).

15. "Liberty is never more pleasing than under a pious king." Claudian, *De Consulatu Stilichonis* 3.114–15.

16. "Vulgar speech."

17. "Rome was" (i.e., it existed no more).

18. See n. 8.

19. The thought, although a truism, may have been derived from a passage in Boswell's life of Johnson: "Johnson's *London* was published in May, 1738; and it is remarkable, that it came out on the same morning with Pope's satire, entitled '1738;' so that England had at once its Juvenal and Horace as poetical monitors." *Life of Johnson*, ed. R. W. Chapman, rev. J. D. Fleeman (London: Oxford University Press, 1970), pp. 91–92.

THE SIMPLE SPELLING MANIA

With the possible exception of slang and *vers libre*, the most pernicious literary crime of this unsettled age is the attempted destruction of standard English spelling by fanatical so-called reformers. In the younger days of our language every man was his own orthographical authority. Not only were the works of different authors marked by dissimilar spelling, but one writer would frequently vary his usage within the compass of a single sentence, even signing his own name as the fancy of the moment dictated. The ill effects of such a system are obvious, and we need but glance at the early colonial documents of New England to perceive how confusing it was.

But increasing civilisation, acting as a check to the vagaries of individuals, gradually evolved an approximately uniform orthography, which was well established by the works of the exact and polished Augustan writers, and settled with fair definitiveness by Dr. Johnson's epoch-making dictionary.[1] This process of adjustment was by no means abrupt, radical, or artificial; being a mere selection and perpetuation of the best models, with the almost imperceptible abandonment of the less desirable forms. Of the benefits of this crystallisation it is scarce necessary to speak. The use of correct English, now become uniform, spread with marvellous facility throughout all classes of society; reaching every home in our northern American colonies by means of the famous old New-England Primer.[2] The spelling-bee arose as a recognised Yankee institution, and the isolated farmer attained an orthographical level equal to that of his more cultivated urban brother.

Another and less rational side of the situation, however, had existed since the reign of Queen Elizabeth. Sir Thomas Smith, Secretary of State to that splendid monarch, brought forward a radical and artificial scheme of phonetic spelling which defied every law of conservatism and natural growth.[3] Part of his system required new alphabetical characters which cannot be exhibited here, but as specimens the following may be given: *priesthood*, "*prestud*"; *name*, "*nam*"; *glory*, "*glori*"; *shame*, "*zam*".

After England had ceased laughing at the eccentric precepts of Sir Thomas, there arose a celebrated teacher, one Dr. Gill, who became even more ridiculous in his departures from good taste.[4] Some of his few innovations which can be spelled with ordinary letters are: *gracious*, "*grasius*"; *seem*, "*sjm*"; *love*, "*luv*"; *cannot*, "*kanot*"!

In 1634 Mr. Charles Butler published a treatise on bees wherein he displayed a freakish mode of spelling which he had invented, and which approached, though scarcely equalled, the follies of Smith and Gill.[5]

During the reign of Charles I there was a phonetic tendency which broke out in such forms as "*erth*" for *earth*, "*dais*" for *days*, and the like. Soon after this, Bishop Wilkins put forward an "ideal" orthography; which, however, he had the sense to know the public would never adopt.[6]

There is in the author's library an edition of Erasmus Darwin's poems, printed in New York in 1805, and containing a novel system of representing the elision of vowels in verse.[7] *Unmark'd* is here spelled "*unmarkt*"; *parch'd*, "*parcht*"; *touch'd*, "*toucht*"; *lock'd*, "*lockt*", and so on. However, despite all these attempts at disturbing the normal development of our spelling, no radical change has as yet been seriously accepted or considered.

But the present age is eminently one of folly and radicalism. The metrical sins of the contemporary "poets" are grave and manifold; the colloquial atrocities of the prose writer are, if anything, more numerous and abominable still. For the first time in history our orthography is in danger of a deliberate destruction which will, if successful, obliterate all natural uniformity of spelling and plunge us backward three centuries into a state wherein no two men can spell alike. Each particular "reforming" fanatic has his own favourite degree of change; and unless conventional forms be guarded with the greatest assiduity, we shall by the artificial tearing down of our language attain a chaos equal to that of Chaucer's time. Etymology, that invaluable aid to precise expression, would be extirpated, should the modern vagaries come into use.

As yet only America seems tainted by the insidious propaganda of the "spelling reformers", but Old England itself has some very ridiculous examples, and is in ultimate danger. Most offensively does the evil appear in certain of the amateur press associations, whose personnel, mainly youthful, fall an easy prey to new fallacies. While some venture no further into the vice than to write *"thru"*, *"tho"*, and *"thoro"* for *through*, *though*, and *thorough*, others display more serious symptoms, and are liable to commit the worst excesses of perverted orthography. Are there not enough sound critics in amateurdom to conduct a systematic campaign, both by example and precept, against "simplified" spelling? Most of the scholarly element are known to be opposed to the pernicious practice, and most writers in the United refrain commendably from it; but in other associations it runs rampant and unchecked. It is here respectfully suggested that those publishers who, though using normal spelling themselves, yet print "simplified" contributions without amendment, take a definite stand for the purity of their mother-tongue, and revise all matter received to the authoritative forms of Webster, Worcester, or Stormonth.[8]

The radicalism of today will soon become but a memory, and the present generation of free poets, peace advocates, socialistic cranks, users of slang, simplified spellers, and the like, will look back with blushes on their former folly. Is it not best, then, to assist in the extinction of the spark which if unchecked may seriously disturb our etymological and orthographical precision and uniformity? Individual influence is slight among us, but a concerted effort to save amateurdom from corrupt usages may be felt even outside the boundaries of our little world.

EDITOR'S NOTE FP: *United Co-operative* 1, No. 1 (December 1918): 1–3. A learned screed against simplified spelling, a movement that enjoyed a brief vogue in the later 19th and early 20th centuries in both the US and the UK. See HPL's poem "The Simple Speller's Tale" (*Conservative*, April 1915; AT 204–5), with its pungent conclusion: "Yet why on us your anger or wrath use? / We do but ape Professor B—— M——!" (referring to Brander Matthews, a leading American critic and professor who advocated simple spelling). HPL continued to rail at the movement in letters of the late 1920s (see, e.g., SL 3.90–92). But the movement had by then already lost steam (largely because a subsidy granted to the Simplified Spelling Board by Andrew Carnegie abruptly ceased upon his death in 1919). See, in general, H. L. Mencken, *The American Language* (New York: Knopf, 4th rev. ed. 1936), pp. 397–407.

Notes

1. Samuel Johnson (1709–1784), *A Dictionary of the English Language* (1755). HPL owned a 12th edition (1802; LL 479).

2. *The New England Primer; or, An Easy and Pleasant Guide to the Art of Reading* (1727). HPL owned three different editions, but does not identify them; see SL 3.408.

3. Sir Thomas Smith (1513–1577), *De recta et emendata linguae Anglicae scriptione, dialogus* (1568).

4. The most important work by Alexander Gill (1565–1635) is the *Logomania Anglica* (1619).

5. Charles Butler, *The Feminine Monarchy; or, The History of Bees* (1623). Butler (1560–1647) also wrote an *English Grammar* (1634).

6. John Wilkins (1614–1672), *An Essay towards a Real Character, and a Philosophical Language* (1668).

7. Erasmus Darwin (1731–1802), *Beauties of The Botanick Garden* (New York: D. Longworth, 1805; *LL* 222). Cf. *SL* 3.409.

8. HPL alludes to the lexicographers Noah Webster (see *LL* 930–32), Joseph Emerson Worcester, and James Stormonth (see *LL* 850). The last was an Englishman whose *Dictionary of the English Language* (1871) HPL preferred to Webster's American dictionary.

THE CASE FOR CLASSICISM

A Reply to Prof. Philip B. McDonald

In another part of this issue Prof. Philip B. McDonald, Chairman of the Department of Private Criticism, presents some views on amateur journalism which well exhibit his firm belief and constructive interest in our modest institution. At the same time, however, he criticises the United's present literary policy in a manner which calls for immediate reply on the part of those who have laboured to establish existing standards.

Prof. McDonald believes, if we are to accept his verdict literally, that amateurdom's attempts to attain a classical level of expression are the result of a misconception of our province. Averse to the thought that we should perfect ourselves in those tasteful modes of utterance which are eternal and universal in the conservative world outside, he urges that our papers descend to a realm of more intimate subjectivity and personality; including, to quote his own words, "more of the human and American".

Not for a moment can this plea be permitted to pass unchallenged, since it is so likely to affect the multitude of crude and youthful writers who need little to discourage them from the pursuit of urbane scholarship. But in challenging it, one need not impugn in any way the contention that informal and subjective expression is desirable or even necessary in amateurdom. It will be sufficient to insist that such expression belongs solely to the epistolary branch of our activities, leaving our printed publications free for more ambitious experiments in the formation of a real style and a real kinship with standard literature.

The local, intimate, and subjective phase of amateurdom is without a doubt far greater than a member so recent as Prof. McDonald can realise. The correspondence of amateurs, including both personal and circulating letters, is prodigious; and the ever-multiplying array of manuscript magazines and epistolary groups is increasing this informal contact immensely.[1] Members with similar interests or intellectual processes are being banded together in circles like the "Kleicomolo" described in the March *United*

Amateur;[2] and it may be safely said that our thoughts, feelings, and individual reactions to literature and events are pretty generally shared without the necessity of dragging them into print.

Turning now to our regular publications, it must be emphasised that their purpose is not to replace chit-chat or correspondence, but to give publicity to our finished literary products. In our cultural development we must differentiate betwixt processes and results. The subjectivity of our correspondence rightly exemplifies our processes of digesting literature; but the objectivity of our published work exemplifies, also rightly, our results in producing a literature of our own, be it ever so humble. In that literature we have not only the right but the obligation to strive for the best style, and emulate the best authors, within our scope of reading; even though our work must necessarily resemble more or less that of professionals. And why, indeed, should Prof. McDonald deem it so vast a crime for us to parallel standard books and periodicals? Are we, as he fancies, trying to compete with them, merely because we employ them as models? We must needs wonder whether Prof. McDonald realises the immeasurably closer sympathy one can attain with the standard authors and their thoughts, by sedulously following in their footsteps. This keener comprehension of good literature is alone sufficient to justify the experiments of the tyro in conventional expression. Our avowed object is to give the novice training and experience in authorship. Is it not then an occasion for satisfaction rather than for sorrow, that our members should adopt the style of the best authors? Any other course would inevitably result in the acquisition of a vague, objectionable, and irremediably vicious style. By training the novice exclusively in informal subjectivity, we should ruin his ability to write with force, correctness, and dignity. There are many living examples, surviving from cruder ages of amateurdom, to prove this contention.

Another aspect of Prof. McDonald's scholastic thought is revealed in a more incidental way by his article. This is his attitude toward general literature; as evinced by his cautious disparagement of mellowed, broadly representative books, in favour of modern, locally American, and potentially ephemeral writings. He seems to typify the spirit recently referred to by President Faunce of Brown University, who declared that most of us are "too desperately contemporary".[3]

It is not my purpose here to engage in any extensive battle of ancient and modern books, such as that fought in Saint-James's Library and veraciously chronicled by Dean Swift;[4] but I cannot refrain from insisting on the permanent paramountcy of classical literature as opposed to the superficial productions of this disturbed and degenerate age. The literary genius of Greece and Rome, developed under peculiarly favourable circumstances, may fairly be said to have completed the art and science of expression. Unhurried and profound, the classical author achieved a standard of simplicity, moderation, and elegance of taste, which all succeeding time has been powerless to excel or even to equal. Indeed, those modern periods have been most cultivated, in which the models of antiquity have been most faithfully followed. When Prof. McDonald rather proudly points to certain recent great rhetoricians as apparently uninfluenced by the classics, he forgets that the models which they did adopt were indeed strongly influenced by those selfsame classics. Be it directly, as in the case of Mr. Burke, or indirectly, as in the case of Mr. Wilson, classicism is ever the moulder of effective rhetoric.

Prof. McDonald's plea for a more local American flavour in amateur writing, though sustained by an utterance of the eternally quoted Emerson, is in reality an appeal for a rather pernicious provincialism. Not that it is less the patriotic duty of the local writer to immortalise his native place in literature; but that it is undesirable to encourage the growth of dialectic and stylistic variants from the general type which possesses so long and so illustrious an ancestry. Breadth, not narrowness, is the great cultural desideratum. Prof. McDonald's view reminds me of that of a young amateur journalist of five years ago; who complained because two of our members, one in Massachusetts and the other in California, wrote alike—thus disregarding possible opportunities for "local colour" in expression.

As to the applicability of a classical style to present needs, I think no branch of thought today would be the worse for expression in the clear rhetoric of better times. In fact, I cannot but believe that such a course would help greatly to weed out unworthy and unsubstantial things in contemporary life. We moderns have overreached ourselves, and are blundering along with a dislocated sense of values amidst a bustle of heavy trivialities and false emotions which find reflection in the vague, hectic, hurried, and impressionistic language of decadence. Translation of our thoughts into the clearcut, rational phrases of classicism might help to reveal the flimsy fatuity of most of the innovations we so blindly worship.

The assertion of Prof. McDonald that the classical style is too restrained, and lacking in humanity, seems to me scarcely supported by evidence. The vital eloquence of the classics cannot be disputed; and if there be any restraint in their language, it is but for the purpose of strengthening their ultimate effect. Compare, for example, the simple force of Graeco-Roman writing, with the florid emptiness of Oriental effusions. So far as restraint goes, a malicious commentator might easily use Prof. McDonald's own bare and staccato prose style as an illustration of inconsistency betwixt precept and practice. The first thing one remarks on reading his frigid "Engineering English" is its laconic atmosphere of aloofness from vivid feeling and from love of pure harmonic beauty. Noting the rhetorical correctness and literary background possessed by Prof. McDonald, one cannot but wish that he might add to his work the crowning graces of classical fluency and moderate ornamentation.

In conclusion, let me express my position in the matter unequivocally. I am an advocate of the highest classical standard in amateur journalism, and shall continue to bend all my energies toward its maintenance. Printed papers are not suitable repositories for loose informality, nor are the hasty and ill-formed writings of today models for emulation. Should the subject receive further discussion in the amateur press, I should be gratified. Meanwhile I may humbly say to my learned adversary,

"Maxime, si tu vis, cupio contendere tecum."[5]

EDITOR'S NOTE FP: *United Co-operative* 1, No. 2 (June 1919): 3–5. A rebuttal to an article, "A Criticism of Amateur Journalism," by Philip B. McDonald, a professor of Engineering English [*sic*] at the University of Colorado, appearing just previous to HPL's article (pp. 2–3). In the course of the article HPL asserts the "permanent paramountcy of classical literature," which would suggest that the only thing subsequent generations can do is to imitate it— which is exactly what HPL himself was doing at this time, especially in his poetry.

Notes

1. HPL alludes to such epistolary groups as the Kleicomolo and the Gallomo, in which HPL and his colleagues engaged in a round-robin correspondence, and to such manuscript magazines as *Corona* and his own (lost) typewritten journal, *Hesperia*.

2. "The Kleicomolo," *United Amateur* 18, No. 4 (March 1919): 74–76. The unsigned article is probably by Rheinhart Kleiner, then president of the UAPA.

3. William Herbert Perry Faunce (1859–1930), president of Brown University (1899–1930).

4. HPL alludes to Jonathan Swift's *The Battle of the Books* (1710), a satire on contemporary debates as to the relative merits of ancient and modern literature.

5. "I very much wish, if you are willing, to compete with you." Quoted by Thomas Babington Macaulay in his article, "Samuel Johnson" (*Encyclopaedia Britannica,* 1856), from a Scotsman who wished to challenge Johnson to a battle of wits. Macaulay rightly calls the line "a detestable Latin hexameter."

LITERARY COMPOSITION

In a former article our readers have been shewn the fundamental sources of literary inspiration, and the leading prerequisites to expression. It remains to furnish hints concerning expression itself—its forms, customs, and technicalities—in order that the young writer may lose nothing of force or charm in presenting his ideas to the public.

Grammar

A review of the elements of English grammar would be foreign to the purpose of this department. The subject is one taught in all common schools, and may be presumed to be understood by every aspirant to authorship. It is necessary, however, to caution the beginner to keep a reliable grammar and dictionary always beside him, that he may avoid in his compositions the frequent errors which imperceptibly corrupt even the purest ordinary speech. As a general rule, it is well to give close critical scrutiny to all colloquial phrases and expressions of doubtful parsing, as well as to all words and usages which have a strained or unfamiliar sound. The human memory is not to be trusted too far, and most minds harbour a considerable number of slight linguistic faults and inelegancies picked up from random discourse or from the pages of newspapers, magazines, and popular modern books.

Types of Mistakes

Most of the mistakes of young authors, aside from those gross violations of syntax which ordinary education corrects, may perhaps be enumerated as follows.

(1) Erroneous plurals of nouns, as *vallies* or *echos.*

(2) Barbarous compound nouns, as *viewpoint* or *upkeep.*

(3) Want of correspondence in number between noun and verb where the two are widely separated or the construction involved.

(4) Ambiguous use of pronouns.

(5) Erroneous case of pronouns, as *whom* for *who,* and vice versa, or phrases like "between you and I", or "Let *we* who are loyal, act promptly."

(6) Erroneous use of *shall* and *will,* and of other auxiliary verbs.

(7) Use of intransitive for transitive verbs, as "he *was graduated* from college", or vice versa, as "he *ingratiated* with the tyrant".

(8) Use of nouns for verbs, as "he *motored* to Boston", or "he *voiced* a protest".

(9) Errors in moods and tenses of verbs, as "If I *was* he, I should do otherwise", or "He said the earth *was* round."

(10) The split infinitive, as "*to* calmly *glide*".

(11) The erroneous perfect infinitive, as "Last week I expected *to have met* you."

(12) False verb-forms, as "I *pled* with him."

(13) Use of *like* for *as,* as "I strive to write *like* Pope wrote."

(14) Misuse of prepositions, as "The gift was bestowed *to* an unworthy object", or "The gold was divided *between* the five men."

(15) The superfluous conjunction, as "I wish *for* you to do this."

(16) Use of words in wrong senses, as "The book greatly *intrigued* me", "*Leave* me take this", "He was *obsessed* with the idea", or "He is a *meticulous* writer."

(17) Erroneous use of non-Anglicised foreign forms, as "a strange *phenomena*", or "two *stratas* of clouds".

(18) Use of false or unauthorised words, as *burglarise* or *supremest.*

(19) Errors of taste, including vulgarisms, pompousness, repetition, vagueness, ambiguousness, colloquialism, bathos, bombast, pleonasm, tautology, harshness, mixed metaphor, and every sort of rhetorical awkwardness.

(20) Errors of spelling and punctuation, and confusion of forms such as that which leads many to place an apostrophe in the possessive pronoun *its.*

Of all blunders, there is hardly one which might not be avoided through diligent study of simple textbooks on grammar and rhetoric, intelligent perusal of the best authors, and care and forethought in composition. Almost no excuse exists for their persistent occurrence, since the sources of correction are so numerous and so available. Many of the popular manuals of good English are extremely useful, especially to persons whose reading is not as yet extensive; but such works sometimes err in being too pedantically precise and formal. For correct writing, the cultivation of patience and mental accuracy is essential. Throughout the young author's period of apprenticeship, he must keep reliable dictionaries and text-books at his elbow;[1] eschewing as far as possible that hasty extemporaneous manner of writing which is the privilege of more advanced students. He must take no popular usage for granted, nor must he ever hesitate, in case of doubt, to fall back on the authority of his books.

Reading

No aspiring author should content himself with a mere acquisition of technical rules. As Mrs. Renshaw remarked in the preceding article, "Impression should ever precede and be stronger than expression." All attempts at gaining literary polish must begin with judicious *reading,* and the learner must never cease to hold this phase uppermost. In many cases, the usage of good authors will be found a more effective guide than any amount of precept. A page of Addison or of Irving will teach more of style than a whole manual of rules, whilst a story of Poe's will impress upon the mind a more vivid notion of powerful and correct description and narration than will ten dry chapters of a bulky text-book. Let every student read unceasingly the best writers, guided by the admirable Reading Table which has adorned the *United Amateur* during the past two years.

It is also important that cheaper types of reading, if hitherto followed, be dropped. Popular magazines inculcate a careless and deplorable style which is hard to unlearn, and which impedes the acquisition of a purer style.[2] If such things must be read, let them be skimmed over as lightly as possible. An excellent habit to cultivate is the analytical study of the King James Bible. For simple yet rich and forceful English, this masterly production is hard to equal; and even though its Saxon vocabulary and poetic rhythm be unsuited to general composition, it is an invaluable model for writers on quaint or imaginative themes. Lord Dunsany, perhaps the greatest living prose artist, derived nearly all of his stylistic tendencies from the Scriptures; and the contemporary critic Boyd points out very acutely the loss sustained by most Catholic Irish writers through their unfamiliarity with the historic volume and its traditions.[3]

Vocabulary

One superlatively important effect of wide reading is the enlargement of vocabulary which always accompanies it. The average student is gravely impeded by the narrow range of words from which he must choose, and he soon discovers that in long compositions he cannot avoid monotony. In reading, the novice should note the varied mode of expression practiced by good authors, and should keep in his mind for future use the many appropriate synonyms he encounters.[4] Never should an unfamiliar word be passed over without elucidation; for with a little conscientious research we may each day add to our conquests in the realm of philology, and become more and more ready for graceful independent expression.

But in enlarging the vocabulary, we must beware lest we misuse our new possessions. We must remember that there are fine distinctions betwixt apparently similar words, and that language must ever be selected with intelligent care. As the learned Dr. Blair points out in his Lectures, "Hardly in any language are there two words that convey precisely the same idea; a person thoroughly conversant in the propriety of language will always be able to observe something that distinguishes them."[5]

Elemental Phases

Before considering the various formal classes of composition, it is well to note certain elements common to them all. Upon analysis, every piece of writing will be found to contain one or more of the following basic principles: *Description,* or an account of the appearance of things; *Narration,* or an account of the actions of things; *Exposition,* which defines and explains with precision and lucidity; *Argument,* which discovers truth and rejects error; and *Persuasion,* which urges to certain thoughts or acts. The first two are the bases of fiction; the third didactic, scientific, historical, and editorial writings. The fourth and fifth are mostly employed in conjunction with the third, in scientific, philosophical, and partisan literature. All these principles, however, are usually mingled with one another. The work of fiction may have its scientific, historical, or argumentative side; whilst the text-book or treatise may be embellished with descriptions and anecdotes.

Description

Description, in order to be effective, calls upon two mental qualities: observation and discrimination. Many descriptions depend for their vividness upon the accurate reproduction of details; others upon the judicious selection of salient, typical, or significant points.

One cannot be too careful in the selection of adjectives for descriptions. Words or compounds which describe precisely, and which convey exactly the right suggestions to the mind of the reader, are essential. As an example, let us consider the following list of epithets applicable to a *fountain*, taken from Richard Green Parker's admirable work on composition.[6]

> Crystal, gushing, rustling, silver, gently-gliding, parting, pearly, weeping, bubbling, gurgling, chiding, clear, grass-fringed, moss-fringed, pebble-paved, verdant, sacred, grass-margined, moss-margined, trickling, soft, dew-sprinkled, fast-flowing, delicate, delicious, clean, straggling, dancing, vaulting, deep-embosomed, leaping, murmuring, muttering, whispering, prattling, twaddling, swelling, sweet-rolling, gently-flowing, rising, sparkling, flowing, frothy, dew-distilling, dew-born, exhaustless, inexhaustible, never-decreasing, never-falling, heaven-born, earth-born, deep-divulging, drought-dispelling, thirst-allaying, refreshing, soul-refreshing, earth-refreshing, laving, lavish, plant-nourishing.

For the purpose of securing epithets at once accurate and felicitous, the young author should familiarise himself thoroughly with the general aspect and phenomena of Nature, as well as with the ideas and associations which these things produce in the human mind.

Descriptions may be of objects, of places, of animals, and of persons. The complete description of an object may be said to consist of the following elements:

1. When, where, and how seen; when made or found; how affected by time.
2. History and traditional associations.
3. Substance and manner of origin.
4. Size, shape, and appearance.
5. Analogies with similar objects.
6. Sensations produced by contemplating it.
7. Its purpose or function.
8. Its effects—the results of its existence.

Descriptions of places must of course vary with the type of the place. Of natural scenery, the following elements are notable:

1. How beheld—at dawn, noon, evening, or night; by starlight or moonlight.
2. Natural features—flat or hilly; barren or thickly grown; kind of vegetation; trees, mountains, and rivers.
3. Works of man—cultivation, edifices, bridges, modifications of scenery produced by man.
4. Inhabitants and other forms of animal life.
5. Local customs and traditions.
6. Sounds—of water; forest; leaves; birds; barnyards; human beings; machinery.
7. View—prospect on every side, and the place itself as seen from afar.
8. Analogies to other scenes, especially famous scenes.
9. History and associations.
10. Sensations produced by contemplating it.

Descriptions of animals may be analysed thus:

1. Species and size.
2. Covering.
3. Parts.
4. Abode.
5. Characteristics and habits.
6. Food.
7. Utility or harmfulness.
8. History and associations.

Descriptions of persons can be infinitely varied. Sometimes a single felicitous touch brings out the whole type and character, as when the modern author Leonard Merrick hints at shabby gentility by mentioning the combination of a frock coat with the trousers of a tweed suit.[7] Suggestion is very powerful in this field, especially when mental qualities are to be delineated. Treatment should vary with the author's object; whether to portray a mere personified idea, or to give a quasi-photographic view, mental and physical, of some vividly living character. In a general description, the following elements may be found:

1. Appearance, stature, complexion, proportions, features.
2. Most conspicuous feature.
3. Expression.
4. Grace or ugliness.
5. Attire—nature, taste, quality.
6. Habits, attainments, graces, or awkwardnesses.
7. Character—moral and intellectual; place in the community.
8. Notable special qualities.

In considering the preceding synopses, the reader must remember that they are only suggestions, and not for *literal* use. The extent of any description is to be determined by its place in the composition; by taste and fitness. It should be added, that in fiction description must not be carried to excess. A plethora of it leads to dulness, so that it must ever be balanced by a brisk flow of *Narration*, which we are about to consider.

Narration

Narration is an account of action, or of successive events, either real or imagined; and is therefore the basis both of history and of fiction. To be felicitous and successful, it demands an intelligent exercise of taste and discrimination; salient points must be selected, and the order of time and of circumstances must be well maintained. It is deemed wisest in most cases to give narratives a climactic form; leading from lesser to greater events, and culminating in that chief incident upon which the story is primarily founded, or which makes the other parts important through its own importance. This principle, of course, cannot be literally followed in all historical and biographical narratives.

Fictional Narration

The essential point of fictional narration is *plot*, which may be defined as a *sequence of incidents designed to awaken the reader's interest and curiosity as to the result*. Plots may be simple or complex; but suspense, and climactic progress from one incident to another, are essential. Every incident in a fictional work should have some bearing on the climax or denouement, and any denouement which is not the inevitable result of the preceding incidents is awkward and unliterary. No formal course in fiction-writing can equal a close and observant perusal of the stories of Edgar Allan Poe or Ambrose Bierce. In these masterpieces one may find that unbroken sequence and linkage of incident and result which mark the ideal tale. Observe how, in "The Fall of the House of Usher", each separate event foreshadows and leads up to the tremendous catastrophe and its hideous suggestion. Poe was an absolute master of the mechanics of his craft. Observe also how Bierce can attain the most stirring denouements from a few simple happenings; denouements which develop purely from these preceding circumstances.

In fictional narration, verisimilitude is absolutely essential. A story must be consistent and must contain no event glaringly removed from the usual order of things, unless that event is the main incident, and is approached with the most careful preparation. In real life, odd and erratic things do occasionally happen; but they are out of place in an ordinary story, since fiction is a sort of idealisation of the average. Development should be as life-like as possible, and a weak, trickling conclusion should be assiduously avoided. The end of a story must be stronger rather than weaker than the beginning; since it is the end which contains the denouement or culmination, and which will leave the strongest impression upon the reader. It would not be amiss for the novice to write the last paragraph of his story first, once a synopsis of the plot has been carefully prepared—as it always should be. In this way he will be able to concentrate his freshest mental vigour upon the most important part of his narrative; and if any changes are later found needful, they can easily be made. In no part of a narrative should a grand or emphatic thought or passage be followed by one of tame or prosaic quality. This is *anticlimax*, and exposes a writer to much ridicule. Notice the absurd effect of the following couplet—which was, however, written by no less a person than Waller:

> "Under the tropic is our language spoke,
> And part of *Flanders hath receiv'd our yoke*."[8]

Unity, Mass, Coherence

In developing a theme, whether descriptive or narrative, it is necessary that three structural qualities be present: Unity, Mass, and Coherence. Unity is that principle whereby every part of a composition must have some bearing on the central theme. It is the principle which excludes all extraneous matter, and demands that all threads converge toward the climax. Classical violations of Unity may be found in the *episodes* of Homer and other epic poets of antiquity, as well as in the digressions of Fielding and other celebrated novelists; but no beginner should venture to emulate such liberties. Unity is the quality we have lately noted and praised in Poe and Bierce.

Mass is that principle which requires the more important parts of a composition to occupy correspondingly important places in the whole composition, the paragraph, and the sentence. It is that law of taste which insists that emphasis be placed where emphasis is due, and is most strikingly embodied in the previously mentioned necessity for an emphatic ending. According to this law, the end of a composition is its most important part, with the beginning next in importance.

Coherence is that principle which groups related parts together and keeps unrelated parts removed from one another. It applies, like Mass, to the whole composition, the paragraph, or the sentence. It demands that kindred events be narrated without interruption, effect following cause in a steady flow.

Forms of Composition

Few writers succeed equally in all the various branches of literature. Each type of thought has its own particular form of expression, based on natural appropriateness; and the average author tends to settle into that form which best fits his particular personality. Many, however, follow more than one form; and some writers change from one form to another as advancing years produce alterations in their mental processes or points of view.

It is well, in the interests of breadth and discipline, for the beginner to exercise himself to some degree in every form of literary art. He may thus discover that which best fits his mind, and develop hitherto unsuspected potentialities.

We have so far surveyed only those simpler phases of writing which centre in prose fiction and descriptive essays. Hereafter we hope to touch upon didactic, argumentative, and persuasive writing; to investigate to some extent the sources of rhetorical strength and elegance; and to consider a few major aspects of versification.

EDITOR'S NOTE FP: *United Amateur* 19, No. 3 (January 1920): 56–60. An elementary but on the whole sound guide to prose composition, emphasising principles to which HPL himself adhered (and recommended to others) for the whole of his life. His citation of such writers as Bierce and Dunsany (both of whom he had read in 1919) is to be noted.

Notes

1. See n. 8 to "The Simple Spelling Mania" for some of the dictionaries owned by HPL. Among the "text-books" HPL used were Abner Alden's *The Reader* (1802; LL 16), read when he was seven (SL 2.107–8), Richard Green Parker's *Aids to English Composition* (1844; LL 673), and William Chauncey Fowler's *English Grammar* (1866; LL 327). When HPL resumed the writing of fiction in 1917, he may have utilised such works as Henry Seidel Canby, Frederick Erastus Pierce, and Willard Higley Durham's *Facts, Thought, and Imagination: A Book on Writing* (1917; LL 151) and Joseph Berg's Esenwein's *Writing the Short-Story* (1918; LL 301).

2. HPL fails to reveal that he himself devoured enormous quantities of these popular magazines as a youth (including the entire run of the *All-Story* from 1905 until at least 1914, as well as the *Argosy* and other Munsey magazines), and would later read every issue of *Weird Tales* from its inception in 1923 until his death in 1937, along with other pulp magazines.

3. See Ernest A. Boyd, "Lord Dunsany—Fantaisiste," in *Appreciations and Depreciations* (New York: John Lane, 1918), pp. 71–100.

4. HPL owned an edition of George Crabb's *English Synonyms* (1816; LL 201).

5. See n. 5 to "Metrical Regularity."

6. See n. 1 above.

7. Leonard Merrick (1864–1939) was a British novelist and short story writer who enjoyed a vogue in the 1910s and 1920s.

8. Edmund Waller (1605–1687), "Upon the Death of the Lord Protector," ll. 21–22.

EDITOR'S NOTE TO "A SCENE FOR *MACBETH*" BY SAMUEL LOVEMAN

The ensuing suppositious scene, designed for the tragedy of *Macbeth*, displays anew the almost uncanny genius of Samuel Loveman in the field of Elizabethan scholarship. Shakespearian students will find in these lines an identification of the author and his chosen period which constitutes a notable achievement in the annals of archaic imitation, and will marvel at the depth of insight which makes possible a reflection not only of the form but of the spirit of a literature three centuries behind us.

This is the second of Mr. Loveman's Shakespearian scenes to appear in the amateur press, the first having been published in *The Sprite* for August, 1917.[1] We are here given an important dramatic moment missing from all existing texts of *Macbeth*; the death of Lady Macbeth, oppressed by fear and conscience, and with a mind haunted by remorseful images, chiefly of the murdered wife and children of Macduff. Herself a mother, she suffers most of all from the memory of the helpless children slain by her husband's men; a thought embodied and phrased with supreme skill by Mr. Loveman in her brief utterance:

> "Here's where it hurts!
> O little baby hands that pluck me close,
> Poor wandering atoms in this night of pitch—
> Fordone, fordone, fordone!"

The death itself is poignantly realistic, revealing the author as always an artist even when most an archaist.

We now approach the scene, which may be taken as following Scene III of the fifth Act, in which Macbeth has asked the Doctor of Physic:

> Canst thou not minister to a mind diseas'd;
> Pluck from the memory a rooted sorrow;
> Raze out the written troubles of the brain;
> And, with some sweet oblivious antidote,
> Cleanse the stuff'd bosom of that perilous matter
> Which weighs upon the heart?"

EDITOR'S NOTE FP: *United Amateur* 20, No. 2 (November 1920): 17 (unsigned). A note presumably written by HPL (he was the official editor of the *United Amateur* at this time) prefacing "A Scene for Macbeth," a work by Samuel Loveman (1887–1976), a poet and playwright whose work HPL had admired even before coming into epistolary contact with him in 1917. See the poem "To Samuel Loveman, Esquire, on His Poetry and Drama, Writ in the Elizabethan Style" (1915; AT 94–95).

Notes

1. See "A Scene for *King Lear*," *Sprite* 8, No. 3 (August 1917): [1–10].

WINIFRED VIRGINIA JACKSON:
A "DIFFERENT" POETESS

In these days of unrestrained licence in poetry, it would at first sight seem difficult to single out any one bard as the possessor of ideas and modes of expression so unique and original that the overworked adjective "different" is merited. Every poetaster of the modern school claims to be "different", and bases his claim to celebrity upon this "difference"; an effect usually achieved by the adoption of a harsh, amorphous style, and a tone of analytical, introspective subjectivity so individual that all the common and universal elements of beauty and poetry are excluded. Indeed, eccentricity has come so completely into fashion, that he who follows up the wildest vagaries is actually the least different from the hectic scribbling throng about him.

But notwithstanding this malady of the times, there does remain among us an ample field for genius and artistic distinctiveness. The laws of human thought are unchangeable, and whenever there is born a soul attuned to real harmony, and inspired by that rare sensitiveness which enables it to feel and express the latent beauty and hidden relationships of Nature, the world receives a new poet. Such an one will of necessity break through the decadent customs of the period; and falling back to the forms of true melody, sing a spontaneous song which cannot help being original, because it represents the unforced reaction of a keen and delicate mind to the panorama of life. And when this reaction is enabled to bring out in the simplest and most beautiful style fancies and images which the world has not received or noted before, we are justified in claiming that the bard is "different".

Such a bard is Winifred Virginia Jackson, whose poetry has for six years been the pride of the United Amateur Press Association. Born in Maine, and through childhood accustomed to the mystical spell of the ancient New-England countryside, Miss Jackson for a long period quietly and unconsciously absorbed a prodigious store of beauty and phantasy from life. Having no design to become a poet, she accepted these ethereal gifts as a matter of course; until about a decade ago they manifested themselves in a burst of spontaneous melody which can best be described as a sheer overflowing of delightful dreams and pictures from a mind filled to the brim with poetic loveliness. Since that time Miss Jackson has written vast quantities of verse; always rich and musical, and if one may speak in paradox, always artless with supreme art. None of these poems is in any sense premeditated or consciously composed; they are more like visions of the fancy, instantaneously photographed for the perception of others, and unerringly framed in the most appropriate metrical medium.

When we peruse the poetry of Miss Jackson we are impressed first by its amazing variety, and almost as quickly by a certain distinctive quality which gives all the varied specimens a kind of homogeneity. As we analyse our impressions, we find that both of these qualities have a common source—the complete objectivity and almost magical imagination of supreme genius. Objectivity and imagination, the gifts of the epic bards of classical antiquity, are today the rarest of blessings. We live in an age of morbid emotion and introspectiveness; wherein the poets, such as they are, have sunk to the level of mere pathologists engaged in the dissection of their own ultra-sophisticated spirits. The fresh touch of Nature is lost to the majority, and rhymesters rant endlessly and realistically about the relation of man to his fellows and to himself; overlooking the real foundations of art and beauty—wonder, and man's relation to the unknown cosmos. But Miss Jackson is not of the majority, and has not overlooked these things. In her the ancient and unspoiled bard is refulgently reincarnated; and with an amazing universality and freedom from self-consciousness she suppresses the ego completely, delineating Nature's diverse moods and aspects with an impersonal fidelity and delicacy which form the delight of the discriminating reader, and the despair of the stupid critic who works by rule and formula rather than by brain. There is no medium which the spirit of Miss Jackson cannot inhabit. The same mind which reflects the daintiest and most gorgeous phantasies of the faery world, or furnishes the most finely wrought pictures of refined pathos and sentiment, can abruptly take up its abode in some remote Maine timber region and pour out such a wild, virile chantey of the woods and the river that we seem to glimpse the singer as the huskiest of a tangle-bearded, fight-scarred, loud-shouting logging crew sprawling about a pine campfire.

A critic[1] has grouped the poetical work of Miss Jackson into six classes: lyrics of ideal beauty, including delightful Nature-poems replete with local colour; delicate amatory lyrics; rural dialect lyrics and vigorous colloquial pieces; poems of sparkling optimism; child verse; and poems of potent terror and dark suggestion. "With her," he adds, "sordid realism has no place; and her poems glow with a subtle touch of the fanciful and the supernatural which is well sustained by tasteful and unusual word-combinations, images, and onomatopoeic effects." This estimate is confirmed by the latest productions of the poetess, and we shall endeavour to shew by certain specimens lately published or about to be published, selected almost at random:

"The Bonnet" is a characteristic bit of Jacksonian delicacy and originality. We here behold a sustained metaphor of that striking type which the author so frequently creates; a metaphor which draws on all Nature and the unseen world for its basis, and whose analogies are just the ones which please us most, yet which our own minds are never finely attuned enough to conceive unaided. The swain in the poem tells of his intention to make a bonnet for his chosen nymph to wear. He will fashion it with "golden thimble, scissors, needle, thread"; taking velvet from the April sky as a groundwork, stars for trimming, moonlight for banding, and a web of dreams for lining. He will scent it with the perfume of "the reddest rose that the singing wind finds sweetest where it farthest blows", and "will take it at the twilight for his love to wear". Here we have nothing of the bizarre or the conspicuous, yet in the six little stanzas of quaintly regular metre there is suggested all of that world of faery beauty which the eye can glimpse beyond the leaden clouds of reality; a world which exists because it can be dreamed of. The poem is "different" in the truest way; it is original because it conveys beauty originally in an inconspicuous and harmonious vehicle.

But turn now to "Ellsworth to Great Pond" and marvel! True, we still find the vivid delineation of human feelings, but what a distance we have travelled! Gone is the young dreamer with his world of moonshine, for here roars the Maine lumberjack with all the uncouth vigour and rude natural expressiveness of the living satyr. It is life; primal, uncovered, and unpolished—the ebullient, shouting vitality of healthy animalism.

> "Drink hard cider, swig hard cider,
>   Swill hard cider, Boys!
> Throw yer spikers, throw yer peavies,
>   Bellow out yer noise!"

We have drifted from the aether of Keats to the earth of Fielding, yet under the guidance of the same author. Greater proof of Miss Jackson's absolute objectivity and marvellous imagination could not be produced or asked.

Yet who shall say that the Jackson pendulum is powerful only at the extremes of its sweeping arc? In "Workin' Out" we discover a pastoral love-lyric which for quaintness and graphic humanness could not well be surpassed. Here the distinctive and spontaneous inventiveness of Miss Jackson's fancy is displayed with especial vividness. The rural youth, "workin' out" far from his loved Molly, enumerates the prosaic chores he can perform with easy heart; but mentions in each case some more poetic thing which stirs his emotions and gives him loneliness for the absent fair. He can cut and husk corn, but the golden-rod reminds him of his Molly's golden hair. He can milk cows, but the gentian reminds him of his Molly's blue eyes. Aside from their intrinsic ingeniousness, these images possess an unconscious lesson for the poet who can read it. They expose with concrete illustrations the fallacy of the so-called "new poetry", which disregards the natural division between beautiful and unbeautiful things and rhapsodises as effusively over a sewer-pipe as over the crescent moon.

"The Token" exhibits Miss Jackson in her airiest lyrical mood; a mood original because it possess the rare lyrism of pure music and fancy rather than the common lyrism of unsubtilised emotion. There is bounding music in thought and medium alike, whilst the naive plunge into the theme without introduction or explanation is a stroke savouring of the simplicity of genius. Equally effective is the simple metrical transition whereby the chorus assumes the trochaic measure of a childhood chant or carol:

> "Lightly O, brightly O,
> Down the long lane she will go!
> Dancing she, glancing she,
> Down the lane with eyes aglow!"

In "Assurance" and "It's Lovetime", the author displays a lyrical fervour of more conventional type; adding the touch of originality by means of melodious simplicity and reiteration in the one case, and pure lyric ecstasy in the other.

The metrical originality of Miss Jackson, displayed in all classes of her work, should not be slighted amidst the enthusiasm one entertains for her magical mastery of thoughts and images. No other conservative poet of the period is more versatile and individual in choice of numbers, or in adaptation of measure to mood. "Driftwood", a wonderfully original poem of imagination describing the fancies which arise from the smoke of logs wafted from far mysterious lands where once the trees grew under strange suns, moons, and rainbows, is as remarkable in form as in idea. One may judge by a sample pair of stanzas:

> "You warm your hands
> And smile
> Before the fire of driftwood.
>
> I feel old lands'
> Wan guile
> That writes in fire of driftwood."

We have so far viewed poetry which would lead us to classify Miss Jackson as a delineator of moods rather than of character; yet knowing her versatility, we naturally expect to find among her works some potent character studies. Nor are we disappointed. "Joe", a song of the Maine woods, describes in admirably appropriate verbiage—as simple and as nearly monosyllabic as possible—the typical Anglo-Saxon stoic of far places, who faces comfort and disaster, life and death, with the same unemotional attitude which Miss Jackson sums up so skilfully in the one ejaculatory bit of colloquial indifference—"Dunno!"

"The Song of Jonny Laughlin" is a highly unusual ballad relating the history of a peculiarly good and self-sacrificing river character. The story is simple, but the piece gains distinctiveness from its absolutely faithful reproduction of the spirit of frontier balladry. In words, swing, and weird refrain, there exists every internal evidence of traditional authenticity; and that such a bit of Nature could be composed by a cultivated feminine author is an overwhelming testimonial to Miss Jackson's unique gifts.

That Miss Jackson can reflect the spirit of the most dissimilar characters is further proved by the two immensely powerful studies of the vagabond type entitled "The Call" and "John Worthington Speaks". These things are masterpieces of their kind; the self-revealing narratives of restless wanderers by land and sea, crammed to repletion with details and local colour which no one but their author could command without actual experience as a derelict of five continents and as many oceans. They leave the reader veritably breathless with wonder at the objectivity and imagination which can enable a New-England poetess to mirror with such compelling vividness in thought and language the sentiments of so utterly opposite a type. Not even the narrowly specialised genius of such rough-and-ready writers as Service and Knibbs,[2] working in their own peculiar field, can surpass this one slight phase of Miss Jackson's universal genius.

It remains to speak of the singular power of Miss Jackson in the realm of the gruesome and the terrible. With that same sensitiveness to the unseen and the unreal which lends witchery to her gayer productions, she has achieved in darker fields of verse results inviting comparison with the best prose work of Ambrose Bierce or Maurice Level. Among her older poems the ghastly and colourful phantasy "Insomnia"[3] and the grimly realistic rustic tragedy "Chores" excited especial praise, a critic referring as follows to the latter piece:

> "It has all the compelling power which marks Miss Jackson's darker productions, and is conveyed in an arresting staccato measure which emphasises the homely horror of the theme. The phraseology, with its large proportion of rural and archaic words and constructions, adds vastly to the general effect and atmosphere."[4]

This reference to Miss Jackson's unusual vocabulary deserves elaboration, for one of the secrets of her effective poetry is the wide and diverse array of words and word-combinations which she commands. Recondite archaisms and ruralisms, together with marvellously apt and original descriptive compounds, are things which perpetually astonish and delight her readers. Of recent specimens of Miss Jackson's darker verse, "Finality", "The Song", and "Fallen Fences" deserve especial praise. The horrible picture conjured up in the closing lines of the first named piece is one well calculated to haunt the dreams of the imaginative.

As we conclude this survey of rich and varied poetry, our dominant impression aside from admiration is that of wonder at the tardiness with which the author has been recognised by the non-amateur public. As yet the name of Jackson is a comparative novelty to the literary world, a thing explainable only by the reluctance of its possessor to adopt that species of trumpeting which helps less modest and less genuine poets into the glare of celebrity. But genius such as Miss Jackson's cannot remain for-ever hidden, however slight be her striving for fame; so that we may reasonably expect the next few years to witness her establishment among the leading literary figures, as one of the ablest, broadest, and most original of contemporary bards.

EDITOR'S NOTE   FP: *United Amateur* 20, No. 4 (March 1921): 48–52. A much expanded and revised version of the article "Winifred Virginia Jordan: Associate Editor" (*Silver Clarion*, April 1919; *CE1*). Jackson (1876–1959), formerly married to Horace Jordan but now divorced, was thought to have engaged in a romance with HPL during the period 1918–21 (see Joshi, *Life* 199–201). The magazine appearances of most of the poems cited by HPL have not been located, but they probably appeared in various amateur journals or in her two books, *Backwoods: Maine Narratives, with Lyrics* (1927) and *Selected Poems* (1944).

Notes

1. The critic was HPL himself in his earlier article. The subsequent quotation ("With her . . .") is also from that article.

2. HPL refers to the Anglo-Canadian poet Robert Service (1874–1958), and the American poet Henry Herbert Knibbs (1874–1945). They are also cited in DPC (March 1919; *CE1*).

3. "Insomnia" was published in HPL's *Conservative* (October 1916).

4. "Chores" appeared in Jackson's amateur journal *Eurus* (February 1918). The quotation is from HPL's DPC (May 1918).

THE POETRY OF LILIAN MIDDLETON

Assuming that conditions in amateur journalism duplicate in miniature those of the general literary world, there is significance in the consistent conservatism of its foremost figures. Art, after all, is founded on the unchanging qualities and funda-mental experiences of mankind; and despite the occasional adoption of novel phases is always most genuine when it adheres most closely to the normal tradition. Nowhere is this truer than in the poetic field, where we find normality and rational aesthetic proportion in almost every truly dominant artist. Of amateurdom's three preëminently notable poets of the last decade, Samuel Loveman, Winifred Virginia Jackson, and "Lilian Middleton", not one is lacking in that sense of symmetry, relativity, fulness, and structural harmony which constitutes true conservatism. Impressionism, if ever occurring in these bards, is present only so far as it is an accurate reflection of Nature. Of "imagism", the abnormal expression of partial and non-rational perception, there is hardly a trace.

Samuel Loveman has for nearly twenty years symbolised the high-water mark of amateur art. Winifred V. Jackson, entering amateurdom in 1915, has recently received the acclamation of the larger literary sphere as one of America's new poets of genius. This article will attempt to survey the merits of "Lilian Middleton", former United Lau-reate, whose increasing array of excellent verse has assured her a place of eminence beside the two just mentioned.

S. Lilian Middleton-McMullen, whose works are now distinguished by publication in poetry magazines all over the country, is a discovery of Winifred V. Jackson's, and an added plume in the cap of that noted poetess. She is a native of Ireland, of a loyal British Unionist family, and inherits a trace of French blood through a great-grandmother. In her heredity there is a definitely artistic element, as shewn by the fact that both her mother and sister are poets of no mean skill.[1]

Mrs. McMullen was educated in English private schools, and originally specialised in music; being a violoncellist and pianiste of great ability, and to some degree a composer. At an early age she was given to the writing of verse, but these older specimens are notable only for grace and correctness. Amateurdom has seen two of them—"Late Autumn" in The Tryout, and "The 'Cellist" in The United Co-operative. They are, quite obviously, juvenilia; though of unusual merit for such work.

Not until after Mrs. McMullen's removal to the United States and acquaintance with Mrs. Jackson was her later and richer poetic vein uncovered. In 1918, at Miss Jackson's suggestion, she wrote as a credential to the United the poem "My Mistress—Music", which excited such favourable notice in manuscript that it was at once featured in The United Amateur.[2] Critical comment was unanimously approving, for it was clear that amateurdom had at last acquired another real singer—one with that distinct individuality and facility which make true art. The rest we know, for the partial pseudonym of "Lilian Middleton" has since become associated with one of the most poignant and beautiful elements of our literature.

The poetry of Mrs. McMullen, like all authentic art, possesses qualities of individuality which can be isolated and defined only by close analysis. Lesser writers may have mannerisms—affectations of form put on or put off at will—but only real artists can have style; that subtle and unmistakable uniqueness of expression which never comes save as the result of an absolute originality of perception, appraisal, and comparison. Style Mrs. McMullen has in abundance, and style of so piquant and truly lyrical a nature that a foreigner might derive pleasure from the cadence of her verses without understanding their purport. Much of this lyrism is certainly due to her intelligent musical education, but that factor is not enough to account for the curiosa felicitas[3] whereby all harsh effects are instinctively rejected, and all lines modulated with a Tennysonian liquidity quite uncommon in amateurdom. To achieve such results one must have an innate lyrical genius; a sensitiveness to beauty of spoken sound as connected with beauty of imagery which a purely musical training can hardly supply in full.

Mrs. McMullen's inspiration is gratifyingly free from the taint of modernism, whether in the sense of imagistic affiliations, unpoetic realism, or sloppy emotional waste. Her lyrics, perhaps influenced by some Celtic heritage, are things of infinite daintiness and witchery; often homely and familiar in theme, but invariably raised above the commonplace by the piquant originality of treatment and masterly refinement of rhythm. Original genius, it may incidentally be remarked, is found quite as often in method as in subject-matter; so that in judging a simple genre poem one must not cavil till he has investigated the kind of fancy animating the various images. Only if this fancy be commonplace, will condemnation be justified. Mrs. McMullen gives to a simple scene or sentiment that indefinable charm and faery glamour which belong to genius, as the moonlight gives charm and glamour to a landscape which by day is prosaic and undistinguished.

With literary sources as varied as Chaucer, Browning, Tennyson, and Austin Dobson[4]—to name a few—Mrs. McMullen has evolved an original style whose keynotes are exquisite lightness and buoyancy, quaint delicacy, and gentle pathos. She has, perhaps unconsciously as yet, a daintily coloured vision of life in its true proportions; for even in writing from the conventional point of view she glimpses the world's absence of substance—the need to retreat into the more tenuous upper regions of the fancy to escape pain and sordidness, and the underlying sadness which pursues one even to that ethereal haven. This apparent preoccupation with externals should not be judged as shallowness, but rather as a mark of aesthetic soundness in conformity with the truth emphasised by Schopenhauer, that the world is *beautiful as an object but ugly as a source of experience.*[5]

The variety of Mrs. McMullen's work is considerable; ranging from Dresden-China bits of *vers de société* and Gallic ballades, triolets and villanelles about Watteau shepherdesses, to serious pieces of greater length, imagination, and wistfulness. Her song-poetry, which includes some delectable child verse, has already found favour with composers and publishers; while her occasional departures into the realm of the sombre are, though not equal to her lighter productions, by no means infelicitous. Mrs. McMullen's Muse is still in a state of active growth, so that it will not do to impose too rigid a classification upon her art at this juncture.

It is illuminating to glance at some typical McMullen poems with an eye for their peculiar beauties. In sheer exuberance of sprightly melody and whimsicality, the Parisian trifle "Dans la Rue" is rich. A stanza or two illustrates how much piquancy can be extracted from the sheerest material:

> How I love you, Petite,
>   With your gay little air,
> As you pass down the street!
>
> I shall hasten!—*toute suite*
>   You will hear me declare
> How I love you, Petite,
> As you pass down the street!

France is in Mrs. McMullen's blood, and appears deliciously in occasional French phrases and subjects. Note such vivacious stanzas as the following, taken from the poem "Petit à Petit, L'Oiseau Fait Son Nid":

> 'Tis many months since first I saw you smile,
>   (The dullest day your sunny smile would hallow!)
> *Tout transporte,* I stood and watch'd you, while
>   *Vite comme le vent,* you pass'd me at St. Malo;
> One flashing glance from sloe-black eyes, *Petite,*
> And *tout à coup,* my heart was at your feet!

But it is in other poems—poems with the element of pathos more emphasised—that one finds Mrs. McMullen's fancy at its best. In such verse there is all the distinctiveness which results from viewing the eternal human tragedy through the diminishing-glass of romantic selection, and transfiguring it with the gentle glow of music, restraint, and a singularly original quaintness. "The Token" is a good sample—telling of how a dweller in "a little house of stone" received a loved one's messages from the evening star that shone in the west across the fields, and how sadness came when a mansion was built and shut out the light of the star. "In My Wee Room" is perhaps even better, giving a picture of a transition from joy to sadness with a few deft touches describing articles of furniture and decoration. "Desirée Logier" is a masterpiece—extremely simple in plot, relating only an idyllic courtship in war-torn France which ended in the weeping of Desirée by the poppied grave of the young Fusilier Dennis O'Toole, it derives from its skilfully breathed atmosphere and inherent music a charm and brooding sadness which scores of more hectic and apparently intense emotional outbursts fail to exhibit. Later fragments of McMullen verse shew the same qualities in even more mature form—the following stanzas are from different poems:

> But oh! my shadows are so sweet
> That I must sing which grasses sway—
> What matters *now*, that soon my feet
> Shall not pass here on any day?

> Out to the west with a full sail
> Eagerly fare the ships,
> And into the crest of the white foam
> Lightly the sea-gull dips.
> But I would plunge to the grey deeps
> In search of a dead man's lips.

> But they say that on the mountain where I've lain among the heather,
> With the plover's note a-mourning thro' the haze of blue,
> That the cold and dead are lying in the soft-cheek'd Irish weather,
> And oh! my heart is breaking for the mountain that I knew.

The same musical and atmospheric qualities can be found in documents of other moods, among which the gentle domestic affections, sometimes associated with picturesque Irish scenes, hold a large place. "When I Am a Lady, Old and Gray" has won a Laureateship—and deserved it. A few lines will suggest its magic:

> I shall smile at things the young folks do,
> And shall counsel give, so kind and wise!
> All dress'd in a gown of soft old blue,
> Old blue to match my faded eyes!

"The Fairy-Maiden" has an elfin, elusive quality:

> Ah! yes; you may woo me—and win me—enfold me
> But when the dew glistens, and starlight is falling,
> And all the night-voices are whisp'ring—are calling,
> Then you never can keep me—you never can hold me!

Childhood has a charm for Mrs. McMullen, as shewn in the quaintly grave long narrative poem "Understanding", the haunting lyric "In the Far Field", and others as yet unpublished. For this subject her lightness of touch fits her preëminently. Of plain amatory verse the bard does not produce a great quantity, but what she does write is of inimitable grace and musical tenderness, as we may see by pieces like "Eventide", whose final stanza reads as follows:

> Now up a pathway steep
> Moon mounts the skies—
> Dear, let me long and deep

> Drink of your eyes.
> Ah! what the bliss to know
> Your sweet head pillow'd, so!

The poetry of spiritual revolt—the eternal cry of man at the limitations of Nature—is another phase of the McMullen genius. "In Rein" is familiar to all amateurs. Less so, perhaps, is "The Prisoner", which begins:

> My soul would be for ever free
> Of this dull body where it hides!
> My body wanders stumblingly
> While light as air my spirit rides!

With these varied samples, it will perhaps be needless to speak in detail of Mrs. McMullen's especial gift for vivid metrical effects. Her mastery of quaint and captivating metres is notable, irregular anapaests being perhaps her favourite form. We see this skill illustrated in many unusual compositions, among them "My Mistress—Music", which is its author's first poem of maturity:

> I have a Mistress fair to see,
> But oh! she's fickle as she is fair.
> What would you do if you were me?
> Let my passion seem
> But a cherish'd dream
> That fades away into thinnest air?

The following is very recent—from a lyric entitled "On the Heart of the Spring":

> O! Birdie a-swing
> On the heart of the spring,
> As you lightsomely hover
> And skim o'er the clover.
> What a torrent of rapturous, lyrical madness
> In a frenzy of turbulent spring-blossom gladness
> You fling!

The individuality of Mrs. McMullen's subtler metrical qualities is infinite—one might point out a delightfully quaint habit of accenting adjectives instead of the nouns they modify, as, for example,

> And a *white* bird mounts on a *strong* wing.

That the growth of this unique genius will be eminently interesting to watch, none may dispute. Mrs. McMullen is already a lyrist of the first order—second to none in amateurdom so far as music of phrase, magic of metre, and buoyancy of fancy are concerned—and from the advances she has already made we may predict much. Young in years, replete with studious energy, and having a background of exceptional cultivation, her expanding special reading and increasing experience promise notable results. Philosophy may temper the serenity of her work with a more poignant note of despair, while sophistication may emphasise the hollowness of sentiments now treated as at least presumable actualities. But always there will be an airy and exquisite soaring above the commonplace—a lyrical freshness of mood and repudiation of prosaic, un-subtilised realism.

Mrs. McMullen is fortunate in having an appeal which is popular as well as classi-cal. The professional success of her work, while not affecting her pure artistry of method, will serve as an added assurance of excellence and encouragement to progress. She is, it seems quite certain, among the very few amateurs who are destined for an early and cordial recognition by the general literary world.

EDITOR'S NOTE Unpublished (AMS, JHL). Dated 14 January 1922 on the ms. A friendly analysis of the work of S. Lilian McMullen, who published her work in the amateur press under the pseudonym "Lilian Middleton." McMullen lived in Newton Centre, MA, and was a friend of Winifred Virginia Jackson. HPL met her in August 1921 (see HPL to Rheinhart Kleiner, 30 August 1921; AHT). HPL prepared a condensed version of this essay as his contribution to "The Vivisector" (March 1922; CE1).

Notes

1. HPL discusses Middleton's sister, Mrs. Stella L. Tully, in DPC (March 1919; CE1).

2. *United Amateur*, January 1919. HPL discusses it in DPC (May 1919; CE1).

3. "Studied happiness [of style]," a comment made by Petronius (*Satyricon* 118.5) on Horace.

4. HPL owned the selected or collected poetical works of all these poets: Geoffrey Chaucer (*LL* 170), Robert Browning (*LL* 124), Alfred, Lord Tennyson (*LL* 866), and Austin Dobson (*LL* 254).

5. Arthur Schopenhauer (1788–1860), German philosopher who influenced HPL signifi-cantly at this period, especially by way of a selection of essays translated as *Studies in Pessi-mism* (1893). See "Nietzscheism and Realism" (1922; CE5).

LORD DUNSANY AND HIS WORK

The relatively slight recognition hitherto accorded Lord Dunsany, who is perhaps the most unique, original, and richly imaginative of living authors, forms an amus-ing commentary on the natural stupidity of mankind. Conservatives view him with pa-tronage because he does not concern himself with the hoary fallacies and artificialities which constitute their supreme values. Radicals slight him because his work does not display that chaotic defiance of taste which to them is the sole identifying mark of au-thentic modern disillusion. And yet one might hardly err in claiming that he should have the homage of both rather than of neither; for surely if any man has extracted and combined the residue of true art in older and newer schools alike, it is this singular giant in whom the classic, the Hebraic, and Nordic, and the Irish aesthetic traditions are so curiously and admirably combined.

General knowledge of Dunsany seems to be limited to a vague impression that he is a member of the Celtic revival group who writes odd plays. Like most general knowl-edge, this is sadly fractional and incomplete; and in many ways somewhat misleading. Dunsany belongs, properly speaking, to no group whatsoever; while the mere author-ship of dramatic phantasies is a small enough item in the personality of one whose poetic stories and plays reflect the sheer genius of a distinctive philosophy and aesthetic outlook. Dunsany is not a national but an universal artist; and his paramount quality is not simply weirdness, but a certain godlike and impersonal vision of cosmic scope and perspective, which comprehends the insignificance, cloudiness, futility, and tragic absurdity of all life and reality. His main work belongs to what modern critics have called the "literature of escape"; the literature of conscious unreality created out of an intelligent and sophisticated conviction that analysed reality has no heritage save of chaos, pain, and disappointment. He is in this way both a conservative and a modern; a conservative because he still believes that beauty is a thing of golden rememberings and simple patterns, and a modern because he perceives that only in arbitrarily selected fancy can we find fixed any of the patterns which fit our golden rememberings. He is the supreme poet of wonder, but of the intelligently assumed wonder to which one turns after experiencing the fullest disillusion of realism.

Edward John Moreton Drax Plunkett, Eighteenth Baron Dunsany, was born in 1878 at Dunsany Castle, County Meath, Ireland;[1] and is a representative of the oldest and greatest blood in the British Empire. His race-stock is predominantly Teutonic and Scandinavian—Norman and Danish—circumstance which gives to him the frosty heritage of Northern lore rather than the wilder and more mystical Celtic tradition. His family, however, is closely woven into the life of Ireland; and it is his uncle, the statesman Sir Horace Plunkett, who first proposed the Dominion idea now applied in the creation of the Irish Free State. Lord Dunsany himself is a loyalist Imperialist in sympathies; a valiant officer in the British army, and veteran of both Boer and World wars.

Dunsany's earliest youth was spent at the ancestral estate of his mother, Dunstall Priory, Shoreham, Kent, England. He had a room whose windows faced the hills and the sunset, and to these vistas of golden earth and sky he attributes much of his poetic tendency. His unique manner of expression was promoted by his mother's careful choice of his reading; newspapers were wholly excluded, and the King James Bible made the principal article of literary diet. The effect of this reading on his style was permanent and marvellously beneficial. The simplicity and purity of archaic English, and the artistic repetitions of the Hebrew psalmists, all became his without conscious effort; so that to this day he has escaped the vitiation common to most modern prose-writers.

At his first public school, Cheam School, Dunsany received still more of the biblical influence, and obtained his first touch of an influence still more valuable; that of the Greek classics. In Homer he found a spirit of wonder akin to his own, and throughout his work one may trace the inspiration of the Odyssey—an epic, by the way, which is probably of much vaster genius than its more martial antecedent, the Iliad. The Odyssey teems with just that glamour of strange, far lands which is Dunsany's prime attribute.

After Cheam School came Eton, and after that Sandhurst, where the youthful Edward Plunkett was trained to that profession of arms which becomes a scion of nobility. In 1899 the Boer War broke out, and the youth fought with the Coldstream Guards through all its hardships. Also in 1899 he succeeded to his ancient title and his majority; the boy Edward Plunkett had become Lord Dunsany, man and soldier.

Dunsany first appears in literature shortly after the dawn of the new century, as a patron of the work of the Irish literary group. In 1905 he published his first book, "The Gods of Pegāna", in which his original genius shines through the fantastic creation of a new and artificial Aryan mythology; a perfectly developed cycle of nature-allegories with all the infinite charm and shrewd philosophy of natural legendry. After that other books appeared in swift succession, all illustrated by the weird artist Sidney H. Sime. In "Time and the Gods" (1906), the mythic idea was extended with increasing vividness.

"The Sword of Welleran" (1908) sings of a world of men and heroes ruled by Pegāna's gods, as does "A Dreamer's Tales" (1910). We here find the best Dunsanian forms fully developed; the Hellenic sense of conflict and fatality, the magnificently cosmic point of view, the superbly lyrical flow of language, the Oriental splendour of colouring and imagery, the titanic fertility and ingenuity of imagination, the mystical glamour of fabulous lands "beyond the East" or "at the edge of the world", and the amazing facility for devising musical, alluring, and wonder-making proper names, personal and geographical, on classical and Oriental models. Some of Dunsany's tales deal with the objective world we know, and of strange wonders therein; but the best of them are about lands conceivable only in purple dream. These are fashioned in that purely decorative spirit which means the highest art, having no visible moral or didactic element save such quaint allegory as may inhere in the type of legendary lore to which they belong. Dunsany's only didactic idea is an artist's hatred of the ugly, the stupid, and the commonplace. We see it occasionally in touches of satire on social institutions, and bits of lamentation over the pollution of Nature by grimy cities and hideous advertising signs. Of all human institutions, the billboard is most abhorrent to Lord Dunsany.

In 1909 Dunsany wrote his first play, "The Glittering Gate", at the request of W. B. Yeats, who desired something of his for the Abbey Theatre in Dublin. Despite the author's absolute previous inexperience, the result was highly successful; and turned Dunsany toward a steady career of dramatic composition. Though the present writer continues to prefer the stories, most critics unite in giving higher praise to the plays; and certainly the latter possess a brilliancy of dialogue and sureness of technique which place Dunsany among the greatest of dramatists. What simplicity! What fancy! What exalted speech! Like the stories, the best of the plays are of fantastic plot and setting. Most are very short, though at least two, "If" and "Alexander", are of full length.[2] The most esteemed is perhaps "The Gods of the Mountain", which tells of the fate of seven beggars in the city of Kongros, who impersonated the seven green jade gods who sit on the mountain Marma. Green, by the way, is a favourite colour in Dunsany's work; and green jade its most frequent embodiment. In this play the Nietzschean figure of the chief beggar Agmar is drawn with a master's stroke, and is likely to live permanently among the vivid characters of the world's drama. Other marvellously powerful plays are "A Night at an Inn"—a bit worthy of the Parisian Grand Guignol— and "The Queen's Enemies", an elaborated Egyptian incident from Herodotus.[3] It is impossible to exaggerate the pure genius for dramatic utterance and situation which Dunsany shews in his best plays. They are thoroughly classical in every sense.

Dunsany's attitude of wonder is, as we have noted, a consciously cultivated one; overlying a keenly philosophical and sophisticated intelligence. It is therefore not remarkable that with the years an element of visible satire and acute humour began to appear in his work. There is, indeed, an interesting parallelism between him and that other great Irishman Oscar Wilde; whose fantastic and wittily worldly sides were so delightfully blended, and who had the same divine gift of gorgeous prose and exotic imagery. In 1912 appeared "The Book of Wonder", whose brief fantastic tales all hold a certain humorous doubt of their own solemnity and truth. Soon afterward came "The Lost Silk Hat",[4] a one-act comedy of manners equalling in sheer sparkle and cleverness anything even Sheridan could devise; and since then the serious side of Dunsany has been steadily on the wane, despite occasional plays and tales which shew a survival of the absolute beauty-worshipper. "Fifty-One Tales", published in 1915, having something of the urbane prose-poetic spirit of a philosophical Baudelaire, whilst "The Last Book of Wonder" (1916) is like the first volume of kindred title. Only in the scattered fragments forming "Tales of Three Hemispheres" (1919) do we find strong reminders of the older, simpler Dunsany. "If" (1922), the new long play, is mainly satirical comedy with one brief touch of exotic eloquence. "Don Rodriguez", just announced by the publishers, has not been read by the present writer; but may have more of the old Dunsany.[5] It is his first novel, and is highly regarded by those reviewers who have seen it. "Alexander", a full-length play based on Plutarch, was written in 1912 and is considered by the author as his best work. It is to be regretted that this drama has been neither published nor acted. Dunsany's shorter plays are grouped in two volumes. "Five Plays", containing "The Gods of the Mountain", "The Golden Doom", "King Argimēnēs and the Unknown Warrior", "The Glittering Gate", and "The Lost Silk Hat", was published in 1914. In 1917 appeared "Plays of Gods and Men", with "The Tents of the Arabs", "The Laughter of the Gods", "The Queen's Enemies", and "A Night at an Inn."

Dunsany has never forsaken his position as a patron of letters, and was the literary sponsor of the Irish peasant poet Ledwidge[6]—that immortaliser of the blackbird, who fell in the Great War while serving in the Fifth Royal Inniskilling Fusiliers with Dunsany as his captain. The war engrossed much of Dunsany's imagination, since he saw active service in France and in the Dublin revolt of 1916, when he was badly wounded. This engrossment is shewn by a volume of charming and sometimes pathetic stories, "Tales of War" (1918), and a collection of reminiscent essays, "Unhappy Far-Off Things" (1920).[7] His general view of war is the sane one: that conflict is a disaster as inevitable as the tides and the seasons.

America is highly regarded by Dunsany, since it has been readier than the mother country to give him what little appreciation he has. Most of his plays have been acted here by "Little Theatre" companies, especially that of Stuart Walker,[8] and at times considerable enthusiasm has been developed. All such productions have been made with the careful supervision of the author, whose letters of directions are eminently interesting. Dunsany plays are favourites with many collegiate dramatic societies, and justly so. In 1919–20 Dunsany made a lecture tour of the United States, where he was generally well received.

The personality of Lord Dunsany is exceedingly attractive, as can be attested by the present writer, who sat in a front seat directly opposite him when he spoke in the Copley-Plaza ballroom in Boston in October 1919. On that occasion he outlined his literary theories with much charm, and read in full his playlet, "The Queen's Enemies". He is a very tall man—six feet four—of medium breadth, with fair complexion, blue eyes, high forehead, abundant light brown hair, and a small moustache of the same colour. His face is wholesomely and delicately handsome, and his expression is one of charming and whimsical kindliness with a certain boyish quality which no amount of worldly experience or his single eyeglass can efface. There is boyishness also in his walk and bearing; a trace of the stoop and the engaging awkwardness which one associates with adolescence. His voice is pleasant and mellow, and his accent the apex of British cultivation. His whole bearing is easy and familiar, so much so that the *Boston Transcript's* reporter complained of his lack of unctuous platform presence. As a dramatic reader he undoubtedly lacks vividness and animation; obviously, he would be as poor as an actor as he is great as an author. He dresses with marked carelessness, and has been called the worst-dressed man in Ireland. Certainly, there was nothing impressive in the loosely draped evening attire which nebulously surrounded him during his American lecturers. To Boston autograph seekers he proved very accommodating, refusing none despite a severe headache which forced his hand many times to his forehead. When the entered a cab his top hat was knocked off—thus do the small remember the mishaps of the great!

Lord Dunsany is married to a daughter of Lord Jersey, and has one son, the Hon. Randal Plunkett, born in 1906. His tastes, far from being the morbid predilections of the traditional cynic and fantaisiste, are distinctly outdoor and normal; savouring rather of his feudal and baronial side. He is the best pistol shot in Ireland, an ardent cricketer and horseman, a big game hunter, and a confirmed devotee of rural scenes. He has travelled extensively, especially in Africa; and lives alternately at his own Meath castle, at his mother's place in Kent, and at his London home at 55, Lowndes Square. That he has the truly romantic quality of modest heroism, is attested by an incident when he rescued a man from drowning, and refused to reveal his name to the admiring crowds.

Dunsany's writing is always very rapid, and is done mainly in the late afternoon and early evening, with tea as a mild stimulant. He almost invariably employs a quill pen, whose broad, brush-like strokes are unforgettable by those who have seen his letters and manuscripts. His individuality appears in every phase of his activity, and involves not only an utterly unique simplicity of style but an utterly unique scarcity of punctuation which readers occasionally regret. About his work Dunsany spreads a quaint atmosphere of cultivated naiveté and child-like ignorance, and likes to refer to historical and other data with a delightfully artless air of unfamiliarity. His consistent aim is to survey the world with the impressionable freshness of unspoiled youth—or with the closest approach to that quality which his experience will allow. This idea sometimes plays havock with his critical judgment, as was keenly realised in 1920, when he most considerately acted as Laureate Judge of Poetry for the United Amateur Press Association.[9] Dunsany has the true aristocrat's attitude toward his work; and whilst he would welcome fame, he would never think of debasing his art either for the philistine rabble or for the reigning clique of literary chaoticists. He writes purely for self-expression, and is therefore the ideal amateur journalist type.

The ultimate position of Dunsany in literature depends largely on the future course of literature itself. Our age is one of curious transition and divergence, with an increasing separation of art from the past and from all common life as well. Modern science has, in the end, proved an enemy to art and pleasure; for by revealing to us the whole sordid and prosaic basis of our thoughts, motives, and acts, it has stripped the world of glamour, wonder, and all those illusions of heroism, nobility, and sacrifice which used to sound so impressive when romantically treated. Indeed, it is not too much to say that psychological discovery, and chemical, physical, and physiological research have largely destroyed the element of emotion among informed and sophisticated people by resolving it into its component parts—intellectual idea and animal impulse. The so-called "soul" with all its hectic and mawkish attributes of sentimentality, veneration, earnestness, devotion, and the like, has perished on analysis. Nietzsche brought a transvaluation of values, but Remy de Gourmont has brought a wholesale destruction of all values.[10] We know now what a futile, aimless, and disconnected welter of mirages and hypocrisies life is; and from the first shock of that knowledge has sprung the bizarre, tasteless, defiant, and chaotic literature of that terrible newer generation which so shocks our grandmothers—the aesthetic generation of T. S. Eliot, D. H. Lawrence, James Joyce, Ben Hecht, Aldous Huxley, James Branch Cabell, and all the rest. These writers, knowing that life has no real pattern, either rave, or mock, or join in the cosmic chaos by exploiting a frank and conscious unintelligibility and confusion of values. To them it savours of the vulgar to adopt a pattern—for today only servants, churchgoers, and tired business men read things which mean anything or acknowledge any values. What chance, then, has an author who is neither stupid or common enough for the clientele of the *Cosmopolitan, Saturday Evening Post,* Harold Bell Wright, *Snappy Stories, Atlantic Monthly,* and *Home Brew;*[11] nor confused, obscene, or hydrophobic enough for the readers of the *Dial, Freeman, Nation,* or *New Republic,* and the would-be readers of "Ulysses"? At present one tribe rejects him as "too highbrow", whilst the other ignores him as impossibly tame and childishly comprehensible.

Dunsany's hope of recognition lies with the literati and not with the crowd, for his charms are those of a supremely delicate art and a gentle disillusion and world-weariness which only the discriminating can ever enjoy. The necessary step toward such recognition is a rebound which is quite likely to come with a maturer understanding of modern disillusion and all its implications. Art has been wrecked by a complete consciousness of the universe which shews that the world is to each man only a rubbish-heap limned by his individual perception. It will be saved, if at all, by the next and last step of disillusion; the realisation that complete consciousness and truth are themselves valueless, and that to acquire any genuine artistic titillation we must artificially invent limitations of consciousness and feign a pattern of life common to all mankind—most naturally the simple old pattern which ancient and groping tradition first gave us. When we see that the source of all joy and enthusiasm is wonder and ignorance, we shall be ready to play the old game of blindman's buff with the mocking atoms and electrons of a purposeless infinity.

It is then that we shall worship afresh the music and colour of divine language, and take an Epicurean delight in those combinations of ideas and fancies which we know to be artificial. Not that we can resume a serious attitude toward emotion—there is too much intellect abroad for that—but that we can revel in the Dresden-china Arcadia of an author who will play with the old ideas, atmospheres, types, situations, and lighting effects in a deft pictorial way; a way tinged with affectionate reminiscence as for fallen gods, yet never departing from a cosmic and gently satirical realisation of the true microscopic insignificance of the man-puppets and their petty relations to one another. Such an author may well avoid flippancy or vulgarity, but he must keep the intellectual point of view paramount even when hidden, and beware of speaking seriously with the voice of passions proved by modern psychology to be either hypocritically hollow or absurdly animal.

And is not this a virtual description of Dunsany, a liquid prose-poet who writes classic hexameters by accident, with his stage set for relentless deities and their still more relentless conqueror Time; for cosmic chess-games of Fate and Chance; for the funerals of dead gods; for the birth and death of universes; and for the simple annals of that speck in space called the world, which with its poor denizens is but one of countless playthings of the little gods, who are in turn only the dreams of MĀNA YOOD SUSHĀĪ? The balance between conservatism and sophistication in Dunsany is perfect; he is whimsically traditional, but just as conscious of the chaotic nullity of values as any assertive modern. With the same voice that sings god-moving forces he mourns with a child's broken rocking-horse, and tells how a boy's wish for a hoop made a king sacrifice his crown to the stars;[12] nor does he fail to chant of quiet villages, and the smoke of idyllic hearths, and the lights in cottage windows at evening. He creates a world which has never existed and never will exist, but which we have always known and longed for in dreams. This world he makes vivid not by pretending that it is real, but by exalting the quality of unreality and suffusing his whole dream-universe with a delicate pessimism drawn half from modern psychology and half from our ancestral Northern myths of Ragnarock, the Twilight of the Gods. He is at once modern and mythologist, viewing life correctly as a series of meaningless pictures, but investing it with all the ancient formulae and saws which like frozen metaphors in language have become an integral part of our cherished heritage of associations.

Dunsany is like nobody else. Wilde is his nearest congener, and there are points of kinship to Poe, De Quincey, Maeterlinck, and Yeats; but all comparisons are futile. His peculiar combination of matter and manner is unique in its imperious genius. He is not perfect, or not always perfect, but who indeed is continually so? Critics complain that he sometimes mixes satire with the atmosphere of tragedy; but this objection is a conventional one, and argues an unfamiliarity with the Irish tradition which has produced such perversely immortal classics as James Stephens' "Crock of Gold". They cavil, too, at his introduction of walking stone gods and hideous Hindoo idols on the stage; but this cavilling is pitifully blind in its interpretation of apocalyptic visions in terms of theatrical mechanics. Any criticism by the present writer would be of the nature of a plea; urging a less complete metamorphosis of the old myth-making Dunsany into the newer and more sparklingly satirical Dunsany. A reincarnated Sheridan is precious indeed, but the Dunsany of "A Dreamer's Tales" is a wonder twice as precious because it cannot be duplicated or even approached. It is a wonder which has restored to us our childhood's dreams, as far as such things can ever be restored; and that is the most blessed happening which the earth may know.

The future is dark and dubious, and amidst its devastating introspection and analysis there may be no place for art as we know it. But if any existing art does belong to that future, it is the art of Lord Dunsany.

EDITOR'S NOTE FP: *Marginalia* (Arkham House, 1944). Text based on the AMS (JHL), dated 14 December 1922. A lecture written for a meeting of the Hub Club, an amateur group in Boston, in mid-December 1922 (see *SL* 1.203). HPL had been enraptured by Dunsany ever since he read him in the fall of 1919, at which time he also saw Dunsany lecture in Boston (see *SL* 1.91–93). HPL probably derived most of his information on Dunsany from Edward Hale Bierstadt's *Dunsany the Dramatist* (1917; rev. 1919; *LL* 91) and from the abundant newspaper coverage of Dunsany's American tour of 1919–20. The significance of the essay derives from its concluding section, in which HPL ponders the role of art in modern society in a manner that strikingly anticipates Joseph Wood Krutch's *The Modern Temper* (1929), a volume that significantly influenced HPL's later thought.

Notes

1. In fact, Dunsany was born at 15 Park Square near Regent's Park, London, although Dunsany Castle became his primary residence.

2. *If* was published separately in 1921 and included in *Plays of Near and Far (Including If)* (1923); HPL did not own either of these volumes and probably never read *If*. *Alexander* was written in 1912 but first published only in *Alexander and Three Small Plays* (1925).

3. *The Gods of the Mountain* appears in *Five Plays* (1914); *A Night at an Inn* was published separately in 1916 and was included in *Plays of Gods and Men* (1917), which also contained *The Queen's Enemies*. Dunsany read *The Queen's Enemies* in Boston when HPL saw him (see *SL* 1.91).

4. *The Lost Silk Hat* was first published in *Five Plays*.

5. HPL later read *Don Rodriguez* (the American title of the novel *The Chronicles of Rodriguez*, 1922), and it may have influenced "He" (1925) and "The Strange High House in the Mist" (1926). See my article, "Lovecraft and Dunsany's *Chronicles of Rodriguez*," *Primal Sources* (New York: Hippocampus Press, 2003), pp. 177–81.

6. Dunsany wrote introductions to *Songs of the Fields* (1916), *Songs of Peace* (1917), and *Last Songs* (1918) by Francis Ledwidge (1887–1917), as well as to *The Complete Poems of Francis Ledwidge* (1919).

7. *Unhappy Far-Off Things* dates to 1919.

8. Stuart Walker (1888–1941), American director who established the Portmanteau Theatre and staged many of Dunsany's plays. See the letters between Dunsany and Walker reprinted in the revised edition (1919) of Bierstadt's *Dunsany the Dramatist*.

9. See Dunsany's Letter to Mary Faye Durr (10 July 1920), published in the *United Amateur* 20, No. 2 (November 1920): 22–23. Of Dunsany's selections of amateur poems for laureate awards, HPL later wrote "Dunsany's laureate letter was indeed interesting, though his decisions were certainly atrocious" (HPL to Frank Belknap Long, 4 June 1921; AHT).

10. HPL began reading Nietzsche around 1919 (see *SL* 1.86). Of the French philosopher Remy de Gourmont (1858–1915) HPL read at least *A Night in the Luxembourg* (1906) in 1923 (*SL* 1.250).

11. HPL published "Herbert West—Reanimator" (1921–22) and "The Lurking Fear" (1922) in *Home Brew*, a professional humour magazine edited by his amateur journalism associates George Julian Houtain and E. Dorothy (MacLaughlin) Houtain.

12. The references are to the story "Blagdaross" (in *A Dreamer's Tales*) and to the play *The Golden Doom*.

RUDIS INDIGESTAQUE MOLES

The Conservative, observing the complacent indifference of most amateurs toward the present state of literature and general aesthetics, hath frequently wondered how acute be their realisation of just what is taking place. The average amateur paper, when it can spare the space from subjects so titanic as politics, conventions, and personalities, is unique in its allegiance to the accepted art and literature of the past; and in its happy oblivion regarding the menaces offered by the present and future. To read such a paper one would gather that Tennyson and Longfellow are still taken seriously as poets, and that the sentiments and sentimentalities of our fathers are still capable of awakening the Muse and forming the basis of future works of art. A protest against this species of myopia was some time ago uttered by one of our ultra-radicals; but lost force because of its origin and form. Perhaps it would not be improper for a Conservative, whose sympathy with extreme manifestations is little enough, to call renewed attention to the situation.

Do our members realise that the progress of science within the last half-century has introduced conceptions of man, the world, and the universe which make hollow and ridiculous an appreciable proportion of all the great literature of the past? Art, to be great, must be founded on human emotions of much strength; such as come from warm instincts and firm beliefs. Science having so greatly altered our view of the universe and the beliefs attendant upon that view, we are now confronted by an important shifting of values in every branch of art where belief is concerned. The old heroics, pieties, and sentimentalities are dead amongst the sophisticated; and even some of our appreciations of natural beauty are threatened. Just how expansive is this threat, we do not know; and The Conservative hopes fervently that the final devastated area will be comparatively narrow; but in any case startling developments are inevitable.

A glance at the serious magazine discussion of Mr. T. S. Eliot's disjointed and incoherent "poem" called "The Waste Land", in the November *Dial*, should be enough to convince the most unimpressionable of the true state of affairs. We here behold a practically meaningless collection of phrases, learned allusions, quotations, slang, and scraps in general; offered to the public (whether or not as a hoax) as something justified by our modern mind with its recent comprehension of its own chaotic triviality and disorganisation. And we behold that public, or a considerable part of it, receiving this hilarious melange as something vital and typical; as "a poem of profound significance", to quote its sponsors.[1]

To reduce the situation to its baldest terms, man has suddenly discovered that all his high sentiments, values, and aspirations are mere illusions caused by physiological processes within himself, and of no significance whatsoever in an infinite and purposeless cosmos. He has discovered that most of his acts spring from hidden causes remote from the ones hitherto honoured by tradition, and that his so-called "soul" is merely (as one critic puts it) a rag-bag of unrelated odds and ends. And having made these discoveries, he does not know what to do about it; but compromises on a literature of analysis, chaos, and ironic contrast.

What will come of it? This we cannot say; but certainly, great alterations are due amongst the informed. European culture has reached the Alexandrian stage of effeteness, and we probably cannot hope for anything better than diverging streams of barren intellectualism and of an amorphous, passionate art founded on primal instincts rather than delicate emotions. The emotions will be minutely analysed and laughed at; the instincts will be glorified and wallowed in. The hope of art, paradoxically enough, lies in the ability of future generations not to be too well informed; to be able, at least, to create certain artificial limitations of consciousness and enjoy a gently whimsical repetition and variation of the traditional images and themes, whose decorative beauty and quaintness can never be wholly negligible to the sensitive taste. It is, for example, hardly possible that moonlight on a marble temple, or twilight in an old garden in spring, can ever be other than beautiful in our eyes. Bourgeois and plebeian literature, of course, will undoubtedly go on without change; for the thoughts of the great majority are rarely affected by the subtleties of progress. The Edgar A. Guests are secure in their unassuming niches.[2] But it is only by the higher strata that we can judge a literature in its historic perspective, so that the permanent residuum of folk or ballad aesthetics does not figure in the problem. Never before, it is interesting to note, have the popular and the sophisticated types of literature been so widely divergent as at present.

Meanwhile it is singular that so few echoes of the prevailing turbulence should have reached our amateur press. Shall we remain comfortably cloistered with our Milton and Wordsworth, never again to know the amusing buzzing of such quaint irritants as *Les Mouches Fantastiques?*[3] The Conservative confesses himself curious to know what other amateur authors and editors think of "The Waste Land" and its bizarre analogues!

EDITOR'S NOTE FP: *Conservative* No. 12 (March 1923): 6–8 (unsigned). HPL's celebrated denunciation of T. S. Eliot's *Waste Land*, which HPL read when it was first published in the US in the *Dial* (November 1922; LL 238). (It had appeared in the UK in Eliot's magazine, the *Criterion*, in October 1922.) At the same time, however, HPL criticises amateur writers for failing to take note of Eliot and other developments in modern literature and thought. HPL's parody "Waste Paper" (1923?; *AT* 252–55) seeks to embody his opinion of *The Waste Land* as "a practically meaningless collection of phrases, learned allusions, quotations, slang, and scraps in general."

Notes

1. Hence the subtitle of "Waste Paper": "A Poem of Profound Insignificance."

2. Edgar A. Guest (1891–1959), English-born American poet whose work, widely published in newspapers, became a byword for trite and hackneyed poetic expression.

3. *Les Mouches Fantastiques* was a literarily radical amateur journal edited by Elsa A. Gidlow and Roswell George Mills. See HPL's essay "Les Mouches Fantastiques" (1918; *CE1*).

INTRODUCTION [TO *THE POETICAL WORKS OF JONATHAN E. HOAG*]

Penned in this age of chaos and change, fever and flourish, by a man born when Andrew Jackson was President, when Poe was an unknown youth with his second thin volume of verses in the press, when Coleridge, Moore, Crabbe, Southey, and Wordsworth were living bards, and when the memory of Byron, Shelley, Blake, and Keats was still recent; the present collection of poems is probably unique in its defiance of time and whim. Where else, indeed, would one be likely to find such a body of poetry; written almost wholly after the author's eighty-fifth year, and with many of the choicest specimens dating from beyond his ninetieth year, yet exhibiting an uniform grace, vigour, and vividness which place it in competition with the best, irrespective of origin?

Our venerable author, Jonathan E. Hoag, was born February 10, 1831, in a farmhouse at Valley Falls, Rensselaer County, New York. Heredity gave him her best; for in his blood are mingled the Quaker strain of the Hoags, the sturdiness of the Wings, the rugged independence of Ethan Allen, and the high martial spirit of the Giffords, through whom he traces his descent from the Norman Walter Gifford, first Earl of Buckingham, who was standard-bearer to William the Conqueror. The earliest environment of Mr. Hoag, which he has celebrated in so many delightful poems and essays, was an idyllic kind of rural life which has today largely vanished through the incursions of the railway, telephone, and postal system; and which was marked by that lofty and picturesque simplicity formed when a race of fine stock and traditions reverts to the stalwart condition of the pioneer. In such a life there was, despite the proportion of arduous toil, a certain beauty and freshness that sprang from the continuous isolation with varied Nature, and from the acutely visible cycle of fundamental acts and processes—ploughing, sowing, cultivating, reaping, storing; stock-raising, shearing, spinning, weaving; baking, sewing, candle-making—all the simple, homely little deeds which modernity has banished from most individual lives through coöperative effort, yet which the most sophisticated writers like to recall in occasional idyls and delicately etched eclogues. Thousands knew this elder and vanished America, but being bound to the practical, did not feel its loveliness poignantly enough to need to express it in the rhythms and images of poetry. Mr. Hoag, however, was endowed with the true vision and divine sensitiveness of the bard; and vibrated sympathetically to the pastoral scenes around him. Alive to beauty in every form, he found it wherever he looked; and watched the calm agrestic years roll by, with the life of the old farm hoe, and the little school, and the academy, and the general training on the green. He knew, and what is more, he felt, the old America of our fathers; and was in addition a worshipper of those universal powers of grandeur and loveliness which gleam in the woods, hills, valleys, streams, and waterfalls of untenanted Nature. Add to this a keenly active, humorous, and analytical mind, and a disposition of the warmest kindness, tolerance, and sympathy; and you have a picture of the fundamentals on which our poet's art is built.

The titanic background of the past, so pitifully lost to our younger generation, was possessed in all its potency by the growing bard. The Hoags are a long-lived race, and when little Jonathan was six he could sit at the feet of his great-aunt Lydia, who lived to be 103, and hear at first hand the reminiscences of one who had witnessed not only the Revolution, but the last of the French and Indian wars as well.[1] He learned from the very first that essential continuity of life and thought which our moderns learn too late or not at all; and never swerved from conservatism and sanity as he grew to the six feet of sturdy Hoag, Wing, Allen, and Gifford brawn which he has today.

Of books Mr. Hoag was ever an avid reader. Though educated only at the "little red schoolhouse" and the Washington County Academy, he lost no opportunity to enlarge his liberal culture; so that ere long he was master of a wide erudition and discriminating philosophy. Uniting to his studiousness and acute observation of men and scenes, he gradually became stored within an accumulation of ideas and images which in one of his eloquent temperament could not but seek expression in literature. By degrees we find him uttering his thoughts and impressions in essays and poems; though moved somewhat to restraint because of the absence of early technical training in the most rigid literary forms. Of this earlier work very little verse has survived; though from the single specimen here presented we see that its natural merit was indeed great.

Mr. Hoag, maturing, acquired experience, family responsibilities, and varied interests. Poet and dreamer already, he became likewise skilled in law, newspaper correspondence, observant travel, and the several sciences. He developed social and political interests, visited the Philadelphia Exposition of 1876, and rose to a position of commanding influence in the Prohibition party; for his sensitive good taste had always rebelled against the bestial spectacle of drunkenness and its attendant miseries. His letters, signed "Scriba", were always in demand by the press; whether touching on the beauties of some natural vista or historic spot, on some unusual observation pertaining to geology, geography, or meteorology, or on some problem of governmental or economic significance. In 1904, at an age already ripe, Mr. Hoag made an extended tour of the United States; beholding the scenic wonders of the West, and studying the condition of mankind all over the nation. He saw a sunset from Pike's Peak, talked with old Geronimo, that last relic of aboriginal savagery, and accumulated a new fund of beauty and lore to animate his literary products. It is quite possible that the exceptionally powerful impression made on him by the awesome peaks and canyons that lay along his course was the basic impulse behind that renewed poetical flow which shines forth in these pages and which is still flourishing with undiminished lustre. The force of that impression can be attested by all readers of the Greenwich (N.Y.) *Journal* who followed "Scriba's" series of graphic prose articles on the subject.

Late in 1915 Mr. Hoag received his final impulse toward continuous and systematic literary production through his advent to the miniature world of "amateur journalism"; a group of societies formed for the encouragement of the non-professional litterateur, and possessing an amateur press whose columns welcome all qualified comers. Availing himself of the various departments of criticism and encouragement, our bard began to turn out a finished product whose form fully sustained its matter, and which followed correctly those poetical traditions to which he was naturally inclined. The results may be seen in this volume; where the general classification, as shewn in the table of contents, exhibits the various directions taken by the author's Muse. Much of this work is of nocturnal origin, inspired by dreams or waking visions of the darkness, and set to paper as quickly as possible. Scarcely anything is studied or premeditated, since "Scriba" sings for the most purely artistic of reasons—because he cannot help it! Awe, reminiscence, beauty-worship, sorrow, speculation, wonder—any of the countless impulses may move him; and when once moved, he cannot but express himself with that simple and spontaneously selective poignancy which is the truest art. And so he is today, at the age of ninety-two; expressing out of a long life of taste, thought, beauty, honour, and virtue, those images so thoroughly yet delicately coloured by the career they reflect. He resides at "Vista Buena", his delightful village home in Greenwich, New York, where with his son and grandchildren he weaves his dreams, while Dionondawa's cataract pours ceaseless music on his ears.

The poetry of Mr. Hoag is distinguished by a Doric purity and simplicity which, together with the reflective tranquillity and occasional domestic touches, affiliate it conclusively with the earlier American school. It is fresh, Colonial, and free from self-conscious ornamentation. It has escaped not only the abyss of modernism, but the hothouse of Victorian preciosity and affectation as well; keeping the ancient verbal austerity as Bryant kept it, and holding also not a little of that eighteenth-century ease and swing which, as in Dr. Holmes' best work, is a genuine survival from our local tradition of Byles, Sewell, Freneau, Trumbull, Dwight, and Barlow,[2] rather than a pedantic revival of Queen Anne and Georgian piquancy after the manner of the late Austin Dobson. Flexibility, however, is a dominant feature; and leads the poet to adapt his measure to his mood, so that we are occasionally surprised by such variations from the general style as we see in verses like "The Celtic's Dream of His Erin Home". Subtler variations are those which we note between essentially stately pieces, such as the Nature odes and pensive reminiscences; and the playful pieces, such as the juveniles and the jovial reminiscences. When in the lighter vein, Mr. Hoag manages with unusual success to avoid the insipid, the puerile, and the banal; and achieves a kind of simplicity with correct diction and images drawn directly from experience. This image-drawing occasionally attains a felicity amounting to sheer genius, for "Scriba" seems to know by instinct just what sort of unhackneyed allusion will best call up in a few words the vivid pictures his theme demands.

Should a critic attempt to decide which of the several fields of Mr. Hoag's work best suits the author's talents, he would find himself involved in much delicate comparison. There are odes to Nature's primal forces which sometimes reach impressive depths, as where in speaking of the Grand Canyon of the Colorado he refers to black caverns where

"Vast nameless satyrs dance with noiseless feet."

Then, too, there are elegies and poems of pathos and patriotism where sheer natural feeling seems to animate the lines with a radiance more lasting than that of studied phrases. The juvenile pieces are ineffably appealing, while the legends and brighter Nature poems are full of a quaint and characteristic fascination. But in the end it seems certain that a conscientious analyst would award the palm to those reminiscent idyls in which the writer's own rural childhood is mirrored with such inspired fidelity and selective individuality. It is here that the descriptive and lyrical moods are most perfectly united, and here that the poet's gift of original observation is given freest play. In these studies of Old America we have the convincing touch of one who has lived in the scenes he describes; and who consequently avoids the objectivity, inaccuracy, and false stresses of the newer bards whose outlook is purely detached and antiquarian. He knows what to tell, because he writes from living memories and does not need to rely on stock phrases, images, or situations. Who else, in describing the "little red school-house", would refer to the master's tapping on the window to summon the scholars in from recess? Another poet would drag in the traditional bell—but "Scriba" knows his subject from actual experience. The spirit of childhood is very close to him, and he retains with a truly photographic accuracy his original reactions to the rural scene of the thirties; so that we may share the young enthusiasm with which he thrilled so many decades ago. Not a sentiment or perception is missing, and even the outworn, supposedly exploded values of the past take on a new reality as seen again through his unspoiled and ever-youthful eyes.

The present volume includes, besides one earlier piece, the entire output of Mr. Hoag's finished Muse; that is, that portion of his contemporary work which has passed the scrutiny of his more calmly appraising second judgment, including all permanent material written between the winter of 1915–16 and the spring of 1923. What place it may ultimately take in the pastoral minstrelsy of America is not for the writer to predict; since the whole aesthetic order is at present so convulsed with unrest, rebellion, and a virtual transvaluation of values. But we may at least agree that according to accepted standards, our poet has accomplished a marvellous work in capturing the spirit of the buoyant, hopeful past for the benefit of the doubting, pessimistic present. What would we not give for that earlier outlook upon man, the world, and the universe! The esteem in which "Scriba" is held by his contemporaries may plainly be seen from the bulky appendix of tributes, in which the present writer appears as a persistent and periodical offender. It is that writer's hope, both from personal regard and from a disinterested love of beauty in literature, that he may have the privilege of adding some day to these tributes a centennial ode which its venerable subject may read in the full vigour of a lengthened span.

EDITOR'S NOTE   FP: In *The Poetical Works of Jonathan E. Hoag* (New York: Privately printed, 1923), pp. iii–vii. Dated March 1923, but probably written a bit earlier (the volume itself appeared in late April or early May). Hoag (1831–1927) was a resident of the Catskill Mountains region who took to writing poetry quite late in life, appearing widely in amateur journals in the last decade of his life. HPL wrote birthday poems to him every year from 1918 to 1927, as well as an elegy, "Ave atque Vale" (1927; *AT* 382–83); most of these poems appeared not only in various amateur journals, but also in the *Troy Times* and the *Greenwich Journal*. Hoag's *Poetical Works*, edited by HPL (the poems were revised by HPL, James F. Morton, and Samuel Loveman), was funded by Hoag; it constitutes the first appearance of any work by HPL in hardcover. Two poems from the book, "Death" and "To the American Flag," were long attributed to HPL, but seem clearly to be by Hoag (although possibly revised by HPL). See my article, "Two Spurious Lovecraft Poems," *Crypt of Cthulhu* No. 20 (Eastertide 1984): 25–26.

Notes

1. HPL may have been thinking of his own similar encounter with a Mrs. Wood, a woman born in 1796 whom HPL met when she was 100 years old (*SL* 3.409).

2. HPL refers to the early American writers Mather Byles (1707–1788), Jonathan Mitchell Sewall (1748–1808), Philip Freneau (1752–1832), John Trumbull (1750–1831; see *LL* 192), Timothy Dwight (1752–1817), and Joel Barlow (1754–1812).

ARS GRATIA ARTIS

A mongst the lessons which The Conservative has learnt since his advent to the United, is the folly of judging an artist by his subject-matter and spirit. To maintain at all times the proper distinction betwixt art and the field of philosophy and ethics is an accomplishment to be acquired only by degrees, but one which stamps its possessor as having passed a definite milestone on the road to a truly civilised attitude. It is not the sluggish bourgeois mind which can endorse sincerely the dictum of Oscar Wilde, that "No artist is ever morbid. The artist can express everything."[1]

That many of our members have so far failed to reach this important milestone is unfortunately demonstrated by a multitude of stupid moralisings on the part of amateur critics; moralisings almost as stupid as those of The Conservative himself in other days. Sometimes they rise to heights of absurdity which almost redeem them as pieces of unconscious burlesque, as when a certain gentleman lectured Mr. Samuel Loveman on his sombre poetry.[2] At other times, when their object is less brilliant, they are themselves merely dull; as when a well-meaning reformer lectures The Conservative on some weird stories, which were declared to "pollute the pages on which they appear". But always they are discouraging in the mental immaturity they imply, and ominous in their revelation of the natural narrowness of mankind.

Until the progress of civilisation shall have become impossibly complete, we shall never fail to be bored by Boeotian condemnations of sincere art as "gloomy", "morbid", or "unhealthy", as the case may be. These epithets will continue to be hurled about with zeal and blindness as long as sleepy critics persist in judging art as something made to order on a false and conventional pattern for the uplift and amusement of the rabble, instead of something purely in the nature of portrayal and self-expression. Would that the proper teacher might inculcate in the minds of such critics some sentences of Wilde on the subject of "healthiness":

> "From the point of view of style, a healthy work of art is one whose style recognises the beauty of the material it employs, be that material one of words or of bronze, of colour or of ivory; and uses that beauty as a factor in producing the aesthetic effect. From the point of view of subject, a healthy work of art is one the choice of whose subject is conditioned by the temperament of the artist, and comes directly out of it. . . . An unhealthy work of art, on the other hand, is a work whose style is obvious, old-fashioned, and common; and whose subject is deliberately chosen not because the artist has any pleasure in it, but because he thinks that the public will pay him for it."[3]

EDITOR'S NOTE Unpublished (TMS, JHL). An essay probably written in spring or summer 1923 and designed for the *Conservative*, whose last issue had appeared in July 1919; but when HPL finally revived the *Conservative* in March and July 1923, he evidently decided not to include this item. The title is Latin for "Art for art's sake," reflecting the celebrated aesthetic movement begun in France in the mid-19th century and chiefly associated in England with the work of Walter Pater and Oscar Wilde. The long quotation from Wilde that concludes the essay was also cited in "Final Words" (September 1921; CE5), as part of HPL's involvement with the *Transatlantic Circulator*.

Notes

1. From Wilde's preface to *The Picture of Dorian Gray* (1891).
2. The reference is to Michael Oscar White; see the editor's note to "In the Editor's Study" (p. 72).
3. From Wilde's "The Soul of Man under Socialism" (*Fortnightly Review*, February 1891).

IN THE EDITOR'S STUDY

A desperate need of amateurdom today is an enlightened critical standard which shall save us from devotion to false, conventional, and superficial values, and blindness to all that is sincere, vital, penetrating, or genuinely ecstatic in art. The relative rarity of young blood has begun to give us a perilously Philistine bias, so that the path of the un-compromising artist in our midst is much thornier than it should be. These are times when a flash of subtle emotion of a colourful appeal to obscure and fantastic recesses of the imagination is likely to evoke a superior titter if the words sound in the least extravagant or unfamiliar to a mind bred on Dickens or the *Saturday Evening Post*. Good homely common sense, no doubt, but sadly disastrous to amateur literature.

It is time, The Conservative believes, definitely to challenge the sterile and exhausted Victorian ideal which blighted Anglo-Saxon culture for three quarters of a century and produced a milky "poetry" of shopworn sentimentalities and puffy platitudes; a dull-grey prose fiction of misplaced didacticism and insipid artificiality; an appallingly hideous system of formal manners, costume, and decoration; and worst of all, an artistically blasphemous architecture whose uninspired nondescriptness transcends tolerance, comprehension, and profanity alike.

These reflections are elicited by the urbane warfare of Philistine and Grecian so opportunely precipitated by Mr. Michael White's critique of Mr. Samuel Loveman's poetry. Mr. White, taking his stand with the hard-headed and condemning an artist who employs such strange materials as ecstasy or imagination, has naturally aroused the opposition of certain ardent fantaisistes like Mr. Frank Belknap Long, Jun., whose impressionistic reply appeared in these columns.[1] And now we find Mr. Long the recipient of some priceless comic-supplement sarcasm from the admirers of Mr. White, a typical Boston group to whom New England's Puritan heritage has denied that touch of ethereal madness which makes for the creation and appreciation of universal, fundamental art.

Just what do these mild hostilities signify? Should we after all denounce our Eminent Victorians merely because of their support of the critic who classifies Macaulay, Carlisle (sic), Emerson, and Shaw as "great poets", attributes unique limitations to the word *chorus*, and sits stolid in the beams of imaginative art? Is this protest of humorous, sensible clearness against symbolic, colourful intensity indeed a mark of Victorian obtuseness instead of a sane defence of tradition in the face of chaotic innovation? Certainly the position of Mr. White's circle is flawless if we are to accept art as an affair of the external intellect and commonplace, unanalysed emotions alone. The Conservative dissents only because he believes with most of the contemporary world that the actual foundations of art differ widely from those which the prim nineteenth century took for granted.

What is art but a matter of impressions, of pictures, emotions, and symmetrical sensations? It must have poignancy and beauty, but nothing else counts. It may or may not have coherence. If concerned with large externals or simple fancies, or produced in a simple age, it is likely to be of a clear and continuous pattern; but if concerned with individual reactions to life in a complex and analytical age, as most modern art is, it tends to break up into detached transcripts of hidden sensation and offer a loosely joined fabric which demands from the spectator a discriminating duplication of the artist's mood. The Philistine clamour for a literature of plain statement and superficial theme loses force when we assign to literature—especially poetry—its proper place in aesthetics, and compare it to such modes of expression as music and architecture, which do not speak in the language of primers.

The Conservative is no convert to Dadaism. Nothing, on the contrary, seems more certain to him than that the bulk of radical prose and verse represents merely the extravagant extreme of a tendency whose truly artistic application is vastly more limited. Traces of this tendency, whereby pictorial methods are used, and words and images employed without conventional connexions to excite sensations, may be found throughout literature; especially in Keats, William Blake, and the French symbolists. This broader conception of art does not outrage any external tradition, but honours all creations of the past or present which can shew genuine ecstatic fire and a glamour not tawdrily founded on utterly commonplace emotions.

Thus the shrill laughter of the thin-blooded literalist at the ecstatic artist is founded mainly on one-sidedness and conventionality of background; the scoffer being nearly always a follower of an obsolete tradition, steeped in the orthodox English literature of the middle nineteenth century rather than immersed in the universal stream which knows neither time nor country. Such a sage, like the proverbial *homo unius libri,*[2] may prove formidable and witty antagonist; but his parochial limitations obviously unfit him for anything like an authoritative pronouncement on laws touching the entire human spirit. *"Les esprits mediocres,"* says La Rochefoucauld, *"condamnent d'ordinare tout ce qui passe leur portée."*[3] Before intelligently approaching a work of art a critic must absorb at least the rudiments of the background from which it was developed—which takes us back to the problem of dealing with the Victorian scolding and giggling which bid fair to discourage sincere aesthetic endeavour in amateur journalism.

The Conservative would unassumingly urge a slight course of literary research upon those critics who are hurling the English nineteenth century in our faces with so much gusto, finality, and drollery. Without wishing to emulate their own fetching pageantry of mighty names across the learned page, he would bid them consider such titans as Walter Pater, Lafcadio Hearn, Arthur Symons, Arthur Machen, Wilde, Gautier, Flaubert, Baudelaire, Verlaine, Rimbaud, Mallarmé, Laforgue, D'Annunzio, or Croce—titans about whom much may be learnt even through reviews. Once really aware of the existence of this wider field, and of the extent to which it has influenced contemporary ideas of art, our conscientious Philistines could not but enlarge their horizons of tolerance. How much they might actually understand or sympathise, is a temperamental matter alien to the problem.

EDITOR'S NOTE FP: *Conservative* No. 13 (July 1923): 21–24 (unsigned); rpt. *National Amateur* 46, No. 2 (November 1923): 13. An editorial continuing a running debate in which HPL, Frank Belknap Long, and Alfred Galpin severely criticised the amateur critic Michael Oscar White for censuring the poetry of Samuel Loveman in the article "The Poets of Amateur Journalism: III. Samuel Loveman," *Oracle* 3, No. 4 (December 1922): 12–17. See further HPL's "Bureau of Critics," March 1923 (CE1). The essay (along with "[Random Notes]" below) won the Essay Laureateship of the NAPA for 1922–23 (hence its reprinting in the *National Amateur*).

Notes

1. Frank Belknap Long, "An American Humorist," *Conservative* No. 12 (March 1923): 2–5.
2. "The man of a single book."
3. "Mediocre souls usually condemn everything that passes beyond their scope." François de Marsillac, duc de La Rochefoucauld (1613–1680), *Maxims* (1665f.), No. 375.

[RANDOM NOTES]

Among the interesting problems raised by the current Philistine-Grecian controversy in amateurdom is one which both concerns and contains humour—the problem of when and when not to laugh in dissecting an unusual literary production seriously offered by an author whose general achievements set him definitely above the throng of the inept and the extravagant. To many, and especially to the older critics, the answer would appear farcically simple; and would involve an amused insistence on the right of a Cheshire cat to exercise his hereditary prerogative on all occasions, thus establishing the inference that possible ludicrousness in writing, if *unintentional*, is always *unconscious*, and therefore a fatal artistic defect.

This ordinary attitude is at first sight of such weight that the merest questioner exposes himself to a share of its possessors' cachinnations. Examples of really hilarious gravity are so prevalent that their recollection overshadows all the nuances of the ultimate problem. But a dispassionate view, free from the glare of the obvious, reveals one important modifying consideration in the fact that comicality always depends wholly on the system of thought and values held by the perceiver; that, in short, ridiculousness is *relative*, and conditioned by the truth, inflexibility, or paramountcy of certain common ideas which are absolute to the multitude yet merely virtual to the closer inquirer. Intelligence and education, as they open new fields of risibility, close old ones; so that the laughing-stock of one stage of culture is often the gospel of the next, and vice versa.

Remembering these things as we turn to literary criticism, we perceive the difficulty of laying down permanent laws of laughter in an age when all standards are plastic. Much of the serious and accepted literature of the past, especially where human motives and cosmic purposes are involved, is broadly comical to the mind informed in contemporary science and philosophy; and much in modern writing, where the conceptions touch on the subjective and imaginary instead of the real world, is screamingly funny to the mind accustomed to nothing but literal reality and inherited beliefs.

Thus it would seem wise to look before you laugh. A subtle writer's imagery often takes a turn which has its conceivably comic side, yet which is not only admirable but sometimes powerfully original when viewed as part of a fabric as exotic, individual, subjective, and essentially decorative as the pictured phantasmata of Sime or Beardsley.[1] Such an artist is not unconscious of the humorous interpretation which prosaic literalism may give his occasional bizarrerie—often he laughs himself—but he retains his quaintly carven Buddhas and Sivas just as zealously, knowing that they fit his far, strange realm of alien moonlight and incense-perfumed dream, however odd or ludicrous they may appear in the workaday sunshine of Main Street.

Far be it from The Conservative to decry humour in amateur journalism. High Pegāna knows how badly we need the genuine article! But are there not times when its judicious discipline augments our power of creation and appreciation in certain fields? Who will say that Lord Dunsany's delicate Arabesque touch has not suffered as his wit has become less and less detached from it, or that Arthur Machen is not the stronger for the child-like naiveté of his outlook on the dream-world? And is it not possible that some of the Philistine hyperticklishness at unaccustomed whimsies springs from a lack of that deeper and more pervasive humour which sees in all human life and effort an ironic comedy?[2] Verily, laughter is an art for the discriminating!

EDITOR'S NOTE FP: *Conservative* No. 13 (July 1923): 27–28 (unsigned); rpt. *National Amateur* 46, No. 2 (November 1923): 13–14. A further rumination on the Michael Oscar White controversy.

Notes

1. Sidney Sime (1867–1941), British artist best known for illustrating the work of Lord Dunsany; Aubrey Beardsley (1872–1898), celebrated British artist and illustrator. HPL owned many editions of Dunsany with the Sime illustrations, as well as *The Art of Aubrey Beardsley* (1918; LL 71).
2. Cf. "The Defence Remains Open!" (1921; (CE5): "The world is indeed comic, but the joke is on mankind."

[REVIEW OF *EBONY AND CRYSTAL* BY CLARK ASHTON SMITH]

EBONY AND CRYSTAL by CLARK ASHTON SMITH. (4to 152 pp. The Auburn Journal, Auburn, Calif., 1923.)

Between the urbane sterilities of our bearded Brahmins and the psycho-analytical clinics of our younger intellectuals, American poetry fares badly indeed; a condition expressed with melancholy force by George Sterling[1] in his introduction to the third book of verse from Clark Ashton Smith. More truly sensitive to the wilder dreams of men, and more sublimely cosmic in his imaginative sweep of fancy's chartless chaos than any native versifier since Poe, Mr. Smith has remained in relative obscurity outside his Californian domain because of a public trained to distrust beauty and the adventure of the spirit.

"Ebony and Crystal" is an artist's intrepid repudiation of the world of trolleys and cash-registers, Freudian complexes and Binet-Simon tests, for realms of exalted and iridescent strangeness beyond space and time yet real as any reality because dreams have made them so. Mr. Smith has escaped the fetish of life and the world, and glimpsed the perverse, titanic beauty of death and the universe; taking infinity as his canvas and recording in awe the vagaries of suns and planets, gods and daemons, and blind amorphous horrors that haunt gardens of polychrome fungi more remote than Algol and Achernar. It is a cosmos of vivid flame and glacial abysses that he celebrates, and the colourful luxuriance with which he peoples it could be born from nothing less than sheer genius.

The summation of Mr. Smith's exotic vision is perhaps attained in the long phantasmal procession of blank verse pentameters entitled "The Hashish-Eater; or, The Apocalypse of Evil". In this frenzied plunge through nameless gulfs of interstellar terror the Californian presents a narcotic pageant of poisonous vermilion and paralysing shadows whose content is equalled only by its verbal medium; a medium involving one of the most opulent and fastidiously choice vocabularies ever commanded by a writer of English.

Mr. Smith, born in 1893, was the author of an amazing volume at nineteen.[2] He has kept faithful to the splendour that knows no shackles, and whether in his cosmic orgies or his simpler love-poems has always fulfilled the Cabellian aspiration—"to write perfectly of beautiful happenings".[3]

EDITOR'S NOTE FP: *L'Alouette* 1, No. 1 (January 1924): 20–21 (signed "H. P. L."). HPL had come in touch with the California poet and fantaisiste Clark Ashton Smith (1893–1961) in August 1922, initiating a correspondence that would cease only with HPL's death. This review of Smith's third poetry volume, *Ebony and Crystal: Poems in Verse and Prose* (Auburn, CA: Auburn Journal, 1922; erroneously dated to 1923 by HPL) is the only instance in which HPL wrote on Smith aside from a paragraph in "Supernatural Horror in Literature." Smith had given HPL a copy of the book (see *SL* 1.213).

Notes

1. Sterling (1869–1926), a leading Californian poet of the period, had been Smith's mentor since 1911. He also wrote a preface to Smith's second volume, *Odes and Sonnets* (1918).

2. *The Star-Treader and Other Poems* (San Francisco: A. M. Robertson, 1912).

3. James Branch Cabell (1879–1958), American novelist and essayist. The quotation The quotation—"at what cost now, in this fleet hour of my vigor, may one write perfectly of beautiful happenings?"—derives from the "Auctorial Induction" of Cabell's *The Certain Hour* (New York: Robert M. McBride, 1916), p. 17.

THE PROFESSIONAL INCUBUS

It has often been remarked that fiction is the weakest point in amateur literature, and I do not think the belief is a mistaken one. None can deny that we have nothing in the field of the story which may be compared with the poetry of Samuel Loveman, the essays of James F. Morton, Jr., the critical analyses of Edward H. Cole, or the phantasies of Frank Belknap Long, Jr. True, Mrs. Edith Miniter produces work of the highest quality—but unfortunately only the most infinitesimal fraction of this appears in the amateur press. Our loss is the outside world's gain.

The generally assigned cause for our fictional debility is lack of space, and this factor is certainly a potent one. For the adequate development of a story idea, ample room is an absolute essential; and this we are unable to provide for under present financial conditions. But of late I have come to believe that there is another cause; a cause extending very deeply into the composition of the American scene, and affecting us because of our slowness in making a certain distinction. This cause is the hopeless inferiority and inartistry of the entire standard of American bourgeois fiction, and the neglected distinction is that between successful professional fiction and honestly artistic attempts at self-expression in the narrative.

If the object of amateur journalism were to train likely young plodders in the skilled manual labour of professional fiction carpentry, no one might justly protest at the existing condition. But the idea has been held by some that amateurdom is synonymous with aesthetic sincerity, and with the loving craftmanship for its own sake which is art. If this is so, we are on the wrong track; for there is nothing of art or true merit in the "salable short story" which too often forms the model of our efforts. I do not think any meritorious short story could be sold to an average professional magazine of the popular class except by accident. He who strives to produce salable fiction is lost as an artist, for the conditions of American life have made art impossible in the popular professional field.

Editors and publishers are not to blame. They cater to their public, and would suffer shipwreck if they did not. And even when one transfers the blame to this larger unit, one cannot justly be very savage in his blaming; for analysis shews that most of the trouble is absolutely inevitable—as incapable of human remedy as the fate of any protagonist in the Greek drama. Here in America we have a very conventional and half-educated public—a public trained under one phase or another of the Puritan tradition, and also dulled to aesthetic sensitiveness because of the monotonous and omnipresent overstressing of the ethical element. We have millions who lack intellectual independence, courage, and flexibility to get an artistic thrill out of an original and realistic situation, or to enter sympathetically into a story unless it ignores the colour and vividness of actual human emotions and conventionally presents a simple plot based on artificial, ethically sugar-coated values and leading to a flat denouement which vindicates every current platitude and leaves no mystery unexplained by the shallow comprehension of the most mediocre reader.

That is why our professional fiction is unworthy of the emulation of any literary artist. Editors, however, cannot logically be blamed. If any magazine sought and used artistically original types of fiction, it would lose its readers almost to a man. Half the people wouldn't understand what the tales were about, and the other half would find the characters unsympathetic—because these characters would think and act like real persons instead of like the dummies which the American middle classes have been taught and persuaded to consider and accept as human beings. Such is the inevitable condition regarding the enormous bulk of fiction which sets the national standard and determines the type of technical training given all fictional students even in our best universities.

But even this is not all. Added to this, as if by the perversity of a malign fate, is the demand of an overspeeding public for excessive quantity production. Simply put, the American people demand more stories per year than the really artistic authors of America could possibly write. A real artist never works fast except by mood, and never turns out large quantities except by rare chance. He cannot contract to deliver so many words in such and such a time, but must work naturally, gradually, sometimes very slowly, and always as his psychological state determines; utilising favourable states of mind and refraining from putting down the stuff his brain turns out when it is tired or undisciplined to such effort. Now this, of course, will not do when there are hundreds of magazines to fill at regular intervals. So many pages per month or week must be filled; and if the artistic writers lag behind, the publishers must find the next-best thing—persons of mere talent, who can learn certain mechanical rules and technical twists, and put forth stuff of external smoothness, whose sole merit is in conforming to patterns and rehashing the situations and reactions which have been found interesting to the people by previous experience. In many cases these writers achieve popularity— because the public recognises the elements that pleased it before, and is satisfied to receive them again in dexterously transposed form. Actually, the typical reader has very little true taste, and judges by absurd freaks, sentimentalities, and analogies. So it has come to be an accepted tradition that American fiction is not an art but a trade—a thing to be learnt by rule by almost anybody, and demanding above all else a complete submergence of one's own personality and thought in the general stream of conventional patterns which correspond to the bleakly uniform view of life forced on us by mediocre leadership. Success therefore comes not to the man of genius, but to the clever fellow who knows how to catch the public point of view and play up to it. Glittering tinsel reputations are built up, and dumb driven [. . .] hundreds of otherwise honest and respectable plumbers take correspondence courses to crush their individuality and try to be like these scintillant "great ones" whose achievements are really no more than mere charlatanry.

Such is our fictional situation—indiscriminate hordes of writers, mostly without genius, striving by erroneous methods toward a goal which is erroneous to start with! One sees the thing at its zenith in periodicals like *The Saturday Evening Post*, where men of more or less real talent are weighed down with the freely flung gold which forms the price of their originality and artistic conscience. A fearful incubus—which only a few adroit or daring souls ever shake off. But here in amateurdom there is no gold to weigh us down or buy our conscience. Here, if anywhere, we ought to be able to write for the love of writing and the thrill of aesthetic conquest. Shall we not at least strive to do this, in order that our institution may be a thing of real dignity and value instead of a rather ridiculous caricature of the tawdry professional sphere?

EDITOR'S NOTE FP: *National Amateur* 46, No. 4 (March 1924): 35–36. A pungent screed attacking the false literary standards that had emerged in the United States and had, in HPL's judgment, perverted the production of short fiction from an art to a mechanical trade. HPL's comments are fully in consonance with his resolutely amateur stance—a stance he maintained for the whole of his career, even after his own work began appearing professionally in *Weird Tales* in the fall of 1923. The *National Amateur* appearance is full of textual errors and, in the absence of a surviving manuscript, one passage in the penultimate paragraph is so corrupt as to be unintelligible.

THE OMNIPRESENT PHILISTINE

Amateurdom's progress toward a civilised condition is halting and devious. No sooner do we advance a step, than some obstacle in the shape of glorified mediocrity or aesthetic and philosophical reaction appears to block the path; so that half our energy is spent in brushing away false ideas rather than increasing our store of genuine ideas. It is so in most departments of life, hence need call for no especial resentment among us—but it is none the less provoking.

The past official year has witnessed a depressing revival of obsolete notions and parading of outworn theories of art, as conspicuously exemplified by the anti-Loveman criticisms of last December.[1] We were then informed in the best mid-Victorian manner that classical themes are obsolete, that Poe is reprehensively "morbid", that Swinburnian paganism is too "blasphemous" for proper use in a decorous Christian country, that verse must not be above the interests and understanding of the "folksy" throng, that poets must protest against the evils of the age—and much more of the same. This precipitated a controversy yet in its prime, and now there dawns a new effulgence of pale-pink primness and propriety in the shape of *Pauke's Quill*, edited and published by the diverse avatars, aboriginal and otherwise, of that spirited adolescent Paul Livingston Keil, Esq.

Far be it from the undersigned to discourage young Mr. Keil. Indeed, it is our sincere opinion that his vigorous personality will ultimately be of immense benefit in revivifying Amateur Journalism. But certain qualities of his present offering move us to protest in the name of rational thought and artistic progress against a renewed wave of unthinking reaction and emotional Puritanism which cannot but hurt the advance of amateur culture.

Mr. Keil's cry for literary censorship is something particularly dangerous because it excites our sympathy before we fully realise all its implications. Nor many of us, even in this age, have any marked leaning toward public pornography; so that we would generally welcome any agency calculated to banish offences against good taste. But when we come to reflect on the problem of enforcement, and perceive how absurdly any censorship places us in the hands of dogmatic and arbitrary officials with Puritan illusions and no true knowledge of life or literary values, we have to acknowledge that absolute liberty is the lesser evil. The literature of today, with its conscientious striving toward sincerity, must necessarily contain large amounts of matter repugnant to those who hold the hypocritical nineteenth-century view of the world. It need not be vulgarly presented, but it cannot be excluded if art is to express life. That censors actually do seek to remove this legitimate and essential matter, and that they would if given greater power do even greater harm, is plainly shewn by the futile action against "Jurgen", and the present ban on "Ulysses", both significant contributions to contemporary art.[2] And, ironically enough, this same censorship blandly tolerates, through legal technicalities, infinite sewers full of frankly and frivolously nasty drivel without the least pretence of aesthetic or intellectual significance.

But Mr. Keil's major contribution to obscurantism is to be found under the heading "Opinion vs. Fact", where he assiduously strives to prove that the merit of an author's work depends absolutely on the philosophical views he may happen to hold. According to our editor-sage, beauty is not beauty if created by a gentleman who does not belong to our church or bet on our favourite racehorse. No matter how masterful the limning of a picture, it must not hang on our wall unless the painter is endorsed by the Ku Klux Klan, the Y.M.C.A., and the Epworth League.[3] This is quite entertaining, even if not much more luminous than Mr. Keil's masterpiece of meaningless metaphor—the quart of black paint as a tavern night scene. Can it be that people ever believed this sort of thing? It may be so, for anything was possible in Victorian times. There was a tenebrous period, if our grandsires speak truth, when Shelley was banished from the best parlour bookcase because his social and religious principles "weren't quite correct".[4]

But this is 1923—an adult age—and we can ill afford to waste time on chimaeras which perished with Rogers groups and haircloth.[5] Accordingly it is not encouraging to see these periodic recrudescences. Mr. Keil's final air-rifle shot at philosophy is an off-hand distinction between "fact" and "opinion" which makes us wonder what supernal wisdom has decided for him a question which yet baffles the eminent of the earth. We would certainly like to discover that solid and irrefutable body of fact, opinions contrary to which are absolutely and irredeemably worthless. Somehow, though, we fear that a voyage of discovery would only bring us once more against the age-old question-mark, and explain away Mr. Keil's boyish certitudes in a manner already made common property by Herr Nietzsche's "Genealogy of Morals".

Pauke's Quill is a welcome arrival—let us not undervalue it—but it is a pity that its effervescent influence should be lent to the side of obstruction and reaction. It will doubtless mature as Mr. Keil himself matures, and some day we hope to praise it for its virile support of that sounder civilisation which it now opposes with such sprightly ardour.

EDITOR'S NOTE FP: *Oracle* 4, No. 3 (May 1924): 14–17. A somewhat harsh censure of an amateur paper by Paul Livingston Keil, a young amateur. The essay is significant for charting the rapid development of HPL's thought from his early classicist days, his praise of several avant-garde works of contemporary literature, and for his vigorous objections to literary censorship. Keil had met HPL during the latter's New York visit of April 1922 and had taken the celebrated photograph of HPL, James F. Morton, and Frank Belknap Long standing in front of the Poe cottage in Fordham. He later wrote a memoir, "I Met Lovecraft," *Phoenix* 3, No. 6 (July 1944): 149.

Notes

1. See "In the Editor's Study" above.

2. James Branch Cabell's novel *Jurgen* (1919) had been the subject of legal action on the part of the New York Society for the Suppression of Vice, which sought to ban the book for obscenity. A trial in 1922 resulted in an acquittal, and the book was allowed to be distributed. James Joyce's *Ulysses* (1922) was banned in the United States until 1933. HPL later admitted that he never read *Ulysses* (SL 4.14); it is not clear whether HPL ever read *Jurgen*.

3. The Epworth League was founded in 1889 by the Methodist Episcopal Church for the purpose of developing Christian fellowship and promoting social life under church influence.

4. Shelley became notorious for his atheism, expressed in such pamphlets as *The Necessity of Atheism* (1811) and *A Refutation of Deism* (1814).

5. HPL refers to John Rogers (1829–1904), an American sculptor whose mass-produced figures (ranging from Civil War pieces to interpretations of literary works) were popular in the 19th century, and to haircloth, an article of clothing made of hair.

THE WORK OF FRANK BELKNAP LONG, JR.

It is always a bit dangerous to hail an amateur spirit which seems to overtop the general level. That general level is so fastidiously jealous of its dignity, and so terribly quick to pounce on enthusiasts with its nasal accusations of ulterior motives and interested partiality! Wintry-blooded, elephant-footed, the blind suspiciousness of literary senescence and stagnation will ever be with us to cry "puffing", quote old saws, and snicker out of court the subtleties it cannot understand. But because we have a civilised element equally permanent, and even more deserving of attention, it will not do to let values perish altogether. That is why it is fitting at this juncture to call attention to a young writer who has brought us the first new touch of really creative vision we have had in years.

Frank Belknap Long, Jr., poet, critic, and weaver of fantastiques, is the writer in question. He stands above the crowd not because of any ultimate perfection of style or uniqueness of theme, for he is still youthful, changeful, and influenced by external models of varying laudability; but because of a sheer daemonic ecstasy of creation and a passionate sensitiveness to the most delicate and imperceptible nuances of colour and beauty, which not more than one other amateur of today can be said to equal or surpass.

Mr. Long could not have risen to prominence at a more opportune time. With the fires of earlier literary revivals burning low, amateurdom is at present in the grip of a curiously stubborn devotion to outworn ideas and criteria. Generally speaking, we have lacked the vital modern element altogether; for even our ostensible rebels are definitely middle-aged and emotionally grounded in the past which they intellectually reject. It is not hard to define and explode this outworn tradition, for its characteristics are painfully clear. The tradition is one of tameness, imitativeness, and illusion—of exaggerated absorption in the meaningless routine of placid common life, unwarranted belief in vague relations between aesthetic pleasure and intellectual truth, and provincially disproportionate worship of clever little writers like the Longfellow-Holmes clique, who merely conform agreeably to certain stilted backgrounds, affectations, and urbanities, without touching a single authentic emotion or possessing the least shade of truly original perception and insight.

Literary revolutions are not new. Elderly people who smirk complacently and predict the rapid subsidence of modernism forget utterly the Renaissance and even the romantic revival of the early nineteenth century. As in those times, the world has received a colossal influx of new ideas well calculated to remould all our impressions and recast all our utterances. We see the hollowness of things we believed before, and above all the disconnectedness of things we once thought indissolubly joined. It is the birth of a new aesthetic, grounded on the old but going beyond it, and demanding poignant, beautiful, and genuine sensation as the essence of artistic endeavour. Some of the old authors, of course, meet this demand; for the voice of unvarnished Nature never varies. But many fail to do so, because they wrote less from Nature than from false conceptions and interpretations of it, or merely copied those who went before. There is no literary value in a bleak transcript of others' feelings, convictions, and points of view. Paper is too expensive to waste on second-hand thoughts and images, however ambitiously served up. What we want are white-hot projections of individual personality, not cold grey reflections of the Babbitt herd-psychology.[1] Such projections Frank B. Long, almost alone among our newer amateur writers, succeeds in giving us.

The genius of Mr. Long is a spontaneous and self-expressive one. Educated in conventional American schools, and in New York and Columbia Universities, he has been thoroughly dosed with the traditional literature of the fathers; revolting only because he is too acute and aesthetically responsive to be satisfied with the obvious and platitudinous. Unaided he sensed the insincerity of the "museum hush" and the customary genuflection before dead and unmoving gods, and almost unguided he found his own voice among the light and colour and exotic beauty of the Italian Renaissance, the exquisite sensory adventuring of the French symbolists, and the delicate and poly-chrome dream-worlds that his ardent fancy bore out of old legends, childhood moon-glimpses, and faintly reflected memories from the far Mediterranean littoral where the water is deep blue and fragrant winds weave through broken marble colonnades on green seaward hills.

This may sound immature. Perhaps it would be if it were not to be considered as more than a starting-point. But a starting-point is precisely what it is, and its value lies in the perfect repudiation of the commonplace, and the adoption of free pagan beauty as a master, which it involves. For Mr. Long has passed the momentous barrier and learned the momentous lesson—that beauty is pleasure only, and to be taken joyously wherever found, irrespective of all antecedents and sequences. When he expresses himself it is purely to promote his personal aesthetic exaltation by means of beautiful, fantastic, or terrible arabesques, each independent, remote from prosaic life and asso-ciations, and conceived in a spirit essentially decorative; to satisfy with strange and emphatic imaginative symmetries a neural impulse both natural and insistent. And be-cause that impulse is unmixed with love of fame, regard for convention, interest in the public, or any other vulgar ambition, but fulfilled in language of hauntingly original vitality and trippingly musical liquidity, Mr. Long is an artist.

II.

The growth of Mr. Long's taste is keenly interesting to study. Appearing in ama-teurdom early in 1920 with a frankly boyish and elementary story, "Dr. Whitlock's Price",[2] his exceptional gifts were discerned by not more than one critic in all the asso-ciations. That critic, however, saw the single essential thing—that the young author's pictures were all authentic products of an actual visual imagination, and in no case blindly adapted from the lumber-room of previous juvenile reading. About this time Mr. Long wrote fiction voluminously, and with such meteorically rising power that his next published tale, "The Eye Above the Mantel",[3] quite startled those who had judged him by its predecessor. It was in this tale that his intense originality, dramatic sense, and power of fantastic imagery first appeared to a marked degree. In November, 1921, came "In the Tomb of Semenses",[4] an Egyptian phantasy filled with musical and subtly rhythmical phrases, and opiate visions of "multi-coloured lights and the clang-ing-to of brazen portcullises", which proclaimed the genuine poet beneath a dress of prose. Subsequently Mr. Long, though not abandoning the field, wrote less fiction; as if realising that for the nonce his forte lay in the presentation of vivid, isolated, and luxu-rious pictures—single languorous impressions devoid of common thoughts and feelings, spiced with the riches of aloof introspection, and iridescent with extreme bizarrerie. For him was the heritage of Baudelaire.

Mr. Long as a prose-poet has evolved some unforgettable vignettes of grotesque loveliness, alienage, and horror, and has attained heights which few amateurs share. Light, colour, sensation—all these essentials of pure art blend magically in such phan-tasms as "The Migration of Birds", "Flowers of Iniquity", "At the Home of Poe", "Un-happiness", or "Felis".[5] "Felis" marked a new growth of Mr. Long's power, and although he has himself come to regard it as immature, its force and felicity are actually tremen-dous. There are one or two openings for illiterate snickers when it is read with uncom-prehending verbal analysis, but what real critic can miss the sinister spell of the conclusion? . . . .

"Some day I shall drown in a sea of cats. I shall go down, smothered by their embraces, feeling their warm breath upon my face, gazing into their large eyes, hearing in my ears their soft purring. I shall sink lazily down through oceans of fur, between myriads of claws, clutching innumerable tails, and I shall surrender my wretched soul to the selfish and insatiable god of felines."

With this realisation of the artistic value of dissociated pictures and sensations, it is hardly singular that Mr. Long should turn to formal and rather Keatsian poetry. This he has done and is doing more and more; winning at least one prize and exciting considerable notice outside amateurdom, and being represented in our circle by such exquisite sonnets and lyrics as "The Inland Sea", "The Rebel", "Stallions of the Moon", and that inspired bit of elegiac pentameter called "Exotic Quest", which contains the vivid line, "Where golden griffins bathe in midnight meres".[6] If this latter isolated specimen would seem to suggest preciocity, a glimpse at the others quickly dispels that notion; for almost all the recent pieces bear evidences of Mr. Long's entrance into the mood of ironic modernism with its contempt for the grandiose and its sly juxtaposition of the mean and the fine, the commonplace and the exalted. Rhymed efforts in this vein have not been published in amateurdom, but we may grasp the mood equally well from the prose-poem "Ingenue",[7] with its world-weary travesty on pedantry, loftiness, bombast, reverence, chivalry, connected ideas, and the trappings of tradition in general. Just what this ultra-modern saturninity will do to Mr. Long's naive creative energy we cannot say. The tendency in excess would be adverse, but it is probable that the artist's sheer emotional intensity will limit it in the end. For the moment it is perhaps useful in checking what might otherwise be an overdeveloped ingenuousness or juvenile exuberance and extravagance.

It remains to consider Mr. Long as a critic, in which capacity he follows—as might be expected—the purely personal, subjective, and impressionistic method of his favourite John Cowper Powys. He not to be overawed by the "scholastic-veneration-cult", nor is he ever afraid of enthusiasm. With his wide background and more than acute sensibilities he is among the very small group of amateurs really qualified to appraise fantastic and imaginative literature—perceiving points which the average calloused vision overlooks—and we may only hope that he will be given wide opportunities to aid in amateurdom's artistic revival. His few critical weaknesses are such as appear in dealing with cold-blooded analysis and the literature of philosophic intellection as distinguished from art. "An Amateur Humorist" is the title of Mr. Long's best-known critique in our circle.[8] He won Honourable Mention in the N.A.P.A. Essay Laureate contest in 1923.

As a whole, Mr. Long has in him something of the restless, questing, aristocratic spirit of his beloved Italian Renaissance. His visual imagination is prodigious, and his taste for painting and sculpture exceptional. Only in aural imagination and musical appreciation does he feel limitations. He is a young faun strayed out of Arcady, innocent and vibrant, and eager to be himself sincerely in a world of mediocrity, repression, blindness, and stupidity. This is the assertive, unique personality which makes him a well-defined individual instead of a colourless rubber-stamp; which makes him a fearless pagan and a genuine artist. He is not yet mature—fine words and attitudes yet charm him a trifle more than they should, while his youthful ardour still leads him occasionally close to the borders of aesthetic dogmatism and unconscious humour—but he is rapidly maturing. With a finely strung organisation, limitless emotional force, and a mind wholly free from tawdry, sentimentalised tastes and hampering false perspectives, Mr. Long has a future to which only a rash prophet would set limits. He is today the second-greatest creative artist remaining in amateur journalism.

EDITOR'S NOTE FP: *United Amateur* 23, No. 1 (May 1924): 1–4 (unsigned). A paean to HPL's friend and colleague Frank Belknap Long (1901–1994), with whom he had come into contact in early 1920. The essay was probably unsigned because HPL's friendship with Long, well known in the amateur world, might have engendered accusations of partiality or log-rolling, as HPL himself suggests in the opening paragraph.

Notes

1. HPL alludes to Sinclair Lewis's *Babbitt* (1922), a devastating satire on American middle-class psychology. It is not clear, however, that HPL actually read the book.

2. *United Amateur* 19, No. 4 (March 1920): 70–73.

3. *United Amateur* 20, No. 4 (March 1921): 53–56.

4. *United Amateur* 21, No. 2 (November 1921): 13–17.

5. "The Migration of Birds" (a prose poem) appeared in the *United Amateur* 21, No. 4 (March 1922): 41–42. "Flowers of Iniquity" (a poem) appeared in *Home Brew* 1, No. 6 (July 1922): 23–24. "At the Home of Poe: A Poem in Prose" appeared in the *United Amateur* 21, No. 5 (May 1922): 53–54. "Unhappiness" (a poem) appeared in the *Wolverine* (December 1922). "Felis: A Prose Poem" appeared in the *Conservative* No. 13 (July 1923): 3–4. All these items, except "Unhappiness," are included in *The Darkling Tide*, ed. Perry M. Grayson (West Hills, CA: Tsathoggua Press, 1995).

6. The first three poems are included in Long's *A Man from Genoa and Other Poems* (1926); "Exotic Quest" appeared in *The Goblin Tower* (1935); all four are included in *In Mayan Splendor* (1977). "The Inland Sea" appeared in the *United Amateur* 23, No. 1 (May 1924): 9 (also *Weird Tales*, August 1925); "The Rebel" appeared in the *United Amateur* 23, No. 1 (May 1924): 9; "Stallions of the Moon" appeared in the *United Amateur* 23, No. 1 (May 1924): 9 (also *Weird Tales*, August 1925); "Exotic Quest" appeared in the *National Amateur* 45, No. 5 (May 1923): 1.

7. *National Amateur* 45, No. 5 (May 1923): 7; in *The Darkling Tide*.

8. See n. 1 to "In the Editor's Study."

SUPERNATURAL HORROR IN LITERATURE

I. Introduction

The oldest and strongest emotion of mankind is fear, and the oldest and strongest kind of fear is fear of the unknown. These facts few psychologists will dispute, and their admitted truth must establish for all time the genuineness and dignity of the weirdly horrible tale as a literary form. Against it are discharged all the shafts of a materialistic sophistication which clings to frequently felt emotions and external events, and of a naively insipid idealism which deprecates the aesthetic motive and calls for a didactic literature to uplift the reader toward a suitable degree of smirking optimism. But in spite of all this opposition the weird tale has survived, developed, and attained remarkable heights of perfection; founded as it is on a profound and elementary principle whose appeal, if not always universal, must necessarily be poignant and permanent to minds of the requisite sensitiveness.

The appeal of the spectrally macabre is generally narrow because it demands from the reader a certain degree of imagination and a capacity for detachment from every-day life. Relatively few are free enough from the spell of the daily routine to respond to rappings from outside, and tales of ordinary feelings and events, or of common sentimental distortions of such feelings and events, will always take first place in the taste of the majority; rightly, perhaps, since of course these ordinary matters make up the greater part of human experience. But the sensitive are always with us, and sometimes a curious streak of fancy invades an obscure corner of the very hardest head; so that no amount of rationalisation, reform, or Freudian analysis can quite annul the thrill of the chimney-corner whisper or the lonely wood. There is here involved a psychological pattern or tradition as real and as deeply grounded in mental experience as any other pattern or tradition of mankind; coeval with the religious feeling and closely related to many aspects of it, and too much a part of our inmost biological heritage to lose keen potency over a very important, though not numerically great, minority of our species.

Man's first instincts and emotions formed his response to the environment in which he found himself.[1] Definite feelings based on pleasure and pain grew up around the phenomena whose causes and effects he understood, whilst around those which he did not understand—and the universe teemed with them in the early days—were naturally woven such personifications, marvellous interpretations, and sensations of awe and fear as would be hit upon by a race having few and simple ideas and limited experience. The unknown, being likewise the unpredictable, became for our primitive forefathers a terrible and omnipotent source of boons and calamities visited upon mankind for cryptic and wholly extra-terrestrial reasons, and thus clearly belonging to spheres of existence whereof we know nothing and wherein we have no part. The phenomenon of dreaming likewise helped to build up the notion of an unreal or spiritual world; and in general, all the conditions of savage dawn-life so strongly conduced toward a feeling of the supernatural, that we need not wonder at the thoroughness with which man's very hereditary essence has become saturated with religion and superstition. That saturation must, as a matter of plain scientific fact, be regarded as virtually permanent so far as the subconscious mind and inner instincts are concerned; for though the area of the unknown has been steadily contracting for thousands of years, an infinite reservoir of mystery still engulfs most of the outer cosmos, whilst a vast residuum of powerful inherited associations clings around all the objects and processes that were once mysterious, however well they may now be explained. And more than this, there is an actual physiological fixation of the old instincts in our nervous tissue, which would make them obscurely operative even were the conscious mind to be purged of all sources of wonder.

Because we remember pain and the menace of death more vividly than pleasure, and because our feelings toward the beneficent aspects of the unknown have from the first been captured and formalised by conventional religious rituals, it has fallen to the lot of the darker and more maleficent side of cosmic mystery to figure chiefly in our popular supernatural folklore. This tendency, too, is naturally enhanced by the fact that uncertainty and danger are always closely allied; thus making any kind of an unknown world a world of peril and evil possibilities. When to this sense of fear and evil the inevitable fascination of wonder and curiosity is superadded, there is born a composite body of keen emotion and imaginative provocation whose vitality must of necessity endure as long as the human race itself. Children will always be afraid of the dark, and men with minds sensitive to hereditary impulse will always tremble at the thought of the hidden and fathomless worlds of strange life which may pulsate in the gulfs beyond the stars, or press hideously upon our own globe in unholy dimensions which only the dead and the moonstruck can glimpse.

With this foundation, no one need wonder at the existence of a literature of cosmic fear. It has always existed, and always will exist; and no better evidence of its tenacious vigour can be cited than the impulse which now and then drives writers of totally opposite leanings to try their hands at it in isolated tales, as if to discharge from their minds certain phantasmal shapes which would otherwise haunt them. Thus Dickens wrote several eerie narratives; Browning, the hideous poem "Childe Roland"; Henry James, *The Turn of the Screw;* Dr. Holmes, the subtle novel *Elsie Venner;* F. Marion Crawford, "The Upper Berth" and a number of other examples; Mrs. Charlotte Perkins Gilman, social worker, "The Yellow Wall Paper"; whilst the humourist W. W. Jacobs produced that able melodramatic bit called "The Monkey's Paw".

This type of fear-literature must not be confounded with a type externally similar but psychologically widely different; the literature of mere physical fear and the mundanely gruesome. Such writing, to be sure, has its place, as has the conventional or even whimsical or humorous ghost story where formalism or the author's knowing wink removes the true sense of the morbidly unnatural; but these things are not the literature of cosmic fear in its purest sense. The true weird tale has something more than secret murder, bloody bones, or a sheeted form clanking chains according to rule. A certain atmosphere of breathless and unexplainable dread of outer, unknown forces must be present; and there must be a hint, expressed with a seriousness and portentousness becoming its subject, of that most terrible conception of the human brain—a malign and particular suspension or defeat of those fixed laws of Nature which are our only safeguard against the assaults of chaos and the daemons of unplumbed space.[2]

Naturally we cannot expect all weird tales to conform absolutely to any theoretical model. Creative minds are uneven, and the best of fabrics have their dull spots. Moreover, much of the choicest weird work is unconscious; appearing in memorable fragments scattered through material whose massed effect may be of a very different cast. Atmosphere is the all-important thing, for the final criterion of authenticity is not the dovetailing of a plot but the creation of a given sensation. We may say, as a general thing, that a weird story whose intent is to teach or produce a social effect, or one in which the horrors are finally explained away by natural means, is not a genuine tale of cosmic fear; but it remains a fact that such narratives often possess, in isolated sections, atmospheric touches which fulfil every condition of true supernatural horror-literature. Therefore we must judge a weird tale not by the author's intent, or by the mere mechanics of the plot; but by the emotional level which it attains at its least mundane point. If the proper sensations are excited, such a "high spot" must be admitted on its own merits as weird literature, no matter how prosaically it is later dragged down. The one test of the really weird is simply this—whether or not there be excited in the reader a profound sense of dread, and of contact with unknown spheres and powers; a subtle attitude of awed listening, as if for the beating of black wings or the scratching of outside shapes and entities on the known universe's utmost rim. And of course, the more completely and unifiedly a story conveys this atmosphere, the better it is as a work of art in the given medium.

II. The Dawn of the Horror-Tale

As may naturally be expected of a form so closely connected with primal emotion, the horror-tale is as old as human thought and speech themselves.

Cosmic terror appears as an ingredient of the earliest folklore of all races, and is crystallised in the most archaic ballads, chronicles, and sacred writings. It was, indeed, a prominent feature of the elaborate ceremonial magic, with its rituals for the evocation of daemons and spectres, which flourished from prehistoric times, and which reached its highest development in Egypt and the Semitic nations. Fragments like the Book of Enoch[3] and the Claviculae of Solomon[4] well illustrate the power of the weird over the ancient Eastern mind, and upon such things were based enduring systems and traditions whose echoes extend obscurely even to the present time. Touches of this transcendental fear are seen in classic literature, and there is evidence of its still greater emphasis in a ballad literature which paralleled the classic stream but vanished for lack of a written medium. The Middle Ages, steeped in fanciful darkness, gave it an enormous impulse toward expression; and East and West alike were busy preserving and amplifying the dark heritage, both of random folklore and of academically formulated magic and cabbalism, which had descended to them. Witch, werewolf, vampire, and ghoul brooded ominously on the lips of bard and grandam, and needed but little encouragement to take the final step across the boundary that divides the chanted tale or song from the formal literary composition. In the Orient, the weird tale tended to assume a gorgeous colouring and sprightliness which almost transmuted it into sheer phantasy. In the West, where the mystical Teuton had come down from his black Boreal forests and the Celt remembered strange sacrifices in Druidic groves, it assumed a terrible intensity and convincing seriousness of atmosphere which doubled the force of its half-told, half-hinted horrors.

Much of the power of Western horror-lore was undoubtedly due to the hidden but often suspected presence of a hideous cult of nocturnal worshippers whose strange customs—descended from pre-Aryan and pre-agricultural times when a squat race of Mongoloids roved over Europe with their flocks and herds—were rooted in the most revolting fertility-rites of immemorial antiquity.[5] This secret religion, stealthily handed down amongst peasants for thousands of years despite the outward reign of the Druidic, Graeco-Roman, and Christian faiths in the regions involved, was marked by wild "Witches' Sabbaths" in lonely woods and atop distant hills on Walpurgis-Night and Hallowe'en, the traditional breeding-seasons of the goats and sheep and cattle; and became the source of vast riches of sorcery-legend, besides provoking extensive witchcraft-prosecutions of which the Salem affair forms the chief American example.[6] Akin to it in essence, and perhaps connected with it in fact, was the frightful secret system of inverted theology or Satan-worship which produced such horrors as the famous "Black Mass"; whilst operating toward the same end we may note the activities of those whose aims were somewhat more scientific or philosophical—the astrologers, cabbalists, and alchemists of the Albertus Magnus or Raymond Lully[7] type, with whom such rude ages invariably abound. The prevalence and depth of the mediaeval horror-spirit in Europe, intensified by the dark despair which waves of pestilence brought, may be fairly gauged by the grotesque carvings slyly introduced into much of the finest later Gothic ecclesiastical work of the time; the daemoniac gargoyles of Notre Dame and Mont St. Michel being among the most famous specimens. And throughout the period, it must be remembered, there existed amongst educated and uneducated alike a most unquestioning faith in every form of the supernatural; from the gentlest of Christian doctrines to the most monstrous morbidities of witchcraft and black magic. It was from no empty background that the Renaissance magicians and alchemists—Nostradamus, Trithemius, Dr. John Dee, Robert Fludd, and the like—were born.[8]

In this fertile soil were nourished types and characters of sombre myth and legend which persist in weird literature to this day, more or less disguised or altered by modern technique. Many of them were taken from the earliest oral sources, and form part of mankind's permanent heritage. The shade which appears and demands the burial of its bones, the daemon lover who comes to bear away his still living bride, the death-fiend or psychopomp[9] riding the night-wind, the man-wolf, the sealed chamber, the deathless sorcerer—all these may be found in that curious body of mediaeval lore which the late Mr. Baring-Gould so effectively assembled in book form.[10] Wherever the mystic Northern blood was strongest, the atmosphere of the popular tales became most intense; for in the Latin races there is a touch of basic rationality which denies to even their strangest superstitions many of the overtones of glamour so characteristic of our own forest-born and ice-fostered whisperings.

Just as all fiction first found extensive embodiment in poetry, so is it in poetry that we first encounter the permanent entry of the weird into standard literature. Most of the ancient instances, curiously enough, are in prose; as the werewolf incident in Petronius,[11] the gruesome passages in Apuleius,[12] the brief but celebrated letter of Pliny the Younger to Sura, and the odd compilation *On Wonderful Events* by the Emperor Hadrian's Greek freedman, Phlegon.[13] It is in Phlegon that we first find that hideous tale of the corpse-bride, "Philinnion and Machates", later related by Proclus[14] and in modern times forming the inspiration of Goethe's "Bride of Corinth" and Washington Irving's "German Student". But by the time the old Northern myths take literary form, and in that later time when the weird appears as a steady element in the literature of the day, we find it mostly in metrical dress; as indeed we find the greater part of the strictly imaginative writing of the Middle Ages and Renaissance. The Scandinavian Eddas[15] and Sagas[16] thunder with cosmic horror, and shake with the stark fear of Ymir and his shapeless spawn; whilst our own Anglo-Saxon *Beowulf* and the later Continental Nibelung tales are full of eldritch weirdness. Dante is a pioneer in the classic capture of macabre atmosphere, and in Spenser's stately stanzas will be seen more than a few touches of fantastic terror in landscape, incident, and character. Prose literature gives us Malory's *Morte d'Arthur,* in which are presented many ghastly situations taken from early ballad sources—the theft of the sword and silk from the corpse in Chapel Perilous by Sir Launcelot, the ghost of Sir Gawaine, and the tomb-fiend seen by Sir Galahad[17]—whilst other and cruder specimens were doubtless set forth in the cheap and sensational "chapbooks" vulgarly hawked about and devoured by the ignorant. In Elizabethan drama, with its *Dr. Faustus,* the witches in *Macbeth,* the ghost in *Hamlet,* and the horrible gruesomeness of Webster, we may easily discern the strong hold of the daemoniac on the public mind; a hold intensified by the very real fear of living witchcraft, whose terrors, first wildest on the Continent, begin to echo loudly in English ears as the witch-hunting crusades of James the First gain headway.[18] To the lurking mystical prose of the ages is added a long line of treatises on witchcraft and daemonology which aid in exciting the imagination of the reading world.

Through the seventeenth and into the eighteenth century we behold a growing mass of fugitive legendry and balladry of darksome cast; still, however, held down beneath the surface of polite and accepted literature. Chapbooks of horror and weirdness multiplied, and we glimpse the eager interest of the people through fragments like Defoe's "Apparition of Mrs. Veal", a homely tale of a dead woman's spectral visit to a distant friend, written to advertise covertly a badly selling theological disquisition on death.[19] The upper orders of society were now losing faith in the supernatural, and indulging in a period of classic rationalism. Then, beginning with the translations of Eastern tales in Queen Anne's reign and taking definite form toward the middle of the century, comes the revival of romantic feeling—the era of new joy in Nature, and in the radiance of past times, strange scenes, bold deeds, and incredible marvels. We feel it first in the poets, whose utterances take on new qualities of wonder, strangeness, and shuddering. And finally, after the timid appearance of a few weird scenes in the novels of the day—such as Smollett's *Adventures of Ferdinand, Count Fathom*[20]—the released instinct precipitates itself in the birth of a new school of writing; the "Gothic" school of horrible and fantastic prose fiction, long and short, whose literary posterity is destined to become so numerous, and in many cases so resplendent in artistic merit. It is, when one reflects upon it, genuinely remarkable that weird narration as a fixed and academically recognised literary form should have been so late of final birth. The impulse and atmosphere are as old as man, but the typical weird tale of standard literature is a child of the eighteenth century.

III. The Early Gothic Novel

The shadow-haunted landscapes of "Ossian",[21] the chaotic visions of William Blake, the grotesque witch-dances in Burns's "Tam O'Shanter", the sinister daemonism of Coleridge's *Christabel* and *Ancient Mariner,* the ghostly charm of James Hogg's "Kilmeny", and the more restrained approaches to cosmic horror in *Lamia* and many of Keats's other poems, are typical British illustrations of the advent of the weird to formal literature. Our Teutonic cousins of the Continent were equally receptive to the rising flood, and Bürger's "Wild Huntsman" and the even more famous daemon-bridegroom ballad of "Lenore"—both imitated in English by Scott, whose respect for the supernatural was always great—are only a taste of the eerie wealth which German song had commenced to provide. Thomas Moore adapted from such sources the legend of the ghoulish statue-bride (later used by Prosper Mérimée in "The Venus of Ille", and traceable back to great antiquity) which echoes so shiveringly in his ballad of "The Ring"; whilst Goethe's deathless masterpiece *Faust,* crossing from mere balladry into the classic, cosmic tragedy of the ages, may be held as the ultimate height to which this German poetic impulse arose.

But it remained for a very sprightly and worldly Englishman—none other than Horace Walpole himself—to give the growing impulse definite shape and become the actual founder of the literary horror-story as a permanent form. Fond of mediaeval rò-mance and mystery as a dilettante's diversion, and with a quaintly imitated Gothic castle as his abode at Strawberry Hill, Walpole in 1764 published *The Castle of Otranto;* a tale of the supernatural which, though thoroughly unconvincing and mediocre in itself, was destined to exert an almost unparalleled influence on the literature of the weird. First venturing it only as a translation by one "William Marshal, Gent." from the Italian of a mythical "Onuphrio Muralto", the author later acknowledged his connexion with the book and took pleasure in its wide and instantaneous popularity—a popularity which extended to many editions, early dramatisation, and wholesale imitation both in England and in Germany.

The story—tedious, artificial, and melodramatic—is further impaired by a brisk and prosaic style whose urbane sprightliness nowhere permits the creation of a truly weird atmosphere. It tells of Manfred, an unscrupulous and usurping prince determined to found a line, who after the mysterious sudden death of his only son Conrad on the latter's bridal morn, attempts to put away his wife Hippolita and wed the lady destined for the unfortunate youth—the lad, by the way, having been crushed by the preternatural fall of a gigantic helmet in the castle courtyard. Isabella, the widowed bride, flees from this design; and encounters in subterranean crypts beneath the castle a noble young preserver, Theodore, who seems to be a peasant yet strangely resembles the old lord Alfonso who ruled the domain before Manfred's time. Shortly thereafter supernatural phenomena assail the castle in divers ways; fragments of gigantic armour being discovered here and there, a portrait walking out of its frame, a thunderclap destroying the edifice, and a colossal armoured spectre of Alfonso rising out of the ruins to ascend through parting clouds to the bosom of St. Nicholas. Theodore, having wooed Manfred's daughter Matilda and lost her through death—for she is slain by her father by mistake—is discovered to be the son of Alfonso and rightful heir to the estate. He concludes the tale by wedding Isabella and preparing to live happily ever after, whilst Manfred—whose usurpation was the cause of his son's supernatural death and his own supernatural harassings—retires to a monastery for penitence; his saddened wife seeking asylum in a neighbouring convent.

Such is the tale; flat, stilted, and altogether devoid of the true cosmic horror which makes weird literature.[22] Yet such was the thirst of the age for those touches of strangeness and spectral antiquity which it reflects, that it was seriously received by the soundest readers and raised in spite of its intrinsic ineptness to a pedestal of lofty importance in literary history. What it did above all else was to create a novel type of scene, puppet-characters, and incidents; which, handled to better advantage by writers more naturally adapted to weird creation, stimulated the growth of an imitative Gothic school which in turn inspired the real weavers of cosmic terror—the line of actual artists beginning with Poe. This novel dramatic paraphernalia consisted first of all of the Gothic castle, with its awesome antiquity, vast distances and ramblings, deserted or ruined wings, damp corridors, unwholesome hidden catacombs, and galaxy of ghosts and appalling legends, as a nucleus of suspense and daemoniac fright. In addition, it included the tyrannical and malevolent nobleman as villain; the saintly, long-persecuted, and generally insipid heroine who undergoes the major terrors and serves as a point of view and focus for the reader's sympathies; the valorous and immaculate hero, always of high birth but often in humble disguise; the convention of high-sounding foreign names, mostly Italian, for the characters; and the infinite array of stage properties which includes strange lights, damp trap-doors, extinguished lamps, mouldy hidden manuscripts, creaking hinges, shaking arras, and the like. All this paraphernalia reappears with amusing sameness, yet sometimes with tremendous effect, throughout the history of the Gothic novel; and is by no means extinct even today, though subtler technique now forces it to assume a less naive and obvious form. An harmonious milieu for a new school had been found, and the writing world was not slow to grasp the opportunity.

German romance at once responded to the Walpole influence, and soon became a byword for the weird and ghastly. In England one of the first imitators was the celebrated Mrs. Barbauld, then Miss Aikin, who in 1773 published an unfinished fragment called "Sir Bertrand", in which the strings of genuine terror were truly touched with no clumsy hand. A nobleman on a dark and lonely moor, attracted by a tolling bell and distant light, enters a strange and ancient turreted castle whose doors open and close and whose bluish will-o'-the-wisps lead up mysterious staircases toward dead hands and animated black statues. A coffin with a dead lady, whom Sir Bertrand kisses, is finally reached; and upon the kiss the scene dissolves to give place to a splendid apartment where the lady, restored to life, holds a banquet in honour of her rescuer. Walpole admired this tale, though he accorded less respect to an even more prominent offspring of his *Otranto*—*The Old English Baron*, by Clara Reeve, published in 1777.[23] Truly enough, this tale lacks the real vibration to the note of outer darkness and mystery which distinguishes Mrs. Barbauld's fragment; and though less crude than Walpole's novel, and more artistically economical of horror in its possession of only one spectral figure, it is nevertheless too definitely insipid for greatness. Here again we have the virtuous heir to the castle disguised as a peasant and restored to his heritage through the ghost of his father; and here again we have a case of wide popularity leading to many editions, dramatisation, and ultimate translation into French. Miss Reeve wrote another weird novel, unfortunately unpublished and lost.[24]

The Gothic novel was now settled as a literary form, and instances multiply bewilderingly as the eighteenth century draws toward its close. *The Recess*, written in 1785 by Mrs. Sophia Lee, has the historic element, revolving round the twin daughters of Mary, Queen of Scots; and though devoid of the supernatural, employs the Walpole scenery and mechanism with great dexterity. Five years later, and all existing lamps are paled by the rising of a fresh luminary of wholly superior order—Mrs. Ann Radcliffe (1764–1823), whose famous novels made terror and suspense a fashion, and who set new and higher standards in the domain of macabre and fear-inspiring atmosphere despite a provoking custom of destroying her own phantoms at the last through laboured mechanical explanations. To the familiar Gothic trappings of her predecessors Mrs. Radcliffe added a genuine sense of the unearthly in scene and incident which closely approached genius; every touch of setting and action contributing artistically to the impression of illimitable frightfulness which she wished to convey. A few sinister details like a track of blood on castle stairs, a groan from a distant vault, or a weird song in a nocturnal forest can with her conjure up the most powerful images of imminent horror; surpassing by far the extravagant and toilsome elaborations of others. Nor are these images in themselves any the less potent because they are explained away before the end of the novel. Mrs. Radcliffe's visual imagination was very strong, and appears as much in her delightful landscape touches—always in broad, glamorously pictorial outline, and never in close detail—as in her weird phantasies. Her prime weaknesses, aside from the habit of prosaic disillusionment, are a tendency toward erroneous geography and history and a fatal predilection for bestrewing her novels with insipid little poems, attributed to one or another of the characters.

Mrs. Radcliffe wrote six novels; *The Castles of Athlin and Dunbayne* (1789), *A Sicilian Romance* (1790), *The Romance of the Forest* (1791), *The Mysteries of Udolpho* (1794), *The Italian* (1797), and *Gaston de Blondeville*, composed in 1802 but first published posthumously in 1826. Of these *Udolpho* is by far the most famous, and may be taken as a type of the early Gothic tale at its best. It is the chronicle of Emily, a young Frenchwoman transplanted to an ancient and portentous castle in the Apennines through the death of her parents and the marriage of her aunt to the lord of the castle—the scheming nobleman Montoni. Mysterious sounds, opened doors, frightful legends, and a nameless horror in a niche behind a black veil all operate in quick succession to unnerve the heroine and her faithful attendant Annette; but finally, after the death of her aunt, she escapes with the aid of a fellow-prisoner whom she has discovered. On the way home she stops at a chateau filled with fresh horrors—the abandoned wing where the departed chatelaine dwelt, and the bed of death with the black pall—but is finally restored to security and happiness with her lover Valancourt, after the clearing-up of a secret which seemed for a time to involve her birth in mystery. Clearly, this is only the familiar material re-worked; but it is so well re-worked that *Udolpho* will always be a classic. Mrs. Radcliffe's characters are puppets, but they are less markedly so than those of her forerunners. And in atmospheric creation she stands preëminent among those of her time.

Of Mrs. Radcliffe's countless imitators, the American novelist Charles Brockden Brown stands the closest in spirit and method. Like her, he injured his creations by natural explanations; but also like her, he had an uncanny atmospheric power which gives his horrors a frightful vitality as long as they remain unexplained. He differed from her in contemptuously discarding the external Gothic paraphernalia and properties and choosing modern American scenes for his mysteries; but this repudiation did not extend to the Gothic spirit and type of incident. Brown's novels involve some memorably frightful scenes, and excel even Mrs. Radcliffe's in describing the operations of the perturbed mind. *Edgar Huntly* starts with a sleep-walker digging a grave, but is later impaired by touches of Godwinian didacticism. *Ormond* involves a member of a sinister secret brotherhood. That and *Arthur Mervyn* both describe the plague of yellow fever, which the author had witnessed in Philadelphia and New York. But Brown's most famous book is *Wieland; or, The Transformation* (1798),[25] in which a Pennsylvania German, engulfed by a wave of religious fanaticism, hears voices and slays his wife and children as a sacrifice. His sister Clara, who tells the story, narrowly escapes. The scene, laid at the woodland estate of Mittingen on the Schuylkill's remote reaches, is drawn with extreme vividness; and the terrors of Clara, beset by spectral tones, gathering fears, and the sound of strange footsteps in the lonely house, are all shaped with truly artistic force. In the end a lame ventriloquial explanation is offered, but the atmosphere is genuine while it lasts. Carwin, the malign ventriloquist, is a typical villain of the Manfred or Montoni type.

IV. The Apex of Gothic Romance

Horror in literature attains a new malignity in the work of Matthew Gregory Lewis (1775–1818), whose novel *The Monk* (1796) achieved marvellous popularity and earned him the nickname of "Monk" Lewis. This young author, educated in Germany and saturated with a body of wild Teuton lore unknown to Mrs. Radcliffe, turned to terror in forms more violent than his gentle predecessor had ever dared to think of; and produced as a result a masterpiece of active nightmare whose general Gothic cast is spiced with added stores of ghoulishness. The story is one of a Spanish monk, Ambrosio, who from a state of overproud virtue is tempted to the very nadir of evil by a fiend in the guise of the maiden Matilda; and who is finally, when awaiting death at the Inquisition's hands, induced to purchase escape at the price of his soul from the Devil, because he deems both body and soul already lost. Forthwith the mocking Fiend snatches him to a lonely place, tells him he has sold his soul in vain since both pardon and a chance for salvation were approaching at the moment of his hideous bargain, and completes the sardonic betrayal by rebuking him for his unnatural crimes, and casting his body down a precipice whilst his soul is borne off for ever to perdition. The novel contains some appalling descriptions such as the incantation in the vaults beneath the convent cemetery, the burning of the convent, and the final end of the wretched abbot. In the sub-plot where the Marquis de las Cisternas meets the spectre of his erring ancestress, The Bleeding Nun, there are many enormously potent strokes; notably the visit of the animated corpse to the Marquis's bedside, and the cabbalistic ritual whereby the Wandering Jew helps him to fathom and banish his dead tormentor. Nevertheless *The Monk* drags sadly when read as a whole. It is too long and too diffuse, and much of its potency is marred by flippancy and by an awkwardly excessive reaction against those canons of decorum which Lewis at first despised as prudish. One great thing may be said of the author; that he never ruined his ghostly visions with a natural explanation. He succeeded in breaking up the Radcliffian tradition and expanding the field of the Gothic novel. Lewis wrote much more than *The Monk*. His drama, *The Castle Spectre*, was produced in 1798, and he later found time to pen other fictions in ballad form—*Tales of Terror* (1799), *Tales of Wonder* (1801), and a succession of translations from the German.[26]

Gothic romances, both English and German, now appeared in multitudinous and mediocre profusion. Most of them were merely ridiculous in the light of mature taste, and Miss Austen's famous satire *Northanger Abbey* was by no means an unmerited rebuke to a school which had sunk far toward absurdity. This particular school was petering out, but before its final subordination there arose its last and greatest figure in the person of Charles Robert Maturin (1782–1824), an obscure and eccentric Irish clergyman. Out of an ample body of miscellaneous writing which includes one confused Radcliffian imitation called *Fatal Revenge; or, The Family of Montorio* (1807), Maturin at length evolved the vivid horror-masterpiece of *Melmoth the Wanderer* (1820), in which the Gothic tale climbed to altitudes of sheer spiritual fright which it had never known before.[27]

Melmoth is the tale of an Irish gentleman who, in the seventeenth century, obtained a preternaturally extended life from the Devil at the price of his soul. If he can persuade another to take the bargain off his hands, and assume his existing state, he can be saved; but this he can never manage to effect, no matter how assiduously he haunts those whom despair has made reckless and frantic. The framework of the story is very clumsy; involving tedious length, digressive episodes, narratives within narratives, and laboured dovetailing and coincidences; but at various points in the endless rambling there is felt a pulse of power undiscoverable in any previous work of this kind—a kinship to the essential truth of human nature, an understanding of the profoundest sources of actual cosmic fear, and a white heat of sympathetic passion on the writer's part which makes the book a true document of aesthetic self-expression rather than a mere clever compound of artifice. No unbiassed reader can doubt that with *Melmoth* an enormous stride in the evolution of the horror-tale is represented. Fear is taken out of the realm of the conventional and exalted into a hideous cloud over mankind's very destiny. Maturin's shudders, the work of one capable of shuddering himself, are of the sort that convince. Mrs. Radcliffe and Lewis are fair game for the parodist, but it would be difficult to find a false note in the feverishly intensified action and high atmospheric tension of the Irishman whose less sophisticated emotions and strain of Celtic mysticism gave him the finest possible natural equipment for his task. Without a doubt Maturin is a man of authentic genius, and he was so recognised by Balzac, who grouped Melmoth with Molière's Don Juan, Goethe's Faust, and Byron's Manfred as the supreme allegorical figures of modern European literature, and wrote a whimsical piece called "Melmoth Reconciled", in which the Wanderer succeeds in passing his infernal bargain on to a Parisian bank defaulter, who in turn hands it along a chain of victims until a revelling gambler dies with it in his possession, and by his damnation ends the curse. Scott,[28] Rossetti,[29] Thackeray,[30] and Baudelaire[31] are the other titans who gave Maturin their unqualified admiration, and there is much significance in the fact that Oscar Wilde, after his disgrace and exile, chose for his last days in Paris the assumed name of "Sebastian Melmoth".

Melmoth contains scenes which even now have not lost their power to evoke dread. It begins with a deathbed—an old miser is dying of sheer fright because of something he has seen, coupled with a manuscript he has read and a family portrait which hangs in an obscure closet of his centuried home in County Wicklow. He sends to Trinity College, Dublin, for his nephew John; and the latter upon arriving notes many uncanny things. The eyes of the portrait in the closet glow horribly, and twice a figure strangely resembling the portrait appears momentarily at the door. Dread hangs over that house of the Melmoths, one of whose ancestors, "J. Melmoth, 1646", the portrait represents. The dying miser declares that this man—at a date slightly before 1800—is alive. Finally the miser dies, and the nephew is told in the will to destroy both the portrait and a manuscript to be found in a certain drawer. Reading the manuscript, which was written late in the seventeenth century by an Englishman named Stanton, young John learns of a terrible incident in Spain in 1677, when the writer met a horrible fellow-countryman and was told of how he had stared to death a priest who tried to denounce him as one filled with fearsome evil. Later, after meeting the man again in London, Stanton is cast into a madhouse and visited by the stranger, whose approach is heralded by spectral music and whose eyes have a more than mortal glare. Melmoth the Wanderer—for such is the malign visitor—offers the captive freedom if he will take over his bargain with the Devil; but like all others whom Melmoth has approached, Stanton is proof against temptation. Melmoth's description of the horrors of a life in a madhouse, used to tempt Stanton, is one of the most potent passages of the book. Stanton is at length liberated, and spends the rest of his life tracking down Melmoth, whose family and ancestral abode he discovers. With the family he leaves the manuscript, which by young John's time is sadly ruinous and fragmentary. John destroys both portrait and manuscript, but in sleep is visited by his horrible ancestor, who leaves a black and blue mark on his wrist.

Young John soon afterward receives as a visitor a shipwrecked Spaniard, Alonzo de Monçada, who has escaped from compulsory monasticism and from the perils of the Inquisition. He has suffered horribly—and the descriptions of his experiences under torment and in the vaults through which he once essays escape are classic—but had the strength to resist Melmoth the Wanderer when approached at his darkest hour in prison. At the house of a Jew who sheltered him after his escape he discovers a wealth of manuscript relating other exploits of Melmoth including his wooing of an Indian island maiden, Immalee, who later comes to her birthright in Spain and is known as Donna Isidora; and of his horrible marriage to her by the corpse of a dead anchorite at midnight in the ruined chapel of a shunned and abhorred monastery. Monçada's narrative to young John takes up the bulk of Maturin's four-volume book; this disproportion being considered one of the chief technical faults of the composition.

At last the colloquies of John and Monçada are interrupted by the entrance of Melmoth the Wanderer himself, his piercing eyes now fading, and decrepitude swiftly overtaking him. The term of his bargain has approached its end, and he has come home after a century and a half to meet his fate. Warning all others from the room, no matter what sounds they may hear in the night, he awaits the end alone. Young John and Monçada hear frightful ululations, but do not intrude till silence comes toward morning. They then find the room empty. Clayey footprints lead out a rear door to a cliff overlooking the sea, and near the edge of the precipice is a track indicating the forcible dragging of some heavy body. The Wanderer's scarf is found on a crag some distance below the brink, but nothing further is ever seen or heard of him.

Such is the story, and none can fail to notice the difference between this modulated, suggestive, and artistically moulded horror and—to use the words of Professor George Saintsbury—"the artful but rather jejune rationalism of Mrs. Radcliffe, and the too often puerile extravagance, the bad taste, and the sometimes slipshod style of Lewis."[32] Maturin's style in itself deserves particular praise, for its forcible directness and vitality lift it altogether above the pompous artificialities of which his predecessors are guilty. Professor Edith Birkhead, in her history of the Gothic novel, justly observes that with all his faults Maturin was the greatest as well as the last of the Goths.[33] *Melmoth* was widely read and eventually dramatised, but its late date in the evolution of the Gothic tale deprived it of the tumultuous popularity of *Udolpho* and *The Monk*.

V. The Aftermath of Gothic Fiction

Meanwhile other hands had not been idle, so that above the dreary plethora of trash like Marquis von Grosse's *Horrid Mysteries* (1796), Mrs. Roche's *Children of the Abbey* (1796), Miss Dacre's *Zofloya; or, The Moor* (1806), and the poet Shelley's schoolboy effusions *Zastrozzi* (1810) and *St. Irvyne* (1811) (both imitations of *Zofloya*) there arose many memorable weird works both in English and German. Classic in merit, and markedly different from its fellows because of its foundation in the Oriental tale rather than the Walpolesque Gothic novel, is the celebrated *History of the Caliph Vathek*[34] by the wealthy dilettante William Beckford, first written in the French language but published in an English translation before the appearance of the original. Eastern tales, introduced to European literature early in the eighteenth century through Galland's French translation of the inexhaustibly opulent *Arabian Nights*,[35] had become a reigning fashion; being used both for allegory[36] and for amusement. The sly humour which only the Eastern mind knows how to mix with weirdness had captivated a sophisticated generation, till Bagdad and Damascus names became as freely strown through popular literature as dashing Italian and Spanish ones were soon to be. Beckford, well read in Eastern romance, caught the atmosphere with unusual receptivity; and in his fantastic volume reflected very potently the haughty luxury, sly disillusion, bland cruelty, urbane treachery, and shadowy spectral horror of the Saracen spirit. His seasoning of the ridiculous seldom mars the force of his sinister theme, and the tale marches onward with a phantasmagoric pomp in which the laughter is that of skeletons feasting under Arabesque domes. *Vathek* is a tale of the grandson of the Caliph Haroun, who, tormented by that ambition for super-terrestrial power, pleasure, and learning which animates the average Gothic villain or Byronic hero (essentially cognate types), is lured by an evil genius to seek the subterranean throne of the mighty and fabulous pre-Adamite sultans in the fiery halls of Eblis, the Mahometan Devil. The descriptions of Vathek's palaces and diversions, of his scheming sorceress-mother Carathis and her witch-tower with the fifty one-eyed negresses, of his pilgrimage to the haunted ruins of Istakhar (Persepolis) and of the impish bride Nouronihar whom he treacherously acquired on the way, of Istakhar's primordial towers and terraces in the burning moonlight of the waste, and of the terrible Cyclopean halls of Eblis, where, lured by glittering promises, each victim is compelled to wander in anguish for ever, his right hand upon his blazingly ignited and eternally burning heart, are triumphs of weird colouring which raise the book to a permanent place in English letters. No less notable are the three *Episodes of Vathek*, intended for insertion in the tale as narratives of Vathek's fellow-victims in Eblis' infernal halls, which remained unpublished throughout the author's lifetime and were discovered as recently as 1909 by the scholar Lewis Melville whilst collecting material for his *Life and Letters of William Beckford.*[37] Beckford, however, lacks the essential mysticism which marks the acutest form of the weird; so that his tales have a certain knowing Latin hardness and clearness preclusive of sheer panic fright.

But Beckford remained alone in his devotion to the Orient. Other writers, closer to the Gothic tradition and to European life in general, were content to follow more faithfully in the lead of Walpole. Among the countless producers of terror-literature in these times may be mentioned the Utopian economic theorist William Godwin, who followed his famous but non-supernatural *Caleb Williams* (1794) with the intendedly weird *St. Leon* (1799), in which the theme of the elixir of life, as developed by the imaginary secret order of "Rosicrucians",[38] is handled with ingeniousness if not with atmospheric convincingness. This element of Rosicrucianism, fostered by a wave of popular magical interest exemplified in the vogue of the charlatan Cagliostro and the publication of Francis Barrett's *The Magus* (1801), a curious and compendious treatise on occult principles and ceremonies, of which a reprint was made as lately as 1896,[39] figures in Bulwer-Lytton and in many late Gothic novels, especially that remote and enfeebled posterity which straggled far down into the nineteenth century and was represented by George W. M. Reynolds' *Faust and the Demon* and *Wagner, the Wehr-wolf.* *Caleb Williams*, though non-supernatural, has many authentic touches of terror. It is the tale of a servant persecuted by a master whom he has found guilty of murder, and displays an invention and skill which have kept it alive in a fashion to this day. It was dramatised as *The Iron Chest,*[40] and in that form was almost equally celebrated. Godwin, however, was too much the conscious teacher and prosaic man of thought to create a genuine weird masterpiece.

His daughter, the wife of Shelley, was much more successful; and her inimitable *Frankenstein; or, The Modern Prometheus* (1818) is one of the horror-classics of all time. Composed in competition with her husband, Lord Byron, and Dr. John William Polidori in an effort to prove supremacy in horror-making, Mrs. Shelley's *Frankenstein* was the only one of the rival narratives to be brought to an elaborate completion;[41] and criticism has failed to prove that the best parts are due to Shelley rather than to her. The novel, somewhat tinged but scarcely marred by moral didacticism, tells of the artificial human being moulded from charnel fragments by Victor Frankenstein, a young Swiss medical student. Created by its designer "in the mad pride of intellectuality", the monster possesses full intelligence but owns a hideously loathsome form. It is rejected by mankind, becomes embittered, and at length begins the successive murder of all whom young Frankenstein loves best, friends and family. It demands that Frankenstein create a wife for it; and when the student finally refuses in horror lest the world be populated with such monsters, it departs with a hideous threat 'to be with him on his wedding night'. Upon that night the bride is strangled, and from that time on Frankenstein hunts down the monster, even into the wastes of the Arctic. In the end, whilst seeking shelter on the ship of the man who tells the story, Frankenstein himself is killed by the shocking object of his search and creation of his presumptuous pride. Some of the scenes in *Frankenstein* are unforgettable, as when the newly animated monster enters its creator's room, parts the curtains of his bed, and gazes at him in the yellow moonlight with watery eyes—"if eyes they may be called". Mrs. Shelley wrote other novels, including the fairly notable *Last Man;* but never duplicated the success of her first effort. It has the true touch of cosmic fear, no matter how much the movement may lag in places. Dr. Polidori developed his competing idea as a long short story, "The Vampyre"; in which we behold a suave villain of the true Gothic or Byronic type, and encounter some excellent passages of stark fright, including a terrible nocturnal experience in a shunned Grecian wood.

In this same period Sir Walter Scott frequently concerned himself with the weird, weaving it into many of his novels and poems, and sometimes producing such independent bits of narration as "The Tapestried Chamber" or "Wandering Willie's Tale" in *Redgauntlet,* in the latter of which the force of the spectral and the diabolic is enhanced by a grotesque homeliness of speech and atmosphere. In 1830 Scott published his *Letters on Demonology and Witchcraft,* which still forms one of our best compendia of European witch-lore. Washington Irving is another famous figure not unconnected with the weird; for though most of his ghosts are too whimsical and humorous to form genuinely spectral literature, a distinct inclination in this direction is to be noted in many of his productions. "The German Student" in *Tales of a Traveller* (1824) is a slyly concise and effective presentation of the old legend of the dead bride, whilst woven into the comic tissue of "The Money-Diggers" in the same volume is more than one hint of piratical apparitions in the realms which Captain Kidd once roamed. Thomas Moore also joined the ranks of the macabre artists in the poem *Alciphron,* which he later elaborated into the prose novel of *The Epicurean* (1827). Though merely relating the adventures of a young Athenian duped by the artifice of cunning Egyptian priests, Moore manages to infuse much genuine horror into his account of subterranean frights and wonders beneath the primordial temples of Memphis. De Quincey more than once revels in grotesque and arabesque terrors, though with a desultoriness and learned pomp which deny him the rank of specialist.

This era likewise saw the rise of William Harrison Ainsworth, whose romantic novels teem with the eerie and the gruesome. Capt. Marryat, besides writing such short tales as "The Werewolf", made a memorable contribution in *The Phantom Ship* (1839),[42] founded on the legend of the Flying Dutchman, whose spectral and accursed vessel sails for ever near the Cape of Good Hope. Dickens now rises with occasional weird bits like "The Signalman", a tale of ghostly warning conforming to a very common pattern and touched with a verisimilitude which allies it as much with the coming psychological school as with the dying Gothic school. At this time a wave of interest in spiritualistic charlatanry, mediumism, Hindoo theosophy, and such matters, much like that of the present day, was flourishing; so that the number of weird tales with a "psychic" or pseudo-scientific basis became very considerable. For a number of these the prolific and popular Lord Edward Bulwer-Lytton was responsible; and despite the large doses of turgid rhetoric and empty romanticism in his products, his success in the weaving of a certain kind of bizarre charm cannot be denied.

"The House and the Brain", which hints of Rosicrucianism and at a malign and deathless figure perhaps suggested by Louis XV's mysterious courtier St. Germain,[43] yet survives as one of the best short haunted-house tales ever written. The novel *Zanoni* (1842) contains similar elements more elaborately handled, and introduces a vast unknown sphere of being pressing on our own world and guarded by a horrible "Dweller of the Threshold" who haunts those who try to enter and fail. Here we have a benign brotherhood kept alive from age to age till finally reduced to a single member, and as a hero an ancient Chaldaean sorcerer surviving in the pristine bloom of youth to perish on the guillotine of the French Revolution. Though full of the conventional spirit of romance, marred by a ponderous network of symbolic and didactic meanings, and left unconvincing through lack of perfect atmospheric realisation of the situations hinging on the spectral world, *Zanoni* is really an excellent performance as a romantic novel; and can be read with genuine interest today by the not too sophisticated reader. It is amusing to note that in describing an attempted initiation into the ancient brotherhood the author cannot escape using the stock Gothic castle of Walpolian lineage.

In *A Strange Story* (1862) Bulwer-Lytton shews a marked improvement in the creation of weird images and moods. The novel, despite enormous length, a highly artificial plot bolstered up by opportune coincidences, and an atmosphere of homiletic pseudo-science designed to please the matter-of-fact and purposeful Victorian reader, is exceedingly effective as a narrative; evoking instantaneous and unflagging interest, and furnishing many potent—if somewhat melodramatic—tableaux and climaxes. Again we have the mysterious user of life's elixir in the person of the soulless magician Margrave, whose dark exploits stand out with dramatic vividness against the modern background of a quiet English town and of the Australian bush; and again we have shadowy intimations of a vast spectral world of the unknown in the very air about us—this time handled with much greater power and vitality than in *Zanoni*. One of the two great incantation passages, where the hero is driven by a luminous evil spirit to rise at night in his sleep, take a strange Egyptian wand, and evoke nameless presences in the haunted and mausoleum-facing pavilion of a famous Renaissance alchemist, truly stands among the major terror scenes of literature. Just enough is suggested, and just little enough is told. Unknown words are twice dictated to the sleep-walker, and as he repeats them the ground trembles, and all the dogs of the countryside begin to bay at half-seen amorphous shadows that stalk athwart the moonlight. When a third set of unknown words is prompted, the sleep-walker's spirit suddenly rebels at uttering them, as if the soul could recognise ultimate abysmal horrors concealed from the mind; and at last an apparition of an absent sweetheart and good angel breaks the malign spell. This fragment well illustrates how far Lord Lytton was capable of progressing beyond his usual pomp and stock romance toward that crystalline essence of artistic fear which belongs to the domain of poetry. In describing certain details of incantations, Lytton was greatly indebted to his amusingly serious occult studies, in the course of which he came in touch with that odd French scholar and cabbalist Alphonse-Louis Constant ("Eliphas Lévi"),[44] who claimed to possess the secrets of ancient magic, and to have evoked the spectre of the old Grecian wizard Apollonius of Tyana, who lived in Nero's time.

The romantic, semi-Gothic, quasi-moral tradition here represented was carried far down the nineteenth century by such authors as Joseph Sheridan LeFanu, Thomas Preskett Prest with his famous *Varney, the Vampyre* (1847),[45] Wilkie Collins, the late Sir H. Rider Haggard (whose *She* is really remarkably good),[46] Sir A. Conan Doyle, H. G. Wells, and Robert Louis Stevenson—the latter of whom, despite an atrocious tendency toward jaunty mannerisms, created permanent classics in "Markheim", "The Body-Snatcher", and *Dr. Jekyll and Mr. Hyde*. Indeed, we may say that this school still survives; for to it clearly belong such of our contemporary horror-tales as specialise in events rather than atmospheric details, address the intellect rather than the impressionistic imagination, cultivate a luminous glamour rather than a malign tensity or psychological verisimilitude, and take a definite stand in sympathy with mankind and its welfare. It has its undeniable strength, and because of its "human element" commands a wider audience than does the sheer artistic nightmare. If not quite so potent as the latter, it is because a diluted product can never achieve the intensity of a concentrated essence.

Quite alone both as a novel and as a piece of terror-literature stands the famous *Wuthering Heights* (1847) by Emily Brontë, with its mad vista of bleak, windswept Yorkshire moors and the violent, distorted lives they foster. Though primarily a tale of life, and of human passions in agony and conflict, its epically cosmic setting affords room for horror of the most spiritual sort. Heathcliff, the modified Byronic villain-hero, is a strange dark waif found in the streets as a small child and speaking only a strange gibberish till adopted by the family he ultimately ruins. That he is in truth a diabolic spirit rather than a human being is more than once suggested, and the unreal is further approached in the experience of the visitor who encounters a plaintive child-ghost at a bough-brushed upper window. Between Heathcliff and Catherine Earnshaw is a tie deeper and more terrible than human love. After her death he twice disturbs her grave, and is haunted by an impalpable presence which can be nothing less than her spirit. The spirit enters his life more and more, and at last he becomes confident of some imminent mystical reunion. He says he feels a strange change approaching, and ceases to take nourishment. At night he either walks abroad or opens the casement by his bed. When he dies the casement is still swinging open to the pouring rain, and a queer smile pervades the stiffened face. They bury him in a grave beside the mound he has haunted for eighteen years, and small shepherd boys say that he yet walks with his Catherine in the churchyard and on the moor when it rains. Their faces, too, are sometimes seen on rainy nights behind that upper casement at Wuthering Heights. Miss Brontë's eerie terror is no mere Gothic echo, but a tense expression of man's shuddering reaction to the unknown. In this respect, *Wuthering Heights* becomes the symbol of a literary transition, and marks the growth of a new and sounder school.

VI. Spectral Literature on the Continent

On the Continent literary horror fared well. The celebrated short tales and novels of Ernst Theodor Wilhelm Hoffmann (1776–1822) are a byword for mellowness of background and maturity of form, though they incline to levity and extravagance, and lack the exalted moments of stark, breathless terror which a less sophisticated writer might have achieved. Generally they convey the grotesque rather than the terrible.[47] Most artistic of all the Continental weird tales is the German classic *Undine* (1811), by Friedrich Heinrich Karl, Baron de la Motte Fouqué. In this story of a water-spirit who married a mortal and gained a human soul there is a delicate fineness of craftsmanship which makes it notable in any department of literature, and an easy naturalness which places it close to the genuine folk-myth. It is, in fact, derived from a tale told by the Renaissance physician and alchemist Paracelsus in his *Treatise on Elemental Sprites.*

Undine, daughter of a powerful water-prince, was exchanged by her father as a small child for a fisherman's daughter, in order that she might acquire a soul by wedding a human being. Meeting the noble youth Huldbrand at the cottage of her foster-father by the sea at the edge of a haunted wood, she soon marries him, and accompanies him to his ancestral castle of Ringstetten. Huldbrand, however, eventually wearies of his wife's supernatural affiliations, and especially of the appearances of her uncle, the malicious woodland waterfall-spirit Kühleborn; a weariness increased by his growing affection for Bertalda, who turns out to be the fisherman's child for whom Undine was exchanged. At length, on a voyage down the Danube, he is provoked by some innocent act of his devoted wife to utter the angry words which consign her back to her supernatural element; from which she can, by the laws of her species, return only once—to kill him, whether she will or no, if ever he prove unfaithful to her memory. Later, when Huldbrand is about to be married to Bertalda, Undine returns for her sad duty, and bears his life away in tears. When he is buried among his fathers in the village churchyard a veiled, snow-white female figure appears among the mourners, but after the prayer is seen no more. In her place is seen a little silver spring, which murmurs its way almost completely around the new grave, and empties into a neighbouring lake. The villagers shew it to this day, and say that Undine and her Huldbrand are thus united in death. Many passages and atmospheric touches in this tale reveal Fouqué as an accomplished artist in the field of the macabre; especially the descriptions of the haunted wood with its gigantic snow-white man and various unnamed terrors, which occur early in the narrative.

Not so well known as *Undine,* but remarkable for its convincing realism and freedom from Gothic stock devices, is the *Amber Witch* of Wilhelm Meinhold, another product of the German fantastic genius of the earlier nineteenth century. This tale, which is laid in the time of the Thirty Years' War, purports to be a clergyman's manuscript found in an old church at Coserow, and centres round the writer's daughter, Maria Schweidler, who is wrongly accused of witchcraft. She has found a deposit of amber which she keeps secret for various reasons, and the unexplained wealth obtained from this lends colour to the accusation; an accusation instigated by the malice of the wolf-hunting nobleman Wittich Appelmann, who has vainly pursued her with ignoble designs. The deeds of a real witch, who afterward comes to a horrible supernatural end in prison, are glibly imputed to the hapless Maria; and after a typical witchcraft trial with forced confessions under torture she is about to be burned at the stake when saved just in time by her lover, a noble youth from a neighbouring district. Meinhold's great strength is in his air of casual and realistic verisimilitude, which intensifies our suspense and sense of the unseen by half persuading us that the menacing events must somehow be either the truth or very close to the truth. Indeed, so thorough is this realism that a popular magazine once published the main points of *The Amber Witch* as an actual occurrence of the seventeenth century![48]

[In the present generation German horror-fiction is most notably represented by Hanns Heinz Ewers, who brings to bear on his dark conceptions an effective knowledge of modern psychology. Novels like *The Sorcerer's Apprentice* and *Alraune,* and short stories like "The Spider",[49] contain distinctive qualities which raise them to a classic level.]

But France as well as Germany has been active in the realm of weirdness. Victor Hugo, in such tales as *Hans of Iceland,* and Balzac, in *The Wild Ass's Skin, Séraphîta,* and *Louis Lambert,* both employ supernaturalism to a greater or less extent; though generally only as a means to some more human end, and without the sincere and daemonic intensity which characterises the born artist in shadows. It is in Théophile Gautier that we first seem to find an authentic French sense of the unreal world, and here there appears a spectral mastery which, though not continuously used, is recognisable at once as something alike genuine and profound. Short tales like "Avatar", "The Foot of the Mummy", and "Clarimonde" display glimpses of forbidden visits that allure, tantalise, and sometimes horrify; whilst the Egyptian visions evoked in "One of Cleopatra's Nights" are of the keenest and most expressive potency. Gautier captured the inmost soul of aeon-weighted Egypt, with its cryptic life and Cyclopean architecture, and uttered once and for all the eternal horror of its nether world of catacombs, where to the end of time millions of stiff, spiced corpses will stare up in the blackness with glassy eyes, awaiting some awesome and unrelatable summons.[50] Gustave Flaubert ably continued the tradition of Gautier in orgies of poetic phantasy like *The Temptation of St. Anthony,* and but for a strong realistic bias might have been an arch-weaver of tapestried terrors. Later on we see the stream divide, producing strange poets and fantaisistes of the Symbolist and Decadent schools whose dark interests really centre more in abnormalities of human thought and instinct than in the actual supernatural, and subtle story-tellers whose thrills are quite directly derived from the night-black wells of cosmic unreality. Of the former class of "artists in sin" the illustrious poet Baudelaire, influenced vastly by Poe, is the supreme type; whilst the psychological novelist Joris-Karl Huysmans, a true child of the eighteen-nineties, is at once the summation and finale. The latter and purely narrative class is continued by Prosper Mérimée, whose "Venus of Ille" presents in terse and convincing prose the same ancient statue-bride theme which Thomas Moore cast in ballad form in "The Ring".

The horror-tales of the powerful and cynical Guy de Maupassant, written as his final madness gradually overtook him, present individualities of their own; being rather the morbid outpourings of a realistic mind in a pathological state than the healthy imaginative products of a vision naturally disposed toward phantasy and sensitive to the normal illusions of the unseen. Nevertheless they are of the keenest interest and poignancy; suggesting with marvellous force the imminence of nameless terrors, and the relentless dogging of an ill-starred individual by hideous and menacing representatives of the outer blackness. Of these stories "The Horla" is generally regarded as the masterpiece. Relating the advent to France of an invisible being who lives on water and milk, sways the minds of others, and seems to be the vanguard of a horde of extra-terrestrial organisms arrived on earth to subjugate and overwhelm mankind,[51] this tense narrative is perhaps without a peer in its particular department; notwithstanding its indebtedness to a tale by the American Fitz-James O'Brien[52] for details in describing the actual presence of the unseen monster. Other potently dark creations of de Maupassant are "Who Knows?", "The Spectre", "He?", "The Diary of a Madman", "The White Wolf", "On the River", and the grisly verses entitled "Horror".

The collaborators Erckmann-Chatrian enriched French literature with many spectral fancies like The Man-Wolf, in which a transmitted curse works toward its end in a traditional Gothic-castle setting.[53] Their power of creating a shuddering midnight atmosphere was tremendous despite a tendency toward natural explanations and scientific wonders; and few short tales contain greater horror than "The Invisible Eye", where a malignant old hag weaves nocturnal hypnotic spells which induce the successive occupants of a certain inn chamber to hang themselves on a cross-beam. "The Owl's Ear" and "The Waters of Death" are full of engulfing darkness and mystery, the latter embodying the familiar overgrown-spider theme so frequently employed by weird fictionists. Villiers de l'Isle-Adam likewise followed the macabre school; his "Torture by Hope", the tale of a stake-condemned prisoner permitted to escape in order to feel the pangs of recapture, being held by some to constitute the most harrowing short story in literature. This type, however, is less a part of the weird tradition than a class peculiar to itself—the so-called conte cruel, in which the wrenching of the emotions is accomplished through dramatic tantalisations, frustrations, and gruesome physical horrors. Almost wholly devoted to this form is the living writer Maurice Level,[54] whose very brief episodes have lent themselves so readily to theatrical adaptation in the "thrillers" of the Grand Guignol. As a matter of fact, the French genius is more naturally suited to this dark realism than to the suggestion of the unseen; since the latter process requires, for its best and most sympathetic development on a large scale, the inherent mysticism of the Northern mind.

A very flourishing, though till recently quite hidden, branch of weird literature is that of the Jews, kept alive and nourished in obscurity by the sombre heritage of early Eastern magic, apocalyptic literature, and cabbalism. The Semitic mind, like the Celtic

and Teutonic, seems to possess marked mystical inclinations; and the wealth of under-
ground horror-lore surviving in ghettoes and synagogues must be much more considerable than is generally imagined. Cabbalism itself, so prominent during the Middle
Ages, is a system of philosophy explaining the universe as emanations of the Deity, and
involving the existence of strange spiritual realms and beings apart from the visible
world, of which dark glimpses may be obtained through certain secret incantations. Its
ritual is bound up with mystical interpretations of the Old Testament, and attributes
an esoteric significance to each letter of the Hebrew alphabet—a circumstance which
has imparted to Hebrew letters a sort of spectral glamour and potency in the popular
literature of magic. Jewish folklore has preserved much of the terror and mystery of the
past, and when more thoroughly studied is likely to exert considerable influence on
weird fiction. The best examples of its literary use so far are the German novel *The Golem*, by Gustav Meyrink, and the drama *The Dybbuk*, by the Jewish writer using the
pseudonym "Ansky". [The former, with its haunting shadowy suggestions of marvels
and horrors just beyond reach, is laid in Prague, and describes with singular mastery
that city's ancient ghetto with its spectral, peaked gables. The name is derived from a
fabulous artificial giant supposed to be made and animated by mediaeval rabbis according to a certain cryptic formula.[55]] *The Dybbuk*, translated and produced in America in
1925,[56] [and more recently produced as an opera,[57]] describes with singular power the
possession of a living body by the evil soul of a dead man. Both golems and dybbuks are
fixed types, and serve as frequent ingredients of later Jewish tradition.

VII. Edgar Allan Poe

In the eighteen-thirties occurred a literary dawn directly affecting not only the
history of the weird tale, but that of short fiction as a whole; and indirectly moulding
the trends and fortunes of a great European aesthetic school. It is our good fortune as
Americans to be able to claim that dawn as our own, for it came in the person of our
illustrious and unfortunate fellow-countryman Edgar Allan Poe. Poe's fame has been
subject to curious undulations, and it is now a fashion amongst the "advanced intelli-
gentsia" to minimise his importance both as an artist and as an influence; but it would
be hard for any mature and reflective critic to deny the tremendous value of his work
and the pervasive potency of his mind as an opener of artistic vistas. True, his type of
outlook may have been anticipated;[58] but it was he who first realised its possibilities
and gave it supreme form and systematic expression. True also, that subsequent writers
may have produced greater single tales than his;[59] but again we must comprehend that
it was only he who taught them by example and precept the art which they, having the
way cleared for them and given an explicit guide, were perhaps able to carry to greater
lengths. Whatever his limitations, Poe did that which no one else ever did or could
have done; and to him we owe the modern horror-story in its final and perfected state.

Before Poe the bulk of weird writers had worked largely in the dark; without an
understanding of the psychological basis of the horror appeal, and hampered by more
or less of conformity to certain empty literary conventions such as the happy ending,
virtue rewarded, and in general a hollow moral didacticism, acceptance of popular
standards and values, and striving of the author to obtrude his own emotions into the
story and take sides with the partisans of the majority's artificial ideas. Poe, on the
other hand, perceived the essential impersonality of the real artist; and knew that the
function of creative fiction is merely to express and interpret events and sensations as

they are, regardless of how they tend or what they prove—good or evil, attractive or repulsive, stimulating or depressing—with the author always acting as a vivid and detached chronicler rather than as a teacher, sympathiser, or vendor of opinion. He saw clearly that all phases of life and thought are equally eligible as subject-matter for the artist, and being inclined by temperament to strangeness and gloom, decided to be the interpreter of those powerful feeling, and frequent happenings which attend pain rather than pleasure, decay rather than growth, terror rather than tranquillity, and which are fundamentally either adverse or indifferent to the tastes and traditional outward sentiments of mankind, and to the health, sanity, and normal expansive welfare of the species.

Poe's spectres thus acquired a convincing malignity possessed by none of their predecessors, and established a new standard of realism in the annals of literary horror. The impersonal and artistic intent, moreover, was aided by a scientific attitude not often found before; whereby Poe studied the human mind rather than the usages of Gothic fiction, and worked with an analytical knowledge of terror's true sources which doubled the force of his narratives and emancipated him from all the absurdities inherent in merely conventional shudder-coining. This example having been set, later authors were naturally forced to conform to it in order to compete at all; so that in this way a definite change began to affect the main stream of macabre writing. Poe, too, set a fashion in consummate craftsmanship; and although today some of his own work seems slightly melodramatic and unsophisticated, we can constantly trace his influence in such things as the maintenance of a single mood and achievement of a single impression in a tale, and the rigorous paring down of incidents to such as have a direct bearing on the plot and will figure prominently in the climax. Truly may it be said that Poe invented the short story in its present form. His elevation of disease, perversity, and decay to the level of artistically expressible themes was likewise infinitely far-reaching in effect; for avidly seized, sponsored, and intensified by his eminent French admirer Charles Pierre Baudelaire, it became the nucleus of the principal aesthetic movements in France, thus making Poe in a sense the father of the Decadents and the Symbolists.

Poet and critic by nature and supreme attainment, logician and philosopher by taste and mannerism, Poe was by no means immune from defects and affectations. His pretence to profound and obscure scholarship, his blundering ventures in stilted and laboured pseudo-humour, and his often vitriolic outbursts of critical prejudice must all be recognised and forgiven. Beyond and above them, and dwarfing them to insignificance, was a master's vision of the terror that stalks about and within us, and the worm that writhes and slavers in the hideously close abyss. Penetrating to every festering horror in the gaily painted mockery called existence, and in the solemn masquerade called human thought and feelings that vision had power to project itself in blackly magical crystallisations and transmutations; till there bloomed in the sterile America of the 'thirties and 'forties such a moon-nourished garden of gorgeous poison fungi as not even the nether slope of Saturn might boast. Verses and tales alike sustain the burthen of cosmic panic. The raven whose noisome beak pierces the heart, the ghouls that toll iron bells in pestilential steeples, the vault of Ulalume in the black October night, the shocking spires and domes under the sea, the "wild, weird clime that lieth, sublime, out of Space—out of Time"[60]—all these things and more leer at us amidst maniacal rattlings in the seething nightmare of the poetry. And in the prose there yawn open for us the very jaws of the pit—inconceivable abnormalities slyly hinted into a horrible half-knowledge by words whose innocence we scarcely doubt till the cracked tension of the speaker's hollow voice bids us fear their nameless implications; daemoniac patterns and presences slumbering noxiously till waked for one phobic instant into a shrieking revelation that cackles itself to sudden madness or explodes in memorable and cataclysmic echoes. A Witches' Sabbath of horror flinging off decorous robes is flashed before us—a sight the more monstrous because of the scientific skill with which every particular is marshalled and brought into an easy apparent relation to the known gruesomeness of material life.

Poe's tales, of course, fall into several classes; some of which contain a purer essence of spiritual horror than others. The tales of logic and ratiocination, forerunners of the modern detective story, are not to be included at all in weird literature; whilst certain others, probably influenced considerably by Hoffmann, possess an extravagance which relegates them to the borderline of the grotesque. Still a third group deal with abnormal psychology and monomania in such a way as to express terror but not weirdness.[61] A substantial residuum, however, represent the literature of supernatural horror in its acutest form; and give their author a permanent and unassailable place as deity and fountain-head of all modern diabolic fiction. Who can forget the terrible swollen ship poised on the billow-chasm's edge in "MS. Found in a Bottle"—the dark intimations of her unhallowed age and monstrous growth, her sinister crew of unseeing greybeards, and her frightful southward rush under full sail through the ice of the Antarctic night, sucked onward by some resistless devil-current toward a vortex of eldritch enlightenment which must end in destruction? Then there is the unutterable "M. Valdemar",[62] kept together by hypnotism for seven months after his death, and uttering frantic sounds but a moment before the breaking of the spell leaves him "a nearly liquid mass of loathsome—of detestable putrescence".[63] In the *Narrative of A. Gordon Pym* the voyagers reach first a strange south polar land of murderous savages where nothing is white and where vast rocky ravines have the form of titanic Egyptian letters spelling terrible primal arcana of earth; and thereafter a still more mysterious realm where everything is white, and where shrouded giants and snowy-plumed birds guard a cryptic cataract of mist which empties from immeasurable celestial heights into a torrid milky sea.[64] "Metzengerstein" horrifies with its malign hints of a monstrous metempsychosis—the mad nobleman who burns the stable of his hereditary foe; the colossal unknown horse that issues from the blazing building after the owner has perished therein; the vanishing bit of ancient tapestry where was shewn the giant horse of the victim's ancestor in the Crusades; the madman's wild and constant riding on the great horse, and his fear and hatred of the steed; the meaningless prophecies that brood obscurely over the warring houses; and finally, the burning of the madman's palace and the death therein of the owner, borne helpless into the flames and up the vast staircases astride the beast he has ridden so strangely. Afterward the rising smoke of the ruins takes the form of a gigantic horse. "The Man of the Crowd", telling of one who roams day and night to mingle with streams of people as if afraid to be alone, has quieter effects, but implies nothing less of cosmic fear. Poe's mind was never far from terror and decay, and we see in every tale, poem, and philosophical dialogue a tense eagerness to fathom unplumbed wells of night, to pierce the veil of death, and to reign in fancy as lord of the frightful mysteries of time and space.

Certain of Poe's tales possess an almost absolute perfection of artistic form which makes them veritable beacon-lights in the province of the short story. Poe could, when he wished, give to his prose a richly poetic cast; employing that archaic and Orientalised style with jewelled phrase, quasi-Biblical repetition, and recurrent burthen so successfully used by later writers like Oscar Wilde and Lord Dunsany; and in the cases where he has done this we have an effect of lyrical phantasy almost narcotic in essence—an opium pageant of dream in the language of dream, with every unnatural colour and grotesque image bodied forth in a symphony of corresponding sound. "The Masque of the Red Death", "Silence—A Fable", and "Shadow—A Parable" are assuredly poems in every sense of the word save the metrical one, and owe as much of their power to aural cadence as to visual imagery. But it is in two of the less openly poetic tales, "Ligeia" and "The Fall of the House of Usher"—especially the latter—that one finds those very summits of art-istry whereby Poe takes his place at the head of fictional miniaturists. Simple and straightforward in plot, both of these tales owe their supreme magic to the cunning de-velopment which appears in the selection and collocation of every least incident. "Ligeia" tells of a first wife of lofty and mysterious origin, who after death returns through a pre-ternatural force of will to take possession of the body of a second wife; imposing even her physical appearance on the temporary reanimated corpse of her victim at the last mo-ment. Despite a suspicion of prolixity and topheaviness, the narrative reaches its terrific climax with relentless power. "Usher", whose superiority in detail and proportion is very marked, hints shudderingly of obscure life in inorganic things, and displays an abnormally linked trinity of entities at the end of a long and isolated family history—a brother, his twin sister, and their incredibly ancient house all sharing a single soul and meeting one common dissolution at the same moment.[65]

These bizarre conceptions, so awkward in unskilful hands, become under Poe's spell living and convincing terrors to haunt our nights; and all because the author un-derstood so perfectly the very mechanics and physiology of fear and strangeness—the essential details to emphasise, the precise incongruities and conceits to select as pre-liminaries or concomitants to horror, the exact incidents and allusions to throw out innocently in advance as symbols or prefigurings of each major step toward the hideous denouement to come, the nice adjustments of cumulative force and the unerring accu-racy in linkage of parts which make for faultless unity throughout and thunderous ef-fectiveness at the climactic moment, the delicate nuances of scenic and landscape value to select in establishing and sustaining the desired mood and vitalising the de-sired illusion—principles of this kind, and dozens of obscurer ones too elusive to be described or even fully comprehended by any ordinary commentator. Melodrama and unsophistication there may be—we are told of one fastidious Frenchman who could not bear to read Poe except in Baudelaire's urbane and Gallically modulated transla-tion[66]—but all traces of such things are wholly overshadowed by a potent and inborn sense of the spectral, the morbid, and the horrible which gushed forth from every cell of the artist's creative mentality and stamped his macabre work with the ineffaceable mark of supreme genius. Poe's weird tales are *alive* in a manner that few others can ever hope to be.

Like most fantaisistes, Poe excels in incidents and broad narrative effects rather than in character drawing. His typical protagonist is generally a dark, handsome, proud, melancholy, intellectual, highly sensitive, capricious, introspective, isolated, and sometimes slightly mad gentleman of ancient family and opulent circumstances; usually deeply learned in strange lore, and darkly ambitious of penetrating to forbidden secrets of the universe. Aside from a high-sounding name, this character obviously derives lit-tle from the early Gothic novel; for he is clearly neither the wooden hero nor the dia-bolical villain of Radcliffian or Ludovician[67] romance. Indirectly, however, he does possess a sort of genealogical connexion; since his gloomy, ambitious, and anti-social qualities savour strongly of the typical Byronic hero, who in turn is definitely an off-spring of the Gothic Manfreds, Montonis, and Ambrosios. More particular qualities appear to be derived from the psychology of Poe himself, who certainly possessed much of the depression, sensitiveness, mad aspiration, loneliness, and extravagant freakishness which he attributes to his haughty and solitary victims of Fate.

VIII. The Weird Tradition in America

The public for whom Poe wrote, though grossly unappreciative of his art, was by no means unaccustomed to the horrors with which he dealt. America, besides inheriting the usual dark folklore of Europe, had an additional fund of weird associations to draw upon; so that spectral legends had already been recognised as fruitful subject-matter for literature. Charles Brockden Brown had achieved phenomenal fame with his Radcliffian romances, and Washington Irving's lighter treatment of eerie themes had quickly become classic. This additional fund proceeded, as Paul Elmer More has pointed out,[68] from the keen spiritual and theological interests of the first colonists, plus the strange and forbidding nature of the scene into which they were plunged. The vast and gloomy virgin forests in whose perpetual twilight all terrors might well lurk; the hordes of coppery Indians whose strange, saturnine visages and violent customs hinted strongly at traces of infernal origin; the free rein given under the influence of Puritan theocracy to all manner of notions respecting man's relation to the stern and vengeful God of the Calvinists, and to the sulphureous Adversary of that God, about whom so much was thundered in the pulpits each Sunday; and the morbid introspection developed by an isolated backwoods life devoid of normal amusements and of the recreational mood, harassed by commands for theological self-examination, keyed to unnatural emotional repression, and forming above all a mere grim struggle for survival—all these things conspired to produce an environment in which the black whisperings of sinister grandams were heard far beyond the chimney corner, and in which tales of witchcraft and unbelievable secret monstrosities lingered long after the dread days of the Salem nightmare.

Poe represents the newer, more disillusioned, and more technically finished of the weird schools that rose out of this propitious milieu. Another school—the tradition of moral values, gentle restraint, and mild, leisurely phantasy tinged more or less with the whimsical—was represented by another famous, misunderstood, and lonely figure in American letters—the shy and sensitive Nathaniel Hawthorne, scion of antique Salem and great-grandson of one of the bloodiest of the old witchcraft judges.[69] In Hawthorne we have none of the violence, the daring, the high colouring, the intense dramatic sense, the cosmic malignity, and the undivided and impersonal artistry of Poe. Here, instead, is a gentle soul cramped by the Puritanism of early New England; shadowed and wistful, and grieved at an unmoral universe which everywhere transcends the conventional patterns thought by our forefathers to represent divine and immutable law. Evil, a very real force to Hawthorne, appears on every hand as a lurking and conquering adversary; and the visible world becomes in his fancy a theatre of infinite tragedy and woe, with unseen half-existent influences hovering over it and through it, battling for supremacy and moulding the destinies of the hapless mortals who form its vain and self-deluded population. The heritage of American weirdness was his to a most intense degree, and he saw a dismal throng of vague spectres behind the common phenomena of life; but he was not disinterested enough to value impressions, sensations, and beauties of narration for their own sake. He must needs weave his phantasy into some quietly melancholy fabric of didactic or allegorical cast, in which his meekly resigned cynicism may display with naive moral appraisal the perfidy of a human race which he cannot cease to cherish and mourn despite his insight into its hypocrisy. Supernatural horror, then, is never a primary object with Hawthorne; though its impulses were so deeply woven into his personality that he cannot help suggesting it with the force of genius when he calls upon the unreal world to illustrate the pensive sermon he wishes to preach.

Hawthorne's intimations of the weird, always gentle, elusive, and restrained, may be traced throughout his work. The mood that produced them found one delightful vent in the Teutonised retelling of classic myths for children contained in *A Wonder Book* and *Tanglewood Tales*,[70] and at other times exercised itself in casting a certain strangeness and intangible witchery or malevolence over events not meant to be actually supernatural; as in the macabre posthumous novel *Dr. Grimshawe's Secret,* which invests with a peculiar sort of repulsion a house existing to this day in Salem, and abutting on the ancient Charter Street Burying Ground. In *The Marble Faun,*[71] whose design was sketched out in an Italian villa reputed to be haunted, a tremendous background of genuine phantasy and mystery palpitates just beyond the common reader's sight; and glimpses of fabulous blood in mortal veins are hinted at during the course of a romance which cannot help being interesting despite the persistent incubus of moral allegory, anti-Popery propaganda, and a Puritan prudery which has caused the late D. H. Lawrence to express a longing to treat the author in a highly undignified manner.[72] *Septimius Felton,* a posthumous novel whose idea was to have been elaborated and incorporated into the unfinished *Dolliver Romance,* touches on the Elixir of Life in a more or less capable fashion; whilst the notes for a never-written tale to be called "The Ancestral Footstep" shew what Hawthorne would have done with an intensive treatment of an old English superstition—that of an ancient and accursed line whose members left footprints of blood as they walked—which appears incidentally in both *Septimius Felton* and *Dr. Grimshawe's Secret.*

Many of Hawthorne's shorter tales exhibit weirdness, either of atmosphere or of incident, to a remarkable degree. "Edward Randolph's Portrait", in *Legends of the Province House,* has its diabolic moments. "The Minister's Black Veil" (founded on an actual incident) and "The Ambitious Guest" imply much more than they state, whilst "Ethan Brand"—a fragment of a longer work never completed—rises to genuine heights of cosmic fear with its vignette of the wild hill country and the blazing, desolate lime-kilns, and its delineation of the Byronic "unpardonable sinner", whose troubled life ends with a peal of fearful laughter in the night as he seeks rest amidst the flames of the furnace. Some of Hawthorne's notes tell of weird tales he would have written had he lived longer—an especially vivid plot being that concerning a baffling stranger who appeared now and then in public assemblies, and who was at last followed and found to come and go from a very ancient grave.[73]

But foremost as a finished, artistic unit among all our author's weird material is the famous and exquisitely wrought novel, *The House of the Seven Gables,* in which the relentless working out of an ancestral curse is developed with astonishing power against the sinister background of a very ancient Salem house—one of those peaked Gothic affairs which formed the first regular building-up of our New England coast towns, but which gave way after the seventeenth century to the more familiar gambrel-roofed or classic Georgian types now known as "Colonial". Of these old gabled Gothic houses scarcely a dozen are to be seen today in their original condition throughout the United States, but one well known to Hawthorne still stands in Turner Street, Salem, and is pointed out with doubtful authority as the scene and inspiration of the romance. Such an edifice, with its spectral peaks, its clustered chimneys, its overhanging second story, its grotesque corner-brackets, and its diamond-paned lattice windows, is indeed an object well calculated to evoke sombre reflections; typifying as it does the dark Puritan age of concealed horror and witch-whispers which preceded the beauty, rationality, and spaciousness of the eighteenth century. Hawthorne saw many in his youth, and knew the black tales connected with some of them. He heard, too, many rumours of a curse upon his own line as the result of his great-grandfather's severity as a witchcraft judge in 1692.

From this setting came the immortal tale—New England's greatest contribution to weird literature—and we can feel in an instant the authenticity of the atmosphere presented to us. Stealthy horror and disease lurk within the weather-blackened, moss-crusted, and elm-shadowed walls of the archaic dwelling so vividly displayed, and we grasp the brooding malignity of the place when we read that its builder—old Colonel Pyncheon—snatched the land with peculiar ruthlessness from its original settler, Matthew Maule, whom he condemned to the gallows as a wizard in the year of the panic. Maule died cursing old Pyncheon—"God will give him blood to drink"—and the waters of the old well on the seized land turned bitter. Maule's carpenter son consented to build the great gabled house for his father's triumphant enemy, but the old Colonel died strangely on the day of its dedication. Then followed generations of odd vicissitudes, with queer whispers about the dark powers of the Maules, and peculiar and sometimes terrible ends befalling the Pyncheons.

The overshadowing malevolence of the ancient house—almost as alive as Poe's House of Usher, though in a subtler way—pervades the tale as a recurrent motif pervades an operatic tragedy;[74] and when the main story is reached, we behold the modern Pyncheons in a pitiable state of decay. Poor old Hepzibah, the eccentric reduced gentlewoman; child-like, unfortunate Clifford, just released from undeserved imprisonment; sly and treacherous Judge Pyncheon, who is the old Colonel all over again—all these figures are tremendous symbols, and are well matched by the stunted vegetation and anaemic fowls in the garden. It was almost a pity to supply a fairly happy ending, with a union of sprightly Phoebe, cousin and last scion of the Pyncheons, to the prepossessing young man who turns out to be the last of the Maules. This union, presumably, ends the curse. Hawthorne avoids all violence of diction or movement, and keeps his implications of terror well in the background; but occasional glimpses amply serve to sustain the mood and redeem the work from pure allegorical aridity. Incidents like the bewitching of Alice Pyncheon in the early eighteenth century, and the spectral music of her harpsichord which precedes a death in the family—the latter a variant of an immemorial type of Aryan myth—link the action directly with the supernatural; whilst the dead nocturnal vigil of old Judge Pyncheon in the ancient parlour, with his frightfully ticking watch, is stark horror of the most poignant and genuine sort. The way in which the Judge's death is first adumbrated by the motions and sniffing of a strange cat outside the window, long before the fact is suspected either by the reader or by any of the characters, is a stroke of genius which Poe could not have surpassed. Later the strange cat watches intently outside that same window in the night and on the next day, for—something. It is clearly the psychopomp of primeval myth, fitted and adapted with infinite deftness to its latter-day setting.

But Hawthorne left no well-defined literary posterity. His mood and attitude belonged to the age which closed with him, and it is the spirit of Poe—who so clearly and realistically understood the natural basis of the horror-appeal and the correct mechanics of its achievement—which survived and blossomed. Among the earliest of Poe's disciples may be reckoned the brilliant young Irishman Fitz-James O'Brien (1828–1862), who became naturalised as an American and perished honourably in the Civil

War. It is he who gave us "What Was It?", the first well-shaped short story of a tangible but invisible being, and the prototype of de Maupassant's "Horla"; he also who created the inimitable "Diamond Lens", in which a young microscopist falls in love with a maiden of an infinitesimal world which he has discovered in a drop of water. O'Brien's early death undoubtedly deprived us of some masterful tales of strangeness and terror, though his genius was not, properly speaking, of the same titan quality which characterised Poe and Hawthorne.

Closer to real greatness was the eccentric and saturnine journalist Ambrose Bierce,[75] born in 1842; who likewise entered the Civil War, but survived to write some immortal tales and to disappear in 1913 in as great a cloud of mystery as any he ever evoked from his nightmare fancy. Bierce was a satirist and pamphleteer of note, but the bulk of his artistic reputation must rest upon his grim and savage short stories; a large number of which deal with the Civil War and form the most vivid and realistic expression which that conflict has yet received in fiction. Virtually all of Bierce's tales are tales of horror; and whilst many of them treat only of the physical and psychological horrors within Nature, a substantial proportion admit the malignly supernatural and form a leading element in America's fund of weird literature. Mr. Samuel Loveman, a living poet and critic who was personally acquainted with Bierce, thus sums up the genius of the great shadow-maker in the preface to some of his letters:

> "In Bierce, the evocation of horror becomes for the first time, not so much the prescription or perversion of Poe and Maupassant, but an atmosphere definite and uncannily precise. Words, so simple that one would be prone to ascribe them to the limitations of a literary hack, take on an unholy horror, a new and unguessed transformation. In Poe one finds it a *tour de force*, in Maupassant a nervous engagement of the flagellated climax. To Bierce, simply and sincerely, diabolism held in its tormented depth, a legitimate and reliant means to the end. Yet a tacit confirmation with Nature is in every instance insisted upon.
>
> "In 'The Death of Halpin Frayser', flowers, verdure, and the boughs and leaves of trees are magnificently placed as an opposing foil to unnatural malignity. Not the accustomed golden world, but a world pervaded with the mystery of blue and the breathless recalcitrance of dreams, is Bierce's. Yet, curiously, inhumanity is not altogether absent."[76]

The "inhumanity" mentioned by Mr. Loveman finds vent in a rare strain of sardonic comedy and graveyard humour, and a kind of delight in images of cruelty and tantalising disappointment. The former quality is well illustrated by some of the subtitles in the darker narratives; such as "One does not always eat what is on the table", describing a body laid out for a coroner's inquest, and "A man though naked may be in rags", referring to a frightfully mangled corpse.[77]

Bierce's work is in general somewhat uneven. Many of the stories are obviously mechanical, and marred by a jaunty and commonplacely artificial style derived from journalistic models; but the grim malevolence stalking through all of them is unmistakable, and several stand out as permanent mountain-peaks of American weird writing. "The Death of Halpin Frayser", called by Frederic Taber Cooper the most fiendishly ghastly tale in the literature of the Anglo-Saxon race,[78] tells of a body skulking by night without a soul in a weird and horribly ensanguined wood, and of a man beset by ancestral memories who met death at the claws of that which had been his fervently loved mother. "The Damned Thing", frequently copied in popular anthologies, chronicles the hideous devastations of an invisible entity that waddles and flounders on the hills and in the wheatfields by night and day. "The Suitable Surroundings" evokes with singular subtlety yet apparent simplicity a piercing sense of the terror which may reside in the written word. In the story the weird author Colston says to his friend Marsh, "You are brave enough to read me in a street-car, but—in a deserted house—alone—in the forest—at night! Bah! I have a manuscript in my pocket that would kill you!" Marsh reads the manuscript in "the suitable surroundings"—and it does kill him. "The Middle Toe of the Right Foot" is clumsily developed, but has a powerful climax. A man named Manton[79] has horribly killed his two children and his wife, the latter of whom lacked the middle toe of the right foot. Ten years later he returns much altered to the neighbourhood; and, being secretly recognised, is provoked into a bowie-knife duel in the dark, to be held in the now abandoned house where his crime was committed. When the moment of the duel arrives a trick is played upon him; and he is left without an antagonist, shut in a night-black ground floor room of the reputedly haunted edifice, with the thick dust of a decade on every hand. No knife is drawn against him, for only a thorough scare is intended; but on the next day he is found crouched in a corner with distorted face, dead of sheer fright at something he has seen. The only clue visible to the discoverers is one having terrible implications: "In the dust of years that lay thick upon the floor— leading from the door by which they had entered, straight across the room to within a yard of Manton's crouching corpse—were three parallel lines of footprints—light but definite impressions of bare feet, the outer ones those of small children, the inner a woman's. From the point at which they ended they did not return; they pointed all one way." And, of course, the woman's prints shewed a lack of the middle toe of the right foot. "The Spook House", told with a severely homely air of journalistic verisimilitude, conveys terrible hints of shocking mystery. In 1858 an entire family of seven persons disappears suddenly and unaccountably from a plantation house in eastern Kentucky, leaving all its possessions untouched—furniture, clothing, food supplies, horses, cattle, and slaves. About a year later two men of high standing are forced by a storm to take shelter in the deserted dwelling, and in so doing stumble into a strange subterranean room lit by an unaccountable greenish light and having an iron door which cannot be opened from within. In this room lie the decayed corpses of all the missing family; and as one of the discoverers rushes forward to embrace a body he seems to recognise, the other is so overpowered by a strange foetor that he accidentally shuts his companion in the vault and loses consciousness. Recovering his senses six weeks later, the survivor is unable to find the hidden room; and the house is burned during the Civil War. The imprisoned discoverer is never seen or heard of again.

Bierce seldom realises the atmospheric possibilities of his themes as vividly as Poe; and much of his work contains a certain touch of naiveté, prosaic angularity, or early-American provincialism which contrasts somewhat with the efforts of later horror-masters. Nevertheless the genuineness and artistry of his dark intimations are always unmistakable, so that his greatness is in no danger of eclipse. As arranged in his definitively collected works, Bierce's weird tales occur mainly in two volumes, *Can Such Things Be?* and *In the Midst of Life*. The former, indeed, is almost wholly given over to the supernatural.

Much of the best in American horror-literature has come from pens not mainly devoted to that medium. Oliver Wendell Holmes's historic *Elsie Venner*[80] suggests with admirable restraint an unnatural ophidian element in a young woman pre-natally influenced, and sustains the atmosphere with finely discriminating landscape touches. In *The Turn of the Screw* Henry James triumphs over his inevitable pomposity and prolixity sufficiently well to create a truly potent air of sinister menace; depicting the hideous influence of two dead and evil servants, Peter Quint and the governess Miss Jessel, over a small boy and girl who had been under their care. James is perhaps too diffuse, too unctuously urbane, and too much addicted to subtleties of speech to realise fully all the wild and devastating horror in his situations; but for all that there is a rare and mounting tide of fright, culminating in the death of the little boy, which gives the novelette a permanent place in its special class.

F. Marion Crawford produced several weird tales of varying quality, now collected in a volume entitled *Wandering Ghosts*.[81] "For the Blood Is the Life" touches powerfully on a case of moon-cursed vampirism near an ancient tower on the rocks of the lonely South Italian sea-coast. "The Dead Smile" treats of family horrors in an old house and an ancestral vault in Ireland, and introduces the banshee with considerable force. "The Upper Berth", however, is Crawford's weird masterpiece; and is one of the most tremendous horror-stories in all literature. In this tale of a suicide-haunted stateroom such things as the spectral salt-water dampness, the strangely open porthole, and the nightmare struggle with the nameless object are handled with incomparable dexterity.

Very genuine, though not without the typical mannered extravagance of the eighteen-nineties, is the strain of horror in the early work of Robert W. Chambers, since renowned for products of a very different quality.[82] *The King in Yellow*, a series of vaguely connected short stories having as a background a monstrous and suppressed book whose perusal brings fright, madness, and spectral tragedy, really achieves notable heights of cosmic fear in spite of uneven interest and a somewhat trivial and affected cultivation of the Gallic studio atmosphere made popular by Du Maurier's *Trilby*. The most powerful of its tales, perhaps, is "The Yellow Sign", in which is introduced a silent and terrible churchyard watchman with a face like a puffy grave-worm's. A boy, describing a tussle he has had with this creature, shivers and sickens as he relates a certain detail. "Well, sir, it's Gawd's truth that when I 'it 'im 'e grabbed me wrists, sir, and when I twisted 'is soft, mushy fist one of 'is fingers come off in me 'and." An artist, who after seeing him has shared with another a strange dream of a nocturnal hearse, is shocked by the voice with which the watchman accosts him. The fellow emits a muttering sound that fills the head like thick oily smoke from a fat-rendering vat or an odour of noisome decay. What he mumbles is merely this: "Have you found the Yellow Sign?"

A weirdly hieroglyphed onyx talisman, picked up in the street by the sharer of his dream, is shortly given the artist; and after stumbling queerly upon the hellish and forbidden book of horrors the two learn, among other hideous things which no sane mortal should know, that this talisman is indeed the nameless Yellow Sign handed down from the accursed cult of Hastur—from primordial Carcosa, whereof the volume treats, and some nightmare memory of which seems to lurk latent and ominous at the back of all men's minds. Soon they hear the rumbling of the black-plumed hearse driven by the flabby and corpse-faced watchman. He enters the night-shrouded house in quest of the Yellow Sign, all bolts and bars rotting at his touch. And when the people rush in, drawn by a scream that no human throat could utter, they find three forms on the floor—two dead and one dying. One of the dead shapes is far gone in decay. It is the churchyard watchman, and the doctor exclaims, "That man must have been dead for months." It is worth observing that the author derives most of the names and allusions connected with his eldritch land of primal memory from the tales of Ambrose Bierce. Other early works of Mr. Chambers displaying the outré and macabre element are *The Maker of Moons* and *In Search of the Unknown*. One cannot help regretting that he did not further develop a vein in which he could so easily have become a recognised master.[83]

Horror material of authentic force may be found in the work of the New England realist Mary E. Wilkins; whose volume of short tales, *The Wind in the Rose-Bush,* contains a number of noteworthy achievements. In "The Shadows on the Wall" we are shewn with consummate skill the response of a staid New England household to uncanny tragedy; and the sourceless shadow of the poisoned brother well prepares us for the climactic moment when the shadow of the secret murderer, who has killed himself in a neighbouring city, suddenly appears beside it. Charlotte Perkins Gilman, in "The Yellow Wall Paper", rises to a classic level in subtly delineating the madness which crawls over a woman dwelling in the hideously papered room where a madwoman was once confined.

[In "The Dead Valley" the eminent architect and mediaevalist Ralph Adams Cram achieves a memorably potent degree of vague regional horror through subtleties of atmosphere and description.[84]]

Still further carrying on our spectral tradition is the gifted and versatile humourist Irvin S. Cobb, whose work both early and recent contains some finely weird specimens. "Fishhead",[85] an early achievement, is banefully effective in its portrayal of unnatural affinities between a hybrid idiot and the strange fish of an isolated lake, which at the last avenge their biped kinsman's murder. Later work of Mr. Cobb introduces an element of possible science, as in the tale of hereditary memory where a modern man with a negroid strain utters words in African jungle speech when run down by a train under visual and aural circumstances recalling the maiming of his black ancestor by a rhinoceros a century before.[86]

[Extremely high in artistic stature is the novel *The Dark Chamber* (1927), by the late Leonard Cline. This is the tale of a man who—with the characteristic ambition of the Gothic or Byronic hero-villain—seeks to defy Nature and recapture every moment of his past life through the abnormal stimulation of memory. To this end he employs endless notes, records, mnemonic objects, and pictures—and finally odours, music, and exotic drugs. At last his ambition goes beyond his personal life and reaches toward the black abysses of *hereditary* memory—even back to pre-human days amidst the steaming swamps of the Carboniferous age, and to still more unimaginable deeps of primal time and entity. He calls for madder music and takes stronger drugs, and finally his great dog grows oddly afraid of him. A noxious animal stench encompasses him, and he grows vacant-faced and sub-human. In the end he takes to the woods, howling at night beneath windows. He is finally found in a thicket, mangled to death. Beside him is the mangled corpse of his dog. They have killed each other. The atmosphere of this novel is malevolently potent, much attention being paid to the central figure's sinister home and household.

A less subtle and well-balanced but nevertheless highly effective creation is Herbert S. Gorman's novel, *The Place Called Dagon,* which relates the dark history of a western Massachusetts backwater where the descendants of refugees from the Salem witchcraft still keep alive the morbid and degenerate horrors of the Black Sabbat.[87]

Sinister House, by Leland Hall, has touches of magnificent atmosphere but is marred by a somewhat mediocre romanticism.

Very notable in their way are some of the weird conceptions of the novelist and short-story writer Edward Lucas White, most of whose themes arise from actual dreams. "The Song of the Sirens" has a very pervasive strangeness, while such things as "Lukundoo" and "The Snout" rouse darker apprehensions. Mr. White imparts a very peculiar quality to his tales—an oblique sort of glamour which has its own distinctive type of convincingness.]

Of younger Americans, none strikes the note of cosmic terror so well as the California poet, artist, and fictionist Clark Ashton Smith, whose bizarre writings, drawings, paintings, and stories are the delight of a sensitive few. Mr. Smith has for his background a universe of remote and paralysing fright—jungles of poisonous and iridescent blossoms on the moons of Saturn, evil and grotesque temples in Atlantis, Lemuria, and forgotten elder worlds, and dank morasses of spotted death-fungi in spectral countries beyond earth's rim. His longest and most ambitious poem, *The Hashish-Eater,* is in pentameter blank verse; and opens up chaotic and incredible vistas of kaleidoscopic nightmare in the spaces between the stars. In sheer daemonic strangeness and fertility of conception, Mr. Smith is perhaps unexcelled by any other writer dead or living. Who else has seen such gorgeous, luxuriant, and feverishly distorted visions of infinite spheres and multiple dimensions and lived to tell the tale? [His short stories deal powerfully with other galaxies, worlds, and dimensions, as well as with strange regions and aeons on the earth. He tells of primal Hyperborea and its black amorphous god Tsathoggua; of the lost continent Zothique, and of the fabulous, vampire-curst land of Averoigne in mediaeval France. Some of Mr. Smith's best work can be found in the brochure entitled *The Double Shadow and Other Fantasies* (1933).]

IX. The Weird Tradition in the British Isles

Recent British literature, besides including the three or four greatest fantaisistes of the present age, has been gratifyingly fertile in the element of the weird. Rudyard Kipling has often approached it; and has, despite the omnipresent mannerisms, handled it with indubitable mastery in such tales as "The Phantom 'Rickshaw", "'The Finest Story in the World'", "The Recrudescence of Imray", and "The Mark of the Beast". This latter is of particular poignancy; the pictures of the naked leper-priest who mewed like an otter, of the spots which appeared on the chest of the man that priest cursed, of the growing carnivorousness of the victim and of the fear which horses began to display toward him, and of the eventually half-accomplished transformation of that victim into a leopard, being things which no reader is ever likely to forget. The final defeat of the malignant sorcery does not impair the force of the tale or the validity of its mystery.

Lafcadio Hearn, strange, wandering, and exotic, departs still farther from the realm of the real; and with the supreme artistry of a sensitive poet weaves phantasies impossible to an author of the solid roast-beef type. His *Fantastics,* written in America, contains some of the most impressive ghoulishness in all literature; whilst his *Kwaidan,* written in Japan, crystallises with matchless skill and delicacy the eerie lore and whispered legends of that richly colourful nation. Still more of Hearn's weird wizardry of language is shewn in some of his translations from the French, especially from Gautier and Flaubert.[88] His version of the latter's *Temptation of St. Anthony* is a classic of fevered and riotous imagery clad in the magic of singing words.

Oscar Wilde may likewise be given a place amongst weird writers, both for certain of his exquisite fairy tales, and for his vivid *Picture of Dorian Gray,* in which a marvellous portrait for years assumes the duty of ageing and coarsening instead of its original, who meanwhile plunges into every excess of vice and crime without the outward loss of youth, beauty, and freshness. There is a sudden and potent climax when Dorian Gray, at last become a murderer, seeks to destroy the painting whose changes testify to his moral degeneracy. He stabs it with a knife, and a hideous cry and crash are heard; but when the servants enter they find it in all its pristine loveliness. "Lying on the floor was a dead man, in evening dress, with a knife in his heart. He was withered, wrinkled, and loathsome of visage. It was not till they had examined the rings that they recognised who it was."

Matthew Phipps Shiel, author of many weird, grotesque, and adventurous novels and tales, occasionally attains a high level of horrific magic. "Xélucha" is a noxiously hideous fragment, but is excelled by Mr. Shiel's undoubted masterpiece, "The House of Sounds",[89] floridly written in the "yellow 'nineties", and re-cast with more artistic restraint in the early twentieth century.[90] This story, in final form, deserves a place among the foremost things of its kind. It tells of a creeping horror and menace trickling down the centuries on a sub-arctic island off the coast of Norway; where, amidst the sweep of daemon winds and the ceaseless din of hellish waves and cataracts, a vengeful dead man built a brazen tower of terror. It is vaguely like, yet infinitely unlike, Poe's "Fall of the House of Usher".[91] [In the novel *The Purple Cloud* Mr. Shiel describes with tremendous power a curse which came out of the arctic to destroy mankind, and which for a time appears to have left but a single inhabitant on our planet. The sensations of this lone survivor as he realises his position, and roams through the corpse-littered and treasure-strown cities of the world as their absolute master, are delivered with a skill and artistry falling little short of actual majesty. Unfortunately the second half of the book, with its conventionally romantic element, involves a distinct "letdown".]

Better known than Shiel is the ingenious Bram Stoker, who created many starkly horrific conceptions in a series of novels whose poor technique sadly impairs their net effect. *The Lair of the White Worm,* dealing with a gigantic primitive entity that lurks in a vault beneath an ancient castle, utterly ruins a magnificent idea by a development almost infantile.[92] *The Jewel of Seven Stars,* touching on a strange Egyptian resurrection, is less crudely written. But best of all is the famous *Dracula,* which has become almost the standard modern exploitation of the frightful vampire myth. Count Dracula, a vampire, dwells in a horrible castle in the Carpathians; but finally migrates to England with the design of populating the country with fellow vampires. How an Englishman fares within Dracula's stronghold of terrors, and how the dead fiend's plot for domination is at last defeated, are elements which unite to form a tale now justly assigned a permanent place in English letters. *Dracula* evoked many similar novels of supernatural horror, among which the best are perhaps *The Beetle,* by Richard Marsh,[93] *Brood of the Witch-Queen,* by "Sax Rohmer" (Arthur Sarsfield Ward), and *The Door of the Unreal,* by Gerald Biss. The latter handles quite dexterously the standard werewolf superstition. Much subtler and more artistic, and told with singular skill through the juxtaposed narratives of the several characters, is the novel *Cold Harbour,* by Francis Brett Young, in which an ancient house of strange malignancy is powerfully delineated. The mocking and well-nigh omnipotent fiend Humphrey Furnival holds echoes of the Manfred-Montoni type of early Gothic "villain", but is redeemed from triteness by many clever individualities. Only the slight diffuseness of explanation at the close, and the somewhat too free use of divination as a plot factor, keep this tale from approaching absolute perfection.

[In the novel *Witch Wood* John Buchan depicts with tremendous force a survival of the evil Sabbat in a lonely district of Scotland. The description of the black forest with the evil stone, and of the terrible cosmic adumbrations when the horror is finally extirpated, will repay one for wading through the very gradual action and plethora of Scottish dialect. Some of Mr. Buchan's short stories[94] are also extremely vivid in their spectral intimations; "The Green Wildebeest", a tale of African witchcraft, "The Wind in the Portico", with its awakening of dead Britanno-Roman horrors, and "Skule Skerry", with its touches of sub-arctic fright, being especially remarkable.]

Clemence Housman, in the brief novelette "The Were-wolf", attains a high degree of gruesome tension and achieves to some extent the atmosphere of authentic folklore. [In *The Elixir of Life* Arthur Ransome attains some darkly excellent effects despite a general naiveté of plot, while H. B. Drake's *The Shadowy Thing* summons up strange and terrible vistas.[95] George Macdonald's *Lilith* has a compelling bizarrerie all its own; the first and simpler of the two versions being perhaps the more effective.[96]]

Deserving of distinguished notice as a forceful craftsman to whom an unseen mystic world is ever a close and vital reality is the poet Walter de la Mare,[97] whose haunting verse and exquisite prose alike bear consistent traces of a strange vision reaching deeply into veiled spheres of beauty and terrible and forbidden dimensions of being. In the novel *The Return* we see the soul of a dead man reach out of its grave of two centuries and fasten itself upon the flesh of the living, so that even the face of the victim becomes that which had long ago returned to dust.[98] Of the shorter tales, of which several volumes exist, many are unforgettable for their command of fear's and sorcery's darkest ramifications; notably "Seaton's Aunt", in which there lowers a noxious background of malignant vampirism; "The Tree", which tells of a frightful vegetable growth in the yard of a starving artist; "Out of the Deep", wherein we are given leave to imagine what thing answered the summons of a dying wastrel in a dark lonely house when he pulled a long-feared bell-cord in the attic chamber of his dread-haunted boyhood; ["A Recluse", which hints at what sent a chance guest flying from a house in the night;] "Mr. Kempe", which shews us a mad clerical hermit in quest of the human soul, dwelling in a frightful sea-cliff region beside an archaic abandoned chapel; and "All-Hallows", a glimpse of daemoniac forces besieging a lonely mediaeval church and miraculously restoring the rotting masonry. De la Mare does not make fear the sole or even the dominant element of most of his tales, being apparently more interested in the subtleties of character involved. Occasionally he sinks to sheer whimsical phantasy of the Barrie order. Still, he is among the very few to whom unreality is a vivid, living presence; and as such he is able to put into his occasional fear-studies a keen potency which only a rare master can achieve. His poem "The Listeners" restores the Gothic shudder to modern verse.

The weird short story has fared well of late, an important contributor being the versatile E. F. Benson, whose "The Man Who Went Too Far" breathes whisperingly of a house at the edge of a dark wood, and of Pan's hoof-mark on the breast of a dead man. Mr. Benson's volume, *Visible and Invisible*, contains several stories of singular power; notably "Negotium Perambulans", whose unfolding reveals an abnormal monster from an ancient ecclesiastical panel which performs an act of miraculous vengeance in a lonely village on the Cornish coast, and "The Horror-Horn", through which lopes a terrible half-human survival dwelling on unvisited Alpine peaks. ["The Face", in another collection,[99] is lethally potent in its relentless aura of doom. H. R. Wakefield, in his collections *They Return at Evening* and *Others Who Return*, manages now and then to achieve great heights of horror despite a vitiating air of sophistication. The most notable stories are "The Red Lodge" with its slimy aqueous evil, "'He Cometh and He Passeth By'", "'And He Shall Sing . . .'", "The Cairn", "'Look Up There!'", "Blind Man's Buff", and that bit of lurking millennial horror, "The Seventeenth Hole at Duncaster". Mention has been made of the weird work of H. G. Wells and A. Conan Doyle. The former, in "The Ghost of Fear",[100] reaches a very high level; while all the items in *Thirty Strange Stories* have strong fantastic implications. Doyle now and then struck a powerfully spectral note, as in "The Captain of the 'Pole-Star'", a tale of arctic ghostliness, and "Lot No. 249", wherein the reanimated mummy theme is used with more than ordinary skill.

Hugh Walpole, of the same family as the founder of Gothic fiction, has sometimes approached the bizarre with much success; his short story "Mrs. Lunt" carrying a very poignant shudder.] John Metcalfe, in the collection published as *The Smoking Leg*, attains now and then a rare pitch of potency; the tale entitled "The Bad Lands" containing graduations of horror that strongly savour of genius. More whimsical and inclined toward the amiable and innocuous phantasy of Sir J. M. Barrie are the short tales of E. M. Forster, grouped under the title of *The Celestial Omnibus*. Of these only one, dealing with a glimpse of Pan and his aura of fright, may be said to hold the true element of cosmic horror. [Mrs. H. D. Everett, though adhering to very old and conventional models, occasionally reaches singular heights of spiritual terror in her collection of short stories. L. P. Hartley is notable for his incisive and extremely ghastly tale, "A Visitor from Down Under".] May Sinclair's *Uncanny Stories* contain more of traditional occultism than of that creative treatment of fear which marks mastery in this field, and are inclined to lay more stress on human emotions and psychological delving than upon the stark phenomena of a cosmos utterly unreal. It may be well to remark here that occult believers are probably less effective than materialists in delineating the spectral and the fantastic, since to them the phantom world is so commonplace a reality that they tend to refer to it with less awe, remoteness, and impressiveness than do those who see in it an absolute and stupendous violation of the natural order.

[Of rather uneven stylistic quality, but vast occasional power in its suggestion of lurking worlds and beings behind the ordinary surface of life, is the work of William Hope Hodgson, known today far less than it deserves to be.[101] Despite a tendency toward conventionally sentimental conceptions of the universe, and of man's relation to it and to his fellows, Mr. Hodgson is perhaps second only to Algernon Blackwood in his serious treatment of unreality. Few can equal him in adumbrating the nearness of nameless forces and monstrous besieging entities through casual hints and insignificant details, or in conveying feelings of the spectral and the abnormal in connexion with regions or buildings.

In *The Boats of the "Glen Carrig"* (1907) we are shewn a variety of malign marvels and accursed unknown lands as encountered by the survivors of a sunken ship. The brooding menace in the earlier parts of the book is impossible to surpass, though a letdown in the direction of ordinary romance and adventure occurs toward the end. An inaccurate and pseudo-romantic attempt to reproduce eighteenth-century prose detracts from the general effect, but the really profound nautical erudition everywhere displayed is a compensating factor.

The House on the Borderland (1908)—perhaps the greatest of all Mr. Hodgson's works—tells of a lonely and evilly regarded house in Ireland which forms a focus for hideous other-world forces and sustains a siege by blasphemous hybrid anomalies from a hidden abyss below. The wanderings of the narrator's spirit through limitless light-years of cosmic space and kalpas of eternity, and its witnessing of the solar system's final destruction, constitute something almost unique in standard literature. And everywhere there is manifest the author's power to suggest vague, ambushed horrors in natural scenery. But for a few touches of commonplace sentimentality this book would be a classic of the first water.

The Ghost Pirates (1909), regarded by Mr. Hodgson as rounding out a trilogy with the two previously mentioned works, is a powerful account of a doomed and haunted ship on its last voyage, and of the terrible sea-devils (of quasi-human aspect, and perhaps the spirits of bygone buccaneers) that besiege it and finally drag it down to an unknown fate. With its command of maritime knowledge, and its clever selection of hints and incidents suggestive of latent horrors in Nature, this book at times reaches enviable peaks of power.

The Night Land (1912) is a long-extended (583 pp.) tale of the earth's infinitely remote future—billions of billions of years ahead, after the death of the sun. It is told in a rather clumsy fashion, as the dreams of a man in the seventeenth century, whose mind merges with its own future incarnation; and is seriously marred by painful verboseness, repetitiousness, artificial and nauseously sticky romantic sentimentality, and an attempt at archaic language even more grotesque and absurd than that in *"Glen Carrig"*.

Allowing for all its faults, it is yet one of the most potent pieces of macabre imagination ever written. The picture of a night-black, dead planet, with the remains of the human race concentrated in a stupendously vast metal pyramid and besieged by monstrous, hybrid, and altogether unknown forces of the darkness, is something that no reader can ever forget. Shapes and entities of an altogether non-human and inconceivable sort—the prowlers of the black, man-forsaken, and unexplored world outside the pyramid—are *suggested* and *partly* described with ineffable potency; while the night-bound landscape with its chasms and slopes and dying volcanism takes on an almost sentient terror beneath the author's touch.

Midway in the book the central figure ventures outside the pyramid on a quest through death-haunted realms untrod by man for millions of years—and in his slow, minutely described, day-by-day progress over unthinkable leagues of immemorial blackness there is a sense of cosmic alienage, breathless mystery, and terrified expectancy unrivalled in the whole range of literature. The last quarter of the book drags woefully, but fails to spoil the tremendous power of the whole.

Mr. Hodgson's later volume, *Carnacki, the Ghost-Finder,* consists of several longish short stories published many years before in magazines. In quality it falls conspicuously below the level of the other books. We here find a more or less conventional stock figure of the "infallible detective" type—the progeny of M. Dupin and Sherlock Holmes, and the close kin of Algernon Blackwood's John Silence—moving through scenes and events badly marred by an atmosphere of professional "occultism". A few of the episodes, however, are of undeniable power; and afford glimpses of the peculiar genius characteristic of the author.]

Naturally it is impossible in a brief sketch to trace out all the classic modern uses of the terror element. The ingredient must of necessity enter into all work both prose and verse treating broadly of life; and we are therefore not surprised to find a share in such writers as the poet Browning, whose "Childe Roland to the Dark Tower Came" is instinct with hideous menace, or the novelist Joseph Conrad, who often wrote of the dark secrets within the sea, and of the daemoniac driving power of Fate as influencing the lives of lonely and maniacally resolute men.[102] Its trail is one of infinite ramifications; but we must here confine ourselves to its appearance in a relatively unmixed state, where it determines and dominates the work of art containing it.

Somewhat separate from the main British stream is that current of weirdness in Irish literature which came to the fore in the Celtic Renaissance of the later nineteenth and early twentieth centuries. Ghost and fairy lore have always been of great prominence in Ireland, and for over an hundred years have been recorded by a line of such faithful transcribers and translators as William Carleton, T. Crofton Croker, Lady Wilde—mother of Oscar Wilde—Douglas Hyde, and W. B. Yeats. Brought to notice by the modern movement, this body of myth has been carefully collected and studied; and its salient features reproduced in the work of later figures like Yeats, J. M. Synge, "A. E.", Lady Gregory, Padraic Colum, James Stephens, and their colleagues.

Whilst on the whole more whimsically fantastic than terrible, such folklore and its consciously artistic counterparts contain much that falls truly within the domain of cosmic horror. Tales of burials in sunken churches beneath haunted lakes, accounts of death-heralding banshees and sinister changelings, ballads of spectres and "the unholy creatures of the raths"—all these have their poignant and definite shivers, and mark a strong and distinctive element in weird literature. Despite homely grotesqueness and absolute naiveté, there is genuine nightmare in the class of narrative represented by the yarn of Teig O'Kane, who in punishment for his wild life was ridden all night by a hideous corpse that demanded burial and drove him from churchyard to churchyard as the dead rose up loathsomely in each one and refused to accommodate the newcomer with a berth. Yeats, undoubtedly the greatest figure of the Irish revival if not the greatest of all living poets, has accomplished notable things both in original work and in the codification of old legends.

X. The Modern Masters

The best horror-tales of today, profiting by the long evolution of the type, possess a naturalness, convincingness, artistic smoothness, and skilful intensity of appeal quite beyond comparison with anything in the Gothic work of a century or more ago. Technique, craftsmanship, experience, and psychological knowledge have advanced tremendously with the passing years, so that much of the older work seems naive and artificial; redeemed, when redeemed at all, only by a genius which conquers heavy limitations. The tone of jaunty and inflated romance, full of false motivation and investing every conceivable event with a counterfeit significance and carelessly inclusive glamour, is now confined to lighter and more whimsical phases of supernatural writing. Serious weird stories are either made realistically intense by close consistency and perfect fidelity to Nature except in the one supernatural direction which the author allows himself, or else cast altogether in the realm of phantasy, with atmosphere cunningly adapted to the visualisation of a delicately exotic world of unreality beyond space and time, in which almost anything may happen if it but happen in true accord with certain types of imagination and illusion normal to the sensitive human brain. This, at least, is the dominant tendency; though of course many great contemporary writers slip occasionally into some of the flashy postures of immature romanticism, or into bits of the equally empty and absurd jargon of pseudo-scientific "occultism", now at one of its periodic high tides.

Of living creators of cosmic fear raised to its most artistic pitch, few if any can hope to equal the versatile Arthur Machen;[103] author of some dozen tales long and short, in which the elements of hidden horror and brooding fright attain an almost incomparable substance and realistic acuteness. Mr. Machen, a general man of letters and master of an exquisitely lyrical and expressive prose style, has perhaps put more conscious effort into his picaresque *Chronicle of Clemendy,* his refreshing essays, his vivid autobiographical volumes,[104] his fresh and spirited translations,[105] and above all his memorable epic of the sensitive aesthetic mind, *The Hill of Dreams,* in which the youthful hero responds to the magic of that ancient Welsh environment which is the author's own, and lives a dream-life in the Roman city of Isca Silurum, now shrunk to the relic-strown village of Caerleon-on-Usk. But the fact remains that his powerful horror-material of the 'nineties and earlier nineteen-hundreds stands alone in its class, and marks a distinct epoch in the history of this literary form.

Mr. Machen, with an impressionable Celtic heritage linked to keen youthful memories of the wild domed hills, archaic forests, and cryptical Roman ruins of the Gwent countryside, has developed an imaginative life of rare beauty, intensity, and historic background. He has absorbed the mediaeval mystery of dark woods and ancient customs, and is a champion of the Middle Ages in all things—including the Catholic faith. He has yielded, likewise, to the spell of the Britanno-Roman life which once surged over his native region; and finds strange magic in the fortified camps, tessellated pavements, fragments of statues, and kindred things which tell of the day when classicism reigned and Latin was the language of the country. A young American poet, Frank Belknap Long, Jun., has well summarised this dreamer's rich endowments and wizardry of expression in the sonnet "On Reading Arthur Machen":

"There is a glory in the autumn wood;
The ancient lanes of England wind and climb
Past wizard oaks and gorse and tangled thyme
To where a fort of mighty empire stood:
There is a glamour in the autumn sky;
The reddened clouds are writhing in the glow
Of some great fire, and there are glints below
Of tawny yellow where the embers die.

I wait, for he will show me, clear and cold,
High-rais'd in splendour, sharp against the North,
The Roman eagles, and thro' mists of gold
The marching legions as they issue forth:
I wait, for I would share with him again
The ancient wisdom, and the ancient pain."[106]

Of Mr. Machen's horror-tales the most famous is perhaps "The Great God Pan" (1894), which tells of a singular and terrible experiment and its consequences. A young woman, through surgery of the brain-cells, is made to see the vast and monstrous deity of Nature, and becomes an idiot in consequence, dying less than a year later. Years afterward a strange, ominous, and foreign-looking child named Helen Vaughan is placed to board with a family in rural Wales, and haunts the woods in unaccountable fashion. A little boy is thrown out of his mind at sight of someone or something he spies with her, and a young girl comes to a terrible end in similar fashion. All this mystery is strangely interwoven with the Roman rural deities of the place, as sculptured in antique fragments. After another lapse of years, a woman of strangely exotic beauty appears in society, drives her husband to horror and death, causes an artist to paint unthinkable paintings of Witches' Sabbaths, creates an epidemic of suicide among the men of her acquaintance, and is finally discovered to be a frequenter of the lowest dens of vice in London, where even the most callous degenerates are shocked at her enormities. Through the clever comparing of notes on the part of those who have had word of her at various stages of her career, this woman is discovered to be the girl Helen Vaughan; who is the child—by no mortal father—of the young woman on whom the brain experiment was made.[107] She is a daughter of hideous Pan himself, and at the last is put to death amidst horrible transmutations of form involving changes of sex and a descent to the most primal manifestations of the life-principle.

But the charm of the tale is in the telling. No one could begin to describe the cumulative suspense and ultimate horror with which every paragraph abounds without following fully the precise order in which Mr. Machen unfolds his gradual hints and revelations. Melodrama is undeniably present, and coincidence is stretched to a length which appears absurd upon analysis; but in the malign witchery of the tale as a whole these trifles are forgotten, and the sensitive reader reaches the end with only an appreciative shudder and a tendency to repeat the words of one of the characters: "It is too incredible, too monstrous; such things can never be in this quiet world. . . . Why, man, if such a case were possible, our earth would be a nightmare."

Less famous and less complex in plot than "The Great God Pan", but definitely finer in atmosphere and general artistic value, is the curious and dimly disquieting chronicle called "The White People", whose central portion purports to be the diary or notes[108] of a little girl whose nurse has introduced her to some of the forbidden magic and soul-blasting traditions of the noxious witch-cult—the cult whose whispered lore was handed down long lines of peasantry throughout Western Europe, and whose members sometimes stole forth at night, one by one, to meet in black woods and lonely places for the revolting orgies of the Witches' Sabbath. Mr. Machen's narrative, a triumph of skilful selectiveness and restraint, accumulates enormous power as it flows on in a stream of innocent childish prattle; introducing allusions to strange "nymphs", "Dôls",[109] "voolas", "White, Green, and Scarlet Ceremonies", "Aklo letters",[110] "Chian language", "Mao games", and the like. The rites learned by the nurse from her witch grandmother are taught to the child by the time she is three years old, and her artless accounts of the dangerous secret revelations possess a lurking terror generously mixed with pathos. Evil charms well known to anthropologists are described with juvenile naiveté, and finally there comes a winter afternoon journey into the old Welsh hills, performed under an imaginative spell which lends to the wild scenery an added weirdness, strangeness, and suggestion of grotesque sentience. The details of this journey are given with marvellous vividness, and form to the keen critic a masterpiece of fantastic writing, with almost unlimited power in the intimation of potent hideousness and cosmic aberration. At length the child—whose age is then thirteen—comes upon a cryptic and banefully beautiful thing in the midst of a dark and inaccessible wood. She flees in awe, but is permanently altered and repeatedly revisits the wood. In the end horror overtakes her in a manner deftly prefigured by an anecdote in the prologue, but she poisons herself in time. Like the mother of Helen Vaughan in The Great God Pan, she has seen that frightful deity. She is discovered dead in the dark wood beside the cryptic thing she found; and that thing—a whitely luminous statue of Roman workmanship about which dire mediaeval rumours had clustered—is affrightedly hammered into dust by the searchers.

In the episodic novel of The Three Impostors, a work whose merit as a whole is somewhat marred by an imitation of the jaunty Stevenson manner, occur certain tales which perhaps represent the high-water mark of Machen's skill as a terror-weaver. Here we find in its most artistic form a favourite weird conception of the author's; the notion that beneath the mounds and rocks of the wild Welsh hills dwell subterraneously that squat primitive race whose vestiges gave rise to our common folk legends of fairies, elves, and the "little people",[111] and whose acts are even now responsible for certain unexplained disappearances, and occasional substitutions of strange dark "changelings" for normal infants. This theme receives its finest treatment in the episode entitled "The Novel of the Black Seal"; where a professor, having discovered a singular identity between certain characters scrawled on Welsh limestone rocks and those existing in a prehistoric black seal from Babylon, sets out on a course of discovery which leads him to unknown and terrible things. A queer passage in the ancient geographer Solinus,[112] a series of mysterious disappearances in the lonely reaches of Wales, a strange idiot son born to a rural mother after a fright in which her inmost faculties were shaken; all these things suggest to the professor a hideous connexion and a condition revolting to any friend and respecter of the human race. He hires the idiot boy, who jabbers strangely at times in a repulsive hissing voice, and is subject to odd epileptic seizures. Once, after such a seizure in the professor's study by night, disquieting odours and evidences of unnatural presences are found; and soon after that the professor leaves a bulky document and goes into the weird hills with feverish expectancy and strange terror in his heart. He never returns, but beside a fantastic stone in the wild country are found his watch, money, and ring, done up with catgut in a parchment bearing the same terrible characters as those on the black Babylonish seal and the rock in the Welsh mountains.

The bulky document explains enough to bring up the most hideous vistas. Professor Gregg, from the massed evidence presented by the Welsh disappearances, the rock inscription, the accounts of ancient geographers, and the black seal, has decided that a frightful race of dark primal beings of immemorial antiquity and wide former diffusion still dwells beneath the hills of unfrequented Wales. Further research has unriddled the message of the black seal, and proved that the idiot boy, a son of some father more terrible than mankind, is the heir of monstrous memories and possibilities. That strange night in the study the professor invoked 'the awful transmutation of the hills' by the aid of the black seal, and aroused in the hybrid idiot the horrors of his shocking paternity. He "saw his body swell and become distended as a bladder, while the face blackened. . . ." And then the supreme effects of the invocation appeared, and Professor Gregg knew the stark frenzy of cosmic panic in its darkest form. He knew the abysmal gulfs of abnormality that he had opened, and went forth into the wild hills prepared and resigned. He would meet the unthinkable 'Little People'—and his document ends with a rational observation: "If I unhappily do not return from my journey, there is no need to conjure up here a picture of the awfulness of my fate."

Also in *The Three Impostors* is the "Novel of the White Powder", which approaches the absolute culmination of loathsome fright. Francis Leicester, a young law student nervously worn out by seclusion and overwork, has a prescription filled by an old apothecary none too careful about the state of his drugs. The substance, it later turns out, is an unusual salt which time and varying temperature have accidentally changed to something very strange and terrible; nothing less, in short, than the mediaeval *Vinum Sabbati*, whose consumption at the horrible orgies of the Witches' Sabbath gave rise to shocking transformations and—if injudiciously used—to unutterable consequences. Innocently enough, the youth regularly imbibes the powder in a glass of water after meals; and at first seems substantially benefited. Gradually, however, his improved spirits take the form of dissipation; he is absent from home a great deal, and appears to have undergone a repellent psychological change. One day an odd livid spot appears on his right hand, and he afterward returns to his seclusion; finally keeping himself shut within his room and admitting none of the household. The doctor calls for an interview, and departs in a palsy of horror, saying that he can do no more in that house. Two weeks later the patient's sister, walking outside, sees a monstrous thing at the sickroom window; and servants report that food left at the locked door is no longer touched. Summons at the door bring only a sound of shuffling and a demand in a thick gurgling voice to be let alone. At last an awful happening is reported by a shuddering housemaid. The ceiling of the room below Leicester's is stained with a hideous black fluid, and a pool of viscid abomination has dripped to the bed beneath. Dr. Haberden, now persuaded to return to the house, breaks down the young man's door and strikes again and again with an iron bar at the blasphemous semi-living thing he finds there. It is "a dark and putrid mass, seething with corruption and hideous rottenness, neither liquid nor solid, but melting and changing". Burning points like eyes shine out of its midst, and before it is despatched it tries to lift what might have been an arm. Soon afterward the physician, unable to endure the memory of what he has beheld, dies at sea while bound for a new life in America.[113]

Mr. Machen returns to the daemoniac "Little People" in "The Red Hand" and "The Shining Pyramid"; and in *The Terror*, a wartime story, he treats with very potent mystery the effect of man's modern repudiation of spirituality on the beasts of the world, which are thus led to question his supremacy and to unite for his extermination. Of utmost delicacy, and passing from mere horror into true mysticism, is *The Great Return*, a story of the Graal, also a product of the war period. Too well known to need description here is the tale of "The Bowmen"; which, taken for authentic narration, gave rise to the widespread legend of the "Angels of Mons"—ghosts of the old English archers of Crécy and Agincourt who fought in 1914 beside the hard-pressed ranks of England's glorious "Old Contemptibles".

Less intense than Mr. Machen in delineating the extremes of stark fear, yet infinitely more closely wedded to the idea of an unreal world constantly pressing upon ours, is the inspired and prolific Algernon Blackwood, amidst whose voluminous and uneven work may be found some of the finest spectral literature of this or any age.[114] Of the quality of Mr. Blackwood's genius there can be no dispute; for no one has even approached the skill, seriousness, and minute fidelity with which he records the overtones of strangeness in ordinary things and experiences, or the preternatural insight with which he builds up detail by detail the complete sensations and perceptions leading from reality into supernormal life or vision. Without notable command of the poetic witchery of mere words, he is the one absolute and unquestioned master of weird atmosphere; and can evoke what amounts almost to a story from a simple fragment of humourless psychological description. Above all others he understands how fully some sensitive minds dwell forever on the borderland of dream, and how relatively slight is the distinction betwixt those images formed from actual objects and those excited by the play of the imagination.

Mr. Blackwood's lesser work is marred by several defects such as ethical didacticism, occasional insipid whimsicality, the flatness of benignant supernaturalism, and a too free use of the trade jargon of modern "occultism". A fault of his more serious efforts is that diffuseness and long-windedness which results from an excessively elaborate attempt, under the handicap of a somewhat bald and journalistic style devoid of intrinsic magic, colour, and vitality, to visualise precise sensations and nuances of uncanny suggestion. But in spite of all this, the major products of Mr. Blackwood attain a genuinely classic level, and evoke as does nothing else in literature an awed and convinced sense of the immanence of strange spiritual spheres or entities.

The well-nigh endless array of Mr. Blackwood's fiction includes both novels and shorter tales, the latter sometimes independent and sometimes arrayed in series. Foremost of all must be reckoned "The Willows", in which the nameless presences on a desolate Danube island are horribly felt and recognised by a pair of idle voyagers. Here art and restraint in narrative reach their very highest development, and an impression of lasting poignancy is produced without a single strained passage or a single false note. Another amazingly potent though less artistically finished tale is "The Wendigo", where we are confronted by horrible evidences of a vast forest daemon about which

North Woods lumbermen whisper at evening. The manner in which certain footprints tell certain unbelievable things is really a marked triumph in craftsmanship. In "An Episode in a Lodging House"[115] we behold frightful presences summoned out of black space by a sorcerer, and "The Listener" tells of the awful psychic residuum creeping about an old house where a leper died. In the volume titled *Incredible Adventures*[116] occur some of the finest tales which the author has yet produced, leading the fancy to wild rites on nocturnal hills, to secret and terrible aspects lurking behind stolid scenes, and to unimaginable vaults of mystery below the sands and pyramids of Egypt;[117] all with a serious finesse and delicacy that convince where a cruder or lighter treatment would merely amuse. Some of these accounts are hardly stories at all, but rather studies in elusive impressions and half-remembered snatches of dream. Plot is everywhere negligible, and atmosphere reigns untrammelled.

John Silence—Physician Extraordinary is a book of five related tales, through which a single character runs his triumphant course. Marred only by traces of the popular and conventional detective-story atmosphere—for Dr. Silence is one of those benevolent geniuses who employ their remarkable powers to aid worthy fellow-men in difficulty— these narratives contain some of the author's best work, and produce an illusion at once emphatic and lasting. The opening tale, "A Psychical Invasion", relates what befell a sensitive author in a house once the scene of dark deeds, and how a legion of fiends was exorcised. "Ancient Sorceries", perhaps the finest tale in the book, gives an almost hypnotically vivid account of an old French town where once the unholy Sabbath was kept by all the people in the form of cats.[118] In "The Nemesis of Fire" a hideous elemental is evoked by new-spilt blood, whilst "Secret Worship" tells of a German school where Satanism held sway, and where long afterward an evil aura remained. "The Camp of the Dog" is a werewolf tale, but is weakened by moralisation and professional "occultism".

Too subtle, perhaps, for definite classification as horror-tales, yet possibly more truly artistic in an absolute sense, are such delicate phantasies as *Jimbo* or *The Centaur*. Mr. Blackwood achieves in these novels a close and palpitant approach to the inmost substance of dream, and works enormous havock with the conventional barriers between reality and imagination.

Unexcelled in the sorcery of crystalline singing prose, and supreme in the creation of a gorgeous and languorous world of iridescently exotic vision, is Edward John Moreton Drax Plunkett, Eighteenth Baron Dunsany, whose tales and short plays form an almost unique element in our literature. Inventor of a new mythology and weaver of surprising folklore, Lord Dunsany stands dedicated to a strange world of fantastic beauty, and pledged to eternal warfare against the coarseness and ugliness of diurnal reality. His point of view is the most truly cosmic of any held in the literature of any period. As sensitive as Poe to dramatic values and the significance of isolated words and details, and far better equipped rhetorically through a simple lyric style based on the prose of the King James Bible, this author draws with tremendous effectiveness on nearly every body of myth and legend within the circle of European culture; producing a composite or eclectic cycle of phantasy in which Eastern colour, Hellenic form, Teutonic sombreness, and Celtic wistfulness are so superbly blended that each sustains and supplements the rest without sacrifice of perfect congruity and homogeneity. In most cases Dunsany's lands are fabulous—"beyond the East", or "at the edge of the world". His system of original personal and place names, with roots drawn from classical, Oriental, and other sources, is a marvel of versatile inventiveness and poetic discrimination; as one may see from such specimens as "Argimēnēs", "Bethmoora", "Poltarnees", "Camorak", "Illuriel", or "Sardathrion".[119]

Beauty rather than terror is the keynote of Dunsany's work. He loves the vivid green of jade and of copper domes, and the delicate flush of sunset on the ivory minarets of impossible dream-cities. Humour and irony, too, are often present to impart a gentle cynicism and modify what might otherwise possess a naive intensity. Nevertheless, as is inevitable in a master of triumphant unreality, there are occasional touches of cosmic fright which come well within the authentic tradition. Dunsany loves to hint slyly and adroitly of monstrous things and incredible dooms, as one hints in a fairy tale. In *The Book of Wonder* we read of Hlo-hlo, the gigantic spider-idol which does not always stay at home; of what the Sphinx feared in the forest; of Slith, the thief who jumps over the edge of the world after seeing a certain light lit and knowing *who* lit it; of the anthropophagous Gibbelins, who inhabit an evil tower and guard a treasure; of the Gnoles, who live in the forest and from whom it is not well to steal; of the City of Never, and the eyes that watch in the Under Pits;[120] and of kindred things of darkness. *A Dreamer's Tales* tells of the mystery that sent forth all men from Bethmoora in the desert; of the vast gate of Perdóndaris, that was carved from a *single piece* of ivory; and of the voyage of poor old Bill, whose captain cursed the crew and paid calls on nasty-looking isles new-risen from the sea, with low thatched cottages having evil, obscure windows.[121]

Many of Dunsany's short plays are replete with spectral fear. In *The Gods of the Mountain* seven beggars impersonate the seven green idols on a distant hill, and enjoy ease and honour in a city of worshippers until they hear that *the real idols are missing from their wonted seats*. A very ungainly sight in the dusk is reported to them—"rock should not walk in the evening"—and at last, as they sit awaiting the arrival of a troop of dancers, they note that the approaching footsteps are heavier than those of good dancers ought to be. Then things ensue, and in the end the presumptuous blasphemers are turned to green jade statues by the very walking statues whose sanctity they outraged. But mere plot is the very least merit of this marvellously effective play. The incidents and developments are those of a supreme master, so that the whole forms one of the most important contributions of the present age not only to drama, but to literature in general. *A Night at an Inn* tells of four thieves who have stolen the emerald eye of Klesh, a monstrous Hindoo god. They lure to their room and succeed in slaying the three priestly avengers who are on their track, but in the night Klesh comes gropingly for his eye; and having gained it and departed, calls each of the despoilers out into the darkness for an unnamed punishment. In *The Laughter of the Gods* there is a doomed city at the jungle's edge, and a ghostly lutanist heard only by those about to die (cf. Alice's spectral harpsichord in Hawthorne's *House of the Seven Gables*); whilst *The Queen's Enemies* retells the anecdote of Herodotus in which a vengeful princess invites her foes to a subterranean banquet and lets in the Nile to drown them.

But no amount of mere description can convey more than a fraction of Lord Dunsany's pervasive charm. His prismatic cities and unheard-of rites are touched with a sureness which only mastery can engender, and we thrill with a sense of actual participation in his secret mysteries. To the truly imaginative he is a talisman and a key unlocking rich storehouses of dream and fragmentary memory; so that we may think of him not only as a poet, but as one who makes each reader a poet as well.

At the opposite pole of genius from Lord Dunsany, and gifted with an almost diabolic power of calling horror by gentle steps from the midst of prosaic daily life, is the scholarly Montague Rhodes James, Provost of Eton College, antiquary of note, and recognised authority on mediaeval manuscripts and cathedral history. Dr. James, long fond of telling spectral tales at Christmastide, has become by slow degrees a literary weird fictionist of the very first rank; and has developed a distinctive style and method likely to serve as models for an enduring line of disciples.

The art of Dr. James is by no means haphazard, and in the preface to one of his collections[122] he has formulated three very sound rules for macabre composition. A ghost story, he believes, should have a familiar setting in the modern period, in order to approach closely the reader's sphere of experience. Its spectral phenomena, moreover, should be malevolent rather than beneficent; since *fear* is the emotion primarily to be excited. And finally, the technical patois of "occultism" or pseudo-science ought carefully to be avoided; lest the charm of casual verisimilitude be smothered in unconvincing pedantry.

Dr. James, practicing what he preaches, approaches his themes in a light and often conversational way. Creating the illusion of every-day events, he introduces his abnormal phenomena cautiously and gradually; relieved at every turn by touches of homely and prosaic detail, and sometimes spiced with a snatch or two of antiquarian scholarship. Conscious of the close relation between present weirdness and accumulated tradition, he generally provides remote historical antecedents for his incidents; thus being able to utilise very aptly his exhaustive knowledge of the past, and his ready and convincing command of archaic diction and colouring. A favourite scene for a James tale is some centuried cathedral, which the author can describe with all the familiar minuteness of a specialist in that field.

Sly humorous vignettes and bits of life-like genre portraiture and characterisation are often to be found in Dr. James's narratives, and serve in his skilled hands to augment the general effect rather than to spoil it, as the same qualities would tend to do with a lesser craftsman. In inventing a new type of ghost, he has departed considerably from the conventional Gothic tradition; for where the older stock ghosts were pale and stately, and apprehended chiefly through the sense of sight, the average James ghost is lean, dwarfish, and hairy—a sluggish, hellish night-abomination midway betwixt beast and man—and usually *touched* before it is *seen*. Sometimes the spectre is of still more eccentric composition; a roll of flannel with spidery eyes, or an invisible entity which moulds itself in bedding and shews *a face of crumpled linen*.[123] Dr. James has, it is clear, an intelligent and scientific knowledge of human nerves and feelings; and knows just how to apportion statement, imagery, and subtle suggestions in order to secure the best results with his readers. He is an artist in incident and arrangement rather than in atmosphere, and reaches the emotions more often through the intellect than directly. This method, of course, with its occasional absences of sharp climax, has its drawbacks as well as its advantages; and many will miss the thorough atmospheric tension which writers like Machen are careful to build up with words and scenes. But only a few of the tales are open to the charge of tameness. Generally the laconic unfolding of abnormal events in adroit order is amply sufficient to produce the desired effect of cumulative horror.

The short stories of Dr. James are contained in four small collections, entitled respectively *Ghost-Stories of an Antiquary*, *More Ghost Stories of an Antiquary*, *A Thin Ghost and Others*, and *A Warning to the Curious*. There is also a delightful juvenile phantasy, *The Five Jars*, which has its spectral adumbrations. Amidst this wealth of material it is hard to select a favourite or especially typical tale, though each reader will no doubt have such preferences as his temperament may determine.

"Count Magnus" is assuredly one of the best, forming as it does a veritable Golconda of suspense and suggestion. Mr. Wraxall is an English traveller of the middle nineteenth century, sojourning in Sweden to secure material for a book. Becoming interested in the ancient family of De la Gardie, near the village of Råbäck, he studies its records; and finds particular fascination in the builder of the existing manor-house, one Count Magnus, of whom strange and terrible things are whispered. The Count, who flourished early in the seventeenth century, was a stern landlord, and famous for his severity toward poachers and delinquent tenants. His cruel punishments were bywords, and there were dark rumours of influences which even survived his interment in the great mausoleum he built near the church—as in the case of the two peasants who hunted on his preserves one night a century after his death. There were hideous screams in the woods, and near the tomb of Count Magnus an unnatural laugh and the clang of a great door. Next morning the priest found the two men; one a maniac, and the other dead, with the flesh of his face sucked from the bones.

Mr. Wraxall hears all these tales, and stumbles on more guarded references to a *Black Pilgrimage* once taken by the Count; a pilgrimage to Chorazin in Palestine, one of the cities denounced by Our Lord in the Scriptures, and in which old priests say that Antichrist is to be born. No one dares to hint just what that Black Pilgrimage was, or what strange being or thing the Count brought back as a companion. Meanwhile Mr. Wraxall is increasingly anxious to explore the mausoleum of Count Magnus, and finally secures permission to do so, in the company of a deacon. He finds several monuments and three copper sarcophagi, one of which is the Count's. Round the edge of this latter are several bands of engraved scenes, including a singular and hideous delineation of a pursuit—the pursuit of a frantic man through a forest by a squat muffled figure with a devil-fish's tentacle, directed by a tall cloaked man on a neighbouring hillock. The sarcophagus has three massive steel padlocks, one of which is lying open on the floor, reminding the traveller of a metallic clash he heard the day before when passing the mausoleum and wishing idly that he might see Count Magnus.

His fascination augmented, and the key being accessible, Mr. Wraxall pays the mausoleum a second and solitary visit and finds another padlock unfastened. The next day, his last in Råbäck, he again goes alone to bid the long-dead Count farewell. Once more queerly impelled to utter a whimsical wish for a meeting with the buried nobleman, he now sees to his disquiet that only one of the padlocks remains on the great sarcophagus. Even as he looks, that last lock drops noisily to the floor, and there comes a sound as of creaking hinges. Then the monstrous lid appears very slowly to rise, and Mr. Wraxall flees in panic fear without refastening the door of the mausoleum.

During his return to England the traveller feels a curious uneasiness about his fellow-passengers on the canal-boat which he employs for the earlier stages. Cloaked figures make him nervous, and he has a sense of being watched and followed. Of twenty-eight persons whom he counts, only twenty-six appear at meals; and the missing two are always a tall cloaked man and a shorter muffled figure. Completing his water travel at Harwich, Mr. Wraxall takes frankly to flight in a closed carriage, but sees two cloaked figures at a crossroad. Finally he lodges at a small house in a village and spends the time making frantic notes. On the second morning he is found dead, and during the inquest seven jurors faint at sight of the body. The house where he stayed is never again inhabited, and upon its demolition half a century later his manuscript is discovered in a forgotten cupboard.[124]

In "The Treasure of Abbot Thomas" a British antiquary unriddles a cipher on some Renaissance painted windows, and thereby discovers a centuried hoard of gold in a niche half way down a well in the courtyard of a German abbey. But the crafty depositor had set a guardian over that treasure, and something in the black well twines its arms around the searcher's neck in such a manner that the quest is abandoned, and a clergyman sent for. Each night after that the discoverer feels a stealthy presence and detects a horrible odour of mould outside the door of his hotel room, till finally the clergyman makes a daylight replacement of the stone at the mouth of the treasure-vault in the well—out of which something had come in the dark to avenge the disturbing of old Abbot Thomas's gold. As he completes his work the cleric observes a curious toad-like carving on the ancient well-head, with the Latin motto *"Depositum custodi— keep that which is committed to thee."*

Other notable James tales are "The Stalls of Barchester Cathedral", in which a grotesque carving comes curiously to life to avenge the secret and subtle murder of an old Dean by his ambitious successor; "'Oh, Whistle, and I'll Come to You, My Lad'", which tells of the horror summoned by a strange metal whistle found in a mediaeval church ruin; and "An Episode of Cathedral History", where the dismantling of a pulpit uncovers an archaic tomb whose lurking daemon spreads panic and pestilence. Dr. James, for all his light touch, evokes fright and hideousness in their most shocking forms; and will certainly stand as one of the few really creative masters in his darksome province.

For those who relish speculation regarding the future, the tale of supernatural horror provides an interesting field. Combated by a mounting wave of plodding realism, cynical flippancy, and sophisticated disillusionment, it is yet encouraged by a parallel tide of growing mysticism, as developed both through the fatigued reaction of "occultists" and religious fundamentalists against materialistic discovery and through the stimulation of wonder and fancy by such enlarged vistas and broken barriers as modern science has given us with its intra-atomic chemistry, advancing astrophysics, doctrines of relativity, and probings into biology and human thought. At the present moment the favouring forces would appear to have somewhat of an advantage; since there is unquestionably more cordiality shewn toward weird writings than when, thirty years ago, the best of Arthur Machen's work fell on the stony ground of the smart and cocksure 'nineties. Ambrose Bierce, almost unknown in his own time, has now reached something like general recognition.[125]

Startling mutations, however, are not to be looked for in either direction. In any case an approximate balance of tendencies will continue to exist; and while we may justly expect a further subtilisation of technique, we have no reason to think that the general position of the spectral in literature will be altered. It is a narrow though essential branch of human expression, and will chiefly appeal as always to a limited audience with keen special sensibilities. Whatever universal masterpiece of tomorrow may be wrought from phantasm or terror will owe its acceptance rather to a supreme workmanship than to a sympathetic theme. Yet who shall declare the dark theme a positive handicap? Radiant with beauty, the Cup of the Ptolemies was carven of onyx.[126]

EDITOR'S NOTE FP: *Recluse* No. 1 (1927): 27–59. Rev. ed. in *Fantasy Fan* (October 1933– February 1935; incomplete) and *The Outsider and Others* (Sauk City, WI: Arkham House, 1939), pp. 509–53. HPL's landmark essay on weird fiction, initially written at the urging of W. Paul Cook. HPL began writing it in late 1925, working desultorily on it all the way up to its setting in type in the summer of 1927. Almost upon the appearance of the *Recluse* later in 1927, HPL began gathering data on additional works to mention in a revised version of the essay. HPL finally got a chance to prepare a revised edition for the *Fantasy Fan*, but the serialisation had proceeded only up to the middle of Chapter VIII when the fanzine folded.

HPL (who had made all his contemplated revisions by early 1933, sending a marked-up copy of the *Recluse*, along with typewritten sheets containing new passages, to the *Fantasy Fan's* editor, Charles D. Hornig) made some further revisions in 1934–35, when he stumbled upon the work of William Hope Hodgson. He thought that the serialisation would resume (or commence from the beginning) in Willis Conover's *Science-Fantasy Correspondent* in 1936, but Conover did not begin publication of the essay before HPL's death in 1937. HPL's fully revised text did not appear until *The Outsider and Others*. The text as presented here prints HPL's additions to his original essay in brackets. For a more exhaustively annotated edition (including full bibliographical information on all works cited here), see *The Annotated Supernatural Horror in Literature*, ed. S. T. Joshi (Hippocampus Press, 2000).

Notes

1. The following anthropological analysis is probably derived from HPL's reading of such important scholarly volumes as E. B. Tylor's *Primitive Culture* (1871), John Fiske's *Myths and Myth-Makers* (1872), and Sir James George Frazer's *The Golden Bough* (1890–1915). See further the essay "Idealism and Materialism—A Reflection" (CE5).

2. This idea is also expressed in "Notes on Writing Weird Fiction" (see p. 175).

3. The reference is presumably to the first Book of Enoch; there are two others. Enoch was the seventh patriarch from Adam (Genesis 5:18), around whose name many works and legends clustered. The Book of Enoch (part of the Pseudepigrapha of the Old Testament) is a composite work dating roughly to the second and first centuries B.C.E. and relates Enoch's voyages through the heavens; one section contains a prophetic account of the dissolution of the universe. For a translation see R. H. Charles, *The Apocrypha and Pseudepigrapha of the Old Testament* (Oxford, 1913; rpt. 1963), Vol. II.

4. The Clavicula (singular) or Key of Solomon is a book of Jewish magic of unknown date; it claims to date to great antiquity, but has been known only since the 16th century. Its two books (the Greater Key and the Lesser Key) discuss such things as magic spells, rituals, talismans, and evocations of spirits. The first English translation was *The Key of Solomon the King*, tr. S. Liddell MacGregor Mathers (London: Redway, 1889).

5. This idea was derived by HPL from Margaret A. Murray's *The Witch-Cult in Western Europe* (Oxford: Clarendon Press, 1921); cf. SL 3.181. It is no longer accepted by anthropologists.

6. For HPL's connexion of Murray's witch-cult theory with the Salem witch trials see SL 3.178f.

7. Albertus Magnus (1193?–1280), French Aristotelian and tutor of St. Thomas Aquinas, was said to have communed with the devil and practised magic. Twenty-one volumes of alchemy are attributed to him; few are probably authentic. Raymond Lully (1235?–1316), or Ramon Lull, Spanish Platonist, wrote a number of alchemical works and was renowned throughout Europe. His works have been edited in Catalan by M. Obrador et al. (1905–32; 21 vols.).

8. Nostradamus (Michel de Notredame, 1503–1566) wrote a series of prophecies that were ultimately published as the *Centuries* and placed on the *Index Expurgatorius*. Johannes Trithemius (1462–1516), German abbot and mystic, wrote several curious religious and philosophical works, including *Steganographia* (1500; publ. 1606) and *De Lapide Philosophorum* (1619), the latter cited (inaccurately) by HPL in *The Case of Charles Dexter Ward* (MM 121). John Dee (1527–1608) was the celebrated English statesman, mathematician, and royal astrologer for Queen Elizabeth. Frank Belknap Long in "The Space-Eaters" (1927) made him the first English translator of HPL's *Necronomicon*, and HPL follows Long (see "History of the *Necronomicon*" [1927; MW 53]). Robert Fludd (1574–1637), English physi-

cian and Rosicrucian, influenced strongly by Paracelsus, wrote a number of astrological and alchemical works, including *Clavis Philosophiae et Alchymiae* (1633) and *Philosophia Moysaica* (1638). He is also mentioned by HPL in *The Case of Charles Dexter Ward* (MM 121).

9. From the Greek *psychopompos* or "conveyer of the dead" (attribute of Hermes). Used by HPL in the poem "Psychopompos" (1917–18) and in "The Dunwich Horror" (1928), where whippoorwills are the psychopomps. See also below on Hawthorne's *House of the Seven Gables* (p. 106).

10. Sabine Baring-Gould (1834–1924), *Curious Myths of the Middle Ages* (1866; LL 66). For the influence of this volume on HPL's "The Rats in the Walls" see Steven J. Mariconda, "Baring-Gould and the Ghouls", *Crypt of Cthulhu* (St John's Eve 1983); rpt. in Mariconda's *On the Emergence of "Cthulhu" and Other Observations* (West Warwick, RI: Necronomicon Press, 1995), pp. 53–56. A modern reprint of this work (London: Jupiter Books, 1977) is greatly abridged.

11. I.e., chapters 61–62 of the *Satyricon*.

12. Presumably the novel, the *Metamorphoses* or *Golden Ass*; other of Apuleius' works are philosophical.

13. Almost nothing is known about Phlegon of Tralles, freedman of the Emperor Hadrian (r. 117–38 C.E.). Since Phlegon's work has never been fully translated into English, HPL probably derived his information on it from Lacy Collison-Morley's *Greek and Roman Ghost Stories* (1912; rpt. Chicago: Argonaut, 1968), where the story of Philinnion and Machates is translated on pp. 67–71.

14. Proclus, a fifth-century Platonist, apparently retold the tale of Phlegon in a work called "How One Ought to Believe the Soul Enters and Leaves the Body" (*Pos dei noein eisienai kai exienai psychen apo somatos*); see Lacy Collison-Morley, *Greek and Roman Ghost Stories*, pp. 65f.

15. The Eddas are two works of Old Icelandic literature (the *Elder Edda*, in verse, and the *Younger Edda*, in prose) dealing with Norse mythology; the first dates from the 8th to the 12th centuries C.E., and the second from the 13th century.

16. The Sagas are a variety of Icelandic works composed in the 12th and 13th centuries C.E. relating Norse myth, history, and other accounts. Contrary to what HPL suggests, they are in prose.

17. These episodes come, respectively, from Book V, Chapter 15; Book XXI, Chapter 3; and Book XIII, Chapter 12.

18. James I of England (r. 1603–25) himself wrote a treatise on witchcraft, *Daemonologie* (1597).

19. Viz., Charles Drelincourt's *Christian's Defence against the Fears of Death* (1675). This account of the genesis and purpose of Defoe's tract has now been discredited; see R. M. Baine, *Daniel Defoe and the Supernatural* (Athens: University of Georgia Press, 1968), pp. 105f.

20. See esp. ch. 47 ("The Art of Borrowing further explained, and an Account of a Strange Phenomenon") and ch. 62 ("His [Fathom's] Return to England and Midnight-Pilgrimage to Monimia's Tomb").

21. "Ossian" is an invention of the Scottish poet James Macpherson, who attempted to pass off some poetry he had written as translations of the fragments of the ancient Scottish poet Ossian. The chief works he produced were *Fingal* (1762) and *Temora* (1763). The hoax was exploded in the early 19th century.

22. For HPL's opinion of the deficiencies of *Otranto*, see SL 2.231–32.

23. For Walpole's remarks on "Sir Bertrand" see Walpole to William Mason, 8 April 1778 (*Correspondence*, Yale Ed., 28.382) and Walpole to Robert Jephson, 27 January 1780 (*Cor-*

respondence, Yale Ed., 41.410). Walpole discusses *The Old English Baron* in the above two letters as well as in letters to William Cole, 17 August 1778 and 22 August 1778 (*Correspondence*, Yale Ed., 11.107–10).

24. This was *Castle Connor, an Irish Story*.

25. HPL later confessed (HPL to R. H. Barlow, 1 December 1934; ms., JHL) that he never read the entirety of *Wieland* but only the excerpt printed in Vol. 9 of Julian Hawthorne's *The Lock and Key Library* (1909), which he acquired in New York in 1922 (*LL* 400).

26. Actually, *Tales of Wonder* is an anthology of ballads edited by Lewis and containing the work of Southey, Sir Walter Scott, Lewis himself, and others. *Tales of Terror* (1801, not 1799) is a parody of *Tales of Wonder*, and was probably not written or edited by Lewis at all.

27. HPL later admitted that he never read the entirety of *Melmoth* either, but only "two anthology excerpts" (*SL* 2.36)—i.e., Hawthorne's *Lock and Key Library* and George Saintsbury's *Tales of Mystery* (1891; *LL* 755).

28. Scott corresponded with Maturin between 1812 and 1824 (see *The Correspondence of Sir Walter Scott and Charles Robert Maturin* [Austin: University of Texas Press, 1937]), and also reviewed Maturin's *Fatal Revenge* (*Quarterly Review* 3 [1810]: 339f.) and his *Women* (*Edinburgh Review* 30 [1818]: 234f.).

29. Henry Dunn, friend and associate of Dante Gabriel Rossetti, records: "According to his brother, any writing about devils, spectres, or the supernatural generally, whether in poetry or prose, had a fascination for him; at one time—say 1844—his supreme delight was the blood-curdling romance of Maturin, *Melmoth the Wanderer*" (Gale Pedrick, *Life with Rossetti* [London: Macdonald, 1964], p. 96).

30. In recounting to George Henry Lewes his meeting with Goethe in 1830, Thackeray says the following: "His [Goethe's] eyes [were] extraordinarily dark, piercing and brilliant. I felt quite afraid before them, and recollect comparing them to the eyes of the hero of a certain romance called *Melmoth the Wanderer*, which used to alarm us boys thirty years ago; eyes of an individual who had made a bargain with a Certain Person, and at an extreme old age retained these eyes in all their awful splendour." Letter to George Henry Lewes, 28 April 1855; quoted in Lewes' *The Life and Works of Goethe* (Boston: Ticknor & Fields, 1856), 2.450–51.

31. In his essay "De l'essence du rire et géneralement du comique dans les arts plastiques" [On the Essence of Laughter and, in General, the Comic in the Plastic Arts] Baudelaire speaks of Melmoth, "La grande création satanique du reverend Maturin" [the great Satanic creation of the reverend Maturin], and goes on to say: "Quoi du plus grand, quoi de plus puissant relativement à la pauvre humanité que ce pâle et ennuyé Melmoth?" [What could be greater, what could be more powerful in relation to feeble humanity than this pale and weary Melmoth?] *Curiosités esthétiques*, ed. F.-F. Gautier (Paris: Editions de la Nouvelle Revue Française, 1925), p. 342.

32. George Saintsbury, "Introduction" to *Tales of Mystery: Mrs. Radcliffe, Lewis, Maturin* (New York: Macmillan, 1891), p. xxviii.

33. Edith Birkhead, *The Tale of Terror* (New York: E. P. Dutton, 1921), p. 93.

34. For Beckford's influence on HPL see Peter Cannon, "The Influence of *Vathek* on H. P. Lovecraft's *The Dream-Quest of Unknown Kadath*," in *H. P. Lovecraft: Four Decades of Criticism*, ed. S. T. Joshi (Athens: Ohio University Press, 1980), pp. 153–57. HPL also remarks that his unfinished work "Azathoth" (1922) was to have been a "weird Vathek-like novel" (*SL* 1.185). HPL first read *Vathek* around July 1921 (HPL to Rheinhart Kleiner, 30 July 1921; AHT).

35. *The Arabian Nights' Entertainments* were translated into French by Antoine Galland (1704–12), and his rendition was then translated into English (1706f.).

36. A reference, perhaps, to Samuel Johnson's short novel *Rasselas, Prince of Abissinia* (1759).

37. HPL later lent his copy of *The Episodes of Vathek* (1912) to Clark Ashton Smith and urged him to complete the unfinished third episode, which Smith did.

38. A band of mystics arising in the late 16th century and believing in alchemy, astrology, and the occult in general. The term is probably derived from the Latin *rosa* (rose) and *crux* (cross); the symbol of the order was a rose crucified in the centre of a cross. A. E. Waite's *The Real History of the Rosicrucians* (1887) brought the order into publicity.

39. As *The Book of the Magi* (Boston: W. W. Harmon, 1896).

40. George Colman, *The Iron Chest: A Play in Three Acts* (Dublin, 1796), with music to the songs by Stephen Storace. Henry Irving staged the play in 1879.

41. Byron conceived the idea for a ghost story but wrote only a few pages (see Leslie A. Marchand, *Byron: A Biography* [New York: Knopf, 1947], 2.628f.). These are reprinted in E. F. Bleiler, ed., *The Castle of Otranto* [et al.] (New York: Dover, 1966). Polidori apparently lifted the plot of this fragment for his "The Vampyre." P. B. Shelley apparently never began a work.

42. Actually, "The Werewolf" is only a chapter from *The Phantom Ship*.

43. The Comte de Saint-Germain (d. 1784?), whose real name is not known, practised feats of magic at the court of Louis XV from 1748 to about 1755. According to Cagliostro he later went to Germany and became the founder of freemasonry.

44. See such of Constant's writings as *The History of Magic* (1913) and *Transcendental Magic* (1896), both tr. A. E. Waite; the former was used by HPL for the incantations in *The Case of Charles Dexter Ward*.

45. Most scholars now believe that the author of *Varney the Vampire* was James Malcolm Rymer (1814–1881).

46. HPL did not read *She* until late 1926: "I've recently begun reading the work of Sir H. Rider Haggard *for the first time*. 'She' is very good, & if the others are at all commensurate, I have quite a treat ahead" (HPL to August Derleth, 31 October 1926; ms., SHSW).

47. In the first publication of SHL appears a sentence at this point—"Adalbert von Chamisso, in his famous *Peter Schlemihl*, (1814) tells of a man who lost his own shadow as the consequence of a misdeed, and of the strange developments that resulted"—that HPL removed in later versions.

48. A précis of the novel appeared under the title "The Convent Witch" in *Fraser's Magazine* 38 (October 1848): 363–78. The editor-translator is unknown.

49. The tale bears a clear resemblance to HPL's "The Haunter of the Dark" (1935) and must have influenced it. It appeared in Hammett's *Creeps by Night* (1931), which also included HPL's "The Music of Erich Zann."

50. The tale was probably an influence upon HPL's "Under the Pyramids" (1924).

51. This description makes it clear that "The Horla" was a dominant influence upon the conception and development of HPL's "The Call of Cthulhu" (1926). The mention of the "invisible being" perhaps suggests an influence also on "The Dunwich Horror" (1928), although the attributes of the creature in that tale are perhaps more directly derived from Blackwood's "The Wendigo."

52. "What Was It?" See below (p. 107).

53. The four works by Erckmann-Chatrian cited here are all included in Vol. 5 of Hawthorne's *The Lock and Key Library* (1909).

54. HPL owned two volumes by Level, the story collection *Tales of Mystery and Horror,* tr. Alys Eyre Macklin (1920; LL 528) and the novel *Those Who Return,* tr. B. Drillien (1923; LL 529), a translation of *L'Ombre* (1921).

55. In the first publication of SHL the above passage read: "The former, widely popular through the cinema a few years ago, treats of a legendary artificial giant animated by a mediaeval rabbin of Prague according to a certain cryptic formula." HPL comments on this change in January 1937: "To explain that Golem business I must confess that when I wrote the treatise I hadn't read the novel. I had seen the cinema version, and thought it was faithful to the original—but when I came to read the book only a year ago [actually in April 1935; cf. SL 5.138] . . . Holy Yuggoth! The film had nothing of the novel save the mere title and the Prague ghetto setting—indeed, in the book the Golem-monster never appeared at all, but merely lurked in the background as a shadowy symbol. That was one on the old man!" (SL 5.389). The novel had been lent to him by R. H. Barlow. HPL saw the film version of *The Golem* in 1921.

56. HPL saw it in New York on 17 December 1925 (HPL to Lillian D. Clark, 22 December 1925; ms., JHL).

57. The opera, in Italian, was entitled *Il dibuk* (1934), and was composed by Lodovico Rocca. The first production was at the Teatro alla Scala in Milan, 24 March 1934.

58. HPL presumably refers to Poe's extensive borrowing of aesthetic theories from Coleridge and such German theoreticians as A. W. Schlegel.

59. Here HPL may be referring to Blackwood's "The Willows" and Machen's "The White People," which he regarded as the two finest tales in the history of weird fiction.

60. HPL refers to the poems "The Raven," "Bells," "Ulalume," "The City in the Sea," and "Dream-Land."

61. It is curious, then, that HPL below cites "The Man of the Crowd," which surely falls into this third category.

62. This tale's influence upon HPL's "Cool Air" would seem to be self-evident; but HPL himself believed his tale to have been more directly influenced by Machen's "Novel of the White Powder" (HPL to Henry Kuttner, 29 July 1936; *Letters to Henry Kuttner* [West Warwick, RI: Necronomicon Press, 1990], p. 21).

63. The final word in the most authoritative version of Poe's text—a copy made by Sarah Helen Whitman of the text in the *Broadway Journal* (20 December 1845) with manuscript revisions—is "putridity"; many other texts, including many collected editions of Poe, read "putrescence." Late in life HPL came upon the revised reading and found it unsatisfying: "The loss in power—as connected with prose *rhythm*—is obvious. It is curious—almost incredible—how deaf & callous the moderns are to one of the most important factors in prose writing—i.e., cadence or rhythm. Much of the magic of Poe resides in his masterful employment of this element—hence his work is gravely impaired if any part of the text be tampered with" (HPL to R. H. Barlow, [10 February 1935]; ms., JHL).

64. *Pym* has frequently been said to have influenced HPL's *At the Mountains of Madness* (1931), but any connexions between the two tales aside from the Antarctic setting are hard to distinguish.

65. See T. O. Mabbott ("Lovecraft as a Student of Poe," *Fresco* 8, No. 3 [Spring 1958]: 37–39) for a discussion of this interpretation of "Usher," representing HPL's greatest contribution to Poe studies (see also Mabbott's edition of Poe's *Tales and Sketches* [1978], 1.393).

66. I have not been able to ascertain the source for HPL's knowledge of this anecdote.

67. A Latinised adjectival form of "Lewis," referring to M. G. Lewis.

68. See Paul Elmer More (1864–1937), "The Origins of Hawthorne and Poe," in *Shelburne Essays: First Series* (New York: Putnam, 1904): "The unearthly visions of Poe and Hawthorne are in no wise the result of literary whim or of unbridled individualism, but are deeprooted in American history" (p. 53). Cf. *SL* 2.140: "It is easy to see how the critic Paul Elmer More traces the horror-element in American literature to the remote New England countryside with its solitude-warped religious fanaticism."

69. Viz., Judge John Hathorne (1641–1717), son of William Hathorne, earliest American settler of the Hathorne family, who came to Massachusetts in 1630.

70. These two volumes, read by HPL at the age of seven, were the ultimate sources for his abiding interest in classical antiquity (see *SL* 1.7).

71. Entry 129 of the Commonplace Book ("strange & prehistoric Italian city of stone") is explicitly derived from this novel.

72. Presumably a reference to two chapters on Hawthorne in *Studies in Classic American Literature* (1923) by D. H. Lawrence (1885–1930); but I have not been able to identify the remark to which HPL here alludes.

73. See HPL's Commonplace Book (entry 46): "Hawthorne—unwritten plot[:] Visitor from tomb—stranger at some publick concourse followed at midnight to graveyard where he descends into the earth." The Hawthorne note is in his *American Notebooks* for 6 December 1837.

74. This analogy may point to HPL's absorption of the Wagnerian operatic form, with its employment of the *leitmotiv*; the average opera does not employ a recurring motif or theme.

75. HPL first read Bierce in 1919, at the suggestion of Samuel Loveman (*SL* 2.222).

76. From the preface to *Twenty-one Letters of Ambrose Bierce* (Cleveland: George Kirk, 1922; *LL* 89), p. 4.

77. These are the subtitles, respectively, for the first and third chapters of "The Damned Thing."

78. "In all imaginative literature it would be difficult to find a parallel for this story in sheer, unadulterated hideousness." Frederic Taber Cooper, "Ambrose Bierce," in *Some American Story Tellers* (New York: Henry Holt, 1911), p. 352.

79. A character named Joel Manton is featured in HPL's "The Unnamable" (1923).

80. "About 'Elsie Venner'—it has a subtly haunting power, though I'm not sure whether the horror element is concentrated enough to make it a major weird classic. Some, of course, might consider it all the greater on that account. It certainly has atmosphere. I haven't read it in years, but can still recall the malign aura that hangs over the great hill against which the town is built. Possibly that suggested my Yuggothian fungus 'Zaman's Hill' [*Fungi from Yuggoth VII*]" (HPL to R. H. Barlow, [26 October 1934]; ms., JHL).

81. "It may interest you to know that in an XIth hour codicil I amplified my F. Marion Crawford paragraph . . .; this enlarged horizon resulting from the perusal of a collection called *Wandering Ghosts*, lent me by my newest prodigy great-grandchild, Donald Wandrei of St. Paul, Minn." (*SL* 2.123).

82. "I made some eleventh-hour inserts in the proofs [of SHL] which you won't find in the carbon—mainly regarding the forgotten early work of *Robert W. Chambers* (can you believe it?) who turned out some powerful bizarre stuff between 1895 and 1904" (*SL* 2.127). HPL alludes to the endless array of best-selling shopgirl romances produced by Chambers after his early fantasy period.

83. HPL (see SL 3.187) was especially fond of "The Harbor-Master" (originally a short story but later rewritten as the first five chapters of In Search of the Unknown), a tale that may have influenced "The Shadow over Innsmouth" in its depiction of a hybrid fish-man.

84. Included in Cram's rare collection of weird tales, Black Spirits and White, although HPL read it in Joseph Lewis French's anthology Ghosts Grim and Gentle (1926).

85. HPL read this tale in its original appearance in the Argosy, 11 January 1913; in the 8 February 1913 issue was published a letter of comment on the tale by HPL: "It is the belief of the writer that very few short stories of equal merit have been published anywhere during recent years. It is easy to imagine with what genuine regret the editors to whom it was submitted declined to print it." The tale was clearly an influence upon "The Shadow over Innsmouth."

86. "The Unbroken Chain," in On an Island That Cost $24.00 (1926). HPL read the story in its first appearance (Cosmopolitan, September 1923), and it clearly influenced "The Rats in the Walls."

87. The novel is a probable influence upon HPL's "The Shadow over Innsmouth" and "The Dreams in the Witch House."

88. Hearn translated Gautier's One of Cleopatra's Nights and Other Fantastic Romances (1882), Maupassant's Saint Anthony and Other Stories (1924) and The Adventures of Walter Schnaffs (1931), and Anatole France's The Crime of Sylvestre Bonnard (1890). His translation of Flaubert's Temptation of St. Anthony was first published in 1910.

89. First read by HPL in 1923 in the collection The Pale Ape and Other Pulses (1911), lent to him by W. Paul Cook (SL 1.255). See also HPL's letter to the editor of Weird Tales for January 1924, where he speaks of the story in virtually the same terms as he does here. Entries 115 and 116 of the Commonplace Book appear to derive from HPL's reading of the work.

90. "The House of Sounds" originally appeared as "Vaila" in Shapes in the Fire (1896); revised and retitled, it appeared in The Pale Ape.

91. HPL refers to the fact that in both tales a house and its inhabitants appear to share a common soul (on Poe see above, p. 103), so that both the house and its occupants experience a common dissolution.

92. "[W. Paul] Cook . . . hath lent me . . . Stoker's last production, The Lair of the White Worm. The plot idea is colossal, but the development is so childish that I cannot imagine how the thing ever got into print—unless on the reputation of Dracula. The rambling and unmotivated narration, the puerile and stagey characterisation, the irrational propensity of everyone to do the most stupid possible thing at precisely the wrong moment and for no cause at all, and the involved development of a personality afterward relegated to utter insignificance—all this proves to me either that Dracula . . . and The Jewel of Seven Stars were touched up Bushwork-fashion by a superior hand which arranged all the details, or that by the end of his life . . . he trickled out in a pitiful and inept senility" (SL 1.255). Entry 79 of the Commonplace Book ("Shapeless living thing forming nucleus of ancient building") may derive from HPL's reading of this novel.

93. As both Dracula and The Beetle were published in 1897, there may be some question as to whether the former directly influenced the latter.

94. All three stories cited are in The Runagates Club (1928). HPL read the volume in the late summer of 1928 (HPL to August Derleth, 12 August and 5 October 1928; mss., SHSW).

95. The Shadowy Thing was first published in England under the title The Remedy (1925). It clearly influenced "The Thing on the Doorstep."

96. But the earlier version of the novel has yet to be published, and HPL knew of it only in a paraphrase by Greville Macdonald in an introduction to a later edition (London: George Allen & Unwin, 1924). The copy of *Lilith* he owned (*LL* 567) is, of course, the later version.

97. HPL came upon de la Mare's weird work only in the summer of 1926 (*SL* 2.53, 57).

98. The resemblance in plot to HPL's *The Case of Charles Dexter Ward* is obvious. See also entry 194 of the Commonplace Book, which appears to summarise the opening of de la Mare's novel.

99. *Spook Stories* (1928). HPL explains in a letter why he did not cite the volume by name: "No—I don't like the title '*Spook* Stories'. It has a suggestion of triviality" (HPL to August Derleth, 21 August [1932]; ms., SHSW).

100. "The Ghost of Fear" is nothing more than the early story "The Red Room" (in *The Plattner Story and Others* and *Thirty Strange Stories* [both 1897]), apparently retitled by Joseph Lewis French for his anthology, *Ghosts, Grim and Gentle* (1926). HPL had read *Thirty Strange Stories* in 1924 (*SL* 1.287), but evidently the story did not make an impression upon him at that time.

101. Hodgson was brought to HPL's attention only in 1934 by H. C. Koenig (*SL* 5.26, 41). The essay "The Weird Work of William Hope Hodgson" (*Phantagraph*, February 1937), written prior to the passage on Hodgson in SHL, contains the following introductory paragraph: "Mr. H. C. Koenig has conferred a great service on American 'fandom' by calling attention to the remarkable work of an author relatively unknown in this country, yet actually forming one of the few who have captured the illusive inmost essence of the weird. Among connoisseurs of phantasy fiction William Hope Hodgson deserves a high and prominent rank; for triumphing over a sadly uneven stylistic quality, he now and then equals the best masters in his vague suggestions of lurking worlds and beings behind the ordinary surface of life." The rest of the essay appears without substantial alteration in SHL, although HPL has here added a discussion of *The Ghost Pirates*, which does not appear in the essay.

102. It is not entirely clear which works by Conrad HPL read, nor is it certain that he read the celebrated *Heart of Darkness*, which some have classed as a weird tale. Consider this discussion of *Lord Jim*, in which he remarks that he had "previously read only the shorter and minor productions of Conrad": "Conrad is at heart supremely a poet, and though his narration is often very heavy and involved, he displays an infinitely potent command of the soul of men and things, reflecting the tides of affairs in an unrivalled procession of graphic pictures which burn their imagery indelibly upon the mind. . . . No artist I have yet encountered has so keen an appreciation of the essential *solitude* of the high-grade personality . . ." (HPL to Lillian D. Clark, 25 May 1925; *LNY* 129).

103. First read by HPL, at Frank Belknap Long's suggestion, in the summer of 1923 (*SL* 1.228, 233–34).

104. *Far-Off Things* (1922; *LL* 570), *Things Near and Far* (1923; *LL* 577), and *The London Adventure; or, The Art of Wandering* (1924; *LL* 574).

105. Machen translated the complete *Memoirs* of Casanova (1894) as well as the *Heptameron* of Marguerite of Navarre (1886) and random works by Cervantes, Beroalde de Verville, and others.

106. Originally published in *The Man from Genoa and Other Poems* (Athol, MA: W. Paul Cook, 1926), p. 28; rpt. in *In Mayan Splendor* (Sauk City, WI: Arkham House, 1977), p. 14. Long was, of course, a close associate of HPL.

107. The root conception of this story was clearly borrowed by HPL in "The Dunwich Horror" (1928), where Wilbur Whateley and his twin are also the offspring of a human woman and a non-human father, Yog-Sothoth.

108. Cf. the similar diary kept by Wilbur Whateley in "The Dunwich Horror"; where, indeed, such terms from "The White People" as "Aklo" and "Voorish sign" occur (see n. 110 below).

109. HPL mentions creatures named "Doels" in "The Whisperer in Darkness" (DH 256), evidently a borrowing from Machen, although HPL's direct source appears to have been Frank Belknap Long's "The Hounds of Tindalos," where "Doels" are also mentioned. Creatures named "dholes" were formerly thought to be cited in The Dream-Quest of Unknown Kadath, but this proves to have been a textual error for "bholes."

110. Cf. Wilbur Whateley's diary in "The Dunwich Horror": "Today learned the Aklo for the Sabaoth" (DH 184).

111. Cf. Wilmarth's remark in "The Whisperer in Darkness": "Most of my foes, however, were merely romanticists who insisted on trying to transfer to real life the fantastic lore of lurking 'little people' made popular by the magnificent horror-fiction of Arthur Machen" (DH 214).

112. C. Lucius Solinus, Latin writer of the third century C.E., author of the Collectanea Rerum Memorabilium or the Polyhistor (as it is more commonly known), a compendium of natural history and geography largely derived from the Natural History of Pliny the Elder. There was an early English translation by Arthur Golding (1587). The Latin text has been edited by Theodor Mommsen (Berlin, 1895; rev. 1958).

113. For the influence of this tale on "Cool Air" see above (n. 62). See also entry 191 of the Commonplace Book.

114. HPL's first exposure to Blackwood occurred in early 1920, and it was not favourable (see HPL to the Gallomo, [January? 1920]; Letters to Alfred Galpin [Hippocampus Press, 2003], p. 73). But HPL later read "The Willows" in The Listener and Other Stories (1907) and became a Blackwood devotee for life (see HPL to Lillian D. Clark, 29–30 September 1924; LNY 64).

115. More properly "Smith: An Episode in a Lodging House."

116. "A weird story, to be a serious aesthetic effort, must form primarily a picture of a mood—and such a picture certainly does not call for any clever jack-in-the-box fillip. There are weird stories which more or less conform to this description . . . especially in Blackwood's Incredible Adventures" (SL 5.160).

117. HPL refers to the stories "The Regeneration of Lord Ernie," "The Sacrifice," and "A Descent into Egypt."

118. Probably an influence on HPL's "The Shadow over Innsmouth."

119. These names are, respectively, from King Argimēnēs and the Unknown Warrior (in Five Plays [1914]), "Bethmoora" (in A Dreamer's Tales [1910]), "Poltarnees, Beholder of Ocean" (in A Dreamer's Tales), "Carcassonne" (in A Dreamer's Tales), King Argimēnēs and the Unknown Warrior, and "Time and the Gods" (in Time and the Gods [1906]).

120. HPL refers to "Distressing Tale of Thangobrind the Jeweller," "The House of the Sphinx," "Probable Adventure of the Three Literary Men" (probably an influence on HPL's "The Terrible Old Man" [1920]), "The Hoard of the Gibbelins," "How Nuth Would Have Practised His Art upon the Gnoles," and "How One Came, as Was Foretold, to the City of Never."

121. HPL refers to "Bethmoora," "Idle Days on the Yann" (he borrowed the detail in "The Doom That Came to Sarnath"), and "Poor Old Bill."

122. "Preface" to More Ghost Stories of an Antiquary (1911).

123. HPL refers to "The Ash-Tree" and "'Oh, Whistle, and I'll Come to You, My Lad.'" HPL makes an almost exact quotation from the story: ". . . it is a horrible, an intensely horrible, face of crumpled linen."

124. For the influence of this story upon HPL, see Richard Ward, "In Search of the Dread Ancestor: M. R. James' 'Count Magnus' and Lovecraft's *The Case of Charles Dexter Ward*," *Lovecraft Studies* No. 36 (Spring 1997): 14–17.

125. But only six years previous HPL had written: "And nine persons out of ten *never heard of* Ambrose Bierce, the greatest story writer except Poe whom America ever produced" ("The Defence Reopens!" [1921]; CE5).

126. "The cup of the Ptolemies, formerly known as the cup of St Denis, is preserved in the Cabinet des Médailles of the Bibliothèque Nationale in Paris. It is a cup 4¾ in. high and 5⅛ in. in diameter, and richly decorated with Dionysiac emblems and attributes in relief." Alexander Murray Stuart and Arthur Hamilton Smith, "Gem," *Encyclopaedia Britannica*, 11th ed. (1910–11), 11:567.

PREFACE [TO *WHITE FIRE* BY JOHN RAVENOR BULLEN]

What truly constitutes a poet it is very hard to say. Nowadays, when intellect elbows for more than its allotted space in the aesthetic field, we are prone to analyse profoundly, seek for fundamentals, and discourse sagely of the unique insight, individual point of view, and personally selective imagination of the essential bard. We affect to demand that he see nothing undivested of its traditional associations, and that he present to us only the nuclear, isolated, and austerely unadorned imaginative content of his random reactions to experience and emotion. The result is a jarring jumble of academic schools, each based upon sterile theory rather than artistic feeling, which favour us with carefully roiled chaoticisms of varying cast; from the chromatic sensation-vortices of the imagists to the frozen mental detritus of Mr. T. S. Eliot and his followers. Amidst this welter of scientific psychology the art impulse is expected to survive as best it may; and too often its absence is pardoned out of deference to a theoretical form which current yardsticks coolly measure and pronounce real poetry on strictly philosophical grounds.

The late John Ravenor Bullen, in the profusion of delightful lyric poetry on which his increasing literary recognition was founded, wholly repudiated the bondage of contemporary theory and was the more genuine artist thereby. Acknowledging the debt owed by all present beauty to the generations of inherited impressions whence springs its existing relation to human emotion, he was too wise to discard the music, rhythms, symmetries, aspects of vision, and turns of thought and phrase with which spontaneous aesthetic feeling has coloured its expression down the long ages that Nature has forced it to find an outlet. Sensitive to the equal artistic significance of moods and matter, dreams and diurnalities, the fata morgana and facts, he did not neglect to treasure that rare quality of *glamour* which, scorned though it is by realists, yet embodies perhaps the better part of all the loveliness we know in the illusory comedy of appearances called life. A sound instinct kept him closely within the main line of the great English tradition, thus fitting him for the harmonious reflection of those fancies, conceptions, and perspectives which with us must always be strongest because they are the simple aggregate and heritage of a thousand years of our continuous racial and cultural experience.

Mr. Bullen's particular secret as a poet lay, apart from his keen visual imagination and the natural sense of sound which gave melody and limpidity to all his lines and set him unerringly on the trail of the perfectly symphonic word, in the fact that he has preserved his golden illusions and faculty of wonder and values in life. For him the zest and dewiness of the May morning have never departed, and amidst our prevailing desert of cynical sophistication he is able to feel that thrill of pleasure, novelty, and ecstasy in the daily round of terrestrial phenomena which animated the freshly vigorous bards of a brighter time. That thrill alone, so difficult of achievement today, is the one ultimate determinant of the true poet. It is the quality of youth—a youth with Endymion-like independence of chronology—which with a magic quite distinct from anything else we know has the unshared power of animating with grace, marvellousness, and the aspect of significance a world and universe visible to the modern prose mind only as a dull, purposeless, and unsatisfying cycle of electronic, atomic, and molecular rearrangements.

Keeping these sources of inspiration in mind, it is interesting to speculate on the precise methods whereby Mr. Bullen secured his felicitous effects. That *simplicity* was a strong factor is at once obvious; for no one can fail to note how carefully the snares of linguistic complexity, impressionistic chaos, and intellectual involution have been avoided. The author was determined that his pictures stand out in a clear, full light; and that not a particle of their final effect be sacrificed through useless diversions of the reader's vision and attention. Moreover, so skilfully did he manage this point, that there is no outward appearance of strained simplification; no artificial naiveté, no affectedly primerish gestures, and none of the slashing contempt for finenesses and subtleties which marks many writers' efforts at directness. The language is the language of civilised society, with no lack of the colour, richness, and variety necessary to full and flexible utterance; but it is not cast in riddles for riddles' sake, or tortured into meaningless attempts to express the inexpressible—which latter, despite the celebrated Gallic dictum, cannot be considered as wholly banished from life and thought. When ecstasy is demanded, it is created not by a lapse into exclamatory incoherence but by choice of precisely the most graphic and forcible words, all used in normal fashion; for to a connoisseur and colourist like Mr. Bullen, there are enough vivid vocables at command to obviate all need for extravagant distortions. In most cases, the favoured words are the common, beloved ones, to which tradition has bequeathed its mellowest and most enduring overtones; but when the exotic or the unusual was demanded, the poet was not slow to rise to the occasion.

Another source of Mr. Bullen's wide appeal is the quality of *universality*; whereby he tended to touch upon those moods and sentiments which are shared by all the race, rather than harp as most lyrists do upon the subjective emotional phenomena peculiar to themselves. This is, indeed, the authentic attitude of classicism; and is powerful in our poet's work because it was absolutely genuine with him. It here figures as no mere theory or result of conscious straining, but as the natural product of an imagination attuned to the universal emotions. With Mr. Bullen it was this general body of sentiment which possessed the prime elements of glamour, witchery, and loveliness; and because his response to its stimulus was absolutely sincere, he was able to reflect it with all the splendours he himself found twined about it, achieving just as poignant results as does the more personal poet with his highly individualised reactions. Here, indeed, we have an illuminatingly definite proof of the fact that real poetry springs not from any fine-wrought formula or choice of theme, but purely and exclusively from the degree of wonder and ecstasy in the poet's mind, irrespective of subject or type of medium.

Mr. Bullen's general attitude toward life and the universe was one of optimistic acceptance, achieved through a preoccupation with the beauties of orthodox tradition which prevented more than a fleeting glimpse of the stern scientific background. Only once—in the haunting and alluringly Poe-like song called "The Music of the Spheres"—did this defensive armour threaten to give way and admit the despair or resignation of the philosophic modern; for the most part the poet was genuinely able to retain the point of view of the great Victorians, to whose style he was so unmistakably an heir. It is not, of course, to be imagined for a moment that Mr. Bullen's orthodoxy led him into absurdities and insipidities. Working within a cosmos mapped out by the dreams of generations, he displayed a flawless psychological consistency, and ran the gamut of the more beautiful moods and emotions without discords or extravagances. To Tennyson he was probably most keenly indebted for his outlook and method, and he surely formed a disciple in whom the famous nineteenth-century laureate might justly take pride. Here and there a trace of gentle wistfulness crops out to lend a delicate minor note to the symphony, but in the main there predominates an intense delight in present loveliness and in visions of a rosily imagined futurity which gives the work its characteristic tone. The sometimes wearying didacticism of the nineteenth century is not often found in Mr. Bullen's verse. When a moral does appear, it is urbanely insinuated rather than hammered in; and for the most part the author was content to let his images speak for themselves in beauty, the reader to draw whatever lesson—if any—he might feel prompted to draw.

If any fault be discernible in Mr. Bullen's writing, it is a slight tendency to overwork those archaic forms which Pre-Raphaelitism restored to English verse for a season, but at which a more classical taste is again beginning to look at least questioningly. It would, of course, be hyper-critical to deny any authentic poet of the Victorian tradition an occasional *ere, nay, 'tis, doth, thou, hath,* or expletive *do* or *did;* but one may pardonably pause before recommending these forms for constant employment. This applies likewise to the inversions and characteristically crystallised words and phrases which Mr. Bullen sometimes used—poetic licences like *recollections fond; throng, whom restlessly I seek among; bubbling swift their course along; who sanction lent,* and so on; stock expressions like *merry month of May, sun-caressed, feathered songsters, bitter sacrifice, white-plumed, Dame Nature, merry pipes of Pan,* and the like; and single words like *entrancing,* which excessive and inappropriate popular usage has unfortunately stripped of their pristine freshness and value. All these, however, are merely tendencies against which the author usually succeeded in guarding himself; as are the infrequent rusty patches in the metre, and the very rare rhymes which might not win the entire endorsement of Walker's celebrated dictionary. They do not hamper the flow of song and imagery, nor could they ever have suggested any further admonition to the poet than that he exercise at all times that perfect—though to him perhaps fatiguing—fastidiousness which appears in his technical masterpieces.

Mr. Bullen's work seems divisible into seven major classes, each ably and appropriately handled. There is, to begin with, the purely lyrical response to Nature's sheer beauty, opulently displayed in such tuneful shouts as "The Copse" or such irradiate musings as "Evening at the Lakeside", and forming to the present editor's mind the finest flowering of our author's genius. One might consume columns in listing the choice titles which fall under this head, so that we may here do no more than recall a few salient triumphs like the aforementioned two, the perfumed magic of "My Garden", the quaint piquancy of "Where Mayflies Dance", the impressive majesty of "The Storm",[1] the vivid breathlessness of "The Seagull", and the early poems—less assured, perhaps, yet full of golden radiance—"A Country Lane" and "In the Woods". In all these verses the glamour and ecstasy are secured in the simplest possible way, yet are of the utmost poignancy because of the poet's sharp visual imagination and effective command of words.

A second division of Mr. Bullen's work is closely allied to the first, and identical with it so far as most of the imagery is concerned. This is the nature-poetry in which a philosophical strain is embodied, but in which the elements of colour and atmosphere always predominate over the superimposed idea. Excellent instances of this class are afforded by "Thy Perfect Peace", "Far-Distant Bells", "Hope", and above all by that magnificently elfin masterpiece "The Music of the Spheres", which in the opinion of at least one critic forms the absolute high-water mark of its author's talent.

A third type of Bullen verse is the frankly philosophical, with ideas straightforwardly presented, and having only as much of imagery as is necessary to the graphic and graceful illustration of those ideas. This is a sort of poetry which can easily become barren and prosy in the hands of an inexperienced bard; but Mr. Bullen generally managed to ward off the daemon Dulness and to display in even the most homiletic of his lines a mastery of form and development whose architectural quality makes it art in spite of its subject-matter. "Meredith was a prose Browning," wrote Oscar Wilde, *"and so was Browning."*[2] Mr. Bullen had obviously read the great nineteenth-century verse-psychologist well, but was far too astute to follow him into the dreariest mazes of his rugged aridity and prosaic perversity. Of our author's didactic pieces, one might prominently mention "My Creed", "God's Answer", and best of all, the sonnet entitled "God".

As a "fourthly" we may cite a large body of amatory verse extending over a long period of time and containing some marvellously moving touches of human feeling. Less distinctive perhaps than other phases of Mr. Bullen's Muse, it nevertheless has a rare stamp of intensity and sincerity; and not infrequently an almost Elizabethan tinge of balladry. Notable in this field are "Love's Anguish", "The Quest", and "Pluck One Rose and Give to Me".

A fifth though by not means numerous class includes Mr. Bullen's war verse, which contains the same lyric fire that animates the love-poetry, and which reaches its apex in brief utterances like "'Reported Missing'". Still slenderer, and unrepresented in the present collection, is the sixth category of *vers de société*, which finds exemplification in a number of clever acrostics and breezy metrical sallies. Seventh and last, also unrepresented here, comes the bulk of Mr. Bullen's humorous productions, mostly in the dialect of the Canadian oil fields which he knew so well. Here we find exhibited an astonishing versatility; for if in his serious poetry our author shared the delicacy of a Tennyson, he was in his comic efforts proportionately well endowed with the kindly grotesquerie and robust whimsicality of a Dickens. His humour was genuinely unforced, and often almost rollicking; friendly in essence, and virtually untouched by satire or irony. It was, in short, the characteristic "healthy" humour of the nineteenth century; its chief fault—when faulty at all—being a sort of picturesque extravagance to which the greatest of the Victorian jesters were equally prone.

The general recognition of Mr. Bullen's poetic ability has been gradual but gratifyingly steady. He was a constant victor in every kind of literary contest, winning notable awards in the Philadelphia Society of Arts and Letters, the American Poetry Association, the United and National Amateur Press Associations, and the Quill Club of London, of which latter he was for years the American representative. He has to his credit lines and passages that ought never to be forgotten, and had he lived longer we might have expected a mellowing and technical perfection well calculated to seat him among the actual leaders of his craft. In the merit of his work we may see a renewed demonstration of the soundness of conservative fundamentals, and of the basic truth that art's secret lies not in theme or medium, but in the artist's degree of genuinely glamorous or ecstatic vision, whatever be its mood or direction. Clear, unaffected, and rich without eccentricity, Mr. Bullen's best poetry might profitably be taken as a text by the striver against contemporary faddism. He has shewn us by example that wonder is not confined to the uniquely perverted, or true aesthetic feeling to the hectically distorted.

John Ravenor Bullen, born in 1886 as the eldest son of Mr. and Mrs. N. R. H. Bullen, was reared in a delectably embowered ancestral home of Jacobean construction in Bampton, Oxfordshire, England; a seat and garden of beauty which he has potently described in many of his verses and in the languorous prose-poem "Ronevar's Cottage". His first poetry, written in schooldays, shews many signs of the qualities which were later to distinguish it. In early manhood he migrated with his family to Petrolea, in the oil districts of Western Ontario, where he held forth as a cultural pioneer, with increasing interests in the literary activity of North America. He was a lifelong sufferer from ill-health, a circumstance which he valiantly bore and minimised amidst a plenitude of intellectual and aesthetic labours and a judicious series of travels in the wilder parts of Southern Canada. A prose writer as well as a poet, he was the author of many acute criticisms and of at least one unpublished novel, a refreshing romance of old seaways and pirate treasure entitled "From the Mouth of the Golden Toad".[3] The present volume, with its Shelleyan title,[4] was long planned by Mr. Bullen himself; posthumous editing being confined to minor matters of arrangement wholly in consonance with the author's known intention.

On February 28, 1927, Mr. Bullen succumbed to a long siege of endocarditis following a severe attack of grippe. His courage and spirits were always unbroken, and his mother has found in this sonnet an almost perfect expression of the high heart which would wish no shadows even at the last:

> "When I am dead chant no sad songs for me,
> And let no funeral dirge disturb the air.
> Oh, let there be no blackness of despair,
> Or aught that makes my faith a mockery.
> I, who have loved evenings on land and sea,
> That evening when I pass from Here to There,
> Would have my going gladsome—free from care—
> I, who so fondly love this earth and thee!
>
> So think upon our dear ecstatic hours,
> Of books we've loved, and thoughts we've pondered o'er,
> And let each thought a sense of nearness bring;
> For, while my earthly form lies mute 'mid flowers,
> My soul, still loving thee, shall, singing, soar
> On wings of joy into Eternal Spring."

The poet rests now under a white marble cross, on which is carved that supreme utterance of his well-loved brother-singer Rupert Brooke; expressing what they both felt for the mighty, ancient, and beautiful land of their birth and deepest dreams:

> *If I should die, think only this of me:*
> *That there's some corner of a foreign field*
> *That is for ever ENGLAND.*[5]

EDITOR'S NOTE FP: In *White Fire* by John Ravenor Bullen (Athol, MA: The Recluse Press, 1927), pp. 7–13. Bullen was an Englishman who had emigrated to Canada; HPL had been acquainted with him since at least 1921, when they were both involved in the Transatlantic Circulator, an Anglo-American group of amateur writers who criticised one another's manuscripts. HPL's preface is an extensive revision of the article "The Poetry of John Ravenor Bullen" (*United Amateur*, September 1925; see Appendix for text), resurrected by HPL for this selection of Bullen's poetry, funded by Bullen's friend Archibald Freer as a memorial to Bullen, who had died in February 1927. W. Paul Cook of the Recluse Press printed a second edition in 1929, but it was never bound or distributed.

Notes

1. Published in HPL's *Conservative* No. 13 (July 1923): 9–10.

2. The statement is found in the essay "The Critic as Artist" (*Nineteenth Century*, July 1890).

3. Cf. HPL's "Final Words" (1921), in which he hopes that "Messrs. Munday and Bullen will have the abounding charity to shew me the remainder of their respective novels, concerning whose terminations I am in a wholesome state of surprise" (CE5).

4. The phrase "white fire" occurs three times in Shelley: "The Cloud" (l. 45), "Letter to Maria Gisborne" (l. 70), and *Prometheus Unbound* (1.432).

5. Rupert Brooke (1887–1915), "The Soldier" (1914), ll. 1–3.

NOTES ON "ALIAS PETER MARCHALL", BY A. F. LORENZ

This story shews an encouraging fluency and assurance in the handling of narration and dialogue; its chief needs being a greater adherence to life and probability, and a greater freedom from artificiality and conventionality in plot, incidents, and motivation. In other words, the prime effort of the author in revision should be to avoid the reflection of phraseology, situations, character-types, and plot-developments found in the field of popular reading, and to arrive at a more direct and first-hand contact with life and events themselves. Let the source of ideas be not the stories one has read, but the happenings one has noticed in real life; either through direct observation and report, or through the authentic presentation of life in the press, and in scientific books or articles on history, biography, sociology, psychology, and so on. What a good story ought to reflect is not what people are *popularly supposed* to think, feel, say, want, and do, but what people *really* think, feel, say, want, and do. The habit of dealing with life on these authentic terms can be gained from a faithful reading of the truly solid as opposed to the frothy authors. Dreiser, Sherwood Anderson, Edith Wharton, John Galsworthy, Joseph Conrad, De Maupassant, Thomas Mann, Dostoievsky, Turgeniev—these are only a few of the writers whose influence is in the right direction.

In this particular story, the chief trouble is with what we call *motivation*—that is, the art of *having things happen from adequate and probable causes*, just as they would have to happen in real life. When a writer sets down a certain thing as happening or existing, he must arrange the *other* events and conditions of his tale in such a way as to make the given thing not only *reasonably likely* but *almost inevitable*. When he does not do this, the result is to leave the reader impressed with the unreality and artificiality of the whole story. The most extreme violations of this principle occur in the form of *coincidences*—stretched, in the work of many literary beginners, to such a vast distance beyond all human probability or possibility that they become matters of unconscious humour.

The present story has many strained coincidences which need elimination—indeed, its central incident involves such a thing. We may outline this offending coincidence by asking certain questions:

(a) why did Evelyn happen to choose the same town for residence which Peter had chosen, unknown to her?

(b) why did her motor accident happen to bring her to the door of a friend of Peter's?

The fact that such coincidences do occur once in an age in real life, does not make them sufficiently typical of life to warrant their use in fiction. In removing this coincidence from the story, the way to start would be to give Peter and Evelyn some special interest in common; some interest especially connected with the city in which the final reunion occurs. In that case, it would be the same tie which had originally drawn them together, that would bring about the reunion. It might be some historical enthusiasm in which the given city had a prominent place, some art or science especially cultivated in that city, or some form of social study or work in which this city offered a particularly specialised field. But the point is that there must be some reason for both characters' choice—unknown to each other—of the same town to live in. The matter of the accident ought to be smoothed out on similar principles—or removed altogether, with the substitution of some other vivid and dramatic form of confrontation.

In the matter of the priest's recognition of his visitor as the fiancée of his friend, more clearness ought to be observed. It must be made plain, if this incident is retained, that the priest identifies Evelyn by her *name,* and not by any vague, troubled look which draws forth a tale. In real life it would be absurd to suppose that a "troubled look" would be obvious—or that it would lead a sensible and non-meddlesome clergyman into asking a guest for the latter's life-story. Indeed—the accident itself would account for any troubled look that might be present! The *name* is the only possible link—for Peter *might* have told his friend that. Then the priest could elicit the story for verification purposes.

Apart from this matter of incident-motivation, the story needs attention from the standpoint of sound *psychological probability.* That is, we must ask whether the characters really do what living people do under similar conditions, or whether they behave like artificial puppets according to hackneyed, false patterns devised by former popular writers. Here it must greatly be doubted whether the principals of the tale feel and act in a life-like way. The ancient and trite fictional device of the "proud lover" may have some basis of fact under certain conditions, but it is more often found to be a sheer trick of romantic invention. In the present story it is quite conceivable that Peter would have offered his fiancée a release upon losing his money, but it is altogether *inconceivable* that he would have gone to the grotesque length of changing his name and going into hiding. What an average man with the average amount of delicacy would clearly have done, is to offer release—and upon the fiancée's refusal of that, to consider the marriage as simply *postponed* until he might get on his feet again. He would not flee like a melodrama hero, or expect such a frantic pursuit as to necessitate his taking an alias! As a matter of fact, the very element of 'undying devotion' on both sides in this tale is a rather dubious piece of psychology. People are not so naturally monogamous as to ponder forever over one "lost love", except in cases of definite emotional unbalance or extreme intellectual naiveté. When the stir of one affair blows over, they follow the line of least resistance and seek new alignments if the obstacles in the way of the old are too great. Altogether, the only rational way to motivate the separation of Peter and Evelyn, and to account for the avoidance of the latter by the former, is to introduce a normal and ordinary *quarrel* in place of the hackneyed "proud lover" device. Such a thing could be so arranged as to make the evasion, pursuit, final reconciliation, etc., seem at least measurably plausible. But the assumed-name matter is going rather far, and ought to be removed. Rather, let the hero live *obscurely* as a result of his reduced fortunes, and let the city of meeting be so *large* that the previous inquiries of Evelyn failed merely through the ordinary needle-in-a-haystack principle. Also—don't have those inquiries quite so *assiduous*. With time, the poignancy of Evelyn's emotion will inevitably have worn off somewhat. The matter will have receded into a half-dreamlike sentimentalised borderland—which will, however, make the final reunion all the more glamorous; partaking of the nature of a reincarnation, or the recapture of a lost reality from the domain of myth and dream.

Other touches of artificiality and stereotyped convention in place of reality are found in numerous incidents and characterisations—as well as in occasional excesses of phraseology. Close analysis will reveal any of the following pictures as distinctly *artificial*—bits of ready-made colour lifted bodily from the common stock-room of popular fiction, instead of things actually derived from life or proceeding from the individual imagination of the author:

> Typical "society" scene and atmosphere—p. 1
> Typical accident *pathos*—"small dark bundle", etc.—p. 3
> Typical benevolent priest—pp. 4 et seq.
> Typical adolescent romance and characters—Pittsburgh steel heiress and generalised Harvard youth—p. 6
> Typical treatment of authorship as glib mechanical acquirement—p. 7
> Typical stage reunion—"Peter! Evelyn!"—p. 9
> Typical use of identifying scar—p. 10 et ante
> Typical reconciler role as enacted by priest—p. 10

Some of these cases of literary insincerity or "emotional short cuts" are not extreme ones, while others approach the point of what is known as "hokum". The way to get rid of them all is to cast aside the idea of drawing material from one's light fictional reading, and to subject every incident in the tale to the acid test of *what ordinarily happens in actual life*. No author can be ignorant of the prosaic daily life around him. What do people normally do and say from day to day—how so they react to this and that situation? It is from this kind of knowledge, and not from one's recollections of novels and magazine tales, that the material for sound fiction must be drawn. In drawing a character or a scene, don't try to do it as some other author has done, but use original judgment and observation—set down simply your own idea of what such a character or scene is *really* like. A *real* account of a literary lecture, for example, would have different stresses and selections of incidents and descriptions from those in a purely conventional and imitative account. So would a *real* account of an accident, or a priest, or a romance, or a reunion, and so on. Write as you would in a diary or a personal letter—not as you would in preparing a dime novel!

However—don't let it be assumed that this estimate of the story is an unrelievedly unfavourable one. As stated at the outset, there is no question of the tale's assurance and fluency; or of the author's power to handle the essentials of language, narration, and dialogue, once his attention to adequate motivation and correct psychology becomes closer. These assets are very considerable ones—assets which many have to study years to gain and which some never gain perfectly—so that the author need not feel that his imperfect care in plot-elements involves any reduction to the foot of his class. What is needed is merely a little more penetrating vision, realistic analysis, and discrimination in narrative selection—a slight raising of the standard of life-like convincingness all along the line. Such an improvement is not difficult to effect, nor does it imply any long course of training or study. Merely a *readjustment of perspective*—and the trick is accomplished. The very next tale of the same author is perfectly likely to be free from most of the flaws noted in this one.

EDITOR'S NOTE FP: *Lovecraft Studies* No. 28 (Spring 1993): 20–22. Text based on the AMS (JHL). The occasion of this essay's writing is unclear; it was possibly written as an outgrowth of HPL's work with pupils of Anne Tillery Renshaw ("our old-time fellow-amateur Mrs. Renshaw has reappear'd on the horizon with a lot of overflow theme papers from her school to be criticis'd and graded": SL 3.130) or Maurice W. Moe. The date of the essay's composition is unknown, but the handwriting dates it to the late 1920s or early 1930s. The essay reveals HPL's cogent analysis of short story technique and his emphasis on proper motivation of characters' actions and on lifelike (as opposed to formulaic or melodramatic) depiction of character and events.

FOREWORD [TO *THOUGHTS AND PICTURES* BY EUGENE B. KUNTZ]

Readers of the Southwestern dailies, the Presbyterian denominational press, and the journals of the National Amateur Press Association need no introduction to the poetry of the Reverend Eugene B. Kuntz, D.D.

For many years Dr. Kuntz has reflected the thoughts and experiences of a full and active life in verse, and lately his productiveness has reached an astonishing level. It is only fitting, then, that a group of his informal metrical musings be preserved in a medium less ephemeral than the periodical press.

Dr. Kuntz is best known—and justly so—for his vivid and original poems on aspects of mountain grandeur. Unusually sensitive to this form of beauty, and fortunate enough to have lived for a long time in Colorado, where it is supremely exemplified, he has celebrated the changeless majesty and kaleidoscopic moods of earth's peaks in words and cadences that echo much of the mystic stateliness of their themes. Some day, it is to be hoped, a collection of this mountain poetry can be published.

The dominant style of Dr. Kuntz is a long iambic line—often an Alexandrine— exhibiting apt and stately compound words sometimes coined with vast originality and spontaneousness. Though traditional in cast, the poems shew in their images a fresh and individual perception and strong and sincere artistic emotion. Even when some sententious reflection occurs toward the close, it is seldom obtruded so baldly as to dilute the poetry.

In the present collection many of the pieces represent a somewhat different side of Dr. Kuntz's work; homely and familiar newspaper verse in which phases of life are touched upon with thoughtful observation and reflection. Most of these, very naturally, are meant to be judged by the canons of good sense and general taste rather than by those laws of abstract aesthetics which rule out everything savouring of the conventional in atmosphere and phraseology.

Dr. Kuntz, though born in the Rhineland district of Germany, was brought to America as an infant and reared on the edge of the old South. Entering the Presbyterian ministry, he has held many important pastorates in the West and Southwest. His literary activities have increased from year to year, and his verse now forms an almost daily feature in the press in his region. He belongs to several prominent literary organisations, and is represented in the International Poets' Anthology for 1929.

EDITOR'S NOTE FP: In *Thoughts and Pictures* by Eugene B. Kuntz (Haverhill, MA: "Co-operatively published by H. P. Loveracft [sic] and C. W. Smith," 1932), pp. [1–2]. A kindly preface to the selected poems of a longtime amateur, issued by the typographically challenged editor of the *Tryout*. HPL discusses the pamphlet briefly in "Notes on Verse Technique" (p. 152), confirming that it appeared before the writing of that essay.

NOTES ON VERSE TECHNIQUE

In trying to decide what real poetry, as distinguished from mere rhyming prose, actually is, we conclude that the essential marks of poetry are sincere and intense emotion, the use of delicate suggestion, symbolism, and depiction rather than bald statement as a medium of presentation, musically rhythmical language with sound expressive of the theme, and a tremendously exact and intelligent choice of words based on their associative value, literary and colloquial, and on their fresh unhackneyedness in connexion with the given purpose.

Naturally, so general a definition is of only vague help in enabling the amateur to discriminate between good and bad verse in specific cases; hence it would be well to inquire further about the earmarks of poetic merit. Roughly, we may say that any piece of intendedly poetic composition, whether one's own or another's, ought to be studied with a keen eye for at least four points: (1) suitability of the rhythmical form; (2) appropriateness of the vocabulary, language, and manner of approach; (3) sincerity, relevance, and vividness of the symbols, images, or figures of speech employed; and (4) sincerity and truth to human nature of the theme, mood, and plan of presentation.

The first point—about suitability of form—need not be taken as an argument for regular verse against intelligently irregular or free verse; for it means only that the basic harmony between thought and rhythm ought never to be broken, and that when a certain type of cadence-pattern is once decided on, it ought not to be blindly, carelessly, and capriciously violated by deviations inherently alien to it.

In free verse, of course, only a sort of natural taste or instinct can tell the beginner exactly what rhythms are or are not suited to certain passages in a given poem. That is one reason why the indiscriminate use of this medium is not to be highly recommended to the novice except when he has a spontaneous inclination toward it. The lack of guiding rules is a severe handicap at an early stage of poetic growth. In metrical verse, however, it is easy to envisage the various parts of any chosen rhythm-pattern, whether regular or irregular, and to see that the number of accentual beats in any given line complies with the understood requirements of a pattern.

Any good poetic manual like Brander Matthews' "A Study of Versification",[1] or any standard textbook on composition and rhetoric, will give the beginner a full idea of the various English metres, their names, their rules, and their relative fitness for different types of poetic use. It remains for him to see just how these metres are to be applied in practice. Many novices appear to think that the management of line-lengths is a wholly free-and-easy, hit-or-miss process; so that we often find in the amateur papers something like the following:

> "My eyes doth behold the tawdry sky,
> My thoughts doth soar up very high,
> I study, I meditate, my soul opens wide
> Like the rushing and rolling of the daily flood tide."

Now this will never do. When we agree on a certain pattern, assigning so many beats to a line, we must stick to it. In the case cited, the author undoubtedly wanted to use iambic tetrameter, or iambic verse with four beats to a line, thought he succeeded in doing it only in his second line. A more correct version—with certain points other than metre also straightened out—might read:

> My eyes behold the vaulted sky,
> While every thought ascends on high;
> My brooding soul is opened wide
> To Truth's incessant mounting tide.

It will be noted that the amended version has exactly the same number of *syllables,* as well as of *beats,* to a line; and one may add that of course this must tend to be so, dominantly, in all regular metre, since each metrical beat is usually associated with a certain number of syllables. Thus four-beat iambic verse, since the iambic foot is traditionally an unstressed syllable followed by a stressed one, will always tend to have just eight syllables per line—as the foregoing revised specimen has. In general, it is safest for the beginner to count his syllables and plan his metrical pattern on a syllabic basis; though experienced poets, with a trained ear for subtle harmonies, are able to vary the number of *unstressed* syllables provided they keep to the prescribed number of beats per line. Thus Coleridge, in a specimen of four-beat iambics:

> "A snake's small eye blinks dull and shy,
> And the lady's eyes they shrunk in her head;
> Each shrunk up to a serpent's eye,
> And with somewhat of malice and more of dread
> At Christabel she looked askance. . . ."[2]

Here a genuine poetic master is syllabically irregular without spoiling the regularity of the underlying metrical pattern; but as in free verse, it takes a very sensitive and well-trained ear to decide just how to manage the irregular syllables. No beginner is likely to be able to "get away with it", hence the advisability of sticking at first to a regular number of syllables per line. Many, of course, prefer always to retain this absolute regularity; so that some of the world's foremost poetry is in lines which may be largely measured by syllable-counting. Everyone, however, should strive to educate his ear to such a point that he can discriminate between artistic, basically rhythmical irregularity and the irregularity which is irresponsible and violative of rhythm.

This applies not only to irregularity of syllables, but to such deviations from the main *accent* plan as cause one metrical foot to be substituted for another. In the midst of iambic verse we often insert a line which begins with a trochaic foot (with accents reversed) or a spondee (with two equally accented syllables), but we must learn to do this intelligently if we do it at all. Thus the following from Keats is wholly artistic, even though the lines do not all consist of alternating unstressed and stressed syllables as implied by the dominant iambic metre:

> "Then Lamia breathed death-breath; the sophist's eye,
> Like a sharp spear, went through her utterly;
> Keen, cruel, perceant, stinging: she as well
> As her weak hand could any meaning tell,
> Motioned him to be silent. . . ."[3]

Were it not for this variety of accent, a long piece of verse might readily become highly monotonous, yet it is only too easy to make careless variations which are not permissible at all. Thus the following is only harsh and ridiculous because of its irregularities:

> Bright shines the sun over the serene wold,
> And adorns every hedge with refined gold.

Clearly the original plan of an unstressed followed by a stressed syllable should be more closely adhered to—perhaps like this:

> Bright shines the sun above the quiet wold,
> Decking each hedge with transcendental gold.

Here the regularity is not absolute, but the exceptions are confined to places where they do not halt the rhythm. The learner should strive his utmost, by cultivating a rhythmic instinct and by studying the best poetic models, to develop a subconscious taste in the matter of cadences in poetry. Also, he should learn to shun freakish and arbitrary variations in his metrical plan, such as the insertion of lines of one kind of metre in the midst of a poem designed to be in another metre. All too many amateurs are careless in this respect; irresponsibly putting occasional tetrameter or hexameter lines in intendedly pentameter verse, and so on.

Now as for the second earmark of good verse—appropriateness of vocabulary, language, and manner of approach—here we must rely almost entirely on a developed taste, for the specific guiding rules are very few. We have noted before that certain archaic and affectedly "poetic" words are taboo—*yclept, quoth, doth, 'gan, charger, morn,* and things of that kind. It may be added that other words or alleged words such as *galore, enthused, doped, disgruntled,* etc., are taboo because they either do not properly exist or are parts of a lame, feeble type of tame, trite, and stupid colloquialism or "Babbitt English" without standing in any real art of expression. Further taboos exist against definitely slang words except in consciously light or comic verse; against the *oh's, ah's, alas's, dear's, sweet's,* and *tender's* of spurious emotion; and above all, against technical or technically-suggesting words such as *psychology, process, inhibition, educational, economics, terrain, parallax, citizenship, civics, maximum, stabalisation,* and the like, which are utterly and irrevocably confined to prose and the thought-processes peculiar to prose. Thus the following extracts are hopelessly unpoetical:

> "And don't make your trip purely educational,
> But let it be rather somewhat recreational."

> "Service and knowledge solve problems we share,
> More applied Religion leads to the goal,
> Character, Citizenship, Conduct fair,
> Build genuine Peace to master the whole,
> Coöperation with duty and care
> Will make Better Homes the joy of the soul."

In the same class are words or terms of expression suggestive of prose logic rather than poetic symbolism—*hence, therefore, thus, namely, respective, corollary,* and their kith.

It is, of course, but a step from this matter of vocabulary to the question of manner and approach. Here we may only say that poetry must convey its message simply and concretely; using plain, universal, and appropriately symbolic words, and speaking in images, comparisons, suggestions, and implications rather than in coldly explanatory statements or logical expositions. Thus the following line (referring to the Mound-Builders of prehistoric America), though taken from an intended poem, is certainly prose and nothing else:

> "And that whole population disappeared without leaving a physical trace."

To change this into poetry one would have to alter the whole method of diction and approach; untechnicalising the language, substituting pictures, comparisons, or emotional effects for dry statements, and producing something more like this:

> And like a cloud that melts in mystery
> Before the breath of summer's sun-charged wind,
> That race, whose walls had towered from sea to sea,
> Vanished, and left a lifeless void behind.

Often the contrast between prosaic and poetic expression is not as clear-cut as in this example; so that we must look sharply to see whether the poet is really speaking in symbols and images, or merely "bluffing" by writing literal prose statement in language otherwise fairly acceptable to poetry. For example, note the relative flatness and tameness of the following entirely correct verse:

> Her mouth is sweet and music-fraught,
> And on her fair face beams the glow
> Of amorous guile and subtle thought
> Bequeathed from Egypt long ago.

This is smooth enough, but there is no life in it because it merely *states* something instead of *picturing* it. It is really a paraphrase of the opening of Swinburne's "Cleopatra", and when we turn to the original we may instantly see how the concrete and figurative language vitalises and makes poetry of the description:

"Her mouth is fragrant as a vine,
   A vine with birds in all its boughs;
Serpent and scarab for a sign
   Between the beauty of her brows
And the amorous deep lips divine."[4]

    The third earmark of good verse—sincerity, relevance, and vividness of the symbols, images, or figures employed—is an infinitely subtler point than either of the preceding ones; and can be perfectly understood only through the development of one's own inmost taste. Often a poem may be as wholly figurative as the Swinburne original just quoted, yet it will fail to ring true because the symbols, images, and comparisons are forced, artificial, inapplicable, or not deeply felt. A figure of speech, to be really effective, must directly, powerfully, naturally, and genuinely symbolise the actual object, condition, or occurrence which the poet intends it to tell about. If it does not, the effect can never ring true, but will always be bad poetry. It is better to drop into figureless prose than to concoct flimsy and artificial figures which really apply very little to the thing depicted. Such pseudo-figures always reveal their irrelevance to the reader and make a poem feebler instead of stronger. Thus in the first specimen quoted in this article the final image is a palpably false one—a mere rhetorical flourish without relevance or meaning:

"... my soul opens wide
Like the rushing and rolling of the daily flood tide."

Does the *wide opening* of anything bear any resemblance to the *rolling of a tide?* If we have a symbol, it must be an applicable one. Had the poet compared the opening of his soul to the unfolding of flower-petals, the raising of a portcullis, or better still, the opening of a flood-gate, his parallel would have been an applicable and therefore potentially effective one. Some cases, of course, are far subtler than this. It is so easy in poetry to perpetrate passages like:

The roseate dawn at last flared up
Like wine within a magic cup;
While on the green the shadows fell
Like Titans half-invisible. . . .

Yet when we look closely at such concoctions we can easily see that the comparisons are forced, inept, and obviously devised merely of the sake of creating a poetic-looking exterior. They are not real because they are not exact, natural, and spontaneously generated in the poet's subconscious. They are no more real to the poet than to the reader. It will be useful to contrast a bit of typically pompous "hokum" with a piece of genuinely poignant concrete expression on the same subject; hence at the risk of consuming too much space the following pair of Memorial Day verses—collated some years ago by B. K. Hart, Literary Editor of the *Providence Journal*—are given in full.[5] A is smooth, and even free from really false figures, but the symbols are in this case ruined by sheer tameness and triteness. Notice the tremendously increased vitality of B, whose symbols and images are really living and potent ones:

A

Sleep, comrades, sleep and rest
  On this Field of the Grounded Arms,
Where foes no more molest,
  Nor sentry's shot alarms.

Ye have slept on the ground before,
  And started to your feet
At the cannon's sudden roar
  Or the drum's redoubling beat.

Rest, comrades, rest and sleep!
  The thoughts of men shall be
As sentinels to keep
  Your rest from danger free.

Your silent tents of green
  We deck with fragrant flowers;
Yours has the suffering been;
  The memory shall be ours.

B

Do not cry!
But gather buds! And with them greenery
Of slender branches taken from a tree
Well bannered by the Spring that saw them fall,
And you, for you are cleverest of all,
Who have slim fingers and are pitiful!
Brimming your lap with bloom that you may cull,
Will sit apart and weave for every head
A garland of the flowers you gathered.

Be green upon their graves, O happy Spring!
For they were young and eager who are dead!
Of all things that are young and quivering
With eager life, be they remembered
They move not here. They have gone to the clay.
They cannot die again for liberty!
Be they remembered of their land for aye!
Green be their graves, and green their memory!

But the fourth earmark of good verse—the sincerity and truth to human nature of the theme, mood, and plan of presentation—is the hardest one of all for the amateur to define and identify. Literature is so full of favourite stock subjects and conventional modes of treatment that it is really hard sometimes for a novice to know whether he is singing his own mood or the mood of an endless crowd of other writers whose style he relishes and tends to echo. If he is wise, he will beware of trusting himself to be original and sincere in any piece of work except one born directly out of his deepest personal feelings as distinguished from his polite and palpably acquired literary feelings. One ought not to make a show of great emotion where little or none exists. This sort of deception always results in feebleness, unconvincingness, and mushy sentimentality as distinguished from actual warmth. It is fairly easy to detect in the novice, for he usually reveals his hollowness by parading the long string of false-sentiment adjectives and ejaculations—*fond, grand, rare, mighty, wonderful, beauteous, sweet, oh, ah, hark, lo,* etc., etc.—with which he has whipped up a spurious enthusiasm for something that may or may not merit any enthusiasm at all. Much is revealed by choice of subject, as well—for we are on guard against saccharine and perfervid rhapsodings about home, mother, spring, pure love, snow, righteousness, pearly gates, the moon, courage, success, and all the rest of the old standbys.

Even worse than the insincere treatment of a theme which may in itself be intrinsically sound, is the juggling of false ideas and values which have no relation whatever to any form of life or reality. By this is meant, for one thing, the personification or attribution of feeling and consciousness to things utterly incapable of such treatment—the process by which mawkish poets speak of *tender* rocks that *dream* in the *sweet* twilight, or tell about the *song* of the *fond* blossom that *woos* the nightingale. Another form of this insincerity is the display of extravagant emotion over things which do not warrant it—as when the poetaster avers he is *ravished* and *transported* by the fact that a robin has laid an egg in his bird-house, or wails of being *plunged into abysses of grief* by the death of the day at sunset or that of the year in autumn. These are the kind of fellows whom beauty *hurts,* and who cannot see a butterfly without *chanting a hymn of praise.* A recent example of this type of artificial sentiment addresses the much-overworked moon as follows:

> "But to me—you're like a beautiful prayer—
> Something aloof—marvelous and rare."

Only wide reading, keen observation, and cultivated sensitivity will enable the novice to draw an exact and instant line between mawkishness and true feeling; but with time and growth the faculty becomes acute and readily available. The other points—form, language, vividness—likewise become clear under such a regimen; so that to the young bard in any stage of evolution we may always safely give one dominant piece of advice—to read, watch, think, feel, and practice for all he is worth; analysing every specimen of verse he writes or encounters, and refusing to be sidetracked by carelessness or inflated with false sentiment.

* * * * *

Recent months have brought such a profusion of good verse in the papers of the National that it will hardly be possible to do more than glance at certain salient examples.

In *Masaka* for October and January Mr. Burton Crane reveals himself as one of the cleverest and most intelligent of our poets, furnishing several specimens of diverse forms and varying degrees of seriousness whose connecting thread is a definite mood of ironic, half-jaunty disillusionment in which easy assurance is faintly touched with traces of light wistfulness. It is a poetry of ideas rather than of images; but the authenticity and distinctiveness of the mood, the mature flow of the language, and the aptness of the turns of thought all give it a lyric grace which places it far outside the field of mere rhyming prose.

Current colloquialism is often used to great advantage, especially in those pieces which frankly belong to the light verse category. "Lipstick", "A Bronx Cheer for Life", the sonnet sequence "In Passing", and others are all worth more than casual mention. The technique is in general so good that one wonders at the presence of two small but slightly irritating flaws—the assigning of a disyllabic value to the monosyllable *hours,* and the accenting of *romance* on the first syllable. Lighter pieces are "The Seal", "Your Love", and "The Ballad of Alexis", all of which contain an especially keen and sophisticated wit. "Little Streets at Night" is in many ways the finest of the offerings from an imaginative point of view, being full of vivid pictures which arouse a horde of pleasantly exotic vistas in the reader's mind. As the lines themselves say,

> "The silver ghosts of old Japan
> Come gliding forth from vase and fan
> And coloured prints live once again in little streets at night."

An additional word of praise is due to Mr. Crane for his brief but very illuminating article on Japanese poetry.

Ripples from Lake Champlain continues to purvey poetry of an exceptionally high order. The contributions of Vrest Orton,[6] mostly in the sonnet form, attain a literary level which puts them in competition with the best of recent American verse, whether inside or outside amateurdom. Mr. Orton's instinctive command of symbols and images expressive of precise shadings of emotion, and of verbal effects which convey worlds of thought in a single deft twist or eloquently significant pause, makes him a poet in the most genuine sense, and causes us to forgive any signs of careless workmanship which may now and then creep into his lines. "Pension" is a remarkably—almost disturbingly—vivid study of old age, which Editor Kelley has honoured by reprinting in a highly tasteful broadside form. "Mirage" is charged with an unusual amount of harmony despite an irregularity in the rhyme scheme and an employment of the somewhat outmoded archaisms 'neath and o'er. But the lyric "To Helen" is probably the most thoroughly poignant example of Mr. Orton's recent verse. The musical cadences of these brief couplets blend magnificently with the graphic and delicate procession of autumnal imagery—so that we quite forget the disyllabic use of *hour* in the first line.

Aptly supplementing Mr. Orton's work in *Ripples* are the twin replies to his "Pension" by Berniece L. Beane-Graham. While scarcely equalling the potency and rhythm of the original, they display much cleverness and observation, and exemplify an irregular metre which generally escapes harshness.

"Water Lily", by Rev. Philip Jerome Cleveland, is rich in visions of natural beauty, and is cast in a metre of alternating Alexandrine and pentameter lines which proves highly satisfactory until the Alexandrines, toward the close of the poem, unaccountably swell into heptameters. "Stars", by Daniel W. Smythe, "The Hell of Wrath", by Marie Tello Phillips, and various brief items by Bettie Margot Cassie, are all clear-cut and adequate in the expression of single ideas. "Eroti", by Ray H. Zorn, has images of genuine power, though the verses as a whole retain vague traces of an immature workmanship betrayed by the conscious rather than unconscious management of the rhythm. "An Evening and a Morning", by William Sheppard Sparks, is a free verse experiment whose panoramic glimpses indicate a very promising selective imagination, while "Universal Ripples", by Leonard Twynham, is exceedingly eloquent and melodious. The work of Miriam Irene Kimball, here as often elsewhere, suffers from a spirit of prose which persists in spite of the use of metre. It is a matter of vocabulary, mode of approach to the subject, type of diction, and the habit of making flat statements instead of using symbolism, association, suggestion, and pictorial imagery in conveying the desired effect. It would pay Miss Kimball to form a completely fresh idea of the province and methods of poetry through the study of some contemporary manual like the recently published works of L. A. G. Strong.[7] A similar criticism might sometimes be applied to the work of Florence Grow Proctor. Another kind of weakness—the weakness of trite, vague phraseology, diffuse, rather imitative stock emotion, and careless, uncritical, and unselective construction—is exhibited in "Oh! Moon", by Hazel Jacobs.

In "The Woodland Smoke" Rev. Eugene B. Kuntz is seen most advantageously as a weaver of exact, delicate images to mirror his sensitive responses to natural beauty. R. Malcolm Beal also shews much eloquence and vividness in his "Syrian Beggar's Prayer", though the form is somewhat irregular. Always graphic and meritorious are the short lyrics and vignettes by Marjorie Tullar, of which an untitled specimen heads the Autumn *Ripples*. Other excellent recent work by Miss Tullar includes "Irony" in the April *Sea Gull*, "Treasure Chest" in the January *New Amateur*, and "Sanctuary" in the November *Goldenrod*.

Scattered through the different papers of the day are many more poems of undoubted value. William Henry Blauvelt's "Evening", in the *New Amateur*, is very graceful except for the use of the awkward pseudo-poetic idiom *does rear*. "After the Christmas Dance", by Mary Elizabeth Mahakey in the December *Reg'lar Fellows*, has a pathos and simplicity belonging to the true poetic tradition. In the ample February *Amateur Affairs* several good verses occur; notably George W. Roberts' artistically sincere though not very polished "Regrets", Max Kaufman's "The Untapped", and Arthur Canto's "Sunset"—which latter would perhaps be more convincing if not so reminiscent of the synthetic "folksiness" of James Whitcomb Riley and his school. "The Beautiful Night", by N. B. McCarter, shews undoubted poetic feeling but an almost complete lack of technical training, which calls for remedy.

At least two poetry brochures of great merit have appeared in the National since the last report. *Thoughts and Pictures* (22 pp.), by Eugene B. Kuntz, D.D., contains a selection of Dr. Kuntz's lighter newspaper verse compiled by the able editor of *The Tryout*, and includes a great deal of highly pleasing material. Perhaps the most notable poem is "Dusk on a Rainy Night", in which the author's responsiveness to delicate visual impressions, and his instant ability to translate a subtle image into a definite mood, are exhibited with particular force.

Poems from the Heart of Vermont (60 pp.) is an ambitious anthology of work both amateur and non-amateur compiled and published by Mr. Stanton C. Muzzy. It is adorned with two delightful illustrations—a woodcut frontispiece by F. Gilbert Hills, "A Vermont Hillside", and a fine halftone view of a steepled hilltop village photographed by Frank H. Craig and entitled "Sabbath Morn". Perhaps the most distinctive original ingredient is Arthur Goodenough's majestic piece of pageantry, "The Clouds", where we see something of the imaginative power which Lord Dunsany praised over a decade ago when awarding Mr. Goodenough a laureateship in a United contest.[8]

EDITOR'S NOTE FP: Louisville, KY: Press of George G. Fetter Co., 1932 (as *Further Criticism of Poetry*), where the essay is dated 18 April 1932. Text (and title) derived from a TMS (JHL), although this TMS does not appear to have been prepared by HPL (it was possibly prepared by R. H. Barlow). The essay was originally designed as a criticism of amateur verse as part of HPL's work with the NAPA's Bureau of Critics, but it became so lengthy that it was issued as a separate pamphlet. Its generalised subject-matter—similar to HPL's evolving views on the nature and function of poetry, as expressed in letters to Elizabeth Toldridge and others of the late 1920s and exemplified in his own late verse (e.g., *Fungi from Yuggoth*, 1929–30)—has led the editor to place it here rather than in *CE1*. See also "What Belongs in Verse" (p. 182).

Notes

1. Brander Matthews, *A Study of Versification* (1911). HPL frequently recommended this book to beginners in poetry.

2. Samuel Taylor Coleridge, *Christabel* (1816), ll. 583–87.

3. John Keats, *Lamia* (1820), 2.299–303.

4. Algernon Charles Swinburne, "Cleopatra" (1866), ll. 1–5.

5. HPL was an occasional correspondent of Bertrand Kelton Hart, especially in 1929–30, when he, August Derleth, and others sent in lists of best weird tales to Hart's column, "The Sideshow"; Hart published HPL's sonnet "The Messenger" in the column of 3 December 1929. Out of apparent shyness, however, HPL rebuffed repeated offers to meet Hart.

6. Orton (1897–1986) had been a friend of HPL's and an occasional member of the Kalem Club since 1925.

7. L. A. G. Strong, *Common Sense about Poetry* (1931).

8. HPL had had a long acquaintance with Goodenough, ever since the latter wrote a poem about him, "Lovecraft—An Appreciation," in 1918. In 1920 Lord Dunsany, serving as the Laureate Judge of Poetry, selected Goodenough's "World-War" as the best poem of the 1919–20 term.

WEIRD STORY PLOTS

Basic skeletons of certain standard classics analysed, with a view to ascertaining elements and situations most universally conducing to effectiveness.

Poe—Usher[1]

Decaying family and house bound up together—perish at same moment. Atmosphere of menace and decay—premature burial of sister—fear and abnormal listening of brother—dramatic appearance of one thought dead—story quoted with hellish double meaning.

Ligeia[2]

Persistent will to live. First wife (mysterious origin) takes possession of body of second after latter dies. Atmosphere—climax of recognition—changed body—taller—falling cerements reveal dark hair.

MS. Found in a Bottle[3]

Ship in distress—run down by *huge* strange ship which looms *above* doomed vessel on a titanic wave, as on a pinnacle. Narrator flung in rigging of strange ship—finds crew aged, charts and instruments decayed and archaic, wood rotten and porous—like Spanish oak unnaturally distended. Crew do not see or notice narrator. Ship's name—

"Discovery". Great age of crew impressive. Ship is swept into antarctic as by some evil fatality—sense of evil tremendous—and finally sucked into a monstrous amphitheatre, gulf, or whirlpool.

Oval Portrait[4]

Painting in deserted castle appears *alive*. Wayfarer later learns it is of artist's bride—who, neglected, died at its completion.

Valdemar[5]

Dying man kept alive by hypnotism falls to instant and extreme decay 7 months later when hypnotism is removed.

Black Cat[6]

Tortured animal proves torturer's undoing by exposing crime (cf. Telltale Heart).

William Wilson[7]

Boy at school has double—in name, aspect, age, voice, et cetera. Gives him good counsel (better self). In later life thwarts his crimes. W. kills double in duel, thenceforward becoming utter monster.

Berenice[8]

After cloudy, morbid childhood narrator betrothed to cousin. Has abnormal fondness for her *teeth*. After her apparent death he rifles tomb (in unconscious madness) and wrests teeth from body—*which was still alive*. He is told of his horror later—and finds teeth of his sister in box.

Metzengerstein[9]

Atmosphere of horror. Metempsychosis suggested. Feud of houses M and B. Old prophecy "a lofty name shall . . . fall when, as rider over horse, mortality of M. shall triumph over immortality of B."

Count B—old man fond of horses. Baron M—young, wild.

Burns beloved stables of B—old B. perishes trying to save horses, but new horse—huge—is found amidst flames. Not recognised as B.'s tho' branded B. M. rides it violently. As it was found, there disappeared from M's tapestry a pictured horse of B.'s ancestor. At length M's palace takes fire as M is madly riding new horse in forest. Horse runs away and bears him to death amidst flames—smoke assuming form of gigantic horse. Preternatural light about. Idea that horse was old B. himself.

Machen—Great God Pan[10]

In occult way, woman sees Pan and bears daughter. Child reared in seclusion—hellish anecdotes—grows up—drives men to suicide and havock—finally exposed and put to death. Brooding atmosphere—intertwined with hints of Britanno-Roman antiquity.

White People[11]

Small girl introduced to hellish witch cult by nurse. Later sees sinister things in landscape and babbles of strange names. Finally comes on a statue in wood which brings horror and suicide. Atmosphere.

Black Seal[12]

Little people under Welsh hills beget strange horrors on mortals. Prof. Gregg hires idiot boy of such a paternity. Witnesses horror in library—epileptic seizure with strange odours and evidence of unnatural presences. Leaves note and goes into hills to face terrible discovery. Later his effects are found wrapt in parchment bearing the cryptic characters of the seal and inscription. Prof. G. notes likeness of symbols on Babylonish seal and Welsh inscription.

White Powder[13]

Youth takes drug by mistake—Vinum Sabbati—brings hideous secret transformation—absent from house often—attends terrible revels—black spot on hand—spreads—shuts self in room—horror at window—dripping on ceiling below—killing of final liquescent horror.

Terror[14]

Beasts revolt against man.

Blackwood—Willows[15]

Lonely Danube island haunted by Outside presences. They want a victim—nocturnal manifestations—other victim found.

Listener[16]

Awful psychic residuum creeps around old house where leper died.

Ancient Sorceries[17]

Traveller stops at strange French village—odd atmosphere—where inhabitants have secret undercurrent of interests. He sleeps deeply at night. Odd *cat* atmosphere everywhere. Town seems to "get" him. Daughter of inn folk captivates him and urges his initiation in cult—"the old, old life" to which all (even he) have belonged. He refuses. At last the Sabbat night. He feels tendency to go on all fours. Everyone sets out for Sabbat leaving town deserted. He finds them in open going up lonely hill—they anoint with Sabbat ointment—he almost joins, but stumbles and is delayed. Leaves. Think town's outline looks like a cat. Finds time awry. Has stayed a week, yet it is only 2 days later. It is later found that he dreamed all (note details), but 2 witches had been burned in 1700 exactly on the site of the inn where traveller stayed.

Nemesis of Fire[18]

Unnatural heat exists around old country house. Owner's brother mysteriously dead 20 yrs before—burned. Druid grove and standing stones nearby. Luminous shapes and hissing noted or rumoured here. Birds and animals avoid. Dogs chase invisible thing. Things often scorched—smoke seen—grass circles burned—*an invisible fire-nucleus pursues people*—steaming as it crosses water. Elemental waked with fresh blood—hounds bay—fearsome black shape appears—seems to have Egyptian influence.

It is found that the dead brother 20 years before had taken an important mummy from Egypt. *This* had been its guardian. It had followed *and remained.* The mummy (which dead brother had tried to bury ceremoniously to lay curse) is found, and induces odd momentary visions in finders. Old lady—sister—restores scarabaeus which she has taken from mummy. This restores balance and lays elemental.

Secret Worship[19]

Man visits the monastic school in Germany which he attended as a boy. Sinister woodland setting. Finds it changed. Brothers act in sinister way. Are about to sacrifice him to devil—then all vanishes in thin air as John Silence (who has followed him) rescues him. It seems that the brothers went over to devil worship years before, and that the building had long been burned down by the neighbours. Brothers all dead—these were ghosts.

De la Mare—Seaton's Aunt[20]

Very subtle. Youth's aunt has sinister influence. He grows feeble—his engagement frustrated by death—vide text.

Mr. Kempe[21]

Near a fabulously ancient chapel on a perilous sea cliff dwells a strange hermit—an ex-cleric in search of proof of the human soul's existence. Has become sinister and unused to mankind. Man explores cliff—great peril of falling—weird atmosphere—round sealed chapel—finds hermit—talks—finally sees hideous photographs of men maimed by falling from cliff—escapes in terror and hears hermit *crying* as he flees.

All-Hallows[22]

Ancient cathedral on seacoast. Traveller arrives at sunset. Strange atmosphere. Verger disturbed. Curious vibratory presences and shadows in night. Takes visitor over edifice under weird conditions to confirm horror. Masonry is gradually becoming firmer—as if restored by some miraculous power. Atmosphere of evil. Are hideous things besieging this lonely place and restoring it for their own use? Rector was suddenly stricken with idiocy some time before.

M. R. James—Canon Alberic's Scrapbook[23]

A 17th century cleric, because of sins (probably sacrilege), has an hideous daemon attached to him. He draws it in a group. Two centuries later a collector visits the cathedral of that cleric and hears a thin evil laugh. Later the sexton sells him a scrapbook of old missal and psalter leaves, collected by the bygone cleric and containing the drawing. Fear is subtly expressed by all. The *thing* appears to purchaser in his hotel room. It is *attached* to picture. He destroys picture and orders masses said for the old cleric's soul. Outstanding point—daemon attached to old book.

Lost Hearts[24]

Old man studies deeply into rites of later pagans—has collection of odd pagan objects and a small temple at his country seat. Has twice "charitably" taken in children without relatives, but they seem to have run away. Adopts small boy cousin. Boy dreams he sees small figure in leaden bathtub beyond locked door of disused bathroom. Later slits found in his nightshirt above heart. Butler now fancies he has heard voice in wine-cellar. Vernal equinox and full moon come. Crucial time in magical lore. Old man asks boy to visit him for important matter at 11 p.m., telling no one else in household. Boy sees odd (magical) preparations going on. At 10 p.m. by moonlight he sees out window figures of boy and girl. Latter is like figure in bath. Former frightens him more. Girl's hand over heart. Boy has gaping wound where heart ought to be.

At 11 goes to see cousin as agreed—no answer to knock. Enters study and finds cousin dead—rage, fright, and pain on face. In left side a wound baring heart. Long knife on table unused. Wildcat?

MS. on table explains. Old man sought magical powers by consuming hearts of 3 children—taken from living body. Has killed two—was about to complete quota when *something happened*. Expected to be troubled by ghosts.

The Mezzotint[25]

Museum curator gets from a dealer a picture of an old manor house, and finds that it *changes* as viewed at different times. A hooded figure is creeping up the lawn toward the house. Later finds it gone but window open. Still later it appears again as a sort of robed skeleton bearing off a child. Later figure is gone. Afterward identity of house ascertained (from difficult torn inscription), and it is found last heir disappeared in 1802. Father was gifted amateur engraver. Found dead on 3d anniversary of son's disappearance—just after completing engraving of house. He used to be hard on poachers, and had one very proud and well-descended one hanged for shooting a keeper. It was *thought* some *friend* of dead poacher kidnapped heir. . . .

Picture never changed again—secret having been deciphered.

The Ash-Tree[26]

A witch, who gathered twigs from an ash by the window of a squire, is executed on his evidence. She curses him on the gallows—"There will be ghosts at the hall". He is found dead later—after observing some small animal running up and down the great tree. Cause obscure—but small punctures on chest. For a generation no one uses room, and no deaths occur—but there is a mortality amongst local animals. Then grandson sleeps in room and dies. A cat sees something of interest in the tree—explores, and comes out frantically crying. Four huge spiders later found in tree, which is burned. Beneath it a hollow—and the bones and hair of a long-buried old woman. The witch's body, incidentally, had been found missing from its grave when church was enlarged. Latest victim had ordered burning of empty coffin.

Number 13[27]

Very ancient inn in Viborg, Jutland. One of few houses that survived fire of 1726. No room #13 listed—as often in Denmark to avoid superstitious aversion. Guest in #14 goes downstairs and back for coat in evening, and notes a door labelled #13—tries it by mistake and hears an occupant within. As he drowses off to sleep he feels a vague change in the proportions of his room—but lays it to imagination. Guest is antiquarian researching on church history of Denmark. Next day prosecutes his researches, and learns that a tenant in a house owned by the last Catholic bishop of Viborg was accused of black magic. The location of this house is doubtful—modern scholars have tried in vain to place it on maps. That night guest again sees door of Room 13, and hears footsteps and voices—excited—inside. Own room seems oddly smaller—and when he tries to find his portmanteau on the side toward #13 it is apparently missing. Windows are toward a dead wall across the street, on which the shadows of occupants of hotel rooms are cast—his own, that of man in #11, and that of occupant of #13—tall, thin, with draped head. Flickering red light seems to be reflected from room. Retires.

Next morning finds portmanteau where it was at first, and notes that room seems *larger*. Oddly, there seems to be an *extra window* toward #13—for he left a cigarette stub on the window he looked out, and it is now the middle instead of right-hand one as he had thought. As he goes out, he sees that Room *14* is next his. No #13 is visible. Bewilderment.

Continues researches, and finds references to bishop's magician tenant incomplete. It is stated that he was "suddenly removed". That night landlord denies that inn has any Room 13. Guest invites him to call in his room later—and returns without looking for #13. Own room seems smaller. Looking out window toward dead wall, sees shadow of a silently *dancing* man in next room. Knows that tenant of 14 is staid lawyer. At this point landlord calls—and seems struck with something unusual in room. Horrible song now proceeds from next room. They think it lawyer in 14—but just then the lawyer himself knocks and enters angrily—thinking *they* are making the noise. More bewilderment. What is singing? Cat? Something stuck in chimney? . . . Singing gives place to laughing. All now see something is oddly amiss. Going out in corridor, they see light under next door. *It is numbered 13.* They try it. Landlord goes to fetch a strong servant to force it. *Suddenly an arm comes forth to snatch at watchers.* Ragged yellowish linen sleeve—long grey hairs. Retreats, door shuts. A low laugh within. Landlord now returns with 2 strong men and crowbars. They refuse to meddle, but are finally persuaded. As they strike the door vanishes—giving place to a blank plaster wall. Just then a cock crows. Dawn. It now appears that #12 and #14 have more windows than they have at night.

Later floor of #12—in area supposedly covered by ghostly #13—is torn up in a search. Copper box found—containing vellum document. Very hard to decipher. In fact, impossible. Inference that it was contract of sale of wizard to Satan, and that the inn was really the house of the old bishop's magician tenant.

Count Magnus[28]

Curious traveller exploring Sweden. Investigates papers of ancient family at their manor house, but stays at inn. Old church nearby—with family mausoleum on eastern end. No access to m. from ch. Finds family papers interesting. Refer to ancestor—Count M.—who put down a peasant revolt and was hard on poachers. Local tradition adverse to Count M. Said to be cruel—and *to have made the Black Pilgrimage,* bringing someone or something back. Reticence regarding nature of Blk. Plg. Reference to it in Count M's papers—statement that he who goes to Chorazin and salutes the prince (of the air?) shall obtain long life, blood of enemies, and a faithful messenger. Finds alchemical books among Count's effects.

While passing church and locked mausoleum, utters whimsical wish to see Count M.—aloud. Hears metallic clang (in locked mausoleum)—but fancies a caretaker in church has dropt something.

Now extorts story from landlord at inn. It seems that Count M. had an influence after his death. His park was unguarded—but evilly famous. Once 2 men poached in it at night . . . . . . and their frightful screams were heard, followed by a *stranger's* loud laugh *and the clanging of a great door's shutting.* Next day the men are found. One is living—but mad. He pushes something imaginary away. Dies soon—still pushing. Other is dead—face sucked away. This story impresses traveller. Next day he gets deacon to shew him interior of locked mausoleum. Notes where key is hung in church—planning later private visit. Among the sarcophagi is that of Count M—the only one without a cross. Effigy on lid—and band with designs suggestive of exploits—battles, an execution, etc. One scene very inexplicable—man fleeing, pursued by nameless and monstrous *object.* Hooded—tentacled—short. Meanwhile another cloaked man looks on with keen interest. A queer view! Traveller notes the 3 padlocks of Count M's sarcophagus. *One is unfastened and fallen to pavement.*

Later he revisits mausoleum to copy epitaphs. Freakishly—and half involuntarily—he chants an invocation to Count M. When in mausoleum finds that *2 padlocks instead of one are unfastened and on the floor.*

On last night of his sojourn he visits mausoleum to bid Count M—who interests him oddly—a whimsical farewell. As he stands over the sarcophagus saying he would like to see Count M., *the 3d and last padlock falls at his feet.*

Then the hinges of the great copper sarcophagus creak, and the lid begins to rise very slowly. He runs—and as he leaves the mausoleum is unable to turn the key in the lock. Feels hideous apprehensions as he leaves Sweden. On the boat is perplexed about number of passengers. Only 26 at meals, but at other times 28 seem to be about. One cloaked and broad-hatted, and other short and hooded. Back in England he sees the two debatable figures at a crossroad. Horse shies violently. Takes lodgings in a small town, and writes jottings indicative of expected pursuit. Fear and doubt. . . . Later found horribly dead. Juror faints at inquest. No solution. House empty afterward. Later demolished, and unfortunate traveller's MSS. found in cupboard.

Whistle and I'll Come to You[29]

Professor goes to seaside for vacation. Sea is encroaching on coast. Has been asked by an archaeologist to look for site of an ancient Templars' preceptory—which must be on beach now, perhaps encroached upon by sea. Finds stony fragments overgrown with turf—evidently site sought. Finds a small artificial cavity in old masonry—and within it a strange old metal tube. As he leaves ruins he seems to note a vague distant figure following him. That evening he examines tube and finds it a whistle. (Someone is on shore outside his window.) There is an inscription in Latin—partly obscure, partly saying "Who is this who is coming?"

He blows—and note has an eerie quality of infinite distance . . . . also tending to form brain-picture of wide, dark expanse at night, wind blowing, and lone figure. A sudden surge of wind—and a white bird's wing glistens outside window. On second blowing no picture ensues—but a tremendous gust of wind occurs. Gust subsides, but wind cries oddly.

That night he hears someone tossing in bed. There is a spare bed in his room. He does not sleep—but sees odd mental pictures—a long stretch of shore on a late winter evening—slight cold rain—man appears running, finally crouches down exhausted. Pursuer appears—pale fluttering object—queer speed and motions. Makes for crouching man, but professor cannot bear to look further. Opens eyes and lights candle. Motions seem to scare something—perhaps rats—for a scurrying is heard.

Next day is told by maid that *both* of his beds have been slept in. Some mistake, no doubt. Man speaks of *wind* of night before—says it is of the sort rustics believe is *whistled for.* Soon afterward sees a frightened boy who has seen something horrible waving at him from his hotel window. Investigating, finds *spare* bed disturbed.

That night, in the moonlight, he sees a figure sitting upright in the spare bed. It moves and checks his egress from the room. Finally he sees it clearly. *It is made of bedclothes, and has a face of crumpled linen*—a horrible one. Friend hears his cry—bursts into room—and thing collapses to floor as inanimate bedclothes. Next day whistle is thrown into sea.

That was all.

Treasure of Abbot Thomas[30]

In an old book it is stated that Abbot T. of Steinfeld Abbey, Germany, left a great golden treasure hidden somewhere. He gave cryptic hints about directions for finding—and died suddenly in 1529.

Modern antiquary solves directions through stained glass windows—installed by Abbot T. Goes abroad with valet.

Later valet sends to England for his master's rector, saying antiquary has had a bad shock at Steinfeld and is confined to bed. Rector goes and finds antiquary badly shaken. Antiquary requests him to do a favour the next day—to *replace* something somewhere, with assistance of valet. Says it is perfectly safe *in the daytime*. Valet will tell what is necessary. That night rector thinks he hears a fumbling around the lower part of his locked door. In morning he and valet perform desired service—replacing a stone over a hole in side of old courtyard well—down 38 steps—and the antiquary is at once relieved. He is able to start home, and in the evening, en route, tells his story. He had solved the obscure directions which read in part "10,000 pieces of gold are laid up in the well—in the court of the abbot's house of Steinfeld by me, Thomas, who have set a guardian over them. Let him beware who touches them." It was known that Abbot T. had restored the abbot's house and dug a well in the court, adorning it with choice marble carvings.

On reaching Steinfeld he had found abbey and well—noting projecting blocks forming steps down well. Arranged to get treasure at night, when unobserved. Full moon. Descending, found marked stone in side. Removed it. Black hole with foul air beyond. Bags seen inside. Put arm in to feel—touched something curved, damp, and leathery (bag?), and drew it out toward him. *It puts its arms around his neck.* Had a sort of face. Several tentacles. Antiquary screams and is pulled up by valet. Thing drops back to step in front of hole. Valet had at first been down with master; but looking up, thought he saw an old man against the sky—laughing. Had gone up to investigate, but found no one. Then heard master cry, and pulled him up by rope that had been attached.

Antiquary and servant had got back to the inn, but thought there were faint voices in dark hours—*and smell of mould*. Fades at dawn. Felt that a night-thing was abroad, but would retire if stone of aperture were replaced. Hence had rector and valet replace it—he could not, and could not send servant alone, for it took 2 men to manage job—there being irons and wedges to fix. Had mud smeared over surface to conceal movable stone.

Rector, in doing job, notices carving on well-head which had eluded antiquary. It is a hideous grotesque figure—vaguely like a toad—with the motto

"Depositum custodi"

"Keep that which is committed to thee."

School Story[31]

Strange new master comes to school. Highland boy unconsciously and undesignedly brings up image of *a well among 4 yews*. Later a paper saying "If you don't come to me, I'll come to you" in an unknown red hand is handed in at an exercise. Master vastly perturbed. Finally the Highlander sees a strange, wet figure by moonlight—outside the master's window beckoning. Next day master is gone—never seen again. He was much travelled and wore a peculiar watch chain. Years later someone finds bones in old well—thin skeleton clutching another. *The other has the odd charm on its person.* Draw own conclusions.

Tractate Middoth[32]

Ghost attached to a book. Eccentric scholar conceals will in library book. Orders self buried dressed and at table in tomb. Apparition (in present costume, and covered with tomb cobwebs) comes to anyone who consults book with a view to destruction of will. (More effective if less prosaic motivation existed.) Finally kills man about to destroy will.

Casting the Runes[33]

A magician may saddle a victim with a horrible and murderous *companion* through the *personal service* (by handing) of a paper with certain cabbalistic symbols. The victim's only salvation is to serve it personally back to the one from whom he received it. Revenge plot—evil alchemist "casts the runes" on those who give his books bad reviews or prevent him from reading papers at the phil. soc. Finally turning of tables.

Barchester Cathedral[34]

Clergyman kills his aged predecessor in archdeaconry by causing him to trip on stairs with loose carpet. No one knows of this but maidservant with whom he was in collusion. He is later much interested in three curiously carved figures on the prayer-desk of the archdeacon's stall at his cathedral. A cat, a nameless daemon, and a nameless muffled death-figure. Said to be carved by a local artist named Austin from a great tree called the Hanging Oak, which had known Druidic worship and had also been a gallows. In time the cleric has a horrible impression of *life* in these effigies as he fingers them during the course of his duties. He also hears whispers about the murder, and seems to notice a strange cat about the house. Very uneasy. Servant who loosened carpet and helped murder is blackmailing him. Has a cousin stay with him—but the cat is seen again—also a muffled figure mistaken for a maid. Finally his own stair carpet is loosened mysteriously and he falls to his death—his body being likewise hellishly clawed and mangled by *something*. Investigators later trace history of odd carvings after their removal during refitting of church. They were picked up in a woodyard and given to children, but a paper that dropped from a hollow one is curious: It is verse, and predicts an evil fate for any blood-guilty person who touches the carving. The prophecy was dreamed on February 26, 1699 by Austin the carver. Predicts "fetching" *on windy February night.* The cleric died—horribly—on Feby. 26, 1818. Hollow figure destroyed because of horror.

Martin's Close[35]

Young squire stabs and drowns a poor halfwit serving wench whose attentions annoy him. Crime unsuspected. Later evidence that wench is still about the place—sings; dress seen caught in closet door. When she appears trapped in closet, only a small ape-like object runs out. Squire is frightened at hearing of wench's continued presence, for he (alone) knows she is dead. Ghost leads to discovery of body in pond with squire's missing knife—for which he has been secretly looking. He is convicted—and the wench's horrible form is seen near him at times until his execution.

Episode of Cathedral History[36]

In 1840, as Southminster Cathedral is restored to Gothick design, a pulpit is demolished—exposing an ancient tomb whose occupant cannot be identified. Immediately a wave of illness sets in, and there are tales of a little red-eyed ape-like shape that steals out of the cathedral at night, visits various houses in turn, and returns at dawn. Lady sitting on tomb has piece eaten out of dress. Dogs are afraid at night. About this time a hideous nocturnal wailing develops—curious, unhuman—"The Southminster Crying". Attempts to patch a large crack in the mysterious tomb are futile. Plaster is queerly "blown out". A choir-boy thinks he sees "something shiny" behind the crack, and pokes in a roll of music to investigate. *Something catches it at other end.* When it is pulled out, the end is found torn off and the edge is smeared with a black sticky substance.

At length the Dean, Canon, and others take action concerning the tomb. They pry it open with a crowbar—and as they do so a paralysing but unaccountable crash occurs. In the tomb are found a fragment of a dress and some torn music paper. Tomb slab now restored and plastered in. Only one man *saw* what caused the crash—an ape-like thing, which left the church by the north door. Metal cross now on tomb, with inscription from Isaiah—

"Ibi cubavit Lamia."

View from a Hill[37]

Old watchmaker finds occult secrets. Exhumes bones of dead men on Gallows Hill and makes masks and lenses capable of revealing bygone objects. Boils bones and fills field-glass lens with solution. Becomes famous as a discoverer of local archaeological antiquities. Had a viewing-mask made out of the front of a skull. Finally borne off one Midsummer-Eve by invisible ghosts of those whose bones he had desecrated. Seen struggling with invisible things—as if dragged along—and body later found with broken neck betwixt foundation stones of ancient gallows. Story opens later, with his evil field-glass used by others. It shews vanished towers on ruined churches, a gallows and clearing on the now wooded hill, and everything of a bygone sort. Ruined when taken into church—hinting devil-pact. When broken, an evil-smelling ichor discovered betwixt lenses. Infamous.

Warning to the Curious[38]

Legend of an old Saxon crown buried on E. coast of England (originally one of 3) to keep off invaders. A certain old family was its guardian, but is now extinct. The last member was vastly worried because he could find no successor as guardian.

Young archaeologist comes across legend, traces burial-place, and exhumes crown. From that moment feels never alone. An unplaceable, half-seen man is always near him—just at the edge of vision. Others also have seen this man. He is frightened—calls on friends for help and re-buries crown—but doom nevertheless overtakes him. He is lured out on the beach in the mist by an unknown figure, which he follows. Pursuing friends see footprints—his, and those of *bare, bony feet.* Near a ruin he is found dead by violence. No one else there. What did he face at last? Sea washes away footprints.

Dunsany—The House of the Sphinx[39]

Man comes to house of Sphinx. Finds occupants in terror of something coming from hideous encircling wood because of a *deed* . . . which lies on the floor covered with a cloak. Attendants try to strengthen and bar doors, etc. Sphinx is apathetic and resigned. Things approach from the forest, screaming and laughing. Traveller finds door rotten. Escapes from upper door that leads to branches of tree. Does not know fate of Sphinx.

E. F. Benson—Negotium Perambulans[40]

In an especially isolated Cornish fishing village—Polearn—the people have a strange Calvinistic theology and seem to share some ancient local rite or secret. In the church are 4 strange carved panels on the altar-rails—angel of annunciation, angel of resurrection, Witch of Endor, and a curious local scene—priest defying a nameless slug-like monster at Polearn churchyard's lich-gate by holding up a cross. The local vicar preaches of nameless presences ready to pounce on sinners, and points to carved monster as typical one. Below it is quotation from the 91st Psalm—"Negotium perambulans in tenebris". When the vicar preaches of this thing, the congregation exchange knowing nods. They recall an old legend faintly perpetuated—one knowing one bit, another another. According to legend, an older church had once existed near present one. Later owner of land tore it down and used stones for house of his own, keeping altar to dine and play dice on. As he grew old, he became afraid of something after dark. One winter night a gale sprang up and he was heard screaming. Servants found him dying—blood streaming from throat, and drained and withered very oddly. As they enter, a huge black shadow seems to leave him—crawling across floor and up wall and vanishing through window abutting on sea. As he dies he screams "Negotium perambulans in tenebris!"

Later house falls to ruin but is rebuilt by a drunkard. This man in a drunken fit breaks into the church and smashes the carving of the Thing to atoms after hearing about it. Fears darkness, and keeps lights burning all the time. Later broken panel found miraculously mended. That night man runs down dark road screaming "Light! Light!" Found dead and sucked dry on the shore. Years later an artist moves into house. In time he becomes coarsened—fat, shambling, Silenus-faced—*and keeps lights going all night*. Has taken to drink, and a sinister, hellish quality has crept into his pictures. One October evening a great blackness of cloud comes over the west. Artist finds house dark—hastens to strike light. Before he can, a Thing slithers toward him—seen by a man who is with him. A gigantic slug, with no head but a glowering orifice. Rears itself to strike—fastens on artist—frightful screams—Visitor grapples, attempting rescue, but hands sink in. Thing is like mud. Gurgling and sucking noises. Thing glides out window. When lamp is lit artist is dead. Sucked dry. A mere rind of skin over bones.

R. W. Chambers—Yellow Sign[41]

Artist while painting in Wash. Sq. N.Y. glances out of window to churchyard. Sees strange, corpsy-looking watchman. Shivers. Is impressed. Painting goes awry—flesh looks gangrenous and decayed. Model sees watchman out window. He is image of one she had dreamed of—as driving a hearse in which artist was (seen from window). Next day artist hears that church has been sold. A bellboy who had a scuffle with watchman tells horrible story—one of the man's fingers came off in his hand. Soon artist has hideous dream like model's . . . . of being in coffin in hearse and hearing window opened. Looking out, sees model in window. Then hearse is driven into black lane and stops. Driver—the sinister watchman—looks at artist. Artist wakes.

Later—as artist is returning home at dawn—watchman accosts him with thick words. Hellish voice of decay. "Have you found the Yellow Sign?" Next day model gives artist an odd clasp with an unknown symbol—which she found in the street *on the day she first had hellish dream*. Later artist finds the monstrous book—"The King in Yellow"—unaccountably in his library. Despite warning, artist and model both read hideous volume and receive the shocking knowledge it imparts. They want to throw away the Yellow Sign, but cannot. Finally they hear crunching of wheels. The hearse is coming. The watchman enters. They cannot bolt him out. W. tears Yellow Sign from coat of artist. Model drops dead. Hideous scream. . . . People enter. Two dead, artist dying. One of the dead—the watchman—must have been dead for months.

Irvin S. Cobb—Fishhead[42]

Mongrel negro in cabin on shore of deserted lake makes friends with huge hideous catfishes—*which he resembles.* Two brothers murder him at lake edge, and fall in water as *something from beneath* capsizes their boat. Catfish attack. Next day all 3 bodies found in lake—nigger's unharmed—those of assassins hideously mauled.

Hanns Heinz Ewers—The Spider[43]

Room in hotel where many men have hanged themselves at the window—spiders being found near body in each case. Young student goes to live there to investigate. Is captivated by sight in window of house across street—apparently young woman spinning at an archaic wheel. Loses interest in other things—but notes an incident outside window . . . a female spider devours a male. Plays a whimsical game with neighbour in opposite window—imitating motions. Moves become almost simultaneous—as if telepathic. This game in time becomes an obsession—student is psychologically compelled to pursue it. Fear ensues. Visions of those hanged, and self among them. Finds that figure across street really dictates all the moves of game. Compelled by spectacle of neighbour doing some thing, cuts telephone wire which connected him with police headquarters. Then she goes through motions of hanging herself with cord at window—he does same, leaving interrupted written record. At the last he feels a strange rapture, but fears a horrible revelation. . . .

Found hanged by police. Fear on face. Bitten, between lips, is huge spider whose odd markings resemble dress of neighbour described in victim's record. Police read record and search opposite house. The apartment of the window has been vacant for months.

W. Elwyn Backus—Phantom Bus[44]

Youth's fiancee killed in bus accident. Had told him she would return for him if she died first. Year later he notes a strange and sinister bus which precedes his regular bus to town. Dreams about it. It has a strange sickly odour when boarded, and passengers seem asleep. His fiancee is aboard, and suddenly screams. Though bus is a rattletrap, it seems to *glide* smoothly. Wakes in terror. Dream repeated—first did not carry action so far. Tries to board bus in actuality, but always oversleeps. Once when he does not oversleep it fails to appear. Later dream—action repeated and carried further. Crash with truck impends—driver's face seen *fully* at last—half is missing. . . .

Youth's body found hideously mangled in bed. Had screamed in the night.

An old bus—not in service—is found next morning on road twisted and splintered. No one can explain how it got there. Signs of death—but no body.

Conrad Aiken—Mr. Arcularis[45]

After a perilous operation man finds self on ocean liner. Body said to be in hold below. Man has dreams and sleepwalking—finds self repeatedly headed for somewhere—presumably the hold where body is. Actually, he is still in hospital under ether. He dreams all this and dies.

Paul Suter—Beyond the Door[46]

Scientist repulses young woman in house in love with him. She kills self. He fears accusation of murder and buries body in disused well in cellar. Things happen. He finds draughts in house. Ratty rustlings. Things clutch at heels. Pale fingers along floor. He is drawn irresistibly toward well. He thinks something sits on covering slab. Finally opens well when alone in house—but slab of stone (propped up) falls on him and paralyses him. Dies. Horror revealed by diary. Police find his victim's body in well.

John Buchan—Green Wildebeest[47]

Old Kaffir priest—blind hermit—lives in a strange grove on berg above native village in Transvaal. Controls all local water—which comes from strange spring (curb of hewn stone indicating unknown pre-negro antiquity) in wall-enclosed grove full of wild animals including an abnormal and gigantic green wildebeest. Impressive atmosphere. Natives hold priest and grove in vast awe—believe some tremendous force or entity is contained within the enclosure. Two copper prospectors stop at village. One—a youth—resents old priest's control of water and beards him in his den—using whip, forcing his way into sacred enclosure, and shooting the strange green wildebeest therein. Fear seizes him, however (negro blood implied), and he runs away. After that the prospectors are fearfully shunned by all the natives. The elder and pure white one visits the old priest and pleads with him, but the priest sadly says that atonement—vengeance—must be done. He allows man to enter sacred enclosure, but adds that "What was there is there no more. It has gone to the fulfilling of the law." The wildebeest is not seen. Later youth has brain fever, but manages to get home. He is haunted by the feeling that he has loosed something terrible on the world. He sets out to find and kill the wildebeest—or what it represents—and at last shoots at *something*. He thinks he has killed the terror, and fancies the track of the wildebeest is visible—but what he has done is to shoot and kill his travelling companion. Is hanged for murder. Later on the man who was with him on the first trip revisits the region of the blind priest and finds enclosure and village alike gone. There had been an all-obliterating landslide on the cliff or berg. No one there. But the convulsion has opened up new watercourse which replaces the strange spring or well. Ultimate explanations left to reader.

The Wind in the Portico[48]

Odd region in Shropshire where ancient influences subtly linger. Landscape and nomenclature suggest dark strangeness. Shadowy rumours about a squire dwelling in ancient house fronting hollow and lake. Said to worship strange things. Classic temple with portico added to front of house, and a strange hot wind seems always to play about the portico. Inspires beholder with fear as sunset portentously strikes it. One does not wish to be overtaken there at night. Fear exists in all the servants about the place. Squire combines fear with morbid expectancy.

It seems that this squire has been a lifelong antiquary—specialising in Roman Britain. Has found a temple site in high woods on his domain—containing an altar of the local deity *Vaunus*—whose name figures oddly in local nomenclature. Site always supposed to be haunted. Besides altar, certain carvings and sacrificial implements found. Squire has built the temple at front of his house to accommodate the altar he has found. Says he heats it. Hence wind? Promises to shew visitor temple *by day*.

As time passes, fear gains on squire. Inquires about formula in Sidonius Apollinaris for rededicating pagan altar for Christian use.

A visitor in house one summer night feels nocturnal heat, hears rushing wind somewhere despite stillness of night, and glimpses a glow coming from temple. Thinks steam is on by mistake and investigates. Find cupboard of odd, spicy-smelling packages (which he has seen oddly delivered to house at night) labelled *Pro servitio Vauni*. Learns from butler (frightened) *that there is no heating apparatus in house*. Heat, wind, and glow abate and vanish after a time. Next day squire looks ill, but agrees to shew visitor around temple—in the bright sunshine. He says "there are times and seasons for the temple". Visitor finds temple vaguely terrifying—as if nr. imprisoning place, cutting one off from world. Old carvings from ruined temple are set in place. They depict priests bearing branches—half-human faces exhibiting extreme pain . . . *and hair tossed as if by violent wind.* In a prominent place is head of strange male Gorgon—once coloured, with hair and beard green. Very horrible. Altar visible—marked APOLL. VAUN.—bears marks of *recent flames.*

Guest and host both nervous and anxious to leave. *Unwholesomeness* impresses guest, and he makes host promise to close temple and move to inn soon.

That evening host reported ill in bed. At night guest aroused by horrible cries of pain. Crackling of fire and sound of great wind raging, though night outside is still. Guest flees from house and passes temple facade. Temple is brighter than day with a roaring blast of fire. No *flames,* only a burning brightness. Tongue of fire shoots up from altar to roof and spreads there. In front of altar is squire—burned to a crisp—dead. Gorgon's head glows like a sun in hell. Guest tries to enter, but is repelled by fire. Then fire strikes through great oak door into house proper. Guest plunges in lake to ease heat, then returns. Too late to help. All burns down—tho' servants escape. Nothing found of squire. Nothing left of house except a few blackened pillars. Altar and sculptures so cracked and scarred that no museum wants them. Place never rebuilt—stands in ruins to this day.

Skule Skerry[49]

The ancient Saga of Earl Skuli speaks of an Isle of Birds west of Una in the Norlands, where amazing numbers of birds congregate. Once a succession of Holy men lived on it in a cell. A chapel built and endowed by Earl Rognvald, came to an end in time of Malise of Strathearn. So says Adam of Bremen, who adds: "Insula Avium quae est ultima insula et proxima Abysso."

Voyager—ornithologist—looks up isle ("Skule Skerry") as possible landing place in bird migrations. Views it from Una, finds something weird about it—as if it concealed something. Proxima Abysso. . . . . Finds it is regarded as uncanny by people of Una. "Naebody gang there." It is ¼ mile long, low, with one grassy knoll out of reach of highest tides. Remains of monkish cell visible. Despite warnings, visitor camps on Skerry with tent and supplies. Boatman hates to take him, and leaves him a pail of oily waste as a beacon to light if he wishes to come off. Also small dinghy to reach Una in. Visitor thinks of old legends that tell of the Finns—ghouls that live in the deeps of ocean and sometimes come to land in a seal's skin to play havock with mortals. Visitor has trouble with storms and winds, and finally acquires a strange, weird sensation of loneliness—of being at the very edge of things and close to the Abyss that contains only death. It is very cold, and suddenly the vague sensations crystallise into utter terror. Visitor thinks of *meaning* of island—outpost—edge of world—folds and tucks in space—birds know such things—early church knew, and posted sentinels against daemons of darkness—*what did those hermits sometimes see?* Legends tell of Black Silkie, the Finn that haunts this isle.

In panic, Visitor lights the beacon to summon boat from Una. The flare gives things a new eeriness. Someone—some shape—comes suddenly out of the sea—drawing itself heavily on the beach, wallowing, and staring Visitor in face. Great dark head like bull's—old face—wrinkled—enormous broken teeth—dripping beard—Visitor faints and hits head on stone.

Found 3 hrs. later by boatman. Taken to Una and later revived. Recovers from shock in a week. Learns that walrus has been found on beach, and *hopes* that this was what he saw.

Lot #249—By A. Conan Doyle[50]

Unwholesome-looking student of Eastern languages in ancient tower room at Oxford. Has been to Egypt, where the natives shew him surprising deference. Room full of Egyptian curios. Vindictive, cruel, and sometimes tells grandiosely about commanding vast powers for good and evil. Buys an Egyptian mummy and performs incantations over it. Found twice fainted with fright. Neighbours report sound of walking in his room when he is absent. His enemies are strangely attacked by an ape-like thing. Neighbour hears steps when he is calling on him—he excuses self. Also—neighbour returning book sees mummy case empty, then feels something brush by him in hall, and later (door being open) sees mummy in case. This neighbour antagonises student and is pursued at night by a form unmistakably that of the mummy. Oxford now full of talk of an escaped ape. Neighbour takes law into own hands and forces student at pistol's point to burn mummy and destroy papyrus of strange incantations. Student at once leaves the university and is last heard of in the Soudan.

Leonard Cline—The Dark Chamber[51]

Man conceived the idea of recapturing every moment of his life—believing the records of memory, *and even of hereditary memory*, to be graven indelibly upon his brain. Makes exhaustive notes on his own past—keeps files of data, and employs research workers to recover objects and data, and take pictures of scenes, connected with his bygone hours. Employs odours, drugs, and music to open obscure memory-channels and revivify bygone hours. Much of this past-glimpsing comes in *dreams*. Finally the element of *hereditary* memory comes uppermost. He dreams of primal *pre-human* days as a *reptile* in the carboniferous age. His dog becomes afraid of him, and a primal, animal odour encompasses him. He grows vacant and abstracted, as if absent. Drugs and music are used to the limit to induce these shocking resurgences of remote hereditary memory. He seems to have some single grandiose plan of wresting profound and ultimate secrets from infinity. At last he grows sub-human and goes ragged and filthy, and finally naked. Takes to the woods—his great dog having previously fled him in terror and laired in a neighbouring ruin. Howls beneath windows at night. Finally found in a thicket, reeking with an indescribable stench and mangled to death. Beside him is his great dog, also dead and mangled. They have killed each other.

Story has added elements concerning man's sinister household. Very potent atmosphere.

EDITOR'S NOTE   Unpublished (AMS, JHL). Found in the same notebook that contains "[Notes on Weird Fiction]" and an important component of HPL's review of the classics of weird fiction with a view to reinvigorating his own creative fires. In the notes below, information is provided on the full titles and first appearances of the works in question as well as the editions HPL used in reading them (if different from the first appearance).

Notes

1. Edgar Allan Poe, "The Fall of the House of Usher" (*Burton's Gentleman's Magazine*, September 1839). HPL owned *The Works of Edgar Allan Poe*, Raven Edition (New York: P. F. Collier & Son, 1903; 5 vols.; LL 702) as well as *Tales of Mystery and Imagination* (New York: Tudor Publishing Co., 1933). He first read Poe when he was eight years old (SL 2.109).

2. Poe, "Ligeia" ([Baltimore] *American Museum*, September 1838).

3. Poe, "Ms. Found in a Bottle" (*Baltimore Sunday Visiter*, 19 October 1833).

4. Poe, "The Oval Portrait" (*Graham's Magazine*, April 1842).

5. Poe, "The Facts in the Case of M. Valdemar" (*American Review*, December 1845).

6. Poe, "The Black Cat" (*United States Saturday Post*, 19 August 1843).

7. Poe, "William Wilson" (*The Gift for 1840*, 1839).

8. Poe, "Berenice" (*Southern Literary Messenger*, March 1835).

9. Poe, "Metzengerstein" ([Philadelphia] *Saturday Courier*, 14 January 1832).

10. Arthur Machen, "The Great God Pan," in *The Great God Pan and The Inmost Light* (London: John Lane; Boston: Roberts Brothers, 1894). The story is contained in *The House of Souls* (London: Grant Richards, 1906; rpt. New York: Knopf, 1923; *LL* 573).

11. Machen, "The White People" (*Horlick's Magazine*, January 1904); in *The House of Souls*.

12. Machen, "Novel of the Black Seal," a segment of the episodic novel *The Three Impostors* (London: John Lane; Boston: Roberts Brothers, 1895). HPL owned a later edition (Knopf, 1930; *LL* 578) of *The Three Impostors*, but owned an earlier edition (Knopf, 1923) that was lent to Bernard Austin Dwyer and was destroyed in a fire at his home.

13. Machen, "Novel of the White Powder," a segment of *The Three Impostors*.

14. Machen, *The Terror* (London: Duckworth, 1917). HPL read *The Terror* in 1924 (see *SL* 1.304), possibly from a copy lent to him by Frank Belknap Long. He did not own the text.

15. Algernon Blackwood, "The Willows," in *The Listener and Other Stories* (London: Eveleigh Nash, 1907). HPL first read the story in the fall of 1924 (see HPL to Lillian D. Clark, 29–30 September 1924; *LNY* 64), possibly in a copy read at the New York Public Library. He did not own *The Listener*, but had the story in John Gilbert Bohun Lynch's *The Best Ghost Stories* (Boston: Small, Maynard, 1924; *LL* 558).

16. Blackwood, "The Listener," in *The Listener and Other Stories*. HPL owned the text in Joseph Lewis French's *Masterpieces of Mystery* (Garden City, NY: Doubleday, Page, 1920; *LL* 335).

17. Blackwood, "Ancient Sorceries," in *John Silence—Physician Extraordinary* (London: Eveleigh Nash, 1908). HPL owned both this edition (*LL* 96) and a later reprint (New York: E. P. Dutton, [1920] or [1929]; *LL* 97).

18. Blackwood, "The Nemesis of Fire," in *John Silence—Physician Extraordinary*.

19. Blackwood, "Secret Worship," in *John Silence—Physician Extraordinary*.

20. Walter de la Mare, "Seaton's Aunt," in *The Riddle and Other Stories* (London: Selwyn & Blount, 1923). HPL owned a reprint of this volume (New York: Knopf, 1930; *LL* 229).

21. De la Mare, "Mr. Kempe," in *The Connoisseur and Other Stories* (New York: Knopf, 1926; *LL* 228).

22. De la Mare, "All Hallows," in *The Connoisseur and Other Stories*.

23. M. R. James, "Canon Alberic's Scrap-Book," in *Ghost-Stories of an Antiquary* (London: Edward Arnold, 1904). HPL owned an unspecified edition of this volume (*LL* 468).

24. James, "Lost Hearts," in *Ghost-Stories of an Antiquary*.

25. James, "The Mezzotint," in *Ghost-Stories of an Antiquary*.

26. James, "The Ash-Tree," in *Ghost-Stories of an Antiquary*.

27. James, "Number 13," in *Ghost-Stories of an Antiquary*.

28. James, "Count Magnus," in *Ghost-Stories of an Antiquary*.

29. James, "'Oh, Whistle, and I'll Come to You, My Lad,'" in *Ghost-Stories of an Antiquary*.

30. James, "The Treasure of Abbot Thomas," in *Ghost-Stories of an Antiquary*.

31. James, "A School Story," in *More Ghost Stories of an Antiquary* (London: Edward Arnold, 1911). HPL owned an unspecified edition of this volume (*LL* 469)

32. James, "The Tractate Middoth," in *More Ghost Stories of an Antiquary*.

33. James, "Casting the Runes," in *More Ghost Stories of an Antiquary*.

34. James, "The Stalls of Barchester Cathedral," in *More Ghost Stories of an Antiquary*.

35. James, "Martin's Close," in *More Ghost Stories of an Antiquary*.

36. James, "An Episode of Cathedral History," in *A Thin Ghost and Others* (London: Edward Arnold, 1919). HPL owned an unspecified edition of this volume (*LL* 470).

37. James, "A View from a Hill," in *A Warning to the Curious* (London: Edward Arnold, 1925). HPL owned an unspecified edition of this volume (*LL* 471).

38. James, "A Warning to the Curious," in *A Warning to the Curious*.

39. Lord Dunsany, "The House of the Sphinx," in *The Book of Wonder* (London: Heinemann, 1912). HPL owned a reprint, *The Book of Wonder* [and *Time and the Gods*] (New York: Modern Library, [1917]; *LL* 271).

40. E. F. Benson, "*Negotium Perambulans . . .*," in *Visible and Invisible* (New York: George H. Doran, 1923; *LL* 79).

41. Robert W. Chambers, "The Yellow Sign," in *The King in Yellow* (New York: F. Tennyson Neely, 1895). HPL owned an unspecified edition of this volume (*LL* 167).

42. Irvin S. Cobb, "Fishhead" (*All-Story Cavalier*, 11 January 1913), in Cobb's *The Escape of Mr. Trimm* (New York: George H. Doran, 1913). HPL owned the story in T. Everett Harré's *Beware After Dark!* (New York: Macauley, 1929; *LL* 397).

43. Hanns Heinz Ewers, "The Spider," in Dashiell Hammett, ed., *Creeps by Night* (New York: John Day Co., 1931; *LL* 394).

44. W. Elwyn Backus, "The Phantom Bus" (*Weird Tales*, September 1930), in Hammett, *Creeps by Night*.

45. Conrad Aiken, "Mr. Arcularis" (*Harper's*, March 1931), in Hammett, *Creeps by Night*.

46. Paul Suter, "Beyond the Door" (*Weird Tales*, April 1923), in Hammett, *Creeps by Night*.

47. John Buchan, "The Green Wildebeest," in *The Runagates Club* (London: Hodder & Stoughton, 1928). HPL owned the US edition (Boston: Houghton Mifflin, 1928; *LL* 129).

48. Buchan, "The Wind in the Portico," in *The Runagates Club*.

49. Buchan, "Skule Skerry," in *The Runagates Club*.

50. Sir Arthur Conan Doyle, "Lot No. 249" (*Harper's*, September 1892), in Doyle's *Round the Red Lamp* (London: Methuen, 1894). HPL owned the story in Doyle's *Tales of Twilight and the Unseen* (London: John Murray, 1922; *LL* 262).

51. Leonard Cline, *The Dark Chamber* (New York: Viking, 1927; *LL* 183).

[NOTES ON WEIRD FICTION]

1. Suggestions for Writing Story
(The *idea* and plot being tentatively decided on)

1. Prepare synopsis or scenario of events in order of *occurrence*—not order of nar-

ration. Describe with enough fulness to cover all vital points and motivate all incidents planned. Details, comments, and estimates of consequences sometimes desirable.

2. Prepare synopsis or scenario of events in order of *narration,* with ample fulness and detail, and with notes as to changing perspective, stresses, and climax. Change original synopsis to fit if such a change will increase dramatic force or general effectiveness of story. Interpolate or delete incidents at will—never being bound by original conception, even if the ultimate result be a tale wholly different from that first planned. Let additions and alterations be made whenever suggested by anything in the formulating process.

3. Write out the story, rapidly, fluently, and not too critically, following Synopsis 2. Change incidents and plot whenever the developing process seems to suggest such change, never being bound by any previous design. If development suddenly reveals new opportunities for dramatic effect or vivid story-telling, add whatever is thought advantageous—going back and reconciling early parts to new plan. Insert or delete whole sections if necessary or desirable, trying different beginnings and endings till the best is found. But be sure that all references throughout story are thoroughly reconciled with final design. Remove all possible superfluities—words, sentences, paragraphs, or whole episodes or elements—observing usual precautions about the reconciliation of all references.

4. Revise entire text, paying attention to vocabulary, syntax, rhythm or prose, proportioning of parts, niceties of tone, grace and convincingness of transitions (scene to scene, slow and detailed action to rapid and sketchy time-covering action and vice versa. . . . etc. etc. etc.), effectiveness of beginning, ending, climaxes, etc., dramatic suspense and interest, plausibility and atmosphere, and various other elements.

5. Prepare a neatly typed final copy.

In certain cases it is advisable to begin writing a story without either a synopsis or even an idea of how it shall be developed and ended. This is when one feels a need of recording and exploiting some especially powerful or suggestive mood or picture to the full. In such procedure the beginning thus produced may be regarded as a problem to be motivated and explained. Of course, in developing this motivation and explanation it may be well to alter—or even transform, transpose beyond recognition, or altogether eliminate—the beginning first produced.

Once in a while, when a writer has a marked style with rhythms and cadences closely linked with imaginative associations, it is possible to begin *weaving a mood* with characteristic paragraphs and letting this mood dictate much of the tale.

Once in a while it is effective to devise a striking title or series of titles—of such a sort as to evoke poignant imaginative associations—in advance, and write the fictional matter around it or them. Later, when the work is done, title or titles may be changed.

In rare cases, an effective story may be written around a picture.

Often well to spin out a tale at great length in one's head—with notes—before actual formulation. Dream it leisurely—slowly—with any number of changes.

Weird stories are of two kinds—those in which the horror or marvel concerns some *condition* or *phenomenon,* and those in which it concerns some action of persons in connexion with a bizarre condition or phenomenon.

Having decided on a mood, picture, situation, legend, tableau, or climax to express, it is often advisable for the author to explore the list of basic horrors quite thoroughly in order to find one especially adapted to the given framework. This being done, all possible ingenuity must be used in order to develop a logical and naturally motivated explanation for the given effect in terms of the basic horror adopted.

Record all bizarre ideas, moods, images, dreams, conceptions, etc. for future use. Do not despair if they seem to have no logical development. Each one may be worked over gradually—surrounded with notes and synopses, and finally built into a coherent explanatory structure capable of fictional use. Never hurry. The best stories sometimes grow very slowly—over long periods, and with intervals in their formulation.

In a tale involving complex philosophical or scientific principles, try to have all explanations hinted at outset, when thesis is put forward (as in Machen's "White People"), thus leaving narrative and climactic sections unencumbered.

Be willing to spend as much time and care on formulation of synopsis as on writing of actual text—*for the synopsis is the real heart of the story*. The real creative work of fiction-writing is originating and shaping a story in synopsis form.

Have no scruples against introducing two or more separate basic horrors, provided the story's natural and internal logic calls for them. Be sure, however, to keep the tale absolutely logical and realistic except in the directions chosen for departure from reality.

It is occasionally useful to concoct a story half-irresponsibly and spontaneously from some given horror-element, letting it develop as it goes along, changing when desirable, and recording it in the form of a loose, rambling synoptic outline. From this careless outline a real story may often be fashioned.

In order to ensure an adequate climax, it is sometimes advisable to prepare one in considerable detail first, and then construct a main synopsis explaining it.

An utterly bizarre and striking *mode of approach* is sometimes desirable. Time, scene, or other elements wholly remote or non-human.

2. Elements of a Weird Story

(a) Some basic, underlying horror or abnormality—condition, entity, et cetera.
(b) General effects or bearings of the horror.
(c) Mode of manifestation—object embodying the horror and phenomena observed.
(d) Types of fear-reaction pertaining to the horror.
(e) Specific effects of the horror in relation to given set of conditions.

3. Types of Weird Story

(a) Expressing a mode or feeling.
(b) Expressing a pictorial conception.
(c) Expressing a general situation, condition, legend, or intellectual conception.
(d) Explaining a definite tableau or specific dramatic situation or climax.

4. A List of Certain Basic Underlying Horrors Effectively Used in Weird Fiction

[1.]   Unnatural life in a house, and unnatural linkage of lives of separate persons.[1]
[2.]   Premature burial.[2]
[3.]   *Listening* for some approaching horror.[3]
[4.]   Metempsychosis—a dead being forces its personality upon the living.[4]
[5.]   Offspring of a mortal and a daemon.[5]
[6.]   Any mysterious and irresistible march toward a doom.[6]
[7.]   Unnatural life in a picture—transfer of life from person to picture.[7]
[8.]   Prolongation or persistence of an abnormal animation in the dead.[8]
[9.]   Duplication of a personality.[9]
[10.] Ravages on a grave—discovery that the seemingly dead is alive.[10]

[11.] Unnatural connexion betwixt an object and some image of it.[11]

[12.] Membership in hellish cult of witchcraft or daemonolatry.[12]

[13.] Presence of horrible hidden race in lonely region.[13]

[14.] Shocking metamorphosis or decay of living human as induced by taking unknown and evil drug. Idea of monstrous companion.[14]

[15.] Beasts acting deliberately against man.[15]

[16.] Unseen cosmic presences in certain region—idea of genius loci.[16]

[17.] Psychic residuum in old house = ghost.[17]

[18.] Village whose inhabitants all share monstrous secret rites.[18]

[19.] Elemental spirit intrudes or is invoked.[19]

[20.] Holy organisation secretly goes over to diabolism.[20]

[21.] Subtle vampiric preying of one being on another.[21]

[22.] Terrible hermit in lonely place—preys in some way on travellers.[22]

[23.] Powers of darkness (or cosmic outsideness) besiege or take over sacred edifice.[23]

[24.] Hideous daemon attached to some person (& after his death to certain objects pertaining to that person) through sin, incantation, etc.[24]

[25.] Hideous sacrifices attempted through exercise of some bygone paganism. Ghostly reprisal.[25]

[26.] Changes in a picture corresponding to actual events (present or old) in scene it depicts.[26]

[27.] Evil wizard employs metempsychosis to survive in animal forms and carry out revenge.[27]

[28.] Ghostly room in house—sometimes there, sometimes not.[28]

[29.] Wizard acquiring evil companion through trip to strange region of horror.[29]

[30.] A pursuing *thing* called from the grave through an injudicious incantation.[30]

[31.] Blast on an exhumed whistle of unknown antiquity summons vague and hellish presence from the Abyss.[31]

[32.] Monstrous supernatural *guardian* set over treasure or book hidden in ancient ruins.[32]

[33.] A dead man comes from the grave to bear off or punish his murderer.[33]

[34.] Inanimate object acts as living thing to avenge crime.[34]

[35.] Ghost of victim convicts murderer.[35]

[36.] Disturbance of an ancient grave looses a monstrous presence on the world.[36]

[37.] Magical telescope (or cognate device) shews the *past* when looked through.[37]

[38.] Excavation of an ancient and forbidden thing saddles excavator with a hostile shadow, which eventually destroys him.[38]

[39.] A household in great terror of the coming of some unknown doom.[39]

[40.] A sacrilege toward an ancient church summons out of space or the sea an avenging monster which devours the desecrator.[40]

[41.] Perusal of a certain hideous book or possession of a certain awful talisman places person in touch with shocking dream or memory world which brings him eventual destruction.[41]

[42.] Man abnormally akin to lower animals. They avenge his murder.[42]

[43.] Insect hypnotizes man and leads him to his death.[43]

[44.] Ghostly vehicle. Man boards it and is carried into unreal world.[44]

[45.] Sleep-walker drawn nearer and nearer to some horrible place. Tryst with dead, etc.[45]

[46.] Body buried beneath cellar hounds murder (or injurer) to death.[46]

[47.] In savage land, hermit priest guards old shrine containing a very strange and ancient Presence. Accident looses presence, and harm is done to person responsible.[47]

[48.] Remote island region at extreme limit of world—Edge of Abyss. Strange horror appears there.[48]

[49.] Ghouls of the sea that come to land in guise of *seals* and prey upon mankind![49]

[50.] Reconstruction of ancient temple or re-dedication of ancient altar evokes dangerous, unbodied forces.[50]

[51.] Evil student reanimates mummy 4000 years old, and forces it to do his murderous bidding.[51]

[52.] Man tries to recapture *all* of his past, aided by drugs and music acting on memory. Extends process to *hereditary* memory—even to pre-human days. These ancestral memories figure in dreams. Plans stupendous recovery of primal past—but becomes sub-human, develops a hideous primal odour, takes to the woods, and is killed by own dog.[52]

[53.] Traveller coming upon something horrible in strange place—as a horror in a cabin with lighted window found in a forest's depths.[53]

[54.] Dream and waking worlds confused.[54]

[55.] Some past (or future) horror just outside memory (or prescience).[55]

[56.] Entire scene and set of events caused by hypnosis—proceeding either from living person or from corpse or other harbourer of residual psychic force.[56]

[57.] Coming to unknown place and finding one has some hitherto latent memory of it, or hideous connexion with it.[57]

5. List of Primary Ideas Motivating Possible Weird Tales

[1.] Objectivisation of imagination-products
[2.] Metempsychosis
[3.] Return of Spirit
[4.] Return of Body (vampire)
[5.] Hereditary Memory
[6.] Abnormal vision into future
[7.] Advent of alien entity to world
[8.] Daemon summoned by rite
[9.] Vision opened by evil book
[10.] Daemon guardian of a spot
[11.] Evil forces focussed in spot
[12.] Change or vision induced by a drug
[13.] Ghoul
[14.] Monstrous birth
[15.] Lingering influence in house
[16.] Lingering influence in tomb
[17.] Tower or other relique of pre-humans
[18.] World under sea
[19.] Inhabited daemon tower in remote place
[20.] House of horror in old city
[21.] Transposition of mind
[22.] Interference with time
[23.] Archaeological horrors exhumed
[24.] Evil force enters edifice as bat

[25.] Seizure—taking away—of a person by Forces
[26.] Parasitic entity infuses its memory into one it feeds on
[27.] Materialisation of some Thing through rite or magical act
[28.] Distinct tones: intense, clutching, delirious horror; delicate, dream-like fantasy;
       realistic, scientific horror; very subtle adumbration;

EDITOR'S NOTE FP: In *The Notes and Commonplace Book* . . . [ed. R. H. Barlow] (Lakeport, CA: Futile Press, 1938), pp. 1–14. Text based on the AMS (JHL), a notebook (not identical to the notebook containing HPL's Commonplace Book). The notes are a result of HPL's renewed study of the classics of weird fiction, conducted in 1932–33 and the product of his lack of confidence in the merits of his own work. Section 1 is an early version of "Notes on Writing Weird Fiction" (p. 169). "Elements of a Weird Story" and "Types of Weird Story" are abstractions from Section 1; "A List of Certain Basic . . ." is closely related to "Weird Story Plots" (p. 159), following the sequence of stories HPL was reading at that time. (The last five entries apparently were written at a later time, and it is not certain to which stories they apply.) "A List of Primary Ideas Motivating Possible Weird Tales" is a condensation of the previous list.

Notes

1. Edgar Allan Poe, "The Fall of the House of Usher."
2. Poe, "The Fall of the House of Usher" and "The Premature Burial."
3. Poe, "The Fall of the House of Usher."
4. Poe, "Ligeia."
5. Machen, "The Great God Pan."
6. Poe, "MS. Found in a Bottle."
7. Poe, "The Oval Portrait."
8. Poe, "The Facts in the Case of M. Valdemar."
9. Poe, "William Wilson."
10. Poe, "Berenice."
11. Poe, "Metzengerstein."
12. Arthur Machen, "The White People."
13. Machen, "Novel of the Black Seal" (a segment of *The Three Impostors*).
14. Machen, "Novel of the White Powder" (a segment of *The Three Impostors*).
15. Machen, *The Terror.*
16. Algernon Blackwood, "The Willows."
17. Blackwood, "The Listener."
18. Blackwood, "Ancient Sorceries."
19. Blackwood, "The Nemesis of Fire."
20. Blackwood, "Secret Worship."
21. Walter de la Mare, "Seaton's Aunt."
22. De la Mare, "Mr. Kempe."
23. De la Mare, "All-Hallows."
24. M. R. James, "Canon Alberic's Scrapbook."
25. James, "Lost Hearts."
26. James, "The Mezzotint."

27. James, "The Ash-Tree."

28. James, "Number 13."

29. James, "Count Magnus."

30. James, "Count Magnus."

31. James, "'Oh, Whistle, and I'll Come to You, My Lad.'"

32. James, "The Treasure of Abbot Thomas."

33. James, "A School Story."

34. James, "The Tractate Middoth."

35. James, "Martin's Close."

36. James, "An Episode of Cathedral History."

37. James, "A View from a Hill."

38. James, "A Warning to the Curious."

39. Lord Dunsany, "The House of the Sphinx."

40. E. F. Benson, "Negotium Perambulans . . ."

41. Robert W. Chambers, "The Yellow Sign."

42. Irvin S. Cobb, "Fishhead."

43. Hanns Heinz Ewers, "The Spider."

44. R. Elwyn Backus, "The Phantom Bus."

45. Conrad Aiken, "Mr. Arcularis."

46. Paul Suter, "Beyond the Door."

47. John Buchan, "The Green Wildebeest."

48. Buchan, "Skule Skerry."

49. Buchan, "Skule Skerry."

50. Buchan, "The Wind in the Portico."

51. Sir Arthur Conan Doyle, "Lot No. 249."

52. Leonard Cline, The Dark Chamber. August Derleth, unaware of the source of this note, thought it was a plot germ of HPL's and accordingly wrote the "posthumous collaboration" "The Ancestor" based upon it.

53. Possibly Ambrose Bierce, "The Suitable Surroundings."

54. Unidentified.

55. Unidentified.

56. Unidentified.

57. Possibly Ambrose Bierce, "An Inhabitant of Carcosa."

NOTES ON WRITING WEIRD FICTION

My reason for writing stories is to give myself the satisfaction of visualising more clearly and detailedly and stably the vague, elusive, fragmentary impressions of wonder, beauty, and adventurous expectancy which are conveyed to me by certain sights (scenic, architectural, atmospheric, etc.), ideas, occurrences, and images encountered in art and literature. I choose weird stories because they suit my inclination best—one of my strongest and most persistent wishes being to achieve, momentarily, the illusion of some strange suspension or violation of the galling limitations of time, space, and natural law which for ever imprison us and frustrate our curiosity about the infinite cosmic spaces beyond the radius of our sight and analysis. These stories frequently emphasise the element of horror because fear is our deepest and strongest emotion, and the one which best lends itself to the creation of nature-defying illusions. Horror and the unknown or the strange are always closely connected, so that it is hard to create a convincing picture of shattered natural law or cosmic alienage or "outsideness" without laying stress on the emotion of fear. The reason why *time* plays a great part in so many of my tales is that this element looms up in my mind as the most profoundly dramatic and grimly terrible thing in the universe. *Conflict with time* seems to me the most potent and fruitful theme in all human expression.

While my chosen form of story-writing is obviously a special and perhaps a narrow one, it is none the less a persistent and permanent type of expression, as old as literature itself. There will always be a small percentage of persons who feel a burning curiosity about unknown outer space, and a burning desire to escape from the prison-house of the known and the real into those enchanted lands of incredible adventure and infinite possibilities which dreams open up to us, and which things like deep woods, fantastic urban towers, and flaming sunsets momentarily suggest. These persons include great authors as well as insignificant amateurs like myself—Dunsany, Poe, Arthur Machen, M. R. James, Algernon Blackwood, and Walter de la Mare being typical masters in this field.

As to how I write a story—there is no one way. Each one of my tales has a different history. Once or twice I have literally written out a dream; but usually I start with a mood or idea or image which I wish to express, and revolve it in my mind until I can think of a good way of embodying it in some chain of dramatic occurrences capable of being recorded in concrete terms. I tend to run through a mental list of the basic conditions or situations best adapted to such a mood or idea or image, and then begin to speculate on logical and naturally motivated explanations of the given mood or idea or image in terms of the basic condition or situation chosen.

The actual process of writing is of course as varied as the choice of theme and initial conception; but if the history of all my tales were analysed, it is just possible that the following set of rules might be deduced from the *average* procedure:

(1) Prepare a synopsis or scenario of events in the order of their absolute *occurrence*—not the order of their narration. Describe with enough fulness to cover all vital points and motivate all incidents planned. Details, comments, and estimates of consequences are sometimes desirable in this temporary framework.

(2) Prepare a second synopsis or scenario of events—this one in order of *narration* (not actual occurrence), with ample fulness and detail, and with notes as to changing perspective, stresses, and climax. Change the original synopsis to fit if such a change will increase the dramatic force or general effectiveness of the story. Interpolate or delete incidents at will—never being bound by the original conception even if the ultimate result be a tale wholly different from that first planned. Let additions and alterations be made whenever suggested by anything in the formulating process.

(3) Write out the story—rapidly, fluently, and not too critically—following the *second* or narrative-order synopsis. Change incidents and plot whenever the developing process seems to suggest such change, never being bound by any previous design. If the development suddenly reveals new opportunities for dramatic effect or vivid storytelling, add whatever is thought advantageous—going back and reconciling the early

parts to the new plan. Insert and delete whole sections if necessary or desirable, trying different beginnings and endings until the best arrangement is found. But be sure that all references throughout the story are thoroughly reconciled with the final design. Remove all possible superfluities—words, sentences, paragraphs, or whole episodes or elements—observing the usual precautions about the reconciling of all references.

(4) Revise the entire text, paying attention to vocabulary, syntax, rhythm of prose, proportioning of parts, niceties of tone, grace and convincingness or transitions (scene to scene, slow and detailed action to rapid and sketchy time-covering action and vice versa. . . . etc., etc., etc.), effectiveness of beginning, ending, climaxes, etc., dramatic suspense and interest, plausibility and atmosphere, and various other elements.

(5) Prepare a neatly typed copy—not hesitating to add final revisory touches where they seem in order.

The first of these stages is often purely a mental one—a set of conditions and happenings being worked out in my head, and never set down until I am ready to prepare a detailed synopsis of events in order of narration. Then, too, I sometimes begin even the actual writing before I know how I shall develop the idea—this beginning forming a problem to be motivated and exploited.

There are, I think, four distinct types of weird story; one expressing a *mood or feeling*, another expressing a *pictorial conception*, a third expressing a *general situation, condition, legend, or intellectual conception*, and a fourth explaining a *definite tableau or specific dramatic situation or climax*. In another way, weird tales may be grouped into two rough categories—those in which the marvel or horror concerns some *condition* or *phenomenon*, and those in which it concerns some *action of persons* in connexion with a bizarre condition or phenomenon.

Each weird story—to speak more particularly of the horror type—seems to involve five definite elements: (a) some basic, underlying horror or abnormality—condition, entity, etc.—, (b) the general effects or bearings of the horror, (c) the mode of manifestation—object embodying the horror and phenomena observed—, (d) the types of fear-reaction pertaining to the horror, and (e) the specific effects of the horror in relation to the given set of conditions.

In writing a weird story I always try very carefully to achieve the right mood and atmosphere, and place the emphasis where it belongs. One cannot, except in immature pulp charlatan–fiction, present an account of impossible, improbable, or inconceivable phenomena as a commonplace narrative of objective acts and conventional emotions. Inconceivable events and conditions have a special handicap to overcome, and this can be accomplished only through the maintenance of a careful realism in every phase of the story *except* that touching on the one given marvel. This marvel must be treated very impressively and deliberately—with a careful emotional "build-up"—else it will seem flat and unconvincing. Being the principal thing in the story, its mere existence should overshadow the characters and events. But the characters and events must be consistent and natural except where they touch the single marvel. In relation to the central wonder, the characters should shew the same overwhelming emotion which similar characters would shew toward such a wonder in real life. Never have a wonder taken for granted. Even when the characters are supposed to be accustomed to the wonder I try to weave an air of awe and impressiveness corresponding to what the reader should feel. A casual style ruins any serious fantasy.

Atmosphere, not action, is the great desideratum of weird fiction. Indeed, all that a wonder story can ever be is *a vivid picture of a certain type of human mood*. The moment it tries to be anything else it becomes cheap, puerile, and unconvincing. Prime emphasis should be given to *subtle suggestion*—imperceptible hints and touches of selective associative detail which express shadings of moods and build up a vague illusion of the strange reality of the unreal. Avoid bald catalogues of incredible happenings which can have no substance or meaning apart from a sustaining cloud of colour and symbolism.

These are the rules or standards which I have followed—consciously or unconsciously—ever since I first attempted the serious writing of fantasy. That my results are successful may well be disputed—but I feel at least sure that, had I ignored the considerations mentioned in the last few paragraphs, they would have been much worse than they are.

EDITOR'S NOTE FP: *Amateur Correspondent* 2, No. 1 (May–June 1937): 7–10; other versions in *Supramundane Stories* 1, No. 2 (Spring 1938): 11–13 (as "Notes on Weird Fiction-Writing—The 'Why' and 'How'") and *Marginalia* (Arkham House, 1944), pp. 135–39 (as "Notes on the Writing of Weird Fiction"). All three of these texts appear to derive from independent manuscripts, as HPL circulated several handwritten copies of his essay—a revised version of the "Suggestions for Writing Story" in "[Notes on Weird Fiction]," and probably written in 1933—to various correspondents; yet another version is included in a letter to Duane W. Rimel (17 June 1934; ms., JHL). The *Amateur Correspondent* version appears to be the soundest text, and it has largely been followed here. The essay constitutes HPL's definitive statement as to the aims and purposes of weird fiction and his own methods in story writing.

SOME NOTES ON INTERPLANETARY FICTION

Despite the current flood of stories dealing with other worlds and universes, and with intrepid flights to and from them through cosmic space, it is probably no exaggeration to say that not more than a half-dozen of these things, including the novels of H. G. Wells, have even the slightest shadow of a claim to artistic seriousness or literary rank. Insincerity, conventionality, triteness, artificiality, false emotion, and puerile extravagance reign triumphant throughout this overcrowded genre, so that none but its rarest products can possibly claim a truly adult status. And the spectacle of such persistent hollowness had led many to ask whether, indeed, any fabric of real literature can ever grow out of the given subject-matter.

The present commentator does not believe that the idea of space-travel and other worlds is inherently unsuited to literary use. It is, rather, his opinion that the omnipresent cheapening and misuse of that idea is the result of a widespread misconception; a misconception which extends to other departments of weird and science fiction as well. This fallacy is the notion that any account of impossible, improbable, or inconceivable phenomena can be successfully presented as a commonplace narrative of objective acts and conventional emotions in the ordinary tone and manner of popular romance. Such a presentation will often "get by" with immature readers, but it will never approach even remotely the field of aesthetic merit.

Inconceivable events and conditions form a class apart from all other story elements, and cannot be made convincing by any mere process of casual narration. They have the handicap of incredibility to overcome; and this can be accomplished only through a careful realism in every *other* phase of the story, plus a gradual atmospheric or emotional building-up of the utmost subtlety. The emphasis, too, must be kept right—hovering always over *the wonder of the central abnormality itself*. It must be remembered that any violation of what we know as natural law is *in itself* a far more tremendous thing than any other event or feeling which could possibly affect a human being. Therefore in a story dealing with such a thing we cannot expect to create any sense of life or illusion of reality if we treat the wonder casually and have the characters moving about under ordinary motivations. The characters, though they must be natural, should be subordinated to the central marvel around which they are grouped. The true "hero" of a marvel tale is not any human being, but simply a *set of phenomena*.

Over and above everything else should tower the stark, outrageous monstrousness of the one chosen departure from Nature. The characters should react to it as real people would react to such a thing if it were suddenly to confront them in daily life; displaying the almost soul-shattering amazement which anyone would naturally display instead of the mild, tame, quickly-passed-over emotions prescribed by cheap popular convention. Even when the wonder is one to which the characters are assumed to be used, the sense of awe, marvel, and strangeness which the reader would feel in the presence of such a thing must somehow be suggested by the author. When an account of a marvellous trip is presented without the colouring of appropriate emotion, we never feel the least degree of vividness in it. We do not get the spine-tickling illusion that such a thing might possibly have happened, but merely feel that somebody has uttered some extravagant words. In general, we should forget all about the popular hack conventions of cheap writing and try to make our story a perfect slice of actual life except where the one chosen marvel is concerned. We should work as if we were staging a hoax and trying to get our extravagant lie accepted as literal truth.

Atmosphere, not action, is the thing to cultivate in the wonder story. We cannot put stress on the bare events, since the unnatural extravagance of these events makes them sound hollow and absurd when thrown into too high relief. Such events, even when theoretically possible or conceivable in the future, have no counterpart or basis in existing life and human experience, hence can never form the groundwork of an adult tale. All that a marvel story can ever be, in a serious way, is a *vivid picture of a certain type of human mood*. The moment it tries to be anything else it becomes cheap, puerile, and unconvincing. Therefore a fantastic author should see that his prime emphasis goes into subtle suggestion—the imperceptible hints and touches of selective and associative detail which express shadings of moods and build up a vague illusion of the strange reality of the unreal—instead of into bald catalogues of incredible happenings which can have no substance or meaning apart from a sustaining cloud of colour and mood-symbolism. A serious adult story must be true to something in life. Since marvel tales cannot be true to the *events* of life, they must shift their emphasis toward something to which they *can* be true; namely, certain wistful or restless *moods* of the human spirit, wherein it seeks to weave gossamer ladders of escape from the galling tyranny of time, space, and natural laws.

And how are these general principles of adult wonder fiction to be applied to the interplanetary tale in particular? That they *can* be applied, we have no reason to doubt; the important factors being here, as elsewhere, an adequate sense of wonder, adequate emotions in the characters, realism in the setting and supplementary incidents, care in the choice of significant detail, and a studious avoidance of the hackneyed artificial characters and stupid conventional events and situations which at once destroy a story's vitality by proclaiming it a product of weary mass mechanics. It is an ironic truth that no artistic story of this kind, honestly, sincerely, and unconventionally written, would be likely to have any chance of acceptance among professional editors of the common pulp school. This, however, will not influence the really determined artist bent on creating something of mature worth. Better to write honestly for a non-remunerative magazine than to concoct worthless tinsel and be paid for it. Some day, perhaps, the conventions of cheap editors will be less flagrantly absurd in their anti-artistic rigidity.

The events of an interplanetary story—aside from such tales as involve sheer poetic fantasy—are best laid in the present, or represented as having occurred secretly or prehistorically in the past. The future is a ticklish period to deal with; since it is virtually impossible to escape grotesqueness and absurdity in depicting its mode of life, while there is always an immense emotional loss in representing characters as familiar with the marvels depicted. The characters of a story are essentially projections of ourselves; and unless they can share our own ignorance and wonder concerning what occurs, there is an inevitable handicap. This is not to say that tales of the future cannot be artistic, but merely that it is harder to make them so.

A good interplanetary story must have realistic human characters; not the stock scientists, villainous assistants, invincible heroes, and lovely scientist's-daughter heroines of the usual trash of this sort. Indeed, there is no reason why there should be any "villain", "hero", or "heroine" at all. These artificial character-types belong wholly to artificial plot-forms, and have no place in serious fiction of any kind. The function of the story is to express a certain human mood of wonder and liberation, and any tawdry dragging-in of dime-novel theatricalism is both out of place and injurious. No stock romance is wanted. We must select only such characters (not necessarily stalwart or dashing or youthful or beautiful or picturesque characters) as would naturally be involved in the events to be depicted, and they must behave exactly as real persons would behave if confronted with the given marvels. The tone of the whole thing must be realism, not romance.

The crucial and delicate matter of getting the characters off the earth must be very carefully managed. Indeed, it probably forms the greatest single problem of the story. The departure must be plausibly accounted for and impressively described. If the period is not prehistoric, it is better to have the means of departure a secret invention. The characters must react to this invention with a proper sense of utter, almost paralysing wonder, avoiding the cheap fictional tendency of having such things half taken for granted. To avoid errors in complex problems of physics, it is well not to attempt too much detail in describing the invention.

Scarcely less delicate is the problem of describing the voyage through space and the landing on another world. Here we must lay primary stress on the stupendous emotions—the unconquerable sense of astonishment—felt by the voyagers as they realise they are *actually off their native earth*, in cosmic gulfs or on an alien world. Needless to say, a strict following of scientific fact in representing the mechanical, astronomical, and other aspects of the trip is absolutely essential. Not all readers are ignorant of the sciences, and a flagrant contravention of truth ruins a tale for anyone able to detect it.

Equal scientific care must be given to our representation of events on the alien planet. Everything must be in strict accord with the known or assumed nature of the orb in question—surface gravity, axial inclination, length of day and year, aspect of sky, etc.—and the atmosphere must be built up with significant details conducing to verisimilitude and realism. Hoary stock devices connected with the reception of the voyagers by the planet's inhabitants ought to be ruled rigidly out. Thus we should have no overfacile language-learning; no telepathic communication; no worship of the travellers as deities; no participation in the affairs of pseudo-human kingdoms, or in conventional wars between factions of inhabitants; no weddings with beautiful anthropomorphic princesses; no stereotyped Armageddons with ray-guns and space-ships; no court intrigues and jealous magicians; no peril from hairy ape-men of the polar caps; and so on, and so on. Social and political satire are always undesirable, since such intellectual and ulterior objects detract from the story's power as a crystallisation of a mood. What must always be present in superlative degree is a deep, pervasive sense of *strangeness*—the utter, incomprehensible *strangeness* of a world holding nothing in common with ours.

It is not necessary that the alien planet be inhabited—or inhabited at the period of the voyage—at all. If it is, the denizens must be definitely non-human in aspect, mentality, emotions, and nomenclature, unless they are assumed to be descendants of a prehistoric colonising expedition from our earth. The human-like aspect, psychology, and proper names commonly attributed to other-planetarians by the bulk of cheap authors is at once hilarious and pathetic. Another absurd habit of conventional hacks is having the major denizens of other planets always more advanced scientifically and mechanically than ourselves; always indulging in spectacular rites against a background of cubistic temples and palaces, and always menaced by some monstrous and dramatic peril. This kind of pap should be replaced by an adult realism, with the races of other-planetarians represented, according to the artistic demands of each separate case, as in every stage of development—sometimes high, sometimes low, and sometimes unpicturesquely middling. Royal and religious pageantry should not be conventionally overemphasised; indeed, it is not at all likely that more than a fraction of the exotic races would have lit upon the especial folk-customs of royalty and religion. It must be remembered that non-human beings would be wholly apart from human motives and perspectives.

But the real nucleus of the story ought to be something far removed from the specific aspect and customs of any hypothetical outside race—ought, indeed, to be nothing less than the *simple sensation of wonder at being off the earth*. Interest had better be sustained through accounts of bizarre and un-terrestrial natural conditions, rather than through any artificially dramatic actions of the characters, either human or exotic. Adventures may well be introduced, but they should be properly subordinated to realism—made inevitable outgrowths of the conditions instead of synthetic thrills concocted for their own sake.

The climax and ending must be managed very carefully to avoid extravagance or artificiality. It is preferable, in the interest of convincingness, to represent the fact of the voyage as remaining hidden from the public—or to have the voyage a prehistoric affair, forgotten by mankind and with its rediscovery remaining a secret. The idea of any general revelation implying a widespread change in human thoughts, history, or orientation tends to contradict surrounding events and clash with actual future probabilities too radically to give the reader a sense of naturalness. It is far more potent not to make the truth of the story dependent on any condition visibly contradicting what we know—for the reader may pleasantly toy with the notion that *perhaps* these marvels *may* have happened after all!

Meanwhile the deluge of inept interplanetary tosh continues. Whether a qualitative upturn will ever occur on anything like a large scale, this commentator cannot venture to prophesy; but at any rate, he has had his say regarding what he deems the main aspects of the problem. There are, without doubt, great possibilities in the serious exploitation of the astronomical tale; as a few semi-classics like "The War of the Worlds", "The Last and First Men", "Station X", "The Red Brain", and Clark Ashton Smith's best work prove.[1] But the pioneers must be prepared to labour without financial return, professional recognition, or the encouragement of a reading majority whose taste has been seriously warped by the rubbish it has devoured. Fortunately sincere artistic creation is its own incentive and reward, so that despite all obstacles we need not despair of the future of a fresh literary form whose present lack of development leaves all the more room for brilliant and fruitful experimentation.

EDITOR'S NOTE   FP: *Californian* 3, No. 3 (Winter 1935): 39–42. The essay was written around July 1934 for inclusion in one of William L. Crawford's magazines (either *Marvel Tales* or *Unusual Stories*), but did not appear there (see *SL* 5.12); it ended up in Hyman Bradofsky's amateur journal. HPL borrows entire passages from "Notes on Writing Weird Fiction" but slants the discussion toward the burgeoning field of "scientifiction," as represented by such magazines as *Amazing Stories* and *Astounding Stories,* in both of which he himself had appeared.

Notes

1. H. G. Wells, *The War of the Worlds* (1898); Olaf Stapledon, *Last and First Men* (1930); G. MacLeod Winsor, *Station X* (1919; rpt. *Amazing Stories,* July–September 1926); Donald Wandrei, "The Red Brain"(*Weird Tales,* October 1927).

WHAT BELONGS IN VERSE

In reading over a large part of the current amateur verse—as well as many of the ephemeral rhymes in newspapers and minor professional magazines—one is led to wonder just why the writers ever chose a metrical medium for what they had to say. We glance at these more or less measured lines and behold an unlimited number of statements, opinions, and admonitions on a few extremely familiar subjects, each phrased in the literal narrative manner of prose, and reflecting some conventional point of view made popular by copy-book repetition. There may or may not be some valid reason for the writer's wishing to say something. But is there any valid reason why he should depart from unrhymed, continuous prose text when he wishes to state facts, register beliefs and predilections, and make ethical or prudential recommendations?

These processes, notwithstanding the custom of many old-time versifiers of wide household fame, belong essentially to the domains of science, history, administration, and philosophy, and rest basically on intellectual explanation and clear definition. From their very nature they demand embodiment in forms suited to accurate exposition, rather than in those suited to emotional catharsis and imaginative symbolism. Why, then, do so many offerers of statements, doctrines, and sermons persist in assuming the ill-fitting cloak of rhyme and metre which was designed for the poet?

It would be well if every metrical aspirant would pause and reflect on the question of just what, out of the various things he wants to utter, ought indeed to be expressed in verse. The experiences of the ages have pretty well taught us that the heightened rhythms and unified patterns of verse are primarily adapted to *poetry*—which consists of strong feelings sharply, simply, and non-intellectually presented through indirect, figurative, and pictorial images. Therefore it is scarcely wise to choose these rhythms and patterns when we wish merely to tell something or claim something or preach something.

The time to use verse is when some mood or feeling about something becomes so strong and insistent that it calls up various concrete pictures and resemblances and symbols in our minds, and makes us long to shout it or put it on record vividly in terms of these images and symbols. If the sight of the white clouds arouses in us only a wish to point a moral based on their insubstantiality and deceptive aspect, then the best thing for us to do is either to preserve silence or write a sermon, preferably the former. If, on the other hand, such a sight makes us think of things like ships or swans or fleecy flocks or ethereal castles, then we may properly begin to consider whether the feeling is strong enough, and the especial image fresh and original enough, to warrant our breaking into metre.

Poetry, the normal subject-matter of verse, never defines or analyses or asserts or urges or proves anything. It merely depicts, emphasises, symbolises, illuminates, or otherwise expresses some mood or strongly felt object. Therefore when we try to write it we must not state and describe and argue in direct, literal fashion, but must instead convey our meaning through suggested comparisons, elusively symbolic visual images, and—in general—*concrete* associative pictures of some sort.

As a recent specimen of the amateur didactic utterance which could obviously find a more appropriate channel than rhyme, one might cite the following:

"Gossip sometimes does some good
While other times does not but should.
Thus, when it's said with words unkind,
Consider it with a just mind."

Contrasting with this the following quatrain of real poetry from the same magazine—a sample of the kind of emotional utterance which does indeed call for metrical dress:

TO MOTHER
By Albert Chapin

I saw your loving eyes—yet mine were closed;
    I heard your tender voice—though stilled in death;
I felt your gentle touch, and as I dozed
    There came a summer breeze—your sweet, warm breath.[1]

The question of *light verse*, involving some apparent contradictions of the principles here suggested, forms a wholly separate subject, and one which merits subsequent treatment in these columns. Meanwhile it is any case wise to pause carefully before beginning a piece of rhyme—asking oneself whether the subject is indeed fitted for such a vehicle, or whether a prose conveyance could better accommodate its particular bulk and contours.

EDITOR'S NOTE FP: *Perspective Review* (Spring 1935), pp. 10–11. HPL's final utterance as to the nature and purpose of poetry, reflecting the views he had been developing since the late

1920s and focusing on the need to avoid didacticism and to utilise image and symbol rather than plain statement.

Notes

1. Published in the October 1934 issue of *Presque Isle Trail*. HPL discusses it briefly in "Report of the Bureau of Critics" (March 1935; *CEI*).

[SUGGESTIONS FOR A READING GUIDE]

In general, read what interests you most; but within that range choose the things which are recognised as the best literature or soundest scholarship. Do not despise the recommendations of teachers, librarians, authors, and others in a position to judge. Public libraries nowadays offer very valuable advice, based on the individual tastes and needs of each reader. Ask the nearest library for a circular about this service—called "Reading with a Purpose". No other age has been as rich as the present in facilities for adult education.

Try to read at least a few things in each of the great branches of human thought and expression, so that you may have a rough, connected idea of what is known about the universe, matter, the world, organic life, mankind, the stream of history, and the major achievements of the race in philosophy, government, literature, and the various arts. Do not scorn "outlines" and summaries, for it is better to have only a smattering of things than to remain with vast total blanks in your knowledge of what lies around you. Try not to let any article in the better grade of magazines, or any allusion in the course of daily reading, remain utterly meaningless and mystifying to you. Regard each totally unfamiliar subject or reference as a kind of challenge, and do not pass it by until you have dispelled at least the densest clouds of ignorance. Turn constantly to reference books—or make notes for future consultation if no such books are available at the moment. Learn what the best reference books are, and where to find them at the principal libraries.

Read light material in odd moments, but choose fair stretches of time—when you can enjoy the greatest freedom from interruption—for reading things which demand concentration and understanding. Do not persist in reading after fatigue begins to slow up your assimilation rate. It is wasteful to spend time which does not bring results. On the other hand, do not be alarmed or discouraged if you fail to remember everything you read. Nobody can hold all the facts and pictures which have ever entered his head. It is enough if a reasonable residue remains—sufficient basic landmarks to give you a general idea of things, make every-day phenomena and allusions intelligible, and enable you to find more detailed knowledge when you need it. The chief value of reading is the exercise and discipline it gives the mind—the way it teaches us to think, be intelligently curious about things, recognise general principles under varied individual surfaces, compare and correlate seemingly remote subjects and events, know where and how to get information, appreciate and understand history and our environment, employ judgment and proportion, enjoy genuine art and beauty, and transfer our interest from the trivial and meaningless to the significant.

Use your own judgment about balancing the different kinds of reading. Don't feel bound to any logical order, but skip around at will in covering the field of pure literature—unless the works of a certain period make you wish to read more of that period. In covering some of the sciences, it might be well to keep a certain rough sequence in mind, so that the general subjects can come before the more particular ones. You can, if you wish, follow the custom of schools and colleges in conducting parallel lines of reading. Just as they teach ancient and modern literature, science, history, and art at the same time, so can you be reading a book of recent fiction, a translation of Virgil, a summary of history, a popular outline of astronomy, an anthology of poetry, and a manual of Greek sculpture over the same period—picking up one when the mood strikes you, and perhaps choosing another the next time you have a spare quarter-hour. Keep them all going side by side, and one will form an agreeable change from the other. But don't feel bound to do this. If you have a naturally single-track mind you may prefer to read one book—or one sort of book—at a time; or perhaps you will choose to map out definite courses in literature, the arts, history, or the sciences, following each one uninterruptedly until you turn to another. It is all a matter of taste and temperament. In the end one likes to have a connected and workable idea of things—to see the universe whole, and to feel keenly the continuity, drama, and differing moods of human history. But there's no hurry about any of this.

Don't feel bound to "keep up with all the latest books" in order to shew off a superficial up-to-date scholarship. Of the various popular successes of any given season, only a tiny fraction—or perhaps none at all—can usually be of any permanent value. The only books which need to be of recent date are those pertaining to the sciences, where fresh discoveries have to be included—or perhaps to history also, where the modern scientific interpretation of events, and choice of matter for emphasis, are occasionally of great importance. In general literature a large proportion of the most essential books lie in the past—some of them in a past more than two thousand years from the present. However, it will do no harm to keep abreast of recent books and authors by following the reviews in standard periodicals—such as the Book Section of the *New York Times* or the book columns in the front advertising pages of *Harpers* and the *Atlantic*—and reading a few of those volumes which the best critics agree in recommending.

Try to hit certain high spots of general literature. In the classic Greek field, which forms the foundation of our whole structure of western culture, Homer must not be missed—and of all the various translations the prose version formed by Lang and Leaf's *Iliad* and Butcher and Lang's *Odyssey* is probably the closest in spirit to the original. The fascination of these eternal tales is such that their reading will be no duty. Other Greek masterpieces which ought to be read in good translations are the plays of great dramatists—such as Aeschylus' *Prometheus Bound*, Sophocles' *Oedipus the King* and perhaps *Antigone*, Euripides' *Baccantes*, *Electra*, *Alcestis*, and *Medea*, and some of Arisophanes' satiric comedies like *The Clouds*, *The Birds*, and *The Frogs*. Plutarch's *Lives*—or at least some of them—and a few of the Socratic dialogues of Plato (*Apology*, *Crito*, *Phaedo*, and some of the *Republic*—preferably in Jowett's translation) are also good to round out one's Hellenic reading. It might be well to have one's reading of these books come at a time when one is studying about Greek life and customs in the course of one's history reading. A good *abridged* course in Greek reading is formed by William Cleaver Wilkinson's compendium called *A Classic Greek Course in English*.[1]

Roman literature should give us Virgil in Dryden's spirited translation—or perhaps in some good prose version, which would probably get closer to the poet's spirit. One need not read all of Virgil, but a browsing through the *Aeneid*, *Georgics*, and *Eclogues* will reveal numberless passages that hold the imagination and linger in the memory. Read also Horace—supreme master of light verse and playful commentator on human nature, from whom so many of our proverbial sayings (like "golden mean" or "even Homer nods") come. The prose translation published by Macmillan is probably the best one to get. Some of the best orations of Cicero—especially the thunderings against the traitor Catiline—will prove of curiously contemporary interest in this age of social and political turbulence. Nor should one omit the early books of Caesar's *Commentaries,* in which he tells of his conquest of Gaul in prose of the utmost purity and simplicity. Aesop's *Fables*—a famous collection of folk tales which we get from the Latin version of Phaedrus—and some of Marcus Aurelius' philosophic meditations (written in Greek by a Roman emperor of largely Gallic blood) form a good tapering off of our classic reading. It is pleasant to read the Roman classics while studying Roman history; and to make them doubly vivid one may intersperse a few modern novels about Roman life—such as Edward Lucas White's *Unwilling Vestal* and his incomparably fascinating *Andivius Hedulio,* William Stearns Davis's *A Friend of Caesar,* or Robert Graves's twin volumes, *I, Claudius* and *Claudius the God.* Other such modern titles will at once suggest themselves. William Cleaver Wilkinson's *Preparatory Latin Course in English* offers an excellent short cut to Roman literature. In dealing with the ancient world we are also aided by any good manual of mythology—preferably Bulfinch's *Age of Fable.* It is likewise useful to have access to some reference book like *Harper's Dictionary of Classical Literature and Antiquities.*[2]

A third stream of ancient literature profoundly affecting our culture is that included in the Judaeo-Christian Bible, known to us chiefly in the King James version. The classic and Hellenically influenced book of Job should be read as a drama, while the Psalms and the Song of Solomon are pure poetry. Other parts should be read for dramatic, historical, and literary interest—among them the drama of Genesis, the prophetic music of Isaiah, and the simple tragedy and ethical idyllicism of Mark and John. But for a connected knowledge of the whole Scriptural background, it is advisable to seek a summarising and interpreting manual such as Hendrik Willem van Loon's *Story of the Bible.*[3]

Mediaeval literature included some widely separated specimens if we include, as we ought, both European and Oriental. We should read a good bit of Dante—largely in the *Inferno*—in Cary's blank verse translation, enjoying the potent grandeur and beauty, and the touches of human realism. Marco Polo's travels make an absorbing and adventurous story, and throw light on the mediaeval mind. Malory's *Morte d'Arthur* and Froissart's *Chronicles* present a more northern and romantic phase of mediaevalism, but might well be read in summaries or abridgments—such as Bulfinch's book on the Arthurian legends and Singleton's condensation of Froissart. Certain modern novels ably create the spirit of this period—notably Scott's *Ivanhoe* and *The Talisman,* and the late Sir A. Conan Doyle's *White Company* and *Sir Nigel.* Our own ancestral stream in the Middle Ages is vividly represented by the early Anglo-Saxon epic *Beowulf*—a tale of monsters and heroes best read in Clarence Griffin Child's translation. Chaucer's *Canterbury Tales* should be obtained in an edition with the old English slightly modernised for clearness' sake. So read, no more piquant and fascinating tales can be found in literature. Another refreshing bit of mediaevalism—full of naive wonders and grotesqueries—is the quaint volume of Sir John Mandeville's travels. In the Oriental field we do not have to be asked to read the Arabian Nights or Fitzgerald's translation of Omar's *Rubiyat.* All these mediaeval classics will have added interest if we read them simultaneously with books on the history and customs of the period.[4]

Coming down to the Renaissance (a phase of progress which appeared at different dates in different places), we find the short stories of Boccaccio a fundamental classic on which dozens of other writers drew. Some of these should by all means be read. Another classic which epitomises the turbulent Renaissance spirit is Benvenuto Cellini's autobiography. Selections from Rabelais' shapeless and pungent *Gargantua and Pantagruel* are timely, as are goodly slices of Cervantes' immortal *Don Quixote*, and a fair number of Montaigne's *Essays*. Within our own literary stream comes first and foremost William Shakespeare. Read him through, in instalments of not less than fifteen minutes a day. Other books feed different parts of the mind—Shakespeare feeds the entire brain. We have seen in a preceding chapter what a vast proportion of our common conversational phrases spring from him. That is a fair measure of his importance and influence in our civilisation. A useful preliminary to Shakespearian reading is *Tales from Shakespeare*, by Charles and Mary Lamb. If we find Shakespeare especially congenial we may care to investigate some of the other Elizabethan dramatists such as Marlowe, Ben Jonson, Webster, and Beaumont and Fletcher. From Shakespeare it is only a step to Bacon—to whom certain fanatics persistently and groundlessly attribute his plays. Some of his incomparably pithy essays should by all means be read, though his profound *Novum Organum*—one of the major philosophical works of all time—may well be left to specialists. That Bacon was found guilty of bribery in high office is a sad proof that intellect unsupported by ethical taste does not guarantee high character. Don't miss some of Spenser's fantastic allegorical poem *The Faerie Queene*, and the lyrical poems of Ben Jonson, Suckling, Carew, and Herrick. While pursuing this course of reading, it might be pleasant to read also some modern work like Walter Pater's *Renaissance*.[5]

The later seventeenth century has a different mood, or set of moods, and bridges the gulf to modernity. Here Milton dominates. Read all of *Paradise Lost* for unforgettable and inimitable grandeur of concepts, imagery, and language, and revel in the haunting pensiveness of *Lycidas*, the force of the sonnets, and the rare, ethereal felicity of *Comus*, "Il Penseroso", and "L'Allegro". Some of Bunyan's *Pilgrim's Progress* ought to be approached, and the best of Dryden's poems will scarcely bear missing. A typical Restoration comedy or two—such as Wycherley's *Plain-Dealer*, Dryden's *Wild Gallant*, Vanbrugh's *Relapse*, Farquhar's *Beaux' Stratagem*, or Congreve's *Love for Love*—is an admirable key to its period, and will not be found excessively strong meat for a generation reared on James Joyce and Ben Hecht. For quiet rural beauty and naiveté Walton's *Complete Angler* should be read at least in part, while a few couplets of the mordantly satiric *Hudibras*, by Samuel Butler, will not be regretted. Selections from Pepys' *Diary* cannot be skipped, nor can Sir Thomas Browne's quaint *Urn-Burial*. The great Continental luminary of this period is Molière, some of whose plays (such as *Tartuffe*, *Le Bourgeois Gentilhomme*, *Le Misanthrope*, or *Les Precieuses Ridicules*) make delightful reading in translation. Contemporaneous with him are the dramatists Corneille and Racine, and the epigrammatist La Rochefocauld, whose acute and cynical *Maxims* should be read in translation.[6]

As the brilliant eighteenth century dawns literature becomes so prolific that we have to choose from amidst an embarrassment of riches. The novel begins to take form, and we must not miss Defoe's *Robinson Crusoe*, Swift's *Gulliver's Travels*, Fielding's *Tom Jones*, Sterne's *Tristram Shandy*, Smollett's *Humphrey Clinker*, and Goldsmith's *Vicar of Wakefield*. The rise of the essay can best be grasped through a selection of *Spectator* papers by Addison and Steele (preferably those dealing with "Sir Roger de Coverley"), in which English prose attains its height in grace and force. The curious freshness, wit, and vitality of these light comments on contemporary life remind one of the popular "columnists" of today—F. P. A., R. H. L., Christopher Morley, Don Marquis, and the late B. L. T.[7] The drama shines with the sparkling comedies of Sheridan—of which *The Rivals* and *The School for Scandal* must be read. In poetry we shall relish the ringing verses of Pope, the pastoral beauty of parts of Thomson's *Seasons*, the felicity of Goldsmith's "Deserted Village", the deathless *Elegy* of Gray, quiet bits of Cowper, the homely lyrics of Robert Burns, and the prophetic mysticism of William Blake. Boswell's spirited and absorbing life of Johnson needs no recommendation. Benjamin Franklin's *Autobiography* brings America on the scene. The great historians Hume and Gibbon need be read only in selections. Of the political oratory of the time, Burke's speeches afford the best reading. In Germany we see the rise of Goethe and Schiller, both of whom should be noticed. Goethe's *Faust* goes over the line into the nineteenth century. In France the restless intellectual and enlightening forces leading up to the Revolution are perceived. Rousseau's *Social Contract* and *Confessions,* and much of Voltaire, can perhaps be passed over by the hasty reader; but Voltaire's *Candide,* with its ridicule of the hollow philosophy of optimism, is far too good to miss. In the *Zadig* of Voltaire we find an early case of that sort of deductive reasoning which later became the stock in trade of the detective-story writer.[8]

As the eighteenth century passes into the nineteenth we see a culmination of that "romantic revival" which dealt with extravagant individual emotion and looked to the Gothic Middle Ages for inspiration. Important poets now become numerous. We cannot afford to skip the dream-heavy Coleridge, the placidly pantheistic Wordsworth, the martial and resonant Scott, the misanthropic and infuriate Byron, the ethereal Shelley, and the beauty-drugged Keats. Here we have the greatest poetic flowering since the age of Elizabeth. In the essay field we shall delight in the work of Charles Lamb, and of our own graceful countryman Washington Irving. Sir Walter Scott, besides his poems, gives us the Waverly Novels, of which at least a few may pleasurably be sampled. Jane Austen's novels have a quiet and peculiar satiric charm, and a close approach to superficial realism. Read at least *Pride and Prejudice.* Of Thackeray, who sought to depict and lampoon society, read at least *Vanity Fair, The Newcomes,* and that marvellous re-creation of the eighteenth century, *Henry Esmond.* Emily Brontë's titanic *Wuthering Heights* is a work of genius, nor should her sister Charlotte's *Jane Eyre* be passed by. The selected essays of the historian Macaulay should be studied and emulated for force and clearness of style. Equally forceful, though having a choppy, artificial style suggestive of the modern news-magazine *Time,* was Thomas Carlyle, whose *French Revolution* and *Sartor Resartus* might well go on a "must" list. Looking homeward, we should read all the tales and poems of Poe, as well as his essay "The Philosophy of Composition", in which he professes to explain how he wrote "The Raven".[9]

This brings us to the early period of many of the giants of the middle and later nineteenth century. Several of Dickens' novels, especially *David Copperfield,* should be read, while selected poems of Tennyson, Browning, Mrs. Browning, Longfellow, Bryant, Lanier, Lowell, Holmes, Whittier, Emerson, Matthew Arnold, Walt Whitman, and Swinburne will bring rich rewards. Hawthorne should be read extensively, and of Herman Melville at least *Moby-Dick* deserves a hearing. Selected essays of Emerson are refreshing and indispensable, as are the *Walden* and *Cape Cod* of his independent fellow-Concordite Thoreau. Lowell's select essays are as important as his poems, while Holmes' *Autocrat of the Breakfast Table* and its successors form a perennial delight. *The Way of All Flesh,* by the later Samuel Butler, is probably the greatest exposé of domestic sentimentality in all literature. Include *Alice in Wonderland* as a typical specimen of whimsical humour. As the nineteenth century advances we encounter Mark Twain, whose leading works are fruitful, and George Meredith, a psychological novelist whose *Egoist* and *Diana of the Crossways* wear well with the years. Then comes the potent and tragic Thomas Hardy, a growth of the soil who should be judged by such solid master-pieces as *Under the Greenwood Tree* and *The Return of the Native*, or by his poems, rather than by his sentimental and melodramatic *Tess of the d'Urbervilles* or *Jude the Obscure*. Oscar Wilde is best represented by the inimitable light comedy *The Importance of Being Earnest*, the tragedy *Salomé*, the tenuously delightful fairy tales, and the poignant *Ballad of Reading Gaol*. Another writer of the late nineteenth-century aesthetic movement is Walter Pater with his *Marius the Epicurean*—a delicate study of the psychology of the later ancient world. With the nineties comes the late Rudyard Kipling, a fair representation of whose tales and poems are still capable of giving pleasure. The novelist Henry James, with his complex and over-mannered style, runs on into the twentieth century. Read his *Daisy Miller* and *The American*.[10]

The great foreign authors of the nineteenth century begin with Goethe and his *Faust*—Bayard Taylor's translation of which is excellent. Other important German products are the essays of Schopenhauer, the philosophic treatises of Nietzsche, and the glamorous poetry of Heinrich Heine. Turning to France, Balzac's stupendous *Human Comedy* should gradually be read entire, for it is perhaps the most faithful and living portrait of mankind ever painted. Begin with *The Wild Ass's Skin* and *Père Goriot*, and see that *Cesar Birotteau* and *Eugenie Grandet* are early items. Dumas is not so important, but *The Three Musketeers* and *Count of Monte Cristo* may please. Be sure to read at least a few translations form that exquisite stylist Théophile Gautier, and do not miss the *Salammbô* (a stirring tale of ancient Carthage), *Temptation of St. Anthony* (rich in prose-poetry), and *Madame Bovary* (early psychological realism) of his pupil Flaubert. Of Flaubert's pupil de Maupassant read as much as possible—for his stories are the classic models of psychological penetration, intelligent objectivity, and effective handling. Victor Hugo's *Les Miserables*, *Toilers of the Sea*, and *Notre Dame de Paris* are stirring and unforgettable. The *Rouge et Noir* of Stendhal is a curious foretaste of modernism, while Emile Zola (*L'Assomoir*, etc.) is the father of modern realism. In French poetry the supreme giant is Charles Pierre Baudelaire, that dark genius whose work is best sampled through the selected translation in the Modern Library. Mallarmé, Verlaine, and Rimbaud likewise hold a peculiar charm.[11]

In nineteenth-century Scandinavian literature the plays of Ibsen stand almost unrivalled. Begin with *A Doll's House*, *Ghosts*, *Rosmersholm*, or *Brand*, and read as many as you like—not forgetting the curious *Peer Gynt*. Strindberg is another powerful dramatist.

The Russian literature of the nineteenth century includes some of the most poignantly powerful fiction ever written, but sometimes seems remote and alien to us because of its close involvement with the subtleties of the Slavic temperament. Forget the occasional touches which sound mawkish, hysterical, and oversubtilised to western ears, and try to appreciate the psychological power and ruthless emotional portrayal. Turgeniev's *Virgin Soil* and *Fathers and Sons* have great charm despite some overcolouring and artificial contrasts. Chekhov's short stories are vigorous, while Tolstoi's novels *War and Peace*, *Anna Karenina*, *The Kreutzer Sonata*, and others go deep into human emotions. Greatest of all the Russians, however, is Dostoyevsky, with his grim and tense novels *Crime and Punishment*, *The Idiot*, *The Possessed*, and *The Brothers Karamazov*. No one except Shakespeare can excel him in driving force of fancy and emotion.[12]

Crossing into the present century, we are confronted by a flood of books and authors whose relative merits are still undetermined, and from among which we may only make certain tentative choices. English literature gives us Galsworthy's magnificent *Forsyte Saga*, Conrad's novels of the sea (read *Lord Jim* and others), Arnold Bennett's *Old Wives' Tale*, D. H. Lawrence's morbidly emotional novels (*Women in Love, Sons and Lovers,* etc.), W. Somerset Maugham's *Of Human Bondage,* H. G. Wells's serious novels and treatises, Aldous Huxley's disillusioned and prophetic analyses (read *Brave New World* and *Eyeless in Gaza*), William McFee's *Casuals of the Sea,* the incandescent satirical plays of George Bernard Shaw, the biographies of Lytton Strachey, and the vital poems of John Masefield, A. E. Housman, Rupert Brooke, Walter de la Mare, Robert Bridges, and T. S. Eliot. Ireland glows with the lustre of two successive revivals—the earlier giving us W. B. Yeats, today perhaps the greatest living poet, the dramatist Synge (*Riders to the Sea, The Playboy of the Western World*), and the preëminent fantaisiste Lord Dunsany (*A Dreamer's Tales, Plays of Gods and Men*); and the latter intense realists like James Joyce (*Ulysses* is important but difficult), Sean O'Casey, and Sean O'Faolain. In America Frank Norris (*McTeague, The Pit*) and Theodore Dreiser (*Sister Carrie, The Titan, An American Tragedy*) open up a notable line of novelists including Edith Wharton (*Ethan Frome*), Willa S. Cather (*Death Comes for the Archbishop*), Sinclair Lewis (*Arrowsmith, Dodsworth,* etc.), James Branch Cabell (*The Cream of the Jest,* etc.), Ben Hecht (*Erik Dorn*—the first full-length study of the modern temper), Ernest Hemingway (*A Farewell to Arms*), William Faulkner (*Sanctuary*), and Thomas Wolfe (*Look Homeward, Angel*). Poetry has produced Robert Frost, Edgar Lee Masters, Carl Sandburg, Edna St. Vincent Millay, and Archibald MacLeish. All of these are worth exploring.[13]

Modern France boasts the philosophical essayist Remy de Gourmont (read *A Night in the Luxembourg*), who breaks down dozens of nineteenth-century attitudes; the incomparable classical satirist Anatole France, whose *Penguin Island* purges and delights the soul, and the monumental novelists Marcel Proust (read his *Swann's Way* and *Within a Budding Grove*), Romain Rolland (*Jean Christophe* is the foremost philosophical novel of modern times), and Jules Romains (*Men of Good Will*).

Germany has exiled her greatest modern novelist Thomas Mann, whose *Buddenbrooks* and *The Magic Mountain* are landmarks. Other important German moderns are the dramatist Gerhard Hauptmann (*The Sunken Bell*) and the novelist Hermann Suderman (*The Song of Songs, Dame Care*).

The Spanish Ibañez (*The Cathedral*), the Italian D'Annunzio (*The Flame of Life*), the Swedish Selma Lagerlof (*Gosta Berling*), and the Norwegian Sigrid Undset (*Kristin Lavransdatter*—an important study in mediaeval life) seem assured of a permanent place in literature, while in Russia Andreyev (*The Red Laugh, The Seven Who Were Hanged*), Artzibasheff (*Sanine*), and Gorki (*Foma Gordyeff, The Lower Depths, Chelkash*) have vigorously carried the tradition of deep psychological insight and savage, ruthless realism down to the present time.[14]

But these are merely suggestions—which, incidentally, purposely omit most ultramodern experimental material, especially in the field of verse. You aren't forced to read half or a quarter or a tenth of these things. Very few professors of literature have read within twenty or a dozen of the various titles mentioned, to say nothing of those not mentioned. This is merely a rich feast from which you can pick and choose. Nor are you debarred from reading any amount of reasonably good material of a vastly lesser grade. The whimsical trifles of J. M. Barrie, the sociological strainings of Upton Sinclair, the historical and fantastic imaginings of Bulwer-Lytton, the perfumed posturings of Maeterlinck, the urbane preciosities of George Moore, the poems and tales of William Morris, the supernatural romancings of Mrs. Radcliffe, M. G. Lewis, C. R. Maturin, Arthur Machen, Algernon Blackwood, M. P. Shiel, M. R. James, and Walter de la Mare, the scientific fantasies of Jules Verne, H. G. Wells, S. Fowler Wright, and W. Olaf Stapledon, the Victorian imaginings of George Eliot, the Westernisms of Bret Harte, and thousands of other well-written items await the restless browser. The only important thing is to keep away from cheap magazine junk and popular best sellers of the flimsical grade. The better sort of detective stories are far from contemptible—those of A. Conan Doyle, G. K. Chesterton, S. S. van Dine, and others being something like folk classics in their limited way. Don't feel constrained, but follow your own inclinations to a great extent.[15]

Take your literature in mild doses, and don't overdo the poetic side if it is slow to appeal to you. Poetic appreciation sometimes comes quicker through a skimming of anthologies like Palgrave's *Golden Treasury* or the *Oxford Book of English Verse* than through the intensive reading of individual bards. If you feel moved to do some writing yourself, get the best manuals. Kellogg's and W. F. Webster's works on composition are excellent (but look up others at the library or in bookshops), and for the budding poet Brander Matthews' *A Study of Versification* and Gummere's *Handbook of Poetics* cannot be excelled. Always fortify yourself with a good dictionary (Webster's, Standard, Oxford, Century), a Roget's Thesaurus, a Walker's Rhyming Dictionary, a Bartlett's Familiar Quotations, a Brewer's *Dictionary of Phrase and Fable*, a Crabb's *English Synonyms*, a good Encyclopaedia (Britannica, Chambers',[16] Nelson's, International), a modern atlas, *Harper's Dictionary of Classical Literature and Antiquities,* and such other reference works as may prove convenient. If it is not practicable to have these at home, consult them when necessary at the library.

In your survey of literature as a whole, you will often be helped by some of the many excellent books on the history of the subject, which link authors and periods in a dramatic and enlightening way, or reflect the psychology of particular ages. Get books like the following at the library, and scan the shelves and card catalogues for others of the same general sort:

Macy—*Story of the World's Literature*
Quackenbos—*Ancient Literature, Oriental and Classical*
Jebb—*Primer of Greek Literature*
Miller and Kuhns—*Studies in the Poetry of Italy*
Taine—*History of English Literature*
Beers—*Chaucer to Tennyson*
Shaw—*Complete Manual of English Literature*
Backus and Brown—*The Great English Writers*
Baldwin—*Mediaeval Rhetoric and Poetic*
Whipple—*Literature of the Age of Elizabeth*
Clark—*The Seventeenth Century*
Minto—*Literature of the Georgian Era*
Stedman—*Victorian Poets*
Stedman—*Poets of America*
Payne—*History of American Literature*
Boynton—*American Literature*
Trent and Wells—*Pioneer, Colonial, and Revolutionary (Am.) Literature* (3 vols.)
Wilkinson—*Classic French Course in English*
Wilkinson—*Classic German Course in English*

Finally, books of criticism help to perfect one's taste and appreciation. Read H. L. Mencken's *Prejudices*, Arthur Symons' *The Symbolist Movement in Literature*, Matthew Arnold's *Culture and Anarchy*, Bennett's *Literary Taste—How to Form It*, Bushnell's *Historic Background of English Literature*, Cross's *Development of the English Novel*, Shipley's *Quest for Literature*, Untermeyer's *Forms of Poetry*, Wilkinson's *Contemporary Poetry*, Parrington's *Romantic Revolution in America*, Foerster's *Chief American Prose Writers*, W. C. Brownell's various volumes, Lowell's *My Study Windows*, and other items of the sort discoverable at the library. An excellent encyclopaedia covering this ground is Moulton's *Library of Literary Criticism*.

Devotees of the drama will find many volumes especially suited to them. Virtually all the major current plays are easily accessible in book form, while excellent dramatic histories are available. Read Quinn's *The American Drama* (1934–7), Nicoll's *The British Drama* (1933), Dickinson's *Contemporary Drama in England* (1933), and Smith's volumes on *Philosophic Drama, Romantic Drama,* and *Social Comedy* (1928). Collections of recent plays are Mantle's *Best Plays of 1919 to Date*, Watson and Pressey's *Contemporary Drama Series*, Scribner's series of American, English and Irish, and European plays (1931–2), and George Pierce Baker's *Modern American Plays* (1920).

Another phase worth attention is language itself—the study of English words and idioms. Read Trench's old-time classic *On the Study of Words*, and follow it up with more modern works as Lounsbury's *History of the English Language*, L. P. Smith's *English Language*, Mencken's *American Language*, and Barfield's *History in English Words*. One may add that it is advisable to read as many standard works on rhetoric and English usage as one can find time to assimilate, since useful precepts and pointers, some of which may be new to any given reader, are widely scattered through all of them.

But much more important reading is of course outside the field of pure literature. History, science, and art all call for attention. In history we must necessarily be superficial and one-sided. It is enough to have a rough outline knowledge of the history of all lands and ages, and then to specialise in the especial main stream—Greece, Rome, France, England, and America—most directly affecting ourselves. As we approach the present our need for detail increases.

For general history read the latest edition of Wells's splendid and intelligent *Outline*. Cover Greece and Rome with West's or Myers' *Ancient History*, supplementing this superficial study with books like Mahaffy's *Survey of Greek Civilisation*, Wilkins' *Roman Antiquities*, Pellison's *Roman Life in Pliny's Time*, and Osborn's *Heritage of Greece and Legacy of Rome*. For fuller material read William Smith's *History of Greece*, Liddell's *History of Rome*, and Smith's *Student's Gibbon*. For a simpler and more elementary survey, try Barnes' *A Brief History of Ancient Peoples*. Going toward the present, Myers' *Mediaeval and Modern History* is excellent, though Barnes' *Brief History of Mediaeval and Modern Peoples* is shorter and easier. Supplement these with something like Osborn's *The Middle Ages*. The Barnes *Brief History of France*, Harpers' *Student's History of France*, and the more recent Bainville's *History of France* are all useful—the first-named being simplest. In this age of world upheavals, special readings in the history of the affected regions—Spain, Russia, Germany, and so on—may well be arranged. Historic accounts of specific events like the World War or Russian Revolution are likewise valuable. For England a good elementary text-book is Montgomery's *English History*. Larned's *History of England* is also excellent. But our Mother Country deserves a closer study, so one ought eventually to go through J. R. Green's ample *History of the English People*. Historical novels—of which a limitless number exist—and books of English travel and folklore help to make the ancestral land live before our eyes. A good assortment may be unearthed at almost any library. For American history begin with a school text-book like Montgomery's or Muzzey's. Later advance to a scientific and unprejudiced book like James Truslow Adams' *Epic of America*. Follow this with more detailed books on the different historic periods—like those in the *Chronicles of America* series—and wind up with a reading of volumes on the folklore, traditions, antiquities, and social trends of the United States. Try George Cary Eggleston's *Our First Century* and *Life in the Eighteenth Century*, Watson's *Men and Times of the Revolution*, Scudder's *Men and Manners in America a Hundred Years Ago*, Skinner's *Myths and Legends of Our Own Land*, Drake's *Nooks and Corners of the New England Coast*, Eberlein's *Architecture of Colonial America*, Singleton's *Furniture of Our Forefathers*, Dyer's *Early American Craftsmen*, and kindred things. Read still more intensively on the history, folklore, and antiquities of your own state and general region. And do not omit Turner's famous *Frontier in American History* (1921). Finally, give the neighbouring regions of Canada and Latin-America at least a cursory survey. Special books on historic wars and crises are often important, and the reviews should be watched for accounts of new ones. Nowadays we may read of the Revolution, the War between the States, and other debatable questions with infinitely less prejudice and inaccuracy than we could a generation or more ago. Read Andrews' *Colonial Background of the American Revolution* (1924), Van Tyne's *Causes of the War for Independence* (1922), and Beard's *Rise of American Civilisation* (1927), *Economic Interpretation of the Constitution* (1913), and *Economic Origins of Jeffersonian Democracy*. Before concluding our survey of this field let us not forget that we have some magnificent historical novels such as Elizabeth Maddox Roberts' *The Great Meadow*.

Biography is a special form of history extremely fascinating to many. Read Plutarch's *Lives*, and 12 to 20 representative original biographies of world figures like Socrates, Alexander, Aristotle, Caesar, Michaelangelo, Leonardo da Vinci, Voltaire, and Napoleon. Be sure you have not skipped Boswell's *Johnson*, the greatest of all. Investigate the work of Lytton Strachey, André Maurois, Emil Ludwig, and Stefan Zweig. Look up still other eminent lives in a first-class encyclopaedia, and do not forget the great autobiographies—factual or spiritual—such as *The Education of Henry Adams*.

Read a book or two on archaeology, like Magoffin's *Magic Spades*, Woolley's *Digging Up the Past* (1933), or Casson's *Progress of Archaeology* (1934). And do not neglect mythology and folklore. You will be fascinated by Bulfinch's *Age of Fable* and his kindred books on non-classical mythology—all bound together in the "Modern Library" volume. Read John Fiske's *Myths and Myth-Makers*, Baring-Gould's *Curious Myths of the Middle Ages*, Grimm's *Fairy Tales*, Sir Walter Scott's *Demonology and Witchcraft*,[17] and the curious books of the Rev. Montague Summers on dark superstitions. For a thrilling and shuddersome background of a sinister belief read Prof. Margaret A. Murray's *Witch-Cult in Western Europe*. An abridgment of Frazer's *Golden Bough* is valuable as a compendium of odd folk-beliefs, though this encroaches somewhat on the special field of scientific anthropology.

Now turn to the all-important sciences—in which we must, because of the swift march of discovery, seek the latest authorities possible. A good general survey can be obtained from J. Arthur Thomson's four-volume *Outline of Science*, published a few years ago, though this has its weak and now obsolescent points. Another appropriate study at this stage would be mathematics—the basic principles of form and quantity— but as laymen we may well omit this, or restrict it to a review of elementary algebra and plane geometry—the latter a very useful exercise in pure reasoning. Higgs's *Algebra Self-Taught* and Wentworth's *Text-book of Geometry* make an excellent team. In considering the individual sciences we should study the most inclusive and general ones first. Astronomy of course has the widest spread—and ultra-modern discovery has extended the area of that spread to dizzying and inconceivable figures. We should have the latest books for all points touching on the dimensions and nature of the larger universe, though older treatises will serve us well for the general facts of our solar system, and for those parts of the subject which deal merely with apparent aspects of the sky. For basic facts read Bartky's *High Lights of Astronomy* (1936), Stokley's *Stars and Telescopes* (1936), Moulton's *Consider the Heavens* (1935), Baker's *Astronomy* (1933), and Duncan's *Astronomy* (1935). Some of the more spectacular aspects of the larger universe are hinted by Eddington's *Nature of the Physical World* (1928) and Jeans's *Universe Around Us* (1933) and *Through Space and Time* (1934). For amateurs interested in local and traditional aspects of astronomy—constellation study, low-power celestial observation, etc.—Serviss's *Astronomy with the Naked Eye, Astronomy with an Opera Glass,* and *Pleasures of the Telescope* are recommended. An excellent all-around standby is Newcomb's *Astronomy for Everybody.* The best contemporary star-atlas is Upton's, but a quicker working knowledge of the constellations can be obtained by the use of a small revolving planisphere, such as is sold for a quarter at the new Hayden Planetarium in New York.[18]

Physics—the science of matter and its nature and properties—is another subject needing the latest data for its theory-hedged frontier of rays, electrons, neutrons, and quanta, but ably served by older books so far as the surface aspects of its rudiments are concerned. Begin with a popular text-book like Brownell's *First Course in Physics* (1930), or the earlier manuals of Higgins, Sears, or Avery. Even the antediluvian Steele's *Fourteen Weeks in Physics* and prehistoric Ganot's book have their uses in teaching the beginner the first principles of mechanics, optics, acoustics, and so on. All too soon, however, we outgrow such whiskered reliques, and come to require things like Swann's *Architecture of the Universe* (1934), Darwin's *New Conceptions of Matter* (1934), Jeans's *New Background of Science* (1933), Reichenbech's *Atom and Cosmos* (1932), and Infeld's *World in Modern Science* (1934) . . . works already half-outmoded by new concepts and data. Gone is the comfortably static scholarship of yesteryear! The inventive and industrial aspects of modern physics—radio, television, electric eye, and so on—belong more to technology than to the pure science.

Chemistry can scarcely be told from physics in its modern advanced aspects, but its less attenuated side remains differentiated as before as the science of atomic combination. Here once more we need new books for the tenuous fringe, while old ones will do for the practical rudiments. For a sound elementary introduction read Steele's ancient *Fourteen Weeks in Chemistry,* Hessler's *First Year of Chemistry* (1931), or Godfrey's *Elementary Chemistry.* Ampler standard works are Remsen's *Inorganic Chemistry* and *Organic Chemistry.* Beginners who acquire laboratory materials and indulge in actual experiments will appreciate Appleton's *Young Chemist, Easy Experiments of Organic Chemistry,* and (if graduating to more advanced fields) *Qualitative Analysis* and *Quantitative Analysis.* More modern and specialised aspects are presented in Foster's *Romance of Chemistry* (1927), Slosson's *Creative Chemistry,* Findlay's *Spirit of Chemistry* (1934), Howe's *Chemistry in Industry,* and Stieglitz's *Chemistry in Medicine.* Veering sharply away from the modern angle, Johnston's venerable and out-of-print *Chemistry of Common Life* still holds its fascination for anyone lucky enough to encounter it.

Narrowing down to the earth, an old-fashioned but not seriously misleading introduction to geology still unsurpassed for beginners is Geikie's old *Geology Primer.* Another peculiarly congenial veteran is Winchell's *Walks and Talks in the Geological Field*—once a fixture in Chautauqua courses. The present age affords such excellent manuals as Longwell's *Foundations of Geology* (1930), Norton's *Elements of Geology* (1929), and Miller's *Introduction to Geology* (1928). In the special department of mineralogy many popular text-books exist, the best of which are perhaps those furnished by the American Museum of Natural History in New York. Palaeontology, the science of fossil life-forms, belongs as much to biology as to geology, though usually coupled with the latter. Here again the best brochures and manuals can be obtained from the American Museum. Physiography or physical geography grows out of geology but is really separate from it—being the science of land and water, erosion, climate, ocean currents, weathering, and so on. Obviously, this subject does not demand as much modernity as other scientific fields. Geikie's *Physical Geography* and Davis' *Elementary Physical Geography* are as attractive and reliable as ever, though the modernist might prefer Dryer's *Lessons in Physical Geography* (1927). A subdivision of this science is *meteorology*—the study of the weather—which one may approach very fascinatingly though Chambers' *Story of the Weather*. Much lies behind the daily forecasts of our government observers. In connexion with physiography some random reading of general geography and travel material would be appropriate. Books on the subject are innumerable. Prefer volumes which deal with interesting expeditions or which have literary value. Try Dana's *Two Years Before the Mast*, Darwin's *Voyage of the Beagle*, William Beebe's *Arcturus Adventure*, or Sven Hedin's books of explorations in the mysterious Gobi.

We now reach that special form of physical organisation called living matter, thereby entering the domain of *biology*. This is one of the sciences with a bewilderingly forward-moving frontier, but at the moment the admirable and comprehensive *Science of Life* by H. G. Wells and Prof. Julian Huxley (1929) is the finest conceivable introduction for laymen. This lucid exposition goes into ramifications beyond the field of sheer general biology, but the extensions are welcome rather than otherwise. It gives the novice the clearest possible idea of life and vital structure as a whole, explaining many seemingly hard points with a genius-born aptness. More formal text-books are Cole's *Introduction to Biology* (1933) and Moon's *Biology for Beginners* (1933). The special science of vegetable life is not among the swiftest changers, so that Hooker's aged *Botany Primer* still forms a good easy introduction. Bergen's *Introduction to Botany* is another reliable standby. One may, however, be assured of modernity by choosing Campbell's *General Elementary Botany* revised to 1930. Holman's *Elements* come all the way up to 1933. Those caring to follow botany into the special field of agriculture may profitably read Robbins' *Agriculture for High Schools* (1928). The science of the animal world—except on its theoretical frontiers—will also admit of books written day before yesterday. Steele's old *Fourteen Weeks in Zoölogy* is an easy start, and not at all misleading, though one might feel safer with Dakin's *Elements of General Zoölogy* (1927) and Newman's *Outlines of General Zoölogy*. Special fields are covered by such books as Blanchan's *Birds Worth Knowing* (1917), Shoffner's *Bird Book* (1929), Weed's *Butterflies Worth Knowing* (1917), Seton's *Animals Worth Knowing* (1926), and Shimer's *Introduction to the Study of Fossils* (1914). Wood's amiably unscientific *Natural History* still delights the young, and probably conveys far more useful information than wrong impressions. Of books treating solely of the evolution of animal forms, Darwin's epoch-making *Origin of Species* and *Descent of Man* are both pleasantly readable. Haeckel's *Evolution of Man* is technical but simple and clear. In passing, one must pay a special tribute to the useful little books with colour plates issued by the Whitman Publishing Co. of Racine, Wis., and vended very reasonably at the late Frank Winfield Woolworth's widely scattered emporia—the *Red, Green, and Blue Bird Books of America, Butterflies and Moths of America, Wild Flowers of America,* and *Trees of North America.*[19] These small brochures, with their clear and descriptive text, do much toward helping one to identify the flora and aërial fauna of the surrounding landscape.

Working around to what the late B. L. T. described as the so-called human race, we find Vernon Kellogg's *Human Life as the Biologist Sees It* (1922) and J. Arthur Thomson's *What Is Man?* (1924) to be interesting basic treatises. The best popular introduction to anatomy and physiology is Dr. Logan Clendening's *The Human Body*, though the Wells-Huxley *Science of Life* also extends into this field. Insisters on the academic may turn to Kimber's *Text Book of Anatomy and Physiology* (1930). A splendid auxiliary to anatomical study is the *Atlas of Human Anatomy* by Frohse and Broedel, now just on the market in a popular-priced edition (paper $1.25; cloth $2.00) and sold by Barnes and Noble, 105 Fifth Ave., New York City. As we enter the realm of psychology—instincts, emotion, intellect—we find a vociferous multiplicity of rival theories and satellitic charlatanries baying and snapping at our heels, but with care we may pick a sanely conservative course through this tentative and undeveloped science. We soon learn that the major part of the science has nothing to do with sensational "complexes", "inhibitions", "wish-fulfilments", or "subconscious will-power", but deals with the very exact and prosaic business of testing and measuring obscure mental reactions and investigating delicate nervous coördinations and aptitudes. The most representative elementary text-books are Warren and Carmichael's *Introduction to Psychology* (1930), Woodworth's *Psychology* (1934), Moss's *Comparative Psychology* (including lower animals, 1934), and Murphy's *History and Introduction to Psychology* (1929). A more popular sort of treatise is represented by Dr. Dorsey's *Why We Behave Like Human Beings*—a best-seller of 1925—and by the various volumes of H. A. Overstreet. In the highly unsettled and controversy-ridden field of Freudian and behaviouristic theory, several works may interest the layman. Freud's own *General Introduction to Psycho-Analysis* and *The Interpretation of Dreams* are not unreadable, but the popular manuals by André Tridon, Barbara Low, Isidor Coriat, and William J. Fielding are easier to grasp and digest. Dr. John B. Watson's *Behaviourism* presents the case for that extravagant but perhaps truth-containing system, while Dr. Louis Berman's *Glands Regulating Personality* tells how the functioning of the ductless glands determines emotional and mental attitudes as well as regulating many physical characteristics. Another class of books, whose interest is mainly professional, is that dealing with psychiatry, or the measurement of intelligence.

When we begin to consider man in the mass, we find ourselves speculating on the precise way he developed from the lower primates, the reasons why he separated into so many races, the relationship he bears to the various brutish sub-human species whose fossil skulls and bones are found in different parts of the world, the stages he traversed in achieving connected thought, speech, and the use of artifacts, the causes for his existing beliefs, customs, likes, and dislikes, the course of his migrations, clashes, and mixtures before the dawn of history, the principles covering his organisation into groups, the laws by which resources are distributed within these groups, and the manner in which he strikes a balance between individual and collective wishes and needs, and maps out an orderly and mutually helpful path for the multitudinous members of his group. Hence the related and sometimes overlapping fields of research called ethnology, anthropology, sociology, economics, and civics; all of them turbulent areas of dispute.

Regarding biological ethnology or physical anthropology (also called *somatology*)—the development and great divisions of sub-men and true men—we require the absolutely latest books because of the rapid growth of discovery. Every few years a newly excavated primitive skull or correlation of results forces us to change our opinions about man and his subdivisions and relatives. Probably most of the sub-human bones found in ancient strata are not directly ancestral to man, though the Pekin skull discovered in 1931 may be. These lower species were blind alleys of evolution, and the history of surviving races is still obscure. Most believe that all human races have a remote common ancestor within the definite limits of humanity, but Sir Arthur Keith is beginning to dispute this. It is likewise disputed whether the different branches of human civilisation arose independently, or whether all came originally from some common source, probably in Asia. For speculation on these points, and deductions as to the relationships of all the primitive and non-primitive man-like stocks, the best simple books to consult are the latest publications of the American Museum of Natural History. Going beyond these, we should look for the latest volumes by the world's leading authorities—Prof. G. Elliot Smith, Prof. Marcelin Boule, Sir Arthur Keith, Dr. W. K. Gregory, Dr. Arthur Smith Woodward, Dr. Eugene Dubois, Prof. R. S. Lull, J. Deniker, Dr. Ales Hrdlika, or Sir H. H. Johnston.

General anthropology—the study of primitive thought and customs, and of the evolution of racial beliefs, social institutions, and folkways—demands less modernity that ethnology, although new discoveries and interpretations do steadily occur. Kroeber's *Anthropology* (1923) or Lowie's *Introduction to Cultural Anthropology* (1934) forms a good introduction, but many of the older classics like Tylor's *Primitive Culture* and *Early History of Mankind*, or Lubbock's *Prehistoric Times*, are well worth reading. Sir James G. Frazer in *The Golden Bough* has presented the most extensive of all records of tribal beliefs and magical rites (an abridged edition is available), while recent notable researches in special fields are Westermarck's *History of Human Marriage* and Briffault's monumental study in matriarchy—*The Mothers*. When anthropology touches high evolved civilisations it becomes *sociology*, and concerns itself with conditions of life, principles of organisation, and economic and political factors. A good basic work on this phase is Prof. Lester Ward's famous *Outlines of Sociology* (1907), though moderns might look askance at its age. Bogardus' *Introduction to Sociology* (1931), Ross's *Principles of Sociology* (1930), Hiller's *Principles of Sociology* (1933), and Wallis and Willey's *Readings in Sociology* are more comfortably contemporaneous. Other not too specialised or advanced treatises are Lynd's *Middletown* (study of a typical small American city—1929), W. G. Sumner's *Folkways* (1913), W. F. Ogburn's *Social Change* (1923), Burgess' *Urban Community* (1926) and *Personality and the Social Group* (1929), Brown's *Social Psychology* (1934), and Elliott and Merrill's *Social Disorganisation* (1934).

When we reach the stage of economics, the real controversial tornado begins, for here is where greed and conservation clash with certain unmistakable indications. The best popular summary is H. G. Wells's lucid though perhaps opinionated *Work, Wealth, and Happiness of Mankind* (1931), which completes a trilogy with his *Outline of History* and *Science of Life*. More cautious and academic are Taussig's *Principles of Economics* (1925), Garver and Hansen's *Principles of Economics* (1928), Fairchild, Furniss, and Buck's *Elementary Economics* (1932), and Slichter's *Modern Economic Society* (1928). Books which look forward either cautiously or radically are G. D. H. Cole's *Guide Through World Chaos* (1932), Wallace's *New Frontiers* (1934), Beard and Smith's *The Future Comes* (1933), Tugwell's *The Industrial Discipline* (1933), and John Strachey's *Coming Struggle for Power* and *Nature of Capitalist Crisis* (1935). Marx's *Das Kapital* ought to be read in some abridgment, and Adam Smith's eighteenth-century *Wealth of Nations*, the Bible of rugged individualists, has great historic value as a landmark. At the present moment, as the failure of orthodox capitalism to decrease unemployment and the concentration of wealth in a mechanised civilisation becomes increasingly manifest, we must beware of the irresponsible pamphleteering practiced on both sides of the growing breach between conservative "haves" and radical "have-nots". Facts are distorted amidst the tension, and statements and inferences tend to become emotional and undependable. Orthodox Marxism is certainly a grotesque exaggeration of the truth, though orthodox capitalistic laissez-faire can scarcely be less fantastic in the light of present and future conditions.

Getting to the province of civics or political science, we find the tension and confusion still greater. Bewildered as to goals, methods, and conditions, men ask whether economic and social equilibrium can ever be reached without communism on the one hand or fascism on the other, and Continental Europe gives no encouraging reply. Caution and impersonality in choosing authorities are thus imperative for every reader in the field of civics. Haines's *Principles and Problems of Government* (1934) makes a good beginning, as would also Finer's *Theory and Practice of Modern Government* (1931). For the local American angle read Bryce's classic *American Commonwealth* and *Modern Democracies* (1921), Beard's *American Government and Politics*, Odegard's *American Public Mind* (1930), and Holcombe's *State Government in the United States*. For Europe read Ogg's *European Governments and Politics* (1934), Lengyel's *New Deal in Europe* (1934), Laski's *Politics* (1931) and *Problems of Peace* (1932), and Ilin's *New Russia Primer*. Special studies in the politics of each of the great nations can easily be discovered at a good library.

Closely attached to sociology and civics is the subject of *education;* for without intelligent training in facts, skills, taste, judgment, traditions, values, courage, independence, originality, and social responsibility no competent citizenry can ever be developed. A stimulating book in this field is Herbert Spencer's *Education,* which presents certain general principles and values with clearness and vigour. Rousseau's *Emile*—in the form of a rather sentimental novel—is really a thinly disguised educational treatise of considerable historical interest. Among concrete and practical modern treatises may be mentioned Curoe's *Principles of Education* (1924), Averill's *Elements of Educational Psychology* (1924), and Cameron's *Educational Psychology* (1927). Naturally, an abundance of technical and specialised works exist for the professional teacher.

It is now time to look back over what we have read, and see if we can trace amidst the human animal's turbulent emotions, contradictory ideas, confused and shifting aspirations, perpetual hostilities, divided and irreconcilable goals, irrational likes and dislikes, tenacious ignorance and delusions, and generally feverish and bewildered activities any signs of a unity or dominant direction which could justify the concept of a fairly stable set of proximate values, or an approach to the idea of a kind of relative meaning, in the general phenomena of life and social relationships on our planet. In other words, we have arrived at the consideration of philosophy. Of all popular manuals to help us understand the endlessly complex, attenuated, and bitterly partisan speculations which have raged around these problems of reality, value, and meaning since the earliest ages of Greece, the best and clearest is undoubtedly Will Durant's well-known *Story of Philosophy.* It has certain obvious faults and limitations, and makes too many concessions to common bourgeois optimism; but despite all this it presents the principal types and traditions of speculation about ultimate goals, standards, and entity far better than any other book of equal scope. Probably it will lead many readers to study more deeply, and devour at first hand the writings of the great thinkers whose mental battles are related—Plato, Aristotle, Lucretius, Spinoza, Bacon, Hobbes, Locke, Kant, Schopenhauer, Nietzsche, Santayana, Dewey, Bertrand Russell, and all the rest. It will in any case help you to comprehend the vast differences between various streams of thought—rational, practical, or mystical—which are irreconcilable because based on fundamentally different kinds of personality. By learning how others are divided you will come to know where you stand yourself. A short reading course can hardly include the writings of older philosophers, but the simpler works of a few acute contemporaries are worth individual attention. Read Bertrand Russell's *Philosophy* (1927) and *Sceptical Essays* (1928). Santayana's *Winds of Doctrine* (1913) and *Character and Opinion in the United States* (1920) are also of basic importance—and of a gracefulness which will not disappoint admiring readers of his recent first novel, *The Last Puritan. Reason and Nature,* by Prof. Morris Cohen, is highly intelligent and unbiassed. The increasing drift in the United States to the pragmatic instrumentalism of Professor John Dewey—who has taken over and enlarged on the strongest points of the late popular William James without adopting the latter's inconsistencies and bourgeois concessions—makes it wise to glance at his most typical works. Try *Human Nature and Conduct* and *Art as Experience* (1934). The former can be purchased in the Modern Library.

As an example of the opposite school which believes that current knowledge of man and the universe has stripped life of its basic traditional values and rendered most of our familiar emotions (especially that of tragedy) largely meaningless, read Joseph Wood Krutch's *The Modern Temper.* Mr. Krutch believes that existence has been hopelessly impoverished by progress and disillusionment, and adopts a highly pessimistic tone. Another really savage pessimist is the eminent anthropologist Robert Briffault, whose *Breakdown* makes exciting reading. Mr. Briffault's pessimism, however, covers only our existing culture; and he believes that man can become emotionally regenerated and restored to purposeful living by turning to the fresh ideals and way of life of Marxian communism.

In connexion with philosophy a work of two on formal logic would not be amiss— Jevons' *Elements* being particularly good.

There now remain for our notice those fields of taste and human expression not included in literature—the various arts whose modes of conveyance are other than written or spoken words. Before getting to the more recognised ones we ought to consider for a moment a vastly broader field in which the artistic principle vies potently with the utilitarian for dominance—the ancient and still poorly understood field of ethics. That as many factors of civilised human conduct are caused by a form of taste as are caused by utilitarian needs and social pressure, is scarcely to be doubted. It would be odd indeed if man's ingrained craving for rhythm, harmony, form, and continuity did not affect his approach to personal behaviour as considerably as it affects his approach to craftsmanship, written expression, or graphic presentation; and in truth we find this basic aestheticism in all his acts, and all his preferences and opinions concerning his acts. Sociology and civics determine only a skeletonic portion of his total conduct—hence the logical recognition of a separate field of ethics among the arts. The soundest popular manual of modern ethics now available is Walter Lippmann's admirable *Preface to Morals.* Also clear and illuminating is Prof. Irwin Edman's *The Contemporary and His Soul* (1931). Prof. Edman may be recalled as one of the leaders of the late Neo-Humanist movement. John Dewey also approaches the moral field (which indeed lies on the borderline of philosophy) in his collaborated work on *Ethics,* of which a revised addition appeared in 1932.

Approaching the more formal arts, we should first consider the basic and generalised ones including architecture, decoration, the various handicrafts (pottery, silver-smithing, carving, bookbinding, cabinet-making, and so on), and possibly some phases of scenery-appreciation. These, we may roughly say, involve the fundamental and more or less abstract aesthetics of form and colour without literal representation—though of course an extraneous associative element plays a great part in their practical application. We love a beautiful object not only because it embodies abstract harmony, but because it strikes some note of familiarity arousing a chain of pleasant memories or symbolism. Abstract beauty alone would not be sufficient to hold us—hence the tragic fallacy of functionally "modernistic" art, which reminds us of nothing, but leave us homesick, bewildered, and dissatisfied in the absence of landmarks.

We cannot expect to pursue all the individual handicrafts in our reading, for their number is of course legion. Indeed, the details of many belong more to the field of technology than to that of art. Of the various functional and decorative arts architecture is without question the most important. It is indeed one of the greatest of all the arts, being executed on such a scale and in such a manner as to dominate whole regions for vast spaces of time. It is likewise the earliest of the major arts to come to maturity in a growing civilisation. A good introductory volume to read is W. R. Lethaby's *Architecture* in the Home University Library. Read also Rathbun's *Background to Architecture.* For specific handbooks on some of the greatest phases of the art T. Roger Smith's *Classic Architecture* and *Architecture—Gothic and Renaissance,* and Anderson, Spiers, and Dinsmoor's *Architecture of Ancient Greece* may be recommended. Sir Arthur Evans' *Palace of Minos at Knossos* deals with the author's famous rediscovery early in the present century of a forgotten civilisation with a great architectural tradition. For Gothic architecture read Henry Adams' *Mont St. Michel and Chartres,* and Victor Hugo's novel *Notre Dame de Paris*—also the series of illustrated books on English Cathedrals published by George Bell and Sons of London. For the local scene Eberlein's *Architecture of Colonial America* and Cheney's *New World Architecture* (1930) are good. [Sturgis's] *Dictionary of Architecture and Building* is at most libraries to help solve knotty problems.

Any library catalogue will suggest books on such individual decorative crafts as one may wish to study. W. C. Prime's *Pottery and Porcelain,* Moore's *Old Glass, European and American,* and Leitch's *Chinese Rugs* form examples. Books on scenery and its appreciation are scarce to the vanishing point, but a great part of Ruskin's *Frondes Agrestes*—a set of selections from his own monumental *Modern Painters*—amounts to just that. This little volume, though compiled in mid-Victorian times, is still delectable reading, and should not be missed. A book or two on the fascinating art of landscape gardening would suit many tastes—and it is curious to note that the older ones are generally the most delightful. Old Humphrey Repton's *Sketches and Hints on Landscape Gardening* (1794), and Downing's classic American work of the 1840's—*Theory and Practice of Landscape Gardening*—will repay anyone fortunate enough to encounter them.

We should give considerable time to the more specialised arts of graphic and plastic representation, since taste in these fields is of very great importance. Everyone should have a keen appreciation of drawing, painting, and sculpture, and reading should be supplemented by study of the actual objects (or such of them as are available) in galleries and museums, or through accurate pictorial reproductions. Books on painting and sculpture mean little except when read in conjunction with the objects or their reproductions. With such aid, however, descriptive and critical matter is of great educational value. Good preliminary books are Kenyon Cox's *Concerning Painting* (1917) and *The Classic Point of View* (1911). For studying the great painters themselves, nothing can excel the series of brochures called *Masters in Art,* originally published as a magazine thirty years ago by Bates and Guild of Boston, and since issued in collected form. Each of these booklets is devoted to one artist, and contains ten excellent reproductions (unfortunately not in colour) of his best work, plus a portrait of him.

In the letterpress is an ample biographical sketch, followed by a series of several critical estimates of the artist's work, taken from the writings of the best authorities all over the world. Then follows a careful analysis of each reproduced picture; describing the subject, circumstances, and background of the work, indicating the colours, and adding critical notes to aid the learner in grasping all the nuances, details, and implications. The value of such a series—which covers most of the greater masters—is self-evident. It is, indeed, a liberal art education in itself. It is fortunately available in the art departments of most libraries, and isolated booklets occasionally turn up in second-hand bookshops and on remainder counters at grotesquely low prices. Lucky and alert purchasers are often able to form sizeable collections. Another excellent series of art booklets—with small uncoloured pictures alone—is that published at sixpence each by Gowans and Gray in England. The advantage of these brochures is the great number of photographic reproductions—sixty in the Rembrandt book. The extremely useful Perry Pictures—uncoloured reproductions sold singly by the well-known Boston firm at a minimum price—should be largely represented in your collection. But get as many colour prints as you can. One excellent series is *Masterpieces in Colour*—thin books, each devoted to one artist and having several fine coloured reproductions of his chief works—published by Frederick A. Stokes Co. of New York. The letterpress consists of a life of the artist plus brief notes on each picture.[20]

A few books on the eccentric modern forms of painting now so frequently seen will prove value in understanding these manifestations. Read Thomas Craven's *Modern Art* (1934), Morris Davidson's *Understanding Modern Art* (1934), and Sheldon Cheney's *Primer of Modern Art*. Readers desiring to take up graphic art for themselves may find many useful handbooks at the libraries. Here one may mention only a volume or two such as Norton's *Elementary Freehand Perspective*, Lederer's *Drawing Made Easy*, and Arthur L. Guptill's encyclopaedic and prodigiously helpful *Drawing with Pen and Ink*, sold at $8.50 by the Pencil Points Press, 419 Fourth Ave., New York, N.Y. Volumes on sculpture are readily available—some leading treatises on the greatest periods of the art being Miss Richter's *Sculpture and Sculptors of the Greeks* (1930), Tarbell's *History of Greek Art*, Walters' *Art of the Romans*, and Goodyear's *Roman and Mediaeval Art*. Any good life of Michaelangelo perforce sheds light on the best of Renaissance sculpture—while many of the numbers in the *Masters in Art* series treat of sculptors. For general reference in the graphic art field, consult Bryan's *Dictionary of Painters and Engravers* at the library.

Music is a vast field whose surface reading can only scratch. Audition—apart from being an artist oneself—is everything; and he who would acquire, develop, or satisfy musical taste must arrange to hear the best selections rendered in the best manner, whether at concerts, on phonograph records, or over the radio. However, books may guide the beginner most usefully; speeding up his understanding of the art and of specific pieces, and helping him to judge of the "modernistic" changes which seem to be sweeping over it. We have not been a naturally musical race since Tudor and Jacobean times, but there are signs of a revival in the present century. Certainly, we should not allow any major art to remain a blind spot if we can help it. Useful introductory books are Thompson's *How to Understand Music* (1935), Finney's *History of Music* (1935), Moore's *Listening to Music* (1932), McKinney and Anderson's *Discovering Music* (1934), and Spaeth's *Art of Enjoying Music* (1933). For the modern angle read Bauer's *Twentieth Century Music* (1933), Cowell's *New Music Resources* (1930), and John Tasker Howard's *Our American Music* (1931). For operatic understanding and appreciation get the well-known *Book of the Opera* and its sequel, issued in one of the popular series of dollar reprints. And Isaacson's *Face to Face with the Great Musicians* will furnish an agreeable biographical background.[21] Grove's *Dictionary of Music and Musicians,* consulted at the library, should help at times.

An outline of this kind cannot go beyond the arts and pure sciences into the prosaic yet absorbing and dramatic field of mechanised technology. However, for those who feel the fascination of a new age based on strange forces and methods, there are plenty of books to guide. One has only to ask at the library. Of greater cultural interest is the origin of the simple devices we have known for centuries—clocks, telescopes, barometers, and so on—and the story of these is well told in Beckmann's classic *History of Inventions.*

Acquire as many books of the right sort as you can afford to house, for ownership means easy and repeated access and permanent usefulness. Don't be a foppish hoarder of fine bindings and first editions. Get books for what's in them, and be glad enough of that. Marvellous bargains can be found on the dime counters of second-hand shops, and a really good library can be picked up at surprisingly little cost. The one great trouble is housing when one's quarters are limited; though by using many small bookcases—cheap sets of open shelves—in odd corners one can stow away a gratifying number of volumes. Don't despise paper-bound books. Investigate the marvellously cheap pamphlets sold by the Haldemann-Julius Co. of Girard, Kansas, which include many of the most important classics, plus extremely clear outlines of scientific and other subjects prepared (and including the latest developments) by staff writers of the firm. For less humble items, read over the titles of well-known series like "Everyman's Library", "The Modern Library", "The Home University Library", and the various dollar reprints.

Have as good a supply of reference books as possible. If an unabridged dictionary is unfeasible, try something the size and grade of Webster's *Collegiate.* Everything depends on a good encyclopaedia. Get an ancient set of the Britannica or Chambers' (both obtainable cheaply) if you can't afford a new one, and try the handy one-volume *Modern Encyclopaedia* (1934) for $1.98 to furnish the few contemporary references you'll need. You can find Roget's Thesaurus and Crabbe's *Synonyms* among the dollar books, and Bartlett's *Familiar Quotations* can be had for little more. Try for Brewer's *Dictionary of Phrase and Fable,* and get a small classical dictionary if Harper's large one is out of reach. For ready contemporary facts about places, events, and institutions, get the World Almanac every two or three years. Very fair atlases can be obtained at Woolworth's. Pick up all the second-hand books of rhetoric and text-books of history and science that you can find room for. You can never tell when they'll come in handy for the solution of some debatable point. Some literary compendium like Chambers' *Cyclopaedia of English Literature* is also good to have. Be on the lookout at second-hand shops for unusual things like the *Dictionary of Classical Quotations.*

But don't be overawed by your own library, or discouraged by the number of books you ought to read. The preceding list is only to choose from at leisure—nobody is supposed to read it through. But never stop altogether.

EDITOR'S NOTE FP: In *The Dark Brotherhood and Other Pieces* (Sauk City, WI: Arkham House, 1966), pp. 30–63. Text derived from the AMS (JHL). Written in the fall of 1936 as the concluding chapter of Anne Tillery Renshaw's *Well Bred Speech* (Washington, DC: Standard Press, 1936; *LL* 726), which HPL was revising; but Renshaw decided not to use the chapter, along with two or three others that HPL had written. The title was supplied by August Derleth; Renshaw's original chapter (only 4 typewritten pages) was entitled "What

Shall I Read?" (it survives, along with other matter by HPL and Renshaw pertaining to *Well-Bred Speech*, at JHL). Although HPL did much library work in preparing this essay, time constraints forced him to rely on books from his own library for many of his recommendations, especially in general literature, classical literature and scholarship, and the sciences he knew well (astronomy, chemistry, physics). It should by no means be assumed that HPL actually read all the works he cites. In the following notes, reference is made to standard literary texts owned by HPL (numbers in parentheses indicate the numbers in *LL*). A Bibliographical Appendix has been provided to supply full bibliographical information on other works cited; indications are made there as to HPL's ownership of the volumes in question. Some of HPL's citations of titles are either erroneous or condensed; see the Bibliographical Appendix or the index for clarification.

Notes

1. HPL owned Plutarch's *Lives* (697–98); Plato's *Republic* (696); and Wilkinson's *Classic Greek Course in English* (959).

2. HPL owned Dryden's *Vergil* (906) along with other translations; Horace both in Latin and in translation (439–42); some of Cicero's orations (174); Caesar's *Civil War* and *Gallic War* (146–48); and Aesop's fables in translation (11–12).

3. HPL owned several copies of the King James Bible (84–86).

4. HPL owned Dante's *Divine Comedy* in H. F. Cary's translation (218–19); Malory's *Morte d'Arthur* (591); Froissart's *Chronicles* (338); Scott's *Ivanhoe* (769) and *The Talisman* (773); selections from Chaucer (170); and *Arabian Nights* (38).

5. HPL owned several editions of Shakespeare (787–89); the Lambs' *Tales from Shakespeare* (512); selections from Marlowe (494); Jonson's complete plays (486); and selections from Beaumont and Fletcher (72).

6. HPL owned Milton's poetical works (704); Bunyan's *Pilgrim's Progress* (134); Dryden's poetical works (267) and *The Wild Gallant* (268); Butler's *Hudibras* (143); and Pepys' *Diary* (685).

7. HPL refers to various newspaper columnists: F. P. A. is Franklin P. Adams (1881–1960), who chiefly wrote for the *Chicago Tribune* and various New York papers (*Evening Mail*, *Tribune*, *World*, *Herald-Tribune*, *Post*). R. H. L. is Richard Henry Little (1869–1946), who wrote for the *Chicago Tribune*. Christopher Morley (1890–1957) was a columnist for the *New York Evening Post* and *Saturday Review of Literature*. Don Marquis (1878–1937) wrote verse and prose (including poems about "archy and mehitabel") for the *New York Sun* and *Tribune*. B. L. T. is Bert Leston Taylor (1866–1921) who write chiefly for the *Chicago Tribune*.

8. HPL owned Defoe's *Robinson Crusoe* (227); Swift's *Gulliver's Travels* (858); selections from Sterne (843); Goldsmith's *Vicar of Wakefield* (363); the *Spectator* (7, 9–10); Sheridan's plays (796); Pope's poetical works (705); Thomson's *The Seasons* (883); Goldsmith's poems (363); Gray's *Elegy* (372); Burns's poetical works (137); selections from Blake (104); Boswell's *Life of Johnson* (113); Gibbon's *Decline and Fall* and other works (350–52); and Goethe's *Faust* (359–61).

9. HPL owned the poetical works of Coleridge (188), Wordsworth (972), Scott (772), Shelley (794), and Keats (492); Lamb's complete works (510); selected works of Irving (460–64); several of Scott's Waverley novels (766–69, 771, 773–74); Jane Austen's novels (47–50); several works by Thackeray (769–73) including *The Newcomes* and *Henry Esmond*, but not *Vanity Fair*; Emily Brontë's *Wuthering Heights* (611); Charlotte Brontë's *Jane Eyre* (122); Macaulay's miscellaneous works (562); Carlyle's *French Revolution* (153) and *Sartor Resartus* (154); and Poe's complete works (702).

10. HPL owned many of Dickens's novels (241–51), but not *David Copperfield*; the poetical works of Tennyson (866), Browning (124 [selections]), Longfellow (544), Bryant (126), Lowell (553), Holmes (431), Whittier (953), Emerson's *Earlier Poems* (295), Whitman (952 [selections]), and Swinburne (859 [selections]); many works by Hawthorne (401–09); many of Emerson's essays (296–98); some of Lowell's essays (551–52); some of Mark Twain's works (177–79); some works by Wilde (954–57), but not *The Importance of Being Earnest* or *Salomé*; Pater's *Marius the Epicurean* (677); some of Kipling's short stories (502–3); no other work by Henry James aside from *The Turn of the Screw* (467).

11. HPL owned Bayard Taylor's translation of *Faust* (360); Dumas' *Three Musketeers* (269); several works by Gautier (344–47); Flaubert's *Salammbô* (320) and *Temptation of St. Anthony* (321); Hugo's *Hans of Iceland* (448) but no other works; and selections from Baudelaire (69–70).

12. HPL owned Tolstoi's *War and Peace* (888).

13. HPL owned Shaw's *Back to Methuselah* (791); T. S. Eliot's *The Waste Land* (238); many works by Dunsany (270–83); and Cabell's *The Line of Love* (145).

14. HPL owned Andreyev's *The Seven That Were Hanged* and *The Red Laugh* (29).

15. HPL owned many of the supernatural works listed in this paragraph; see my annotated edition of *Supernatural Horror in Literature* (Hippocampus Press, 2000).

16. HPL owned Chambers' *Cyclopaedia of English Literature* (164).

17. HPL owned Grimm's *Fairy Tales* (379) and Scott's *Letters on Demonology and Witchcraft* (770).

18. HPL obtained the planisphere on a trip to the Hayden Planetarium in December 1935.

19. There is no book published by Whitman Publishing Co. under the title *Trees of North America*. HPL may be referring to a well-known work, George Rex Green's *Trees of North America (Exclusive of Mexico)* (Ann Arbor, MI: Edwards Brothers, 1933–34; 2 vols.).

20. HPL owned several volumes in the Stokes series, including those devoted to Frans Hals (392), Bartolome Murillo (632), and Sir Joshua Reynolds (729).

21. This book was written by Charles D. Isaacson, HPL's old amateur journalism nemesis. See DPC (March 1915) and "In a Major Key" (*CE1*).

Bibliographical Appendix

The following list provides bibliographical information on all works (aside from standard literary works) cited by HPL in "Suggestions for a Reading Guide." Information is provided on first editions only unless HPL explicitly refers to a later edition. The abbreviation *LL* refers to HPL's ownership of some edition of the work in his personal library (it should not be assumed that HPL owned the first edition). Information is not supplied when HPL refers only to an author without reference to a specific work.

Adams, Henry. *The Education of Henry Adams*. Cambridge, MA: Riverside Press/Massachusetts Historical Society, 1918.
———. *Mont St. Michel and Chartres*. Cambridge, MA: Houghton Mifflin, 1913.
Adams, James Truslow. *The Epic of America*. Boston: Little, Brown, 1931.
Anderson, William J. R. Phené Spiers, and William Bell Dinsmoor. *The Architecture of Ancient Greece: An Account of Its Historic Development*. New York: Scribner's, 1927.
Andrews, Charles M. *The Colonial Background of the American Revolution*. New Haven: Yale University Press, 1924.

Appleton, John Howard. *Easy Experiments of Organic Chemistry for Students' Laboratory Work.* Providence: Snow & Farnham, 1898.

———. *A Short Course in Qualitative Chemical Analysis.* Philadelphia: Cowperthwait & Co., 1878.

———. *A Short Course in Quantitative Chemical Analysis.* Providence: E. L. Freeman, 1879.

———. *The Young Chemist.* Providence: J. A. & R. A. Reid, 1876. [LL 36]

Arnold, Matthew. *Culture and Anarchy: An Essay in Political and Social Criticism.* London: Smith, Elder, 1869.

Ashbrook, F. G. *The Blue Book of Birds of America.* Racine, WI: Whitman Publishing Co., 1931.

———. *The Green Book of Birds of America.* Racine, WI: Whitman Publishing Co., 1931.

———. *The Red Book of Birds of America.* Racine, WI: Whitman Publishing Co., 1931.

Averill, Lawrence Augustus. *Elements of Educational Psychology.* Boston: Houghton Mifflin, 1924.

Avery, Elroy McKendree. *School Physics.* New York: American Book Co., 1895.

Backus, Truman J., and Helen Dawes Brown. *The Great English Writers from Chaucer to George Eliot.* New York: Sheldon & Co., 1889.

Bainville, Jacques. *History of France.* Tr. Alice Gauss and Christian Gauss. New York: D. Appleton & Co., 1926.

Baker, George Pierce, ed. *Modern American Plays.* New York: Harcourt, Brace & Howe, 1920.

Baker, Robert H. *Astronomy: An Introduction.* New York: D. Van Nostrand & Co., 1930.

Baldwin, Charles Sears. *Medieval Rhetoric and Poetic (to 1400).* New York: Macmillan, 1928.

Barfield, Owen. *History in English Words.* Garden City, NY: George H. Doran, 1926.

Baring-Gould, S. *Curious Myths of the Middle Ages.* London: Rivingtons, 1866. [LL 66]

Bartky, Walter. *Highlights of Astronomy.* Chicago: University of Chicago Press, 1935.

Bartlett, John. *A Collection of Familiar Quotations.* Cambridge: John Bartlett, 1855. (11th ed. 1937.) [LL 67]

Bauer, Marion. *Twentieth Century Music: How It Developed, How to Listen to It.* New York: Putnam, 1933.

Beard, Charles A. *American Government and Politics.* New York: Macmillan, 1910.

———. *An Economic Interpretation of the Constitution of the United States.* New York: Macmillan, 1935.

———. *Economic Origins of Jeffersonian Democracy.* New York: Macmillan, 1915.

———, and Mary A. Beard. *The Rise of American Civilization.* New York: Macmillan, 1927.

———, and George H. E. Smith. *The Future Comes: A Study of the New Deal.* New York: Macmillan, 1933.

Beckmann, Johann. *History of Inventions and Discoveries.* Tr. William Johnston. London: J. Bell, 1797. 3 vols.

Beebe, William. *The Arcturus Adventure.* New York: Putnam, 1926.

Beers, Henry A. *From Chaucer to Tennyson.* New York: Chautauqua Press, 1890.

Bennett, Arnold. *Literary Taste: How to Form It.* New York: George H. Doran Co., 1910.

Bergen, Joseph Young. *Introduction to Botany.* Boston: Ginn & Co., 1914.

Berman, Louis. *The Glands Regulating Personality.* New York: Macmillan, 1921.

Blanchan, Neltje. *Birds Worth Knowing.* Garden City, NY: Doubleday, Page, 1917.

Bogardus, Emory Stephen. *Introduction to Sociology.* Los Angeles: University of Southern California Press, 1917.

Boynton, Percy H. *American Literature.* Boston: Ginn & Co., 1923.

Brewer, Ebenezer Cobham. *Dictionary of Phrase and Fable.* London: Cassell, 1870.

Briffault, Robert. *Breakdown: The Collapse of Traditional Civilisation.* New York: Brentano's, 1932.

———. *The Mothers: A Matriarchal Theory of Social Origins.* New York: Macmillan, 1927.

Brown, Laurence Guy. *Social Psychology: The Nature of Human Nature.* New York: McGraw-Hill, 1934.

Brownell, Herbert. *A First Course in Physics.* Philadelphia: John C. Winston Co., 1929.

Bryan, Michael. *A Biographical Dictionary of Painters and Engravers.* London: Carpenter, 1816. 2 vols.

Bryce, James, Viscount. *The American Commonwealth.* New York: Macmillan, 1888. 3 vols. [LL 128]

———. *Modern Democracies.* New York: Macmillan, 1921.

Bulfinch, Thomas. *The Age of Fable; or, The Beauties of Mythology.* Boston: Sanborn, Carter & Bazin, 1855.

Burgess, Ernest Watson, ed. *Personality and the Social Group.* Chicago: University of Chicago Press, 1929.

———. *The Urban Community.* Chicago: University of Chicago Press, 1926.

Bushnell, Nelson Sherwin. *The Historical Background of English Literature.* New York: Henry Holt & Co., 1930.

Campbell, Elmer Grant. *General Elementary Botany.* New York: Thomas Y. Crowell Co., 1929 (rev. ed. 1930).

Cameron, Edward Herbert. *Educational Psychology.* New York: Century Co., 1927.

Casson, Stanley. *The Progress of Archaeology.* London: George Bell & Sons, 1934.

Chambers, George F. *The Story of the Weather.* London: George Newnes, 1897. [LL 163]

Chambers, Robert, ed. *Cyclopaedia of English Literature.* Edinburgh: W. & R. Chambers, 1844. 2 vols. [LL 164]

Cheney, Sheldon. *The New World Architecture.* London: Longmans, Green, 1930.

———. *A Primer of Modern Art.* New York: Boni & Liveright, 1924.

Clark, Sir G. N. *The Seventeenth Century.* (Oxford History of English Literature.) Oxford: Clarendon Press, 1929.

Clendening, Logan. *The Human Body.* New York: Knopf, 1927.

Cohen, Morris. *Reason and Nature.* New York: Harcourt, Brace, 1931.

Cole, Elbert Charles. *An Introduction to Biology.* New York: John Wiley & Sons, 1933.

Cole, G. D. H. *A Guide through World Chaos.* New York: Knopf, 1932.

Coriat, Isidor. *Abnormal Psychology.* New York: Moffat, Yard, 1914.

Cowell, Henry. *New Musical Resources.* New York: Knopf, 1930.

Cox, Kenyon. *The Classic Point of View: Six Lectures on Painting.* New York: Scribner's, 1911.

———. *Concerning Painting: Considerations Theoretical and Historical.* New York: Scribner's, 1917.

Crabb, George. *English Synonymes.* London: Baldwin, Cradock & Joy, 1816. [LL 201]

Craven, Thomas. *Modern Art: The Men, the Movements, the Meaning.* New York: Simon & Schuster, 1934.

Cross, Wilbur L. *Development of the English Novel.* New York: Macmillan, 1899.

Curoe, Philip Raphael V. *Principles of Education.* New York: Globe Book Co., 1926.

Dana, Richard Henry. *Two Years Before the Mast: A Personal Narrative of Life at Sea.* New York: Harper & Brothers, 1840.

Darwin, Charles. *The Descent of Man, and Selection in Relation to Sex.* London: John Murray, 1871.

————. *Journal of Researches into the Geology and Natural History of the Various Countries Visited by H.M.S. Beagle*. London: H. Colburn, 1839. [Later editions as *The Voyage of the Beagle*.]

————. *On the Origin of Species by Means of Natural Selection*. London: John Murray, 1859.

Darwin, Charles Galton. *The New Conceptions of Matter*. New York: Macmillan, 1931.

Davidson, Morris. *Understanding Modern Art*. New York: Coward-McCann, 1931.

Davis, William Morris. *Elementary Physical Geography*. Boston: Ginn & Co., 1902. [LL 224]

Davis, William Stearns. *A Friend of Caesar*. New York: Macmillan, 1900. [LL 225]

Dewey, John. *Art as Experience*. New York: Minton, Balch & Co., 1934.

————. *Human Nature and Conduct*. New York: Henry Holt & Co., 1922.

————, and James Hayden Tufts. *Ethics*. New York: Henry Holt & Co., 1908 (rev. ed. 1932).

Dickinson, Thomas H. *The Contemporary Drama of England*. Boston: Little, Brown, 1917.

Dorsey, George Amos. *Why We Behave Like Human Beings*. New York: Harper & Brothers, 1925.

Downing, A. J. *A Treatise on the Theory and Practice of Landscape Gardening*. New York: G. P. Putnam, 1849.

Drake, Samuel Adams. *Nooks and Corners of the New England Coast*. New York: Harper & Brothers, 1875. [LL 265]

Dryer, Charles Redway. *Lessons in Physical Geography*. New York: American Book Co., 1901.

Duncan, John Charles. *Astronomy: A Textbook*. New York: Harper & Brothers, 1926.

Durant, Will. *The Story of Philosophy*. New York: Simon & Schuster, 1926. [LL 284]

Dyer, Walter Alden. *Early American Craftsmen*. New York: Century Co., 1915. [LL 287]

Eberlein, Harold Donaldson. *The Architecture of Colonial America*. Boston: Little, Brown, 1915. [LL 290]

Eddington, Sir Arthur S. *The Nature of the Physical World*. Cambridge: Cambridge University Press, 1928.

Eggleston, George Cary. *Life in the Eighteenth Century*. New York: A. S. Barnes & Co., 1905. [LL 292]

————. *Our First Century*. New York: A. S. Barnes & Co., 1905.

Edman, Irwin. *The Contemporary and His Soul*. New York: Jonathan Cape & Harrison Smith, 1931.

Elliott, Mabel A., and Francis Ellsworth Merrill. *Social Disorganization*. New York: Harper & Brothers, 1934.

Evans, Sir Arthur. *The Palace of Minos*. London: Macmillan, 1921–35. 4 vols.

Fairchild, Fred Rogers, Edgar S. Furniss, and Norman Sydney Buck. *Elementary Economics*. New York: Macmillan, 1926.

Fazzini, Lillian Davids. *Butterflies and Moths of America*. Racine, WI: Whitman Publishing Co., 1934.

Fielding, William J. *Health and Self-Mastery through Psychoanalysis and Autosuggestion*. Boston: Lothrop, Lee & Shepard, 1923.

Findlay, Alexander. *The Spirit of Chemistry*. London: Longmans, Green, 1930.

Finer, Herman. *Theory and Practice of Modern Government*. New York: Dial Press, 1932.

Finney, Theodore M. *A History of Music*. New York: Harcourt, Brace, 1935.

Fiske, John. *Myths and Myth-Makers: Old Tales and Superstitions Interpreted by Comparative Mythology*. Boston: Houghton Mifflin, 1872. [LL 317]

Foerster, Norman, ed. *The Chief American Prose Writers*. Boston: Houghton Mifflin, 1916.

Foster, William. *The Romance of Chemistry*. New York: Century Co., 1927.

Frazer, Sir James George. *The Golden Bough.* London: Macmillan, 1890. 2 vols. [Rev. ed. London: Macmillan, 1907–15. 12 vols.]

Freud, Sigmund. *General Introduction to Psychoanalysis.* Tr. G. Stanley Hall. New York: Boni & Liveright, 1920.

———. *The Interpretation of Dreams.* Tr. A. A. Brill. London: George Allen & Co., 1913.

Froissart, Jean. *The Chronicles of Froissart.* Condensed for Young Readers by Adam Singleton [i.e., Edward Singleton Holden]. New York: D. Appleton & Co., 1900.

Ganot, A. *Elementary Treatise on Physics, Experimental and Applied.* London: H. Baillière, 1866.

Garver, Frederic Benjamin, and Alvin Harvey Hansen. *Principles of Economics.* Boston: Ginn & Co., 1928.

Geikie, Sir Archibald. *Text-book of Geology.* London: Macmillan, 1882. [LL 348]

———. *Elementary Lessons in Physical Geography.* London: Macmillan, 1877.

Godfrey, Hollis. *Elementary Chemistry.* New York: Longmans, Green, 1909.

Goodyear, W. H. *Roman and Medieval Art.* Meadville, PA: Flood & Vincent, 1893.

Graves, Robert. *Claudius the God and His Wife Messalina.* New York: Harrison Smith & R. Haas, 1935.

———. *I, Claudius.* New York: Harrison Smith & R. Haas, 1934.

Green, John Richard. *History of the English People.* London: Macmillan, 1877–80. 4 vols. [LL 374]

Grove, Sir George. *A Dictionary of Music and Musicians.* London: Macmillan, 1879–90. 4 vols.

Gummere, Francis Barton. *A Handbook of Poetics.* Boston: Ginn & Co., 1885.

Guptill, Arthur L. *Drawing with Pen and Ink.* New York: Pencil Points Press, 1928.

Haeckel, Ernst. *The Evolution of Man.* London: C. Kegan Paul, 1879. 2 vols.

Haines, Charles Grove. *Principles and Problems of Government.* New York: Harper & Brothers, 1921.

Harbottle, Thomas Benfield. *Dictionary of Quotations (Classical).* London: S. Sonnenschein; New York: Macmillan, 1897.

Harvey, Jane B. *Wild Flowers of America.* Racine, WI: Whitman Publishing Co., 1932.

Hessler, John C. *The First Year of Chemistry.* Chicago: B. H. Sanborn, 1931.

Higgins, Lothrop D. *Lessons in Physics.* Boston: Ginn & Co., 1903. [LL 422]

Higgs, W. P. *Algebra Self-Taught.* London: E. & F. N. Spon, 1876.

Hiller, Ernest Theodore. *Principles of Sociology.* New York: Harper & Brothers, 1933.

Holcombe, Arthur Norman. *State Government in the United States.* New York: Macmillan, 1916.

Holman, Richard M. *Elements of Botany.* New York: John Wiley & Sons, 1928 (rev. ed. 1933).

Hooker, Sir Joseph Dalton. *Botany.* London: Macmillan, 1876. [LL 438]

Howard, John Tasker. *Our American Music: Three Hundred Years of It.* New York: Thomas Y. Crowell Co., 1929.

Howe, Harrison Estell. *Chemistry in Industry.* New York: Chemical Foundation, 1924.

Ilin, M. *New Russia's Primer: The Story of the Five-Year Plan.* Boston: Houghton Mifflin, 1931.

Infeld, Leopold. *The World in Modern Science: Matter and Quanta.* London: Gollancz, 1934.

Isaacson, Charles D. *Face to Face with the Great Musicians.* New York: Boni & Liveright, 1918–21. 2 vols.

Jeans, Sir James. *The New Background of Science.* Cambridge: Cambridge University Press, 1933.

————. *Through Space and Time.* New York: Macmillan, 1934.

————. *The Universe Around Us.* Cambridge: Cambridge University Press, 1929.

Jebb, R. C. *Greek Literature.* London: Macmillan, 1877. [LL 472]

Jervis, William Henley. *A History of France: From the Earliest Times to the Establishment of the Second Empire.* New York: Harper & Brothers, 1862. [LL 474]

Jevons, William Stanley. *The Elements of Logic.* Recast by David J. Hill. New York: Sheldon & Co., 1883. [Based on *Elementary Lessons in Logic.* London: Macmillan, 1870.]

Johnston, James F. W. *The Chemistry of Common Life.* Edinburgh: Blackwood, 1854–55. 2 vols.

Kellogg, Brainerd. *A Text-book on Rhetoric.* New York: Clark & Maynard, 1880.

Kellogg, Vernon L. *Human Life as the Biologist Sees It.* New York: Henry Holt & Co., 1922. [LL 493]

Kimber, Diana Clifford. *Text Book of Anatomy and Physiology.* New York: Macmillan, 1926.

Kroeber, A. L. *Anthropology.* New York: Harcourt, Brace, 1923.

Krutch, Joseph Wood. *The Modern Temper.* New York: Harcourt, Brace, 1929.

Larned, J. N. *History of England.* Boston: Houghton Mifflin, 1900. [LL 515]

Laski, Harold Joseph. *Politics.* Philadelphia: Lippincott, 1931.

————, et al. *Problems of Peace: Sixth Series.* London: George Allen & Unwin, 1931.

Lederer, Charles. *Drawing Made Easy.* Pierre, SD: Capital Supply Co., 1913. [LL 520]

Leitch, Gordon B. *Chinese Rugs.* New York: Dodd, Mead, 1928.

Lengyel, Emil. *The New Deal in Europe.* New York: Funk & Wagnalls, 1934.

Lethaby, W. R. *Architecture: An Introduction to the History and Theory of the Art of Building.* London: Williams & Norgate, 1912.

Liddell, Henry George. *History of Rome from the Earliest Times to the Establishment of the Empire.* London: John Murray, 1855. [LL 532]

Lippmann, Walter. *A Preface to Morals.* New York: Macmillan, 1929.

Lounsbury, Thomas R. *History of the English Language.* New York: Henry Holt & Co., 1879. [LL 546]

Low, Barbara. *Psycho-analysis and Education.* New York: Harcourt, Brace, 1928.

Lowell, James Russell. *My Study Windows.* Boston: J. R. Osgood, 1871. [LL 552]

Lowie, Robert Harry. *An Introduction to Cultural Anthropology.* New York: Farrar & Rinehart, 1934.

Lubbock, Sir John. *Prehistoric Times as Illustrated by Ancient Remains and the Manners and Customs of Modern Savages.* London: Williams & Norgate, 1913.

Lynd, Robert S., and Helen Merrell Lynd. *Middletown: A Study in Cultural Conflicts.* New York: Harcourt, Brace, 1929.

McKinney, Howard D., and W. R. Anderson. *Discovering Music.* New York: American Book Co., 1934.

Macy, John. *Story of the World's Literature.* New York: Boni & Liveright, 1925.

Magoffin, R. V. D., and Emily C. Davis. *Magic Spades: The Romance of Archaeology.* New York: Henry Holt & Co., 1929.

Mahaffy, J. P. *A Survey of Greek Civilization.* Meadville, PA: Flood & Vincent, 1896. [LL 589]

Mantle, Burns, ed. *Best Plays of 1919.* New York: Dodd, Mead, 1920.

Marx, Karl. *Das Kapital.* Hamburg: O. Meissner, 1867. [First Eng. tr. as *Capital.* Tr. Samuel Moore and Edward Aveling. London: S. Sonnenschein, 1886.]

Matthews, Brander. *A Study of Versification.* Boston: Houghton Mifflin, 1911.

Mencken, H. L. *The American Language.* New York: Knopf, 1919.

————. *Prejudices.* New York: Knopf, 1919–27. 6 vols.

Miller, Frank Justus, and O. Kuhns. *Studies in the Poetry of Italy.* Cleveland: Chautauqua Assembly, 1901. [LL 854]

Miller, William J. *An Introduction to Historical Geology.* New York: D. Van Nostrand Co., 1916.

Minto, William. *The Literature of the Georgian Era.* Edinburgh: Blackwood, 1894.

Montgomery, D. H. *The Leading Facts of American History.* New York: Chautauqua Press, 1891.

————. *The Leading Facts of English History.* Boston: Ginn & Co., 1887.

Moon, Thomas Jesse. *Biology for Beginners.* New York: Henry Holt & Co., 1921.

Moore, Douglas. *Listening to Music.* New York: W. W. Norton, 1932.

Moore, N. Hudson. *Old Glass, European and American.* New York: Frederick A. Stokes Co., 1924.

Moss, F. A., and Edward L. Thorndike. *Comparative Psychology.* New York: Prentice-Hall, 1934.

Moulton, Charles Wells, comp. *A Library of Literary Criticism of English and American Authors.* Buffalo: Moulton Publishing Co., 1901–05. 8 vols.

Moulton, Forest Ray. *Consider the Heavens.* Garden City, NY: Doubleday, Doran, 1925.

Murphy, Gardner. *An Historical Introduction to Psychology.* London: Kegan Paul, Trench, Trübner & Co., 1928.

Murray, Margaret A. *The Witch-Cult in Western Europe.* Oxford: Clarendon Press, 1921.

Muzzey, David Saville. *An American History.* Boston: Ginn & Co., 1911.

Myers, P. V. N. *Ancient History.* Boston: Ginn & Co., 1904. [LL 635]

————. *Mediaeval and Modern History.* Boston: Ginn & Co., 1902–04. 2 vols.

Newcomb, Simon. *Astronomy for Everybody.* New York: McClure, Phillips & Co., 1902.

Nicoll, Allardyce. *The British Drama.* London: George G. Harrap, 1925 (rev. ed. 1933).

Norton, Dora Miriam. *Elementary Freehand Perspective.* Pelham, NY: Bridgman, 1927.

Norton, William Harmon. *The Elements of Geology.* Boston: Ginn & Co., 1905.

Odegard, Peter H. *The American Public Mind.* New York: Columbia University Press, 1930.

Ogburn, W. F. *Social Change with Respect to Cultural and Original Nature.* New York: B. W. Huebsch, 1922.

Ogg, Frederic Austin. *European Governments and Politics.* New York: Macmillan, 1934.

Osborn, Edward Bolland. *The Heritage of Greece and the Legacy of Rome.* London: Hodder & Stoughton, 1924. [LL 656]

————. *The Middle Ages.* London: Hodder & Stoughton, 1927. [LL 657]

Palgrave, Francis T., ed. *The Golden Treasury of the Best Songs and Lyrical Poems in the English Language.* London: Macmillan, 1861. [LL 671]

Parrington, V. L. *The Romantic Revolution in America, 1800–1860.* New York: Harcourt, Brace, 1927.

Payne, Leonidas W. *History of American Literature.* Chicago: Rand-McNally, 1919.

Peck, Harry Thurston, ed. *Harper's Dictionary of Classical Literature and Antiquities.* New York: Harper & Brothers, 1896. [LL 680]

Pellisson, Maurice. *Roman Life in Pliny's Time.* Tr. Maud Wilkinson. Meadville, PA: Flood & Vincent, 1897. [LL 681]

Pirsson, Louis V., Charles Schuchert, and Chester R. Longwell. *Foundations of Geology.* New York: John Wiley & Sons, 1931.

Prime, W. C. *Pottery and Porcelain of All Times and Nations.* New York: Harper & Brothers, 1878.

Quackenbos, John D. *Illustrated History of Ancient Literature, Oriental and Classical.* New York: Harper & Brothers, 1878. [LL 713]

Quiller-Couch, Sir Arthur, ed. *The Oxford Book of English Verse: 1250–1900*. Oxford: Oxford University Press, 1900.

Quinn, Arthur Hobson. *A History of the American Drama from the Civil War to the Present Day*. New York: Harper & Brothers, 1927. 2 vols. (rev. ed. 1936).

Rathbun, Seward Hume. *A Background to Architecture*. New Haven: Yale University Press, 1926.

Reichenbach, Hans. *Atom and Cosmos: The World of Modern Physics*. London: George Allen & Unwin, 1932.

Remsen, Ira. *Inorganic Chemistry*. New York: Henry Holt & Co., 1889.

———. *An Introduction to the Study of the Compounds of Carbon; or, Organic Chemistry*. Boston: Ginn, Heath & Co., 1885.

Repton, Humphrey. *Sketches and Hints on Landscape Gardening*. London: W. Bulmer & Co., 1794.

Richter, Gisela Maria Augusta. *The Sculpture and Sculptors of the Greeks*. New Haven: Yale University Press, 1929.

Robbins, Ermon Bev, and Joseph C. Ireland. *Agriculture for High Schools*. Atlanta: Turner E. Smith Co., 1924.

Roberts, Elizabeth Maddox. *The Great Meadow*. New York: Viking Press, 1930.

Roget, Peter Mark. *Thesaurus of English Words and Phrases*. London: Longmans, Brown, Green & Longman, 1852. [LL 741]

Ross, Edward Ailsworth. *The Principles of Sociology*. New York: Century Co., 1920.

Rous, Samuel Holland. *The Victor Book of the Opera*. Camden, NJ: Victor Talking Machine Co., 1912.

Ruskin, John. *Frondes Agrestes*. Sunnyside, UK: George Allen, 1875.

Russell, Bertrand. *Philosophy*. London: George Allen & Unwin, 1927.

———. *Sceptical Essays*. London: George Allen & Unwin, 1928.

Santayana, George. *Character and Opinion in the United States*. New York: Scribner's, 1920.

———. *The Last Puritan*. New York: Scribner's, 1936.

———. *Winds of Doctrine: Studies in Contemporary Opinion*. London: J. M. Dent, 1913.

Scudder, Horace E. *Men and Manners in America a Hundred Years Ago*. New York: Scribner, Armstrong, 1876. [LL 776]

Sears, Frank Edmund. *Essentials of Physics*. New York: Laurel Book Co., 1931.

Serviss, Garrett P. *Astronomy with an Opera Glasss*. New York: D. Appleton & Co., 1888. [LL 779]

———. *Astronomy with the Naked Eye*. New York: Harper & Brothers, 1908. [LL 780]

———. *Pleasures of the Telescope*. New York: D. Appleton & Co., 1901. [LL 781]

Seton, Ernest Thompson. *Animals Worth Knowing*. Selected from "Life Histories of Northern Animals." Arranged by Robert M. McCurdy. Garden City, NY: Doubleday, Page, 1925.

Shaw, Thomas B. *A Complete Manual of English Literature*. Edited by W. Smith. New York: Sheldon & Co., 1865.

Shimer, Hervey Woodburn. *Introduction to the Study of Fossils (Plants and Animals)*. New York: Macmillan, 1914.

Shipley, Joseph T. *The Quest for Literature: A Survey of Literary Criticism and the Theories of Literary Forms*. New York: R. R. Smith, 1931.

Shoffner, Charles Pennypacker. *The Bird Book*. New York: R. Manson, 1929.

Singleton, Esther. *The Furniture of Our Forefathers*. Garden City, NY: Doubleday, Page, 1901. [LL 804]

Skinner, Charles M. *Myths and Legends of Our Own Land.* Philadelphia: Lippincott, 1896. 2 vols. [LL 807]

Slichter, Sumner H. *Modern Economic Society.* New York: Henry Holt & Co., 1931.

Slosson, Edwin Emery. *Creative Chemistry: Descriptive of Recent Achievements in the Chemical Industry.* New York: Century Co., 1919.

Smith, Logan Pearsall. *The English Language.* New York: Henry Holt & Co., 1912.

Smith, Robert Metcalf. *Types of Philosophic Drama.* New York: Prentice-Hall, 1928.

———. *Types of Romantic Drama.* New York: Prentice-Hall, 1928.

———. *Types of Social Comedy.* New York: Prentice-Hall, 1928.

Smith, T. Roger. *Architecture, Gothic and Renaissance.* London: Sampson Low, Marston & Co., 1880. [LL 817]

———, and John Slater. *Architecture, Classic and Early Christian.* London: Sampson Low, Marston & Co., 1882. [LL 818]

Smith, William. *A History of Greece.* New York: Harper & Brothers, 1854. [LL 821]

———, ed. *The Student's Gibbon: The History of the Decline and Fall of the Roman Empire.* New York: Harper & Brothers, 1856. [LL 352]

Spaeth, Sigmund Gottfried. *The Art of Enjoying Music.* New York: Whittlesey House/McGraw-Hill, 1933.

Spencer, Herbert. *Education: Intellectual, Moral and Physical.* London: Ge. Manwaring, 1861.

Stedman, Edmund Clarence. *Poets of America.* Boston: Houghton Mifflin, 1885. [LL 834]

———. *Victorian Poets.* Boston: J. R. Osgood, 1875.

Steele, Joel Dorman. *Fourteen Weeks in Chemistry.* New York: A. S. Barnes & Co., 1873.

———. *Fourteen Weeks in Physics.* New York: A. S. Barnes & Co., 1869.

———. *Fourteen Weeks in Zoology.* New York: A. S. Barnes & Co., 1872. [LL 838]

———, and Esther Dorman Steele. *A Brief History of Ancient Peoples.* New York: A. S. Barnes & Co., 1881.

———. *A Brief History of France.* New York: American Book Co., 1875.

———. *A Brief History of Mediaeval and Modern Peoples.* New York: A. S. Barnes & Co., 1883.

Stieglitz, Julius. *Chemistry in Medicine.* New York: Chemical Foundation, 1928.

Stokley, James. *Stars and Telescopes.* New York: Harper & Brothers, 1936.

Strachey, John. *The Coming Struggle for Power.* London: Gollancz, 1933.

———. *The Nature of Capitalist Crisis.* London: Gollancz, 1935.

Sturgis, Russell. *A Dictionary of Architecture and Building.* London: Macmillan, 1901–02. 3 vols.

Sumner, William Graham. *Folkways: A Study of the Sociological Importance of Usages, Manners, Customs, Mores, and Morals.* Boston: Ginn & Co., 1906.

Swann, W. F. G. *The Architecture of the Universe.* New York: Macmillan, 1934.

Symons, Arthur. *The Symbolist Movement in Literature.* London: Heinemann, 1899.

Taine, Hippolyte. *History of English Literature.* Tr. H. Van Laun. New York: J. W. Lovell, 1873.

Tarbell, Frank Bigelow. *A History of Greek Art.* Meadville, PA: Flood & Vincent, 1896. [LL 862]

Taussig, F. W. *Principles of Economics.* New York: Macmillan, 1911. 2 vols.

Thompson, Oscar. *How to Understand Music.* New York: Dial Press, 1935.

Thomson, J. Arthur. *What Is Man?* London: Methuen, 1913.

———, et al. *The Outline of Science.* London: George Newnes, 1921–22. 2 vols.

Trench, Richard Chevenix. *On the Study of Words.* London: John W. Parker & Son, 1851. [LL 893]

Trent, William P., and Benjamin W. Wells, ed. *Colonial Prose and Poetry*. New York: Thomas Y. Crowell Co., 1901. 3 vols. [Includes *Pioneer Literature, Colonial Literature*, and *Revolutionary Literature*.] [LL 895]

Tridon, André. *Psychoanalysis: Its History, Theory, and Practice*. New York: B. W. Huebsch, 1919.

Tugwell, Rexford G. *The Industrial Discipline and the Governmental Arts*. New York: Columbia University Press, 1933.

Turner, Frederick Jackson. *The Frontier in American History*. New York: Henry Holt & Co., 1920.

Tylor, Edward Burnett. *Researches into the Early History of Mankind and the Development of Civilization*. London: John Murray, 1865.

———. *Primitive Culture*. London: John Murray, 1871.

Untermeyer, Louis. *The Forms of Poetry: A Pocket Dictionary of Verse*. New York: Harcourt, Brace, 1926.

Upton, Winslow. *Star Atlas*. Boston: Ginn & Co., 1896.

Van Loon, Hendrik Willem. *The Story of the Bible*. New York: Boni & Liveright, 1923.

Van Tyne, Claude Halstead. *The Causes of the War of Independence*. Boston: Houghton Mifflin, 1922.

Walker, John. *A Dictionary of the English Language, Answering at Once the Purposes of Rhyming, Spelling, and Pronouncing*. London: T. Becket, 1885. [Later editions (1806f.) as *A Rhyming Dictionary*.]

Wallace, Henry Agard. *New Frontiers*. New York: Reynal & Hitchcock, 1934.

Wallis, Wilson Dallam, and Malcolm Macdonald Willey. *Readings in Sociology*. New York: Knopf, 1930.

Walters, Henry Beachamp. *The Art of the Romans*. London: Methuen, 1911.

Ward, Lester. *Outlines of Sociology*. New York: Macmillan, 1898.

Warren, Howard C., and Leonard Carmichael. *Elements of Human Psychology*. Boston: Houghton Mifflin, 1922.

Watson, E. Bradlee, and Benfield Pressey. *Contemporary Drama*. New York: Scribner's, 1931. 2 vols.

Watson, John B. *Behaviorism*. New York: W. W. Norton, 1925.

Watson, Elkanah. *Men and Times of the Revolution; or, Memoirs of Elkanah Watson*. New York: Dana & Co., 1856. [LL 925]

Webster, Edward Harlan. *Effective English Expression: A High School Text on Oral and Written Composition*. New York: Newson & Co., 1920.

Weed, Clarence M. *Butterflies Worth Knowing*. Garden City, NY: Doubleday, Page, 1917.

Wells, H. G. *The Outline of History*. New York: Macmillan, 1920. [LL 936]

———. *The Work, Wealth, and Happiness of Mankind*. Garden City, NY: Doubleday, Doran, 1931.

———, Julian Huxley, and G. P. Wells. *The Science of Life*. Garden City, NY: Doubleday, Doran, 1931.

Wentworth, G. A. *A Text-book of Geometry*. Boston: Ginn & Co., 1888.

West, Willis Mason. *Ancient History to the Death of Charlemagne*. Boston: Allyn & Bacon, 1902.

Westermarck, Edward. *The History of Human Marriage*. New York: Macmillan, 1891.

Whipple, Edwin P. *The Literature of the Age of Elizabeth*. Boston: Fields, Osgood & Co., 1869. [LL 941]

White, Edward Lucas. *Andivius Hedulio: Adventures of a Roman Nobleman in the Days of the Empire*. New York: E. P. Dutton, 1923. [LL 942]

————. *The Unwilling Vestal: A Tale of Rome under the Caesars.* New York: E. P. Dutton, 1918.

Wilkins, A. S. *Roman Antiquities.* New York: American Book Co., 1877. [LL 985]

Wilkinson, Marguerite. *Contemporary Poetry.* New York: Macmillan, 1923.

Wilkinson, William Cleaver. *Classic French Course in English.* New York: Chautauqua Press, 1886.

————. *Classic German Course in English.* New York: Chautauqua Press, 1887.

————. *A Classic Greek Course in English.* New York: Chautauqua Press, 1892.

————. *Preparatory Latin Course in English.* New York: Phillips & Hunt; Cincinnati: Walden & Stone, 1883.

Williams, Jesse Feiring, Franz Frohse, Max Brödel, and Leon Schlossberg. *Atlas of Human Anatomy.* New York: Barnes & Noble, 1935.

Winchell, Alexander. *Walks and Talks in the Geological Field.* New York: Chautauqua Press, 1886. [LL 964]

Wood, J. G. *The Illustrated Natural History.* London: Routledge, 1859–63. 3 vols. [LL 969]

Woodworth, Robert Sessions. *Psychology.* New York: Henry Holt & Co., 1921.

Woolley, Sir Leonard. *Digging Up the Past.* London: Ernest Benn, 1930.

APPENDIX

THE POETRY OF JOHN RAVENOR BULLEN

Whether such a thing as a double poetry laureateship existed in amateur journalism prior to 1923 is a matter for the old-timer and statistician to say. To the present generation the circumstance had an air of unprecendentedness, and hearty was the prevailing mixture of wonderment and congratulation when, two years ago, the supreme awards for verse in both United and National Amateur Press Associations were captured by the single Muse of Mr. John Ravenor Bullen of Ontario, Canada.

The quiet beauty of Mr. Bullen's poetry had for some time been remarked among us, but so rarely is a strain of merit sufficiently well defined to produce an equal effect on two separate judges that the kindred outcome of the twin contests burst upon us as a surprise and revelation of the most delightful sort. Prize-winning, however, is no novelty for Mr. Bullen. In various seriously artistic competitions all over the continent he has come out with distinguished laurels, and long before his advent to amateurdom his work formed a leading feature in the programmes of such substantial organisations as the American Poetry Association, Philadelphia Society of Arts and Letters, and The Quill Club, of which latter he has for several years been the American representative.

What truly constitutes a poet it is very hard to say. Nowadays, when intellect elbows for more than its allotted space in the aesthetic field, we are prone to analyse profoundly, seek for fundamentals, and discourse sagely of the unique insight, point of view, and personally selective imagination of the essential bard. We affect to demand that he see nothing undivested of its traditional associations, and that he present to us only the nuclear, isolated, and austerely unadorned imaginative content of his random reactions to experience and emotion. The result is a jarring jumble of academic schools, each based upon sterile theory rather than artistic reeling, which favour us with carefully roiled chaoticisms of varying cast; from the chromatic sensation-vortices of the imagists to the frozen mental detritus of Mr. T. S. Eliot and his followers. Amidst this welter of scientific psychology the art impulse is expected to survive as best it may. Too often its absence is pardoned out of deference to a theoretical form which current yardsticks coolly measure and pronounce real poetry on strictly philosophical grounds.

John Ravenor Bullen, in the profusion of delightful lyric poetry on which his increasing literary recognition is founded, has repudiated the bondage of contemporary theory and is the greater artist thereby. Acknowledging the debt owed by all present beauty to the generations of inherited impressions whence springs its existing relation to human emotion, he is too wise to discard the music, rhythms, symmetries, aspects of vision, and turns of thought and phrase with which spontaneous aesthetic feeling has coloured its expression down the long ages that Nature has forced it to find an outlet. Sensitive to the equal artistic significance of moods and matter, dreams and diurnalities, the *fata morgana* and facts, he has not neglected to treasure that rare quality of *glamour* which, scorned though it is by realists, yet embodies perhaps the better part of all the loveliness we know. A sound instinct has kept him closely within the main line of the great English tradition, thus fitting him for the harmonious reflection of those fancies, conceptions, and perspectives which with us must always be strongest because they are the simple aggregate and heritage of a thousand years of our continuous racial and cultural experience.

Mr. Bullen's particular secret as a poet lies, apart from his keen visual imagination and the natural sense of sound which gives melody and limpidity to all his lines and sets him unerringly on the trail of the perfectly symphonic word, in the fact that he has preserved his golden illusions and faculty of wonder and values in life. For him the zest and dewiness of the May morning have never departed, and amidst our prevailing desert of cynical sophistication he is still able to feel that thrill of pleasure, novelty, and ecstasy in the daily round of terrestrial phenomena which animated the freshly vigorous bards of a brighter time. That thrill alone, so difficult of achievement today, is the one ultimate determinant of the true poet. It is the quality of youth—a youth with Endymion-like independence of chronology—which with a magic quite distinct from anything else we know has the unshared power of animating with grace, marvellousness, and the aspect of significance a world and universe visible to the modern prose mind only as a dull, purposeless, and unsatisfying cycle of electronic, atomic, and molecular rearrangements.

Keeping these sources of inspiration in mind, it is interesting to speculate on the precise methods whereby Mr. Bullen secures his felicitous effects. That *simplicity* is a strong factor is at once obvious; for no one can fail to note how carefully the snares of linguistic complexity, impressionistic chaos, and intellectual involution are avoided. The author is determined that his pictures shall stand out in a clear, full light and that not a particle of their final effect shall be sacrificed through useless diversions of the reader's vision and attention. Moreover, he so skilfully manages this point that there is no outward appearance of strained simplification, no artificial naiveté, no affectedly primerish gestures, and none of the slashing contempt for finenesses and subtleties which marks many writers' efforts at directness. The language is the language of civilised society, with no lack of the colour, richness, and variety necessary to full and flexible utterance. However, it is not cast in riddles for riddles' sake or tortured into meaningless attempts to express the inexpressible. When ecstasy is demanded, it is created not by a lapse into exclamatory incoherence but by choice of precisely the most graphic and forcible words, all used in normal fashion; for to a connoisseur and colourist like Mr. Bullen there are enough vivid vocables at command to obviate all need for extravagant distortions. In most cases the favoured words are the common, beloved ones, to which tradition has bequeathed its mellowest and most enduring overtones; but when the exotic or the unusual is demanded, the poet is not slow to rise to the occasion.

Another source of Mr. Bullen's wide appeal is the quality of *universality*, whereby he tends to touch upon those moods and sentiments which are shared by all the race, rather than to harp as most lyrists do upon the subjective emotional phenomena peculiar to themselves. This is, indeed, the authentic attitude of classicism and is powerful in our poet's work because it is absolutely genuine with him. It here figures as no mere theory or result of conscious straining but as the natural product of an imagination attuned to the universal emotions. With Mr. Bullen it is this general body of sentiment which possesses the prime elements of glamour, witchery, and loveliness, and because his response to its stimulus is absolutely sincere, he is able to reflect it with all the splendours he himself finds twined about it, achieving just as poignant results as does the more personal poet with his highly individualised reactions. Here, indeed, we have an illuminatingly definite proof of the fact that real poetry springs not from any fine-wrought formula or choice of theme but purely and exclusively from the degree of wonder and ecstasy in the poet's mind, irrespective of subject or type of medium.

Mr. Bullen's general attitude toward life and the universe is one of optimistic acceptance, achieved through a preoccupation with the beauties of orthodox tradition which prevents more than a fleeting glimpse of the stern scientific background. Only once—in the haunting and alluringly Poe-like song called "The Music of the Spheres"—has this defensive armour threatened to give way and admit the despair or resignation of the philosophic modern. For the most part the poet is genuinely able to retain the point of view of the great Victorians, to whose style he so unmistakably falls heir.

It is not, of course, to be imagined for a moment that Mr. Bullen's orthodoxy leads him into absurdities and insipidities. Working within a cosmos mapped out by the dreams of generations, he displays a flawless psychological consistency and runs the gamut of the more beautiful moods and emotions without discords or extravagances. To Tennyson he is probably most keenly indebted for his outlook and method, and he is surely a disciple in whom the famous nineteenth-century laureate might justly take pride. Here and there a trace of gentle wistfulness crops out to lend a delicate minor note to the symphony, but in the main there predominates an intense delight in present loveliness and in visions of a rosily imagined futurity which gives the work its characteristic tone. The sometimes wearying didacticism of the nineteenth century is not often found in Mr. Bullen's verse. When a moral does appear, it is urbanely insinuated rather than hammered in, and usually the author is content to let his images speak for themselves in beauty—the reader to draw whatever lesson—if any—he feels prompted to draw.

If any fault be discernible in Mr. Bullen's writing, it is a slight tendency to overwork those archaic forms which Pre-Raphaelitism restored to English verse for a season but at which a more classical taste is again beginning to look at least questioningly. It would, of course, be hyper-critical to deny any authentic poet of the Victorian tradition an occasional "ere", "nay", "'tis", "doth", "thou", "hath", or expletive "do" or "did"; but one may pardonably pause before recommending these forms for constant employment. This applies likewise to the inversions and characteristically crystallised words and phrases which Mr. Bullen sometimes uses—poetic licences like "recollections fond", "throng, whom restlessly I seek among", "bubbling swift their course along", "who sanction lent", and so on; stock expressions like "merry month of May", "sun-caressed", "feathered songsters", "bitter sacrifice", "white-plumed", "Dame Nature", "merry pipes of Pan", and the like; and single words like "entrancing", which excessive and inappropriate popular usage has unfortunately stripped of their pristine freshness and value. All these, however, are merely tendencies to be guarded against; as are the infrequent rusty patches in the metre, and the very rare rhymes which might not win the entire endorsement of Walker's celebrated dictionary. They do not hamper the flow of song and imagery, nor do they suggest any further admonition to the poet than that he exercise at all times that perfect—though doubtless provokingly fatiguing—fastidiousness which appears in his technical masterpieces.

Mr. Bullen's work seems divisible into seven major classes, each ably and appropriately handled. There is, to begin with, the purely lyrical response to Nature's sheer beauty, opulently displayed in such tuneful shouts as "The Copse" or such irradiate musings as "Evening at the Lakeside", and forming to the present writer's mind the finest flowering of our author's genius. One might consume columns in listing the choice titles which fall under this head, so that we may here do no more than recall a few outstanding triumphs like the aforementioned two, the perfumed magic of "My Garden", the quaint piquancy of "Where Mayflies Dance", the impressive majesty of "The Storm", the vivid breathlessness of "The Seagull", and the early poems—less assured, perhaps, yet full of golden radiance—"A Country Lane" and "In the Woods". In all these verses the glamour and ecstasy are secured in the simplest possible way, yet are of the utmost poignancy because of the poet's sharp visual imagination and effective command of words. Consider, for example, two specimen stanzas from "The Copse":

"The wooded copse, Oh, rare delight!
  A cool and green sequester'd spot
    Where sighs the scented summer breeze
  Thro' beechen grove and cowslip'd plot;
    Thro' elm and fir and chestnut trees
Where sings the nightingale at night.

* * *

The village chime rings faint and far,
  Rings o'er the meadow land and vale,
    Floats o'er the headland and the lea,
  Drifts o'er the hill and down the dale
    Till Echo in an ecstasy
Flings out an answer from afar."

A second division of Mr. Bullen's work is closely allied to the first, and identical with it so far as most of the imagery is concerned. This is the nature-poetry in which a philosophical strain is embodied, but in which the elements of colour and atmosphere always predominate over the superimposed idea. Excellent instances of this class are afforded by "Thy Perfect Peace", "Far-Distant Bells", "Hope", and above all by that magnificently elfin masterpiece "The Music of the Spheres", which in the opinion of at least one critic forms the absolute high-water mark of its author's talent. One cannot resist quoting fragments:

"Once I wander'd in a sad
  Dreaming mood
In a forest greenly-clad,
  Golden-strew'd.
Thro' the laced aerial ways
  To the undulating ground
Pour'd the mellow sunset-rays
  Glowing softly all around.

Nought I notic'd till a soft
  Wondrous song
Trembled sweetly from aloft,
  Sweet and long.
'Twas as if a thousand chimes
  From a myriad tiny bells
Melted into magic rhymes
  Floating faintly down the dells.

* * *

Were there wizards in that wild
  Woodland lair,
Waving wands that song-beguil'd
  All the air?
'Tis in vain I've ever sought,
  Whisp'ring Nature reigns supreme.
Oh, the anguish of the thought,
Was . . . . oh, was it but a dream?"

A third type of Bullen verse is the frankly philosophical, with ideas straightforwardly presented and having only as much of imagery as is necessary to the graphic and graceful illustration of those ideas. This is a sort of poetry which can easily become barren and prosy in the hands of an inexperienced bard; but Mr. Bullen generally manages to ward off the daemon Dulness and to display in even the most homiletic of his lines a mastery of form and development whose architectural quality makes it art. "Meredith was a prose Browning," wrote Oscar Wilde, *"and so was Browning."* Mr. Bullen has obviously read the great nineteenth-century verse-psychologist well, but has been far too astute to follow him into the dreariest mazes of his rugged aridity and prosaic perversity. Of our author's didactic pieces, one might prominently mention "My Creed", "God's Answer", and best of all, the sonnet entitled "God", which deserves reproduction in full as a perfect example of its kind:

"The Everlasting Universe you scan,
        Stripping it free of God. Your lips declare
The Infinite, Eternal Cosmic plan
        Devoid of purpose. Your bold thoughts lay bare
The secret soul of things, and only find
        Humanity—a fester on Earth's face,
        Man—but a geometric point in space.
God—a cycle of atoms, deaf and blind.

But I with more humility can see
        God in the eyes of laughter and of pain,
In daffodils a-dancing on the lea,
        In white gulls circling where a river flows.
Your God you lose in logic; mine I gain
        Deep in the dreaming glory of a rose."

As a "fourthly" we may cite a large body of amatory verse extending over a long period of time and containing some marvellously moving touches of human feeling. Less distinctive perhaps than other phases of Mr. Bullen's Muse, it nevertheless has a rare stamp of intensity and sincerity; and not infrequently an almost Elizabethan tinge of balladry. Notable in this field are "Love's Anguish", "The Quest", and "Pluck One Rose and Give to Me". A sample stanza of this last is worth quoting for its sprightliness:

"Pluck one rose and give to me
        Fair Lynette.
More I dare not ask of thee,
        Gay Lynette.
Wilt thou pluck the red, red rose,
Stay thy lover as he goes,
Bid him linger—ah! who knows,
        Coy Lynette?"

A fifth though by no means numerous class includes Mr. Bullen's war verse, which contains the same lyric fire that animates the love-poetry, and which reaches its apex in brief utterances like "Reported Missing". Still slenderer so far is the sixth category, *vers de société*, which finds exemplification in clever acrostics and breezy sallies like "Dorothy". Seventh, and in the present system of arrangement the last, comes the bulk of Mr. Bullen's humorous productions, mostly in the dialect of the Canadian oil fields which he

222 🐙 H. P. Lovecraft: Collected Essays

knows so well. Here we find exhibited an astonishing versatility; for if in his serious poetry our author shews the delicacy of a Tennyson, he is in his comic efforts proportionately well endowed with the kindly grotesquerie and robust whimsicality of a Dickens. His humour is genuinely unforced, and often almost rollicking; friendly in essence, and virtually untouched by satire or irony. It was, in short, the characteristic "healthy" humour of the nineteenth century; its chief fault—when faulty at all—being a sort of picturesque extravagance to which the greatest of the Victorian jesters were equally prone.

The general recognition of Mr. Bullen's poetic ability has been gradual but gratifyingly steady. He has been a constant victor in every kind of literary contest, and his double laureateship in amateur journalism is an index of the standing he is likely to achieve. Still young, he has to his credit lines and passages that ought never to be forgotten, and with the years we may expect a mellowing and technical perfection well calculated to seat him among the actual leaders of his craft. A volume of his collected verse, to be entitled "White Fire", has lately been seriously discussed, and numerous magazines already bear evidences of his genius. In the merit of his work we may see a renewed demonstration of the soundness of conservative fundamentals and of the basic truth that art's secret lies not in theme or medium but in the artist's degree of genuinely glamorous or ecstatic vision, whatever be its mood or direction. Clear, unaffected, and rich without eccentricity, Mr. Bullen's best poetry might profitably be taken as a text by the striver against contemporary faddism. He has shewn us by example that wonder is not confined to the uniquely perverted or true aesthetic feeling to the hectically distorted.

John Ravenor Bullen was born in a delectably embowered ancestral home of Jacobean construction in Bampton, Oxfordshire, England; a seat and garden of beauty which he has potently described in many of his verses and in the languorous prose-poem "Ronevar's Cottage". In early manhood he migrated with his family to the oil districts of Western Ontario, where he still holds forth as a cultural pioneer, with increasing interests in the literary life of North America. He is a bachelor and has long suffered the vicissitudes of ill-health; which latter circumstances he has valiantly borne and minimised amidst a plentitude of intellectual and aesthetic labours and a judicious series of travels in the wilder parts of southern Canada. A prose writer as well as a poet, he is the author of many acute criticisms and of at least one unpublished novel, a refreshing romance of old sea ways and pirate treasure entitled "From the Mouth of the Golden Toad".

Mr. Bullen is by no means unconscious of the sources of his inspiration, and has summed up his aesthetic beliefs in a vigorous poetic creed which may well serve as climax and conclusion for this modest appraisal:

> "There is poetry to me in all things:
> A flash of summer lightning o'er the hilltops;
> The muttering cannonade of sullen thunder;
> The moon's pale smile, the sun's hot golden laughter.
> A poem there is in the gale's weird anger.
> Each rose a silent song is in the Junetime.
> The scent of new-mown hay, the river's murmur.
> Far-distant bells, an echo's dying answer;
> The flush of dawn, the sunset's crimson evening;
> The woodland orchestra, the blazing comet
> That swings along its billion-leagued orbit;
> Th' incomprehensible majestic planets,
> The mighty universe's silent movements. . . . . .

All fill my soul with an ecstatic music;
And feeling this, I cannot but affirm that
There is poetry to me in all things."

EDITOR'S NOTE FP: *United Amateur* 25, No. 1 (September 1925): 1–3, 6. An essay on HPL's Anglo-Canadian amateur colleague; later revised as the preface to *White Fire* (pp. 135–39).

THE FAVOURITE WEIRD STORIES OF H. P. LOVECRAFT

Algernon Blackwood: "The Willows"
Arthur Machen: "The Novel of the White Powder"
Arthur Machen: "The Novel of the Black Seal"
Arthur Machen: "The White People"
Edgar Allan Poe: "The Fall of the House of Usher"
M. P. Shiel: "The House of Sounds"
Robert W. Chambers: "The Yellow Sign"
M. R. James: "Count Magnus"
Ambrose Bierce: "The Death of Halpin Frayser"
A. Merritt: "The Moon Pool"

EDITOR'S NOTE FP: *Fantasy Fan* 2, No. 2 (October 1934): 22 (as "The Favorite Weird Stories of H. P. Lovecraft"). Presumably abstracted from a letter sent to H. C. Koenig. The list is based upon an earlier list assembled by HPL at the instigation of B. K. Hart, author of the column "The Sideshow" in the *Providence Journal*. In the column of 23 November 1929, p. 2, HPL listed the first seven of the above stories as "the best"; the next two (along with Bierce's "The Suitable Surroundings" and de la Mare's "Seaton's Aunt") were listed as "a group of second choices." HPL specifies the novelette version of Merritt's "Moon Pool" (*Argosy*, 22 June 1918), not its subsequent incorporation into the novel *The Moon Pool* (1919), which he regarded as an inferior work.

SUPERNATURAL HORROR IN LITERATURE
(for The Science-Fantasy Correspondent)

(Summary of preceding parts published in *The Fantasy Fan*)

I. *Introduction.*

The emotion of fear, and the instinctive revolt of the human ego against the limitations of time, space, and natural law, are so deeply embedded in our personalities that they have always existed and must always exist as motivating elements in art and literature. Fantasy must be reckoned with as a permanent though necessarily restricted element in aesthetics. And because pain is stronger than pleasure, because religions have absorbed the brighter side of our myth-making tendencies, and because the unknown always contains an element of terror despite its fascination, it is the darker side of fantasy which must necessarily remain the most convincing. The universality of a leaning toward dark fantasy is shewn by the fact that most authors of all kinds have occasionally produced specimens of spectral literature. Mere physical gruesomeness or conventional ghosts cannot make true weird art. A certain atmosphere of breathless and unexplainable dread of outer, unknown forces must be present; and there must be a hint, expressed with a seriousness and portentousness becoming its subject, of that most terrible conception of the human brain—a malign and particular suspension or defeat of those fixed laws of Nature which are our only safeguard against the assaults of chaos and the daemons of unplumbed space. The one test of the really weird is simply this—whether or not there be excited in the reader a profound sense of dread, and of contact with unknown spheres and powers; a subtle attitude of awed listening, as if for the beating of black wings or the scratching of outside shapes and entities on the known universe's utmost rim.

II. The Dawn of the Horror Tale.

Elements of cosmic terror appear in the earliest specimens of human literature, largely connected with the darker phases of ancient religions. They are more common, perhaps, in the Oriental and Nordic traditions than in the classic Graeco-Roman tradition. In the Middle Ages they became greatly intensified because of the prevailing superstition, and because of the presence of a persistent "Witch-Cult" of evil and degenerate persons which kept alive certain very primitive rites from pre-Aryan religions and held secret and hideously orgiastic meetings or "Sabbats" in lonely places on traditional dates like May-Eve and Hallowe'en. Another contributing source was the existence of perverse diabolic groups who parodied and inverted the rites of Christianity in repulsive ceremonies like the "Black Mass". Magic and witchcraft were commonly credited, and interest was lent them by the ceaseless quest of alchemists for the secret of gold-making and the formula for an elixir of eternal life. At this period touches of weird horror were scattered all through oral and written literature. They occurred in the Teutonic myths, in the Celtic legends of the Arthurian cycle, in poets like Dante, and in every kind of popular balladry. And this condition continued through the Renaissance, colouring Elizabethan drama and coming down to meet the rapid development of a special horror-literature in the eighteenth century.

The weird or horror story as a definite type begins in the eighteenth century. Its rise was promoted by the translation of the Arabian Nights into European languages, and by that general reaction from classicism toward mediaeval wonder and grotesqueness which formed part of the so-called "romantic movement". Specialised horror-literature first appeared in German balladry, but very soon took up its chief abode in the domain of the novel.

III. The Early Gothic Novel.

The first weird literature in English consisted of novels in which the scene was generally some vast and dismal castle of awesome antiquity, full of terrible secrets, and haunted by apparitions either real or false. Because of their connexion with mediaevalism and the vogue of Gothic architecture, these tales were commonly called "Gothic novels". Most of the Gothic tales seem very flat and artificial to us today, since they relied greatly on mere literary conventions. There was usually a diabolic villain with strange powers, a distressed and insipid heroine, a noble and manly hero, and most of the other hackneyed stage properties. Weirdness was supplied by such standard devices as pallid ghosts, strange lights, damp trap-doors, creaking hinges, extinguished lamps, mouldy hidden manuscripts, shaking arras, and the like. In most of the earlier novels all weird phenomena had a natural (though generally badly strained) explanation, but later on frank supernaturalism had free play. The first of the English Gothic novels was Horace Walpole's *Castle of Otranto*, published in 1764. This seems extremely flat in retrospect, since it has a brisk, cheerful style (like much of the pulp magazine "weird" fiction of today), and is full of naive extravagances. Clara Reeve's *The Old English Baron*, published in 1777, marks a great improvement. Both of these novels involve real ghosts. It was, however, with Mrs. Ann Radcliffe, whose novels had "rational" explanations, that horror-fiction acquired real impetus. Mrs. Radcliffe had phenomenal skill in evoking feelings of deep and genuine horror through the use of certain details, effects, and atmospheric touches, so that her work remains important despite its often tedious length, clumsy explanations, and watery romantic dilutions. Her best and most famous novel is *The Mysteries of Udolpho*, published in 1794. The first American novelist, Charles Brockden Brown, was to some extent an imitator of Mrs. Radcliffe, and his *Wieland; or, the Transformation*, published in 1798, forms a weird classic worth reading.

IV. The Apex of Gothic Romance.

Matthew Gregory Lewis, in *The Monk* (1795), reintroduced the genuine supernatural element into Gothic fiction, and gave an impetus to the type of tale in which the hero-villain sells his soul to the devil. He was, however, surpassed in subtlety and power by Charles Robert Maturin, whose long novel *Melmoth, the Wanderer* (1820) contains touches of true cosmic horror seldom reached in the Gothic school

V. The Aftermath of Gothic Fiction.

Gothic fiction was voluminous beyond all calculation, and existed in Germany as well as in England. Most of it was very naive and poor in quality, and from the first it was powerfully satirised by the unsympathetic. It did, however, exert a tremendous influence, and has left a permanent impress on weird literature. Again and again to this day echoes of some of its characteristics are encountered. *Melmoth* was the last great Gothic novel, but specimens of varying merit continued to appear for many years. Meanwhile the Arabian Nights tradition was occasionally perpetuated; the chief Orientale of this type being William Beckford's colourful and exotic *History of the Caliph Vathek*, originally written in French and published in 1784. Over a century afterward the *Episodes of Vathek* were discovered among Beckford's papers. A wave of interest in "occult" charlatanry—"Rosicrucianism" and the like—gave a new mystical tinge to some of the English fiction of this period; and a rising regard for science shews itself in such works as Mrs. Shelley's *Frankenstein; or, the Modern Prometheus* (1817), in which a young medical student creates, with hideous consequences, an artificial semi-human being from the charnel loot of the churchyards. Dr. Polidori's "The Vampyre" also belongs to this age, as do Thomas Moore's *The Epicurean*, the weird episodes in Scott, and the darker items of Capt. Marryat. Edward Bulwer-Lytton represents the occultist side of the period, and produced "The House and the Brain", *Zanoni*, and *A Strange Story*. Others working in the same essentially romantic and quasi-Gothic tradition from the middle nineteenth century until recent times are Joseph Sheridan Le Fanu, William Harrison Ainsworth, Wilkie Collins, Sir H. Rider Haggard, Robert Louis Stevenson, Sir A. Conan Doyle, and H. G. Wells. Emily Brontë's *Wuthering Heights* stands outside this line in a class by itself—being a tale of life, and of human passions in agony and conflict, with an especially cosmic setting affording room for horror of the most spiritual sort.

VI. Spectral Literature on the Continent.

Horror-literature has not been neglected on the European continent. The German writer Hoffmann (1776–1822) produced a large number of grotesque and fantastic tales which had a wide influence, but which do not strike the profoundest depths of cosmic fear. A more powerful and moving German classic is La Motte Fouqué's *Undine*, in which a water-spirit seeks to acquire a human soul by wedding a human being. Some of the eerie atmospheric touches in this tale are unsurpassed in literature. Wilhelm Meinhold is the earliest German exponent of realistic weirdness, his representative novels being *The Amber Witch* and *Sidonia the Sorceress*. Germany's leading contemporary fantaisiste is Hanns Heinz Ewers, author of *The Sorcerer's Apprentice*, but the greatest singular weird novel modern German authorship is Gustav Meyrink's elusively curious tale of the old Prague ghetto—*The Golem*.

The French take less readily to weirdness than do the northern races, but have nevertheless produced notable classics in that field. Balzac introduced weird touches, and Gautier will be remembered for his "Clarimonde" ("La Morte Amoreuse"). Flaubert's *Temptation of St. Anthony* is in the truest sense a fantasy. Later French authors are divided in their treatment of the weird—some dealing chiefly with dark abnormalities of human psychology, and others continuing the tradition of the actually spectral. In the former class may be mentioned the great poet Baudelaire and the novelist Huysmans; in the latter class the fiction-writer Prosper Mérimée. De Maupassant's weird tales lie on the borderline, and may be regarded as the products of a realistic mind with increasingly morbid predispositions. Another favourite genre of the French is the *conte cruel*, or tale of torture, physical horror, or hideous suspense. In this field, which of course stands only on the outer margin of true weirdness, Villiers de l'Isle Adam and Maurice Level have performed notable work.

VII. Edgar Allan Poe.

Despite all attempts at detraction and belittlement from his own time to ours, the American Edgar Allan Poe (1809–1849) remains the greatest single figure in the history of spectral literature. As an artist and influence alike his power was tremendous. He took the human emotion of cosmic fear out of the realm of namby-pamby romance and moral allegory and gave it its first independent and aesthetically serious exploitation—incidentally devising out of his own genius the potent narrative pattern which has moulded all subsequent short fiction, weird and non-weird alike. Poe was the first to understand the true psychology of man's shadowy mental gropings, and the first to write of them with a purely aesthetic object. He was not without some of the extravagances of his age, and he drew often on the machinery of the Gothic tale; yet as a whole he regenerated and revitalised everything he touched—emerging as the father of the entire subsequent race of weird writers, realistically psychological and spectrally fantastic alike. His own work has a peculiar power over the emotions which quite defies analysis. The whole style—every turn of phrase, every modulation of rhythm, every casual image, every trivial incident and detail, every careless allusion—is saturated with the dark ultimate purpose, and contributes its individually imperceptible effect to the final monstrous climax. No competitor exists—a attempts to minimise this elusive and unholy power by pointing out the limitations of individual stories are little short of pathetic, revealing the blindness and insensitiveness of the critics themselves. In conscious scope, Poe was local rather than literally cosmic. For him, the illimitable abysses of horror lay not outside the universe but within the human mind and spirit. Much of his work deals wholly with morbid psychology, and a whole division of it stands outside the weird realm as the parent of modern detective fiction. But the cosmic touch and feeling are always there—in poems and stories alike. High spots in the pageant are "MS. Found in a Bottle", "Facts in the Case of M. Valdemar", *The Narrative of Arthur Gordon Pym*, "Metzengerstein", "The Man of the Crowd"—and above all else those two incomparable triumphs, "The Fall of the House of Usher" and "Ligeia". Poe's command of those musical, prose-poetic effects later achieved so finely by Wilde and Dunsany is shewn in fantasies like "The Masque of the Red Death", "Silence—a Fable", and "Shadow—a Parable". Detailed and accurate human characterisation was seldom attempted by Poe, since he dealt in dreams and phenomena rather than in personal pictures. His chief type of central figure is a lone, sad, defiant, strangely learned, nobly descended but impoverished seeker after unearthly and forbidden secrets—a type derived partly from the hero-villain of Gothic romance (as was likewise the somewhat similar Byronic hero) and partly from Poe's own character and situation. Poe was from the first much more appreciated in continental Europe than in the Anglo-Saxon world, and in France he formed the primary inspiration of the Symbolist and Decadent schools of poetry represented by Baudelaire, Mallarmé, Leconte de Lisle, and their congeners.

VIII. *The Weird Tradition in America.*

A strong special bias in favour of the weird existed in early America because of the gloomy Puritan heritage and because of the presence on every hand of black, unplumbed woods full of hostile beasts and savages, and suggesting even darker adversaries of mankind. While Poe represents the more modern and scientific aspect of that tradition, the older romantic and morally allegorical aspect is represented most brilliantly by the New England novelist Nathaniel Hawthorne, born in 1804 among the whispered legends and black witchcraft-memories of ancient Salem. Gentle melancholy, dark sorrow and indignation at the baseness of mankind, an inclination to see dark secrets beneath deceptive exteriors, and a keen sensitiveness to the intimations of unreality in every-day objects and scenes, may be said to form the salient Hawthorne characteristics. Add to this a supremely graceful style and a deep saturation in the lore and atmosphere of his native New England, and the sombre artist stands portrayed. Supernaturalism for its own sake is seldom found in Hawthorne. Rather do we meet it as the vehicle for an allegory, or the delicate colouring of some memorable scene, in his pensive and modulated writing. Greatest of Hawthorne's weird works is the novel *The House of the Seven Gables*, which centres around one of those grey-peaked, gloomy dwellings of mediaeval type that preceded the more cheerful and familiar types of colonial architecture in our coast towns, and that may still be found in Salem's obscurer byways. In this subtle masterpiece the age and gloom of the spectral, sagging edifice become attributes of a half-suspected malign life, and the careers of various inmates are strangely moulded by its influence.

Hawthorne left no well-defined literary posterity. His mood and attitude belonged to the age which closed with him, and it is the spirit of Poe which survived and blossomed. Among the earliest of Poe's disciples may be reckoned Fitz-James O'Brien (1828–1862), whose "Diamond Lens" and "What Was It?" have become classics. The latter story forms the first well-shaped narrative of a tangible but invisible being, and is the obvious prototype of de Maupassant's "Horla". O'Brien's early death in the Civil War deprived weird literature of a substantial, though scarcely titanic, figure.

(from this point follow text of original version)

EDITOR'S NOTE FP: Arlington, VA: Carrollton-Clark, 1974 (as *Supernatural Horror in Literature as Revised in 1936* [facsimile of TMS]). A summary of the first eight chapters of "Supernatural Horror in Literature" written for Willis Conover, who was contemplating resuming the serialisation of the essay (suspended when the *Fantasy Fan* folded in February 1935) in his *Science-Fantasy Correspondent*. Conover later decided to run the essay from the beginning, but the two issues of the fanzine that preceded HPL's death did not contain it, and Conover's enthusiasm for the project (and for weird fiction generally) appears to have declined after HPL's death, so that no more issues were published.